FACTS ARE SUBVERSIVE

FACTS ARE SUBVERSIVE

Political Writing from a Decade Without a Name

TIMOTHY GARTON ASH

Yale

UNIVERSITY PRESS

New Haven & London

First published in the United States in 2010 by Yale University Press.
First published in hardback and export trade paperback in Great Britain
in 2009 by Atlantic Books, an imprint of Grove Atlantic Ltd.

The author and publisher would gratefully like to acknowledge the following
for permission to quote from copyrighted material:

'Poem without a Hero', in *The Complete Poems Of Anna Akhmatova* by Anna Akhmatova,
published by Zephyr Press, reprinted by permission of Zephyr Press. Translations of Akhmatova's
poetry copyright © 1989, 1992, 1997 by Judith Hemschemeyer. 'Spain, 1937', from *Collected
Poems of W. H. Auden* by W. H. Auden, copyright © 1940, renewed 1968 by W. H. Auden. Used
by permission of Random House, Inc. 'In Memory of W.B. Yeats', from *Collected Poems of W. H.
Auden* by W. H. Auden, copyright © 1940, renewed 1968 by W. H. Auden. Used by permission
of Random House, Inc. *Manila Manifesto* by James Fenton, copyright © 1989 by James Fenton.
Reprinted by permission of United Agents on behalf of James Fenton. Four lines of 'You Who
Wronged', from *New and Collected Poems: 1931–2001* by Czeslaw Miłosz. Copyright © 1988,
1991, 1995, 2001 by Czesław Miłosz Royalties, Inc. Reprinted by permission of HarperCollins
Publishers. *Homage to Catalonia* by George Orwell, copyright © George Orwell 1937, 1952 and
renewed 1980 by Sonia Brownell Orwell. Reprinted by permission of Houghton Mifflin Harcourt
Publishing Company and of Bill Hamilton as the Literary Executor of the Estate of the Late
Sonia Brownell Orwell and Secker & Warburg Ltd. *Nineteen Eighty-Four* by George Orwell,
copyright © George Orwell. Secker & Warburg Ltd., 1949. *If This Is A Man* by Primo Levi,
published by Jonathan Cape. *Clay: Whereabouts Unknown* by Craig Raine, copyright © 1996
by Craig Raine. Reprinted by permission of David Godwin Associates on behalf of Craig Raine.
My Six Years with Gorbachev by Anatoly Chernyaev, trans. and ed. by Robert D. English and
Elizabeth Tucker. English translation copyright © 2000 by The Pennsylvania State University.
University Park: Pennsylvania State University Press, 2000. Originally published in Russia as
Shest' let s Gorbachevym (Moscow: Progress 'Kultura', 1993).

Yale University Press books may be purchased in quantity for educational, business,
or promotional use. For information, please e-mail sales.press@yale.edu
(U.S. office) or sales@yaleup.co.uk (U.K. office).

Printed in the United States of America
by Sheridan Books, Ann Arbor, Michigan.

Library of Congress Control Number: 2010925059
ISBN: 978-0-300-16117-5 (hardcover : alk. paper)

A catalogue record for this book is available from the British Library.

This paper meets the requirements of ANSI/NISO Z39.48-1992 (Permanence of Paper).

10 9 8 7 6 5 4 3 2 1

In Memory of
Ralf Dahrendorf
1929–2009
Liberal, European, Friend

Contents

3. Islam, Terror and Freedom

4. USA! USA!

5. Beyond the West

6. Writers and Facts

7. Envoi

ORW

Is 'British Intellectual' an Oxymoron?

THE LITERATURE
OF FACT

The Perfect
EU Member

No Ifs and
No Buts

THE BROWN GRASS
OF MEMORY

THE TW
NEW POL

ORWELL'S
LIST

ISLAM IN
EUROPE

'O Chink,
where is
thy Wall?'

Ghosts
in the
Machine

'ICH BIN EIN
BERLINER'

THE STASI ON
OUR MINDS

ANTI-EUROPEANISM
IN AMERICA

Liberalism

WHY BRITAIN IS IN EUROPE

EUROPE'S NEW STORY

1968
and 1989

9/11

Warsaw,
Missouri

MR PRESIDENT

Secularism or
Atheism?

The Mice
in the Organ

Dancing with
History

THE
TOPF
SLOBODA

Decivilization

La Alhambra

Respect?

ARE THERE MORAL FOUNDATION

Beyond
Race

Cities of
No God

000

2010

Political Writing from a Decade without a Name

Preface

Facts are subversive. Subversive of the claims made by democratically elected leaders as well as dictators, by biographers and autobiographers, spies and heroes, torturers and postmodernists. Subversive of lies, half-truths, myths; of all those 'easy speeches that comfort cruel men'.

If we had known the facts about Saddam Hussein's supposed weapons of mass destruction, or merely how thin the intelligence on them was, the British parliament would probably not have voted to go to war in Iraq. Even the United States might have hesitated. The history of this decade could have been different. According to the official record of a top-level meeting with Tony Blair at 10 Downing Street on 23 July 2002, the head of Britain's secret intelligence service, identified only by his traditional moniker 'C', summarized 'his recent talks in Washington' thus: 'Bush wanted to remove Saddam, through military action, justified by the conjunction of terrorism and WMD. But the intelligence and facts were being fixed around the policy.' The facts were being fixed.

In that case, the facts as we now know them are subversive of the justification offered for entering the war of the decade. In the essays that follow, I show how facts can be subversive of the claims of authoritarian rulers (as in Ukraine and Serbia) but also, sometimes, of those of the friends of democratic change (as in Belarus). Facts subvert the lies of oppressors but also the heroic self-images of countries and individuals. Poland's image of itself as a pure victim of history is shaken by the true story of the murder of Jews by Poles in the village of Jedwabne. The United States' cherished claim to moral exceptionalism stumbles over the photographs of torture in the prison at Abu Ghraib. Britain's post-imperial illusions fare little better. Even great political writers, held up to us as moral authorities, are not immune. In this book, I explore the emergence and impact of inconvenient facts in the past lives of both George Orwell and Günter Grass.

The first job of the historian and of the journalist is to find facts. Not the only job, perhaps not the most important, but the first. Facts are cobblestones from which we build roads of analysis. They are mosaic tiles that we fit together to compose pictures of past and present. There will be disagreement about where the road leads and what reality or truth is revealed by the mosaic picture. The facts themselves must be checked against all the available evidence. But some are round and hard – and the most powerful leaders in the world trip over them. So can writers, dissidents and saints.

There have been worse times for facts. In the 1930s, faced with a massive totalitarian apparatus of organized lying, an individual German or Russian had fewer alternative sources of information than today's Chinese or Iranian, with access to a computer and mobile phone. Farther back, even bigger lies were told and apparently believed. After the death in 1651 of the founding spiritual-political leader of Bhutan, his ministers pretended for no less than fifty-four years that the great Shabdrung was still alive, though on a silent retreat, and went on issuing orders in his name. In our time, the sources of fact-fixing are mainly to be found at the frontier between politics and the media. Politicians have developed increasingly sophisticated methods to impose a dominant narrative through the media. In the work of spinmasters in Washington and London, and even more in that of Russia's 'political technologists', the line between reality and virtual reality is systematically blurred. If enough of the people believe it enough of the time, you will stay in power. What else matters? Simultaneously, the media are being transformed by new technologies of information and communications, and their commercial consequences. I work both in universities and in newspapers. In ten years' time, universities will still be universities. Who knows what newspapers will be? For fact-seekers, this brings both risks and opportunities.

'Comment is free, but facts are sacred' is the most famous line of C. P. Scott, a legendary editor of the British newspaper the *Guardian*. In the news business today, that is varied to 'Comment is free, but facts are expensive'. As the economics of newsgathering change, new revenue models are found for many areas of journalism – sports, business, entertainment, special interests of all kinds – but editors are still trying to work out how to sustain the expensive business of reporting foreign news and doing serious investigative journalism. In the meantime, the foreign bureaus of well-known newspapers are closing like office lights being switched off on a janitor's night round.

On the bright side, video cameras, satellite as well as mobile phones, voice recorders and document scanners, combined with the technical ease of uploading their output to the world wide web, create new possibilities for recording, sharing and debating current history – not to mention archiving it for posterity. Imagine that we had digital video footage of the Battle of Austerlitz; a YouTube clip of Charles I being beheaded outside the Banqueting House in Whitehall ('he nothing common did or mean / upon that memorable scene' . . . or did he?); mobile phone snaps of Abraham Lincoln delivering the Gettysburg Address; and, best of all, an audiovisual sampler of the lives of those so-called 'ordinary' people that history so often forgets. (Still almost entirely lost to history is the smell of different places and times, although that is a salient part of the experience when you are there.)

In Burma, one of the most closed and repressive states on earth, the peaceful protests of 2007, led by Buddhist monks, were revealed to the world through photos taken on mobile phones, texted to friends and uploaded to the web. American politicians can no longer get away with saying outrageous things on remote campaign platforms. As the Republican senator George Allen found to his cost, a single video clip posted on YouTube may terminate your presidential aspirations. (The clip showed him dismissing an activist of Indian descent from a rival party as a 'macacca', hence the phrase 'macacca moment'.) In the past, it took decades, if not centuries, before secret documents were revealed. Today, many can be found in facsimile on the world wide web within days, along with court and parliamentary hearings; transcripts of witness testimony; the original police report on the arrest of a drunken Mel Gibson, with the actor's anti-Semitic outburst documented in a Californian policeman's laboured hand – and millions more.

Quantity is not always matched by quality. Behind the recording apparatus there is still an individual human being, pointing it this way or that. A camera's viewpoint also expresses a point of view. Visual lying has become child's play, now that any digital photo can be falsified at the tap of a keyboard, with a refinement of which Stalinist airbrushers could only dream. As we trawl the web, we have to be careful that what looks like a fact does not turn out to be a factoid. Distinguishing fact from factoid becomes more difficult when – as those foreign bureaus close down – you don't have a trained re-porter on the spot, checking out the story by well-tried methods. Yet, taken all in all, these are promising times for capturing the history of the present.

'History of the present' is a term coined by George Kennan to de-scribe the mongrel craft that I have practised for thirty years, combining scholarship and journalism. Thus, for example, producing the essays in analytical reportage that form a significant part of this book is typically a three-stage process. In the initial research stage, I draw on the resources of two wonderful universities, Oxford and Stanford: their extraordinary libraries, specialists in every field, and students from every corner of the globe. So before I go anywhere, I have a sheaf of notes, annotated materials and introductions. In the second stage, I travel to the place I wish to write about, be it Iran under the ayatollahs, Burma to meet Aung San Suu Kyi, Macedonia on the brink of civil war, Serbia for the fall of Slobodan Milošević, Ukraine during the Orange Revolution, or the breakaway para-state of Transnistria. For all the new technologies of record, there is still nothing to compare with being there. Usually I give a lecture or two, and learn from meetings with academic colleagues and students, but for much of the time I work very much like a reporter, observing and talking to all kinds of people from early morning to late at night. 'Reporter', sometimes deemed to be the lowest form of journalistic life, seems to me in truth the highest. It is a badge I would wear with pride.

To be there – in the very place, at the very time, with your notebook open – is an unattainable dream for most historians. If only the historian *could* be a reporter from the distant past. Imagine being able to see, hear, touch and smell things as they were in Paris in July 1789. If I have an advantage over the regular newspaper correspondents, whose work I greatly admire, it is that I may have more time to gather evidence on just one story or question. (Long-form magazine writers enjoy the same luxury.) In Serbia, for example, I was able to cross-examine numerous witnesses of the fall of Milošević, starting within a few hours of the denouement. During the Orange Revolution in Ukraine, I was a witness to the drama as it unfolded.

The final stage is reflection and writing, back in my Oxford or Stanford study: emotion recollected in tranquillity. I also discuss and refine my findings at the seminar table, and in exchanges with colleagues. Ideally, this whole process is iterative, with the cycle of research, reporting and reflection repeated several times. I have written more about this mongrel craft in the introduction to my last collection of essays, which was called *History of the Present*, and – in this volume – in an essay on 'The Literature of Fact'. Most of the longer pieces of analytical reportage that you find between these covers appeared first in the *New York Review of Books*, as did the review essays on writers such as Günter Grass, George Orwell and Isaiah Berlin. Several chapters began life as lectures, including my investigations of Britain's convoluted relationship to Europe and of the (real or alleged) moral foundations of European power. Most of the shorter pieces were originally columns in the *Guardian*. I conceive these mini-essays as an English version of the journalistic genre known in central Europe as a *feuilleton:* a discursive, personal exploration of a theme, often light-spirited and spun around a single detail, like the piece of grit that turns oyster to pearl. Or so the *feuilletonist* fondly hopes.

Many of my regular weekly commentaries in the *Guardian*, by contrast, look to the future, urging readers, governments or international organizations to do something, or, especially in the case of governments, not to do something bad or stupid that they are currently doing or proposing to do. 'We must ...' or 'they must not ...', cry these columns, usually to no effect. Such op-ed pieces have their place, but suffer from built-in obsolescence. They are not reprinted here. Prediction and prescription are both recipes for the dustbin. Description and analysis may last a little longer.

Throughout, I argue from and for a position that I believe can accurately be described as liberal. Particularly in the United States, what is meant by that much abused word requires spelling out (see 'Liberalism'). I write as a European who thinks that the European Union is the worst possible Europe – apart from all the other Europes that have been tried from time to time. And I write as an Englishman with a deep if often frustrated affection for my curious, mixed-up homeland, at once England and Britain.

The heart of my work remains in Europe. In this decade, however, I have gone beyond Europe to report from and analyse other parts of what we used to call the West, and especially the United States, where I now spend three months every year. And I have gone beyond the West, especially to some corners of what we too sweepingly call 'Asia' and 'the Muslim world'. (The map on pp. x–xi plots essays on to places, taking some artistic licence around the edges.)

The biggest limitation for any historian of the present, by comparison with those of more distant periods, is not knowing the longer-term consequences of the events he or she describes. The texts that you read here have been lightly edited, mainly to remove irritating repetitions, as well as anachronisms like 'yesterday' or 'last week', and to harmonize spelling and style. I have also corrected a few errors of fact. (If any remain, please point them out.) Occasionally, I have added a few lines at the end of an essay, from the perspective of the end of the decade. Otherwise the essays are printed as they originally appeared, with the date of first publication at the end. You can thus see what we did not know at the time – and sit in judgement on my misjudgements.

The most painful of these was about the Iraq war. As you will detect from 'In Defence of the Fence', I did not support the Iraq war, but nor did I oppose it forcefully from the start, as I should have. I gave too much credence to the fact-fixers at No. 10, and to Americans I respected, especially Colin Powell. I was wrong.

Since this is the third time I have collected my essays from a decade, let me add a word about the ten-year period from 1 January 2000 to 31 December 2009. Decades are arbitrary divisions of time. Sometimes history chimes with them. Usually it does not. My first book of essays, *The Uses of Adversity*, chronicled central Europe in the 1980s. The 1980s ended with a glorious bang in 1989 – a moment when world history turned on events in central Europe. *History of the Present* chronicled the wider Europe in the 1990s, including some of the Balkan tragedies. The year 1999 was not a turning-point to compare with 1989, but it did see the introduction of the euro, the expansion of NATO to include three central European countries that had previously been behind the Iron Curtain, and what appeared to be the last of the Balkan wars, in Kosovo. The very fact that we were 'entering a new millennium' gave the sense – perhaps the illusion – of a historical caesura.

Unlike 'the 1980s' and 'the 1990s', this has been a decade without a name. I will not embarrass it with 'the noughties'. That is not even a nice try. It is like strapping a frilly frock on to a sweating bull. Somehow it seems more fitting that this decade be left nameless, for not only its character but even its duration remains obscure. It did not begin when it began and it was over before it was over. After the long 1990s, we have the short whatever-we-call-them. With benefit of hindsight, I would argue that the 1990s began on 9 November 1989 (the fall of the Berlin Wall, or 9/11 written European-style) and ended on 11 September 2001 (the fall of the Twin Towers, or 9/11 written American-style). With hindsight, the 1990s seem like an interregnum between one 9/11 and the other, between the end of the twentieth century in 1989 and the beginning of the twenty-first in 2001. If you look at my account of an extended conversation with president George W. Bush in May 2001 ('Mr President'), you will see that the concerns of the most powerful man in the world were, at that point, quite different from what they would soon become. Islamist terrorists did not get a single look-in.

After the terrorist attacks of 11 September 2001, the Bush administration swiftly concluded – and Tony Blair agreed – that a new era had begun, one they defined as the 'Global War on Terror'. The neoconservative writer Norman Podhoretz called it World War IV. But on the unforgettable night of 4 November 2008, which I was lucky enough to witness in Washington (see 'Dancing with History'), as Barack Obama defeated John McCain to become the forty-fourth president of the United States, it turned out that this epoch was over almost before it had begun. Not that we did not still face a grave threat to our lives and liberties from Islamist terrorists – we did and we do – but because other dangers and challenges had emerged, or risen up the agenda. As a seasoned insider once observed: problems are usually not solved, they are just overtaken by other problems.

In this new 'new era', the rise of non-Western powers, especially China, the challenge of global warming, treated with such oil-fired contempt by the Bush administration, and what some saw as a general crisis of capitalism – or was it just of one version of capitalism? – all loomed larger. Meanwhile – but for how long? – the heartwarming phenomenon of Obamaism fed worldwide hopes. So that it looks as if this decade may actually have lasted little more than seven years, from 11 September 2001 to 4 November 2008.

Is this to overestimate the singular importance of the United States? Perhaps. Yet this was a period in which the policies of the United States changed the world as much as they had in any decade since the formative 1940s – but this time round, alas, mainly for the worse. What is more, because of the rise of non-Western powers and America's own self-inflicted financial plight (the two being connected, since Asian savings funded American profligacy), the United States is unlikely to be able to shape the next decade as it did the last.

As for Europe, our old continent has spent most of these nameless years failing to pull together in its dealings with an increasingly non-European world. It has therefore made less difference, for good or ill, than it did in the 1980s, when it was still the central theatre of a global cold war, or in the 1990s. Unless we Europeans wake up to the world we're in, which we show few signs of doing, our influence will continue to dwindle in the years to come.

Yet these are just historically informed guesses, nothing more, and there is some hope that I shall be proved wrong. The kaleidoscope never stops turning. So I look forward to chronicling another decade, which we will presumably call the twenty-tens. Hindsight can wait until it is 2020.

TGA, Oxford, January 2010

I.

Velvet Revolutions, continued . . .

The Strange Toppling of Slobodan Milošević

On Thursday, 5 October 2000, as Serbs stormed the parliament in Belgrade, waving flags from its burning windows, and seized the head-quarters of state television, which an opposition leader had once christened 'TV Bastille', it looked like a real, old-fashioned European revolution. The storming of the Winter Palace! The fall of the Bastille!

Now, surely, the last east European ruler to have remained in power continuously since the end of communism, the 'butcher of the Balkans', would go the way of all tyrants. There were fevered reports that three planes were carrying Slobodan Milošević and his family into exile. Or that he was holed up, Hitler-like, in his bunker. Would he be lynched? Or executed like Ceauşescu? Or commit suicide, as both his parents had done? 'Save Serbia,' the crowds were chanting, 'kill yourself, Slobodan.' Fired by images of revolution, and all the bloody associations of 'the Balkans', hundreds of journalists piled in for a grisly but telegenic denouement.

Instead, late on the evening of Friday, 6 October, Milošević appeared on another national television channel to make the kind of gracious speech conceding election defeat that one expects from an American president or a British prime minister. He had just received the infor-mation, he said, that Vojislav Koštunica had won the presidential election. (This from the man who had spent the last eleven days trying to deny exactly that, by electoral fraud, intimidation, and manipulation of the courts.) He thanked those who voted for him, but also those who did not. Now he planned 'to spend more time with my family, especially my grandson Marko'. Then he hoped to rebuild his Socialist Party as a party of opposition. 'I congratulate Mr Koštunica on his victory,' he concluded, 'and I wish all citizens of Yugoslavia every success in the next few years.'

Neatly dressed, as always, in suit, white shirt and tie, he stood stiffly beside the Yugoslav flag, with his hands crossed very low in front of him, like a schoolboy who had been caught cheating. Or like a penitent before the priest that his father once aspired to be. Sorry, father, I've cheated in the elections, ruined my country, caused immeasurable bloodshed and misery to our neighbours – but I'll be a good boy now. It was incongruous, surreal, ridiculous in the pretence that this was just an ordinary, democratic change of leader.

Yet that is exactly what the new president also wanted to pretend. President Koštunica told me later that Milošević had telephoned him to ask if it was all right to make the broadcast, and he was delighted, because he wished to show everyone in Serbia that a peaceful, democratic transfer of power was possible. Earlier that same evening, Koštunica had appeared on the 'liberated' state television, suited and sober as ever, fielding phone-in questions from the public, and talking calmly about voting systems, as if this were the most normal thing in the world.

Yes, I found young people celebrating in front of the Parliament building that night, blowing whistles and dancing. But most of the friends I talked to – people who had been working against Milošević for years – expressed neither ecstasy nor anger, but a blend of wry delight and residual disbelief. Was he really finished?

That was nothing to the bemusement of the world's journalists. Heck, wasn't this supposed to be a revolution? But the revolution seemed to have started on Thursday night and stopped on Friday morning. No more heroic scenes. No bloodshed. The Serbs had failed to deliver. They had disappointed CNN, and ABC, and NBC. The Palestinians and Israelis were more obliging. They were killing each other. So half the camera crews left for Israel the next day. Those who stayed went on wrestling with the question: what is this?

A very odd mixture it was. On the same morning that President Koštunica moved into the echoing Federation Palace, just a few minutes before receiving the Russian foreign minister, one 'Captain Dragan', a legendary veteran of the Serb insurrection in Krajina, was marching into the Federal Customs building with a bunch of armed men and a Scorpion automatic under his arm. He was there to expel Mihalj Kertes, the Milošević henchman who controlled so many shady deals through the Customs. Captain Dragan told me Kertes was trembling, and begged abjectly for his life.

On Saturday, Koštunica had to stand around for hours in the shabby reception rooms of the 1970s-style Sava Centre, waiting for newly elected parliamentarians from the opposition and Milošević's Socialist Party to resolve their wrangles and allow his formal, constitutional swearing-in. Meanwhile, a shock troop of the 'red berets', State Security special assault forces, including veterans of Serbian actions from Vukovar to Kosovo, was seizing the Interior Ministry. But they were doing this on behalf of the opposition to Milošević. Or at least, one part of it.

As the political parties met for coalition talks about a new federal government, self-appointed 'Crisis Committees' in factories and offices sacked their former bosses – in the name of the people. One minute I watched the paramilitary leader and radical nationalist Vojislav Šešelj denounce the revolution in a session of the Serbian Parliament. The next I was examining the pistol that Captain Dragan took from the hated Kertes. Lightweight, with a handsome, carved rosewood butt. Five soft-tipped bullets and one ordinary one.

Yet all the while, Milošević was quietly sitting in one of his villas in the leafy, hillside suburb of Dedinje, consulting with his old cronies.

On my last day in Belgrade, I drove past these houses on Užićka Street, hidden behind high walls and security fences. Somehow I could not find a doorbell to ring.

I

What was this Serbian revolution? Obviously, much is still unclear about the Serbian events, which have inevitably been compared with the Polish 'self-limiting revolution' of 1980–81 and the central European velvet revolutions of 1989. My very preliminary reading is that what happened in Serbia was a uniquely complex combination of four ingredients: a more or less democratic election; a revolution of the new, velvet, self-limiting type; a brief revolutionary coup of an older kind; and a dash of old-fashioned Balkan conspiracy.

First, the election. What many outsiders failed to appreciate is that Milošević's Serbia was never a totalitarian regime like Ceauşescu's Romania. That is one major reason why his fall was also different. Yes, he was a war criminal, who caused horrible suffering to the Serbs' neighbours in former Yugoslavia. But at home he was not a totalitarian dictator. Instead, his regime was a strange mixture of democracy and dictatorship: a *demokratura*.

There was always politics under Milošević, and it was multiparty politics. Even the regime had two parties: his own and his wife's. Tensions between his post-communist Socialist Party of Serbia and her Yugoslav United Left contributed to the crumbling of his power base. But the opposition parties and politicians now coming to power, including Vojislav Koštunica, have also been involved in politics for a decade. True, there was police and secret police repression, up to and including political assassination. But there were also elections, which Milošević won.

They were not free and fair elections. The single most important pillar of his regime was the state television, which he used to sustain a nationalist siege mentality, especially among people in the country and small towns who had few other sources of information. That is why one of his earliest political opponents, Vuk Drašković, called it TV Bastille. But there were also embattled independent radio stations and privately owned newspapers. People could travel, say almost anything they liked, and demonstrate in the streets. Opposition parties could organize and campaign, and their representatives sat in parliaments and city councils. Another way Milošević stayed in power was to manoeuvre among them, to divide and rule. That same Drašković, for example, accepted power in the Belgrade city government – and, by all accounts, the accompanying sources of enrichment.

Money played a huge part in the politics of this poor and now deeply corrupted country. When I say money I mean huge wads of Deutschmarks stuffed into the pocket of a black leather jacket or carried out of the country in suitcases. The frontiers between politics, business and organized crime were completely dissolved. Milošević's hated son, Marko, was a businessman and a gangster. Among many other properties, he owned a perfume shop in the centre of Belgrade called, appropriately enough, Skandal. On the night of Friday, 6 October, I stood with a crowd contemplating its charred and plundered ruins. He fled to Moscow, taking with him Milošević's grandson, Marko.

The ruling family was at the heart of a larger family, in the mafia sense. Yet the godfather still preserved the outward constitutional forms and periodically sought confirmation in elections. He won them with the help of TV Bastille and a little quiet vote-rigging – but also because he could count on a divided opposition and a significant level of genuine popular support.

Only against this background can one understand why, in early July, Milošević decided to change the constitution and seek direct election for another term as president of the Federal Republic of Yugoslavia. We know now that this was a fatal mistake. Few thought so then.

Why did he lose the election he himself called for 24 September? The first and most unequivocally heartwarming part of the answer is: the mobilization of the other Serbia to defeat him. Against the collective demonization of 'the Serbs', after what 'they' did in Bosnia and Kosovo, one cannot say often and firmly enough that there was always this other Serbia. There are Serbs who have spoken, written, organized and worked against Milošević from the very outset. Their struggle was different from, but no less difficult or dangerous than, the struggle of dissidents under Soviet communism. Soviet dissidents risked imprisonment by the KGB. The Serbian dissidents risked being shot in a dark alley by an unknown assailant. They were not numerous, but they were always there.

One of them is Veran Matić, a thickset, black-bearded, phlegmatic man, always to be found in his office tapping away at a slimline laptop. With a dedicated team of journalists, and a lot of financial aid from the West, Matić built up an independent radio station, B92, which was seized by the authorities at the beginning of the Kosovo war – but continued to provide news on the Internet. He also developed a network called ANEM, supplying independent news and current affairs programmes to provincial radio and television stations not under Milošević's control. Now, while TV Bastille denounced Koštunica and the opposition as NATO lackeys and CIA agents, this network calmly informed the country outside Belgrade about the true facts of the election campaign. There were also less well-known journalists who went to prison for printing what they thought to be true.

Vitally important was the student movement called Otpor, meaning 'resistance', founded in 1998 as a more radical successor to the student protests of 1996 and 1997. One activist told me that the Otpor members learned at seminars organized by Western-funded non-governmental organizations how rights campaigning and civil disobedience had been organized elsewhere, from Martin Luther King to last year in Croatia. These were students majoring in Comparative Revolution. But they added a hundred creative variations of their own. For example, they would appear in the long queues for sugar and oil with T-shirts saying 'Everything in Serbia is OK'. Under their distinctive clenched-fist banner, they confronted the police again, and again, and again. More than 1,500 Otpor activists were arrested during the year leading up to the revolution.

Like civil society activists in the Slovakian elections that toppled Vladimir Mečiar in 1998, they organized a campaign to 'rock the vote'. Popular rock-and-roll concerts were combined with the message to get out and vote. They dreamed up a slogan, 'Vreme je!' – 'It's time!' or 'Now's the time!' – which just happens to be exactly what the crowds chanted in Prague in 1989. Then they found an even better one, 'Gotov je!' – 'He's finished!' That became the motto of this revolution, plastered on Milošević posters, written on caps and banners, scrawled as graffiti on city walls, and roared from 100,000 throats.

Many others in this world of independent activity – what in Slovakia they call 'the third sector' – contributed to the cause. Independent public opinion pollsters, some of them American-funded, did regular surveys that suggested Koštunica was winning. There were countless campaign volunteers and independent election monitors. Millions of Western dollars have been wasted in 'civil society' projects all over post-communist Europe, but this time, in this place, it was surely worth it.

Secondly, there was the fact that the very disparate opposition parties finally united. Not entirely, to be sure. The largest single opposition party, Vuk Drašković's Serbian Renewal Movement, refused to join. Moreover, the Montenegrin president Milo Djukanović called for a boycott of the election, thus allowing Milošević to take virtually all the remaining Montenegrin vote. But still, eighteen parties got together in a Democratic Opposition of Serbia. Much the largest of them was the Democratic Party headed by the long-serving but also compromised and unpopular opposition leader, Zoran Djindjić.

The third reason Milošević lost was that Djindjić and others managed to subdue their own squabbling egos sufficiently to agree on the candidature of Vojislav Koštunica, the leader of the small Democratic Party of Serbia, which had split from the Democratic Party in the early 1990s. Koštunica was reluctant to stand – he self-mockingly says of himself that he was the first undecided voter – but the choice was perfect. For he had a unique combination of four qualities, being anti-communist, nationalist, uncorrupted and dull.

Koštunica never belonged to the Communist Party. A constitutional lawyer and political scientist, he wrote his 1970 doctoral thesis on the role of the opposition in a multiparty system. He subsequently translated *The Federalist Papers* and worked on Tocqueville and Locke. He was fired from Belgrade University for opposing Tito's 1974 constitution as unfair to the Serbs. Unlike most other opposition leaders, he had never even met Milošević – until, on Friday, 6 October, the commander of the army, General Nebojsa Pavković, arranged a brief encounter between outgoing and incoming presidents. 'So,' Koštunica proudly told me, 'I met him for the first time when he lost power.'

He was a moderate nationalist, who had supported the Serb Republic in Bosnia and fiercely criticized NATO's war over Kosovo. Unlike Drašković or Djindjić, he had never been seen hobnobbing with Madeleine Albright. He had stayed in Belgrade throughout the bombing, whereas Djindjić had fled to Montenegro, fearing, perhaps rightly, for his life.

He was uncorrupt. I have rarely seen a more spartan party office than his. He lived in a small apartment with his wife and two cats, and drove a battered old Yugo car. Again, the contrast was acute with other opposition leaders, especially Djindjić and Drašković. With their smart suits and fast cars, they were widely believed to have their hands in the till – in the time-honoured fashion of most politicians in the post-Ottoman world.

His great disadvantage was thought to be his dullness. In the event, even this turned out to be an advantage. Again and again, people told me that they liked his slow, plodding, phlegmatic style. It was such a welcome contrast, they said, to all the heroic-tragic histrionics of Milošević, but also of many of his opponents, such as the ranting Vuk Drašković. 'You know, I want a boring president,' one leading independent journalist told me. 'And I want to live in a boring country.'

And then, Koštunica wasn't so dull after all. Energized – as who would not be? – by finding himself at the head of a crusade for his country's liberation, he produced some brave and memorable moments. His 'Good evening, liberated Serbia', on the night that Parliament and television were stormed, will go straight into the history books.

Of course we can never know the exact compound of motives that made at least 2.4 million Serbs put a circle next to the name of Vojislav Koštunica on Sunday, 24 September. But two striking partial explanations were offered to me.

One concerns the NATO bombing. I asked politicians and analysts when they thought the revolution had begun. Several said, often through pursed lips: well, to be honest, at the end of the Kosovo war. During and immediately after the war, there was a patriotic rallying to the flag, from which Milošević also benefited. But it was too absurdly Orwellian to hear state television proclaiming as a victory what was obviously a historic defeat: the effective loss of Kosovo, Serbia's Jerusalem. Economically, things got worse, and every demand to tighten the belt was justified by the effects of the bombing. The miners in the Kolubara coal mines, whose strike was to give a decisive push to the revolution, told me their wages had sunk after the war from an average of about DM150 a month to as low as DM70. The reduction was explained as a tax for post-war reconstruction. But it made them furious.

Then, as Veran Matić puts it, Milošević 'fought the election not against us but against NATO'. Yet that didn't work either, because at some deeper level people thought, 'Well, he lost against NATO, didn't he?' If Matić is right, then Koštunica was an unconscious beneficiary of the bombing he deplored. This explanation is highly speculative, of course, and can never be proven. But it would not be the first time in history that war had helped to foment revolution.

The other partial explanation is less dramatic, but also convincing and important. It is that a great many people who in the past had voted for Milošević simply decided that enough was enough. The leader had lost touch with reality. Having been there so long, he was to blame for current miseries. It was time for a change. It was, says Ognjen Pribićević, a longtime Milošević critic, like what happened to Margaret Thatcher or Helmut Kohl, after their eleven or sixteen years of power. The comparison with Thatcher or Kohl may seem startling, even insulting. But it's a useful reminder that for many Serbian voters Milošević was not a war criminal or a tyrant. He was just a national leader who did some good things and some bad things, but now had to go.

It was those people, finally, who brought the vote for Vojislav Koštunica just above the 50 per cent needed for him to be elected in the first round.

So that was the election. Already on the night of Sunday, 24 September, a sophisticated and independent election monitoring group – another part of the foreign-funded 'third sector' – told the opposition that Koštunica had won, and people danced in the streets of Belgrade until the early hours. But everyone knew that Milošević would not concede defeat. He would probably try to 'steal the election', fraudulently claiming extra votes from Montenegro and Kosovo. This was only the end of the beginning.

Sure enough, Milošević had the Federal Election Commission declare that Koštunica had won more votes than him, but not enough to secure victory in the first round. There would have to be a run-off second round on 8 October. The opposition now took a giant gamble, against the advice of many Western politicians and supporters. They said: no, we will not go to the second round. Instead, by orchestrating peaceful popular protest, they would force Milošević to concede that he had lost the election. And they set a deadline: 3pm on Thursday, 5 October.

The election campaign already had elements of revolutionary mobilization, like that of the Solidarity election campaign in Poland in the summer of 1989. Revelection, so to speak. But now things developed more clearly towards a new-style peaceful revolution. People came out on the streets of Belgrade and other towns for large demonstrations. The opposition knew that would not be enough. After all, in the winter of 1996–7 Milošević had survived three months of large demonstrations.[1] So they called for a general strike. And they appealed to all the citizens of Serbia to come to Belgrade on Thursday, 5 October, for the demonstration to end all demonstrations.

The general strike was very patchy at first. But in one central place it took hold: in the great opencast coalfields of Kolubara, some thirty miles south of Belgrade, which provide the fuel to generate more than half of Serbia's electricity. It was inevitably compared to the Lenin Shipyard in Gdańsk, birthplace of the Polish revolution in 1980. And to visit the Kolubara mines was indeed to be transported back to the mines and shipyards of Poland twenty years ago. The same plastic wood tables, potted plants, lace curtains, endless glasses of tea and folk music coming over an antiquated radio. The workers in blue overalls, with unshaven, grimy faces and rediscovered dignity.

Here, as there, one of the massive fortresses of communist industrialization – some 17,500 people were at this time employed in the Kolubara complex – was finally turning against its makers. Here, as there, a vital role was played by the more skilled workers and technical staff, who had connections to the democratic opposition: the semiconductors of revolution. People like the 36-year-old engineer Alexander Karić, dubbed the Lech Wałęsa of Kolubara. 'But there are many Lech Wałęsas,' he said, 'we are all Lech Wałęsas.' Sitting in a café, wearing blue overalls and a bright orange baseball cap proclaiming '1 + 1 = 2' – the slogan of Orwell's hero in *Nineteen Eighty-Four*, picked up by an election monitoring group – Karić confided that his favourite pop song was a hit by the famous Yugoslav group Azra. It celebrated the Gdańsk strike of 1980.

As in Gdańsk, economic grievances helped trigger the strike, but the workers immediately subordinated their local and material demands to the national and political one. When the commander of the army, General Pavković, and the government minister accompanying him offered to double the miners' wages if they went back to work, they insisted that they wanted just one thing: recognition of the election results. There was also solidarity, with a small 's'. On the night of 3–4 October, the number of strikers in the coalfields had dwindled and police moved in. So strike leaders called on people to come and support them. And they came in by the thousands, from the nearby town of Lazarevac, and from the capital. Outside one of the mines, the police stood in line, but irresolute. Finally, three old men on a tractor trundled towards them and the police line opened. A scene for a film – or a monument.

One should not exaggerate the similarities with Gdańsk; I could add a long list of differences. But the strike at Kolubara had great symbolic significance. It increased the revolutionary momentum and further broke down the barriers of fear. What followed was purely Serbian.

Early on the morning of Thursday, 5 October, great columns of cars and trucks set out from provincial towns, from Čačak and Užice, from Kragujevac and Valjevo, from the rich plains of the Vojvodina in the north and the Serbian heartland of Šumadija in the south. The convoy from Čačak, headed by its longtime opposition mayor, Velimir Ilić, had a bulldozer, an earthmover and heavy-duty trucks loaded with rocks, electric saws and, yes, guns. They literally bulldozed aside the police cars blocking the road. Other convoys also broke through police blockades, by a mixture of negotiation and muscle.

Many of those who came to Belgrade were ordinary people from opposition-controlled cities, sometimes better informed than their counterparts in the capital, because of the local independent television and radio stations, but often materially worse off than the Belgraders, and so more angry. However, among them were also former policemen and soldiers, veterans of the Serbian campaigns in Croatia, Bosnia and Kosovo, tough, with shaved heads and guns under their leather jackets. Men who knew how to fight and were determined to win this day.

From north and south, east and west, they converged on Belgrade. They joined with the Belgraders who had come out in their hundreds of thousands, further infuriated by the latest absurd and provocative verdict of the constitutional court – which declared the presidential election null and void. So there they stood, massed with flags, and whistles, and banners reading 'He's finished', in front of the impressive parliament building where the Federal Election Commission, which had falsified the election results, was also based.

It was three o'clock – deadline for the revolution. Then it was just past three, and someone in the crowd turned to Professor Žarko Korać, a member of the opposition leadership which had set the deadline, and said, 'Well, Professor, it's seven past . . .'

No one knew what would happen next. Or did they?

2

What happened between about three and seven o'clock on the afternoon of Thursday, 5 October, changed everything. Led by a man in a red shirt, defying police batons and tear gas, a crowd stormed the parliament. Soon thereafter, the nearby state television headquarters was trashed and set alight. A handful of other key media outlets, including the state television studio and transmission centre, and Veran Matić's B92 radio, were more peacefully taken over. Koštunica cried, 'Good evening, liberated Serbia', to an ecstatic crowd, and they celebrated in the streets.

These events invite a moment's reflection on the relationship between image and reality. Those who stormed the parliament created an unforgettable image of liberation – an image that CNN and the BBC sent around the world. This image then became reality. Taking over the state television was itself another compelling television image: the 'TV Bastille' in flames. But it also meant that the opposition now controlled the place that made the images. And that, not the army or police, is the very heart of power in modern politics.

I remember the Polish opposition leader Jacek Kuroń saying in Warsaw in 1989 that if he had to choose between controlling the secret police and television, he'd choose television. Our democracies are television democracies. (In the midst of the revolution, we paused to watch Al Gore and George W. Bush conduct one of the television debates that would decide a more normal presidential election.) Milošević's dictatorship was a television dictatorship. And television was equally central to the revolution. From teledictatorship, via telerevolution, to teledemocracy.

This was a *coup de théâtre* that had the effect of a *coup d'état*. Who was responsible for it? I collected at least a dozen eyewitness accounts of the storming of the parliament, and they differ greatly. Success has many fathers. The ranks of those who did the heroic deed, or planned it, grow like relics of the true cross. About such events, the whole, exact and sober truth will never be known, but there is ample evidence that, beside much spontaneity, there was a strong component of deliberately planned, revolutionary seizure of power.

The mayor of Čačak, Velimir Ilić, described to me how he and his group prepared their trip to Belgrade as if it were a military operation. When I asked one of his vanguard, a burly former paratrooper from the elite 63rd Parachute Regiment, what the object of the operation was, he said crisply, 'That Vojislav Koštunica should appear on state television at 7.30pm.' Before they left, Ilić told them, 'Today, we will be free or die.'

There is doubtless some retrospective self-glorification in these accounts, but other witnesses agree that the boys from Čačak were there in the front line, and well equipped to fight the police. A Belgrade friend who was there recalls a youth of fifteen or sixteen standing before the parliament and taunting the crowd: 'Do you people from Belgrade need us from Čačak to show you how to take your own town hall?' The provincial lad didn't even know what the building was, but he was going to storm it anyway.

Čačak was not alone; there were many angry men from other provincial towns. When the first, heavy waves of tear gas were launched by the police, the intelligentsia of Belgrade mostly fled to nearby apartments, or offices, or cafés. Another friend met an acquaintance who said, 'This is the biggest funeral ever.' She thought the rising was defeated. But the hard men from the provinces came back into the square. They had no nearby apartments to go to, and they were here to finish the job.

The honour of Belgrade was saved by fans of the city's leading soccer club, Red Star. They were, by all accounts, also fighting in the front line. They had practised already in their soccer stadium, taunting the police with their chants of 'Save Serbia, kill yourself Slobodan.' And they knew all about police tactics. Afterwards, the new mayor of Belgrade, the historian and opposition leader Milan St. Protić, thanked them for their heroic role. It must be the only time that a city mayor has thanked his football hooligans for going on the rampage.

Nor was it only Čačak that had made plans. Čačak's mayor Ilić was a member of the coordinated national opposition leadership, and others in that leadership made their own preparations. Zoran Djindjić, the Democratic Party leader, and far more important than his modest title of 'campaign manager' for Koštunica would suggest, told me that he and his opposition colleagues had their own scheme to take parliament from behind – 'but Čačak was too quick for us'. His right-hand man, Čedomir Jovanović, a charismatic former student leader, was on the spot, wearing a bulletproof vest. Another bulldozer was on the job at their request. And Captain Dragan insists that he received instructions from a close aide of Djindjić to seize the Studio B television station – which he duly did, escorting the security guards to safety past an angry crowd. Several opposition figures say they had their own sources inside the police, passing information to them on police tactics. Some time before 7pm, a commander was heard to say, over a captured police radio, 'Give up, he's finished.'

There are a hundred more pieces of the jigsaw to fit into place: retrospective claim and counterclaim about planned and spontaneous action. But the essential point is established. There was, after Serbia's 1989 and its 1980, a brief moment of 1917: a deliberate yet limited use of revolutionary violence. It is hard to imagine the breakthrough coming without it. But the remarkable thing is how limited it was, and how quickly the country returned to new-style, peaceful revolution. Within a week, Otpor activists were organizing an action to encourage people to return the goods they had looted from the shops. One is tempted to say, although the phrase is a dangerous one – recalling as it does Auden's notorious line about 'the necessary murder' – that they used the minimum of necessary violence.

The question remains why the army, and the powerful police and state security special forces built up under Milošević, did not intervene, instead leaving the ordinary police to throw some tear gas and then give up. For those forces, well equipped and battle-hardened, could easily have caused a bloodbath in central Belgrade – although it would probably only have precipitated a far bloodier end of the regime.

Here we enter the murkiest waters. Among the claims made about the army are that its chief, General Pavković, previously known as an arch ally of Milošević, refused to order his tanks to roll; or, rather more plausibly, that, on consulting with his senior commanders, Pavković discovered that they were not willing to risk using their largely conscript forces against their own people. (Reportedly, a clear majority of those who voted from the army and police on 24 September cast their ballot for Koštunica.) Zoran Djindjić told me that the feared 'red berets', formally the Special Operations Unit of the State Security Service under the Serbian Interior Ministry, received a direct order to bomb and retake the parliament and television. They did not carry out the order. Instead, two days later those same 'red berets', commanded by one General Milorad 'Legion' Ulemek (recognizable by the red rose tattooed on his neck), took over the Interior Ministry for – or, at least, in cahoots with – Djindjić.[2]

Belgrade being Belgrade, there are even darker speculations. For as long as I have been travelling here, people have been telling me fantastic tales about conspiracies – internal, but also Western, especially American ones. This is the world capital of conspiracy theories. But, in this case, I think there may just be some truth in them. The speculation is that disaffected former members of the army, secret police and special forces, who had earlier been wondering about trying to overthrow Milošević, now helped to ensure that he was misinformed and the forces unresponsive. In the case of the army, there is little secret. Two very senior former Milošević generals, Momčilo Perišić (dismissed as chief of staff in 1998) and Vuk Obradović, were now leaders of the opposition, and had publicly and privately appealed to their former comrades not to act against the people. But the most important figure mentioned is the former secret police chief Jovica Stanišić, who was fired by Milošević in 1998, but is still believed to wield much influence on those shadowy Belgrade frontiers where secret police, paramilitaries, businessmen, politicians and mafia-style gangsters intermingle.

The motives of such men in the shadows? First, 'just to screw Milošević', as the political analyst Bratislav Grubačić put it to me. Those that Milošević used and then cast aside were taking their revenge. Second, as a source once close to Milošević explained, 'To save their lives. And their money – you know, a lot of money. Perhaps to keep their freedom too.' And to try to make some accommodation with the new powers that be. Which, in this connection, seems to mean primarily Zoran Djindjić, about whom there are persistent rumours of earlier meetings with the former secret police chief. I was struck by the fact that when I asked Djindjić why there was not a popular march on the secret police headquarters, like the East German storming of the Stasi, he hastily replied, 'No, we think there is valuable equipment there, which every state would need.'

This is all, I repeat, no more than informed speculation. To go further would require an investigation which I don't intend to make. This was definitely not like Romania in 1989, where a group of people from inside the former regime organized a coup masquerading as a popular revolution. But Belgrade is a city where people do have the most curious connections. And something more than just the patriotic restraint of the armed forces, and the velvet power of peaceful popular protest, does seem to be required to explain the absence of any serious attempt at repression. If a little old-style Balkan conspiracy contributed to that outcome, well, three cheers for old-style Balkan conspiracy.

On that afternoon of Thursday, 5 October, one woman was crushed under the wheels of a truck. An old man died of a heart attack. The chief editor of state television and a number of policemen and demonstrators were beaten up. There are unconfirmed reports of two police deaths. That was about it. Little short of a miracle in a country still ostensibly ruled by Milošević, and stashed full of guns and men well accustomed to using them.

The combination of these four ingredients – an election drawing on prior multiparty politics, a new-style peaceful revolution, a brief revolutionary *coup de théâtre* and a dash of conspiracy – helps to clarify the puzzle that the world's journalists encountered when they descended on Belgrade. So does the fact that different opposition leaders favoured different blends: Koštunica, the Girondin, always wanting to use peaceful, legal, constitutional means, demonstratively starting as he intends to go on; Djindjić, the Jacobin, more inclined to take direct action; while others were somewhere in between.

3

Four days after Serbia's super-Thursday the opposition still only had in power, formally speaking, the president. 'Yes, at the moment there is only me,' Mr Koštunica wryly remarked, as we sat in the Federation Palace. He was the one figure in the land who was both legal and legitimate. A fortnight later the opposition had reached agreement with Milošević's formerly ruling Socialist Party, and Vuk Drašković's Serbian Renewal Movement, on arrangements for a transitional government in the republic of Serbia, where most of the real executive power lies. This seems likely to include some highly compromised representatives of the old regime.

Everywhere, you hear the quiet flap of turning coats. In one provincial town, Otpor activists are handing out symbolic tubes of Vaseline to the turncoats. But every new democracy needs those greasy opportunists. People still fear a Milošević comeback – the vampire rising from the grave – but already leading members of his own Socialist Party are calling for his resignation. His party probably does have a political future, like post-communist socialist parties elsewhere in post-communist Europe – but only without him.

The world has rushed in to offer congratulations and help, led by France, both as current president of the European Union and cultivating its special relationship with Serbia. Of course, there is a huge task of economic reconstruction: Serbia's gross domestic product is roughly half what it was in 1989. But, to adapt an economist's term, Serbia has the advantages of backwardness. Being last, it can learn from all the other post-communist transitions. Mladjan Dinkić, a representative of the so-called G17 Plus group of economists who were already preparing for a democratic transition, told me they would combine Polish-style shock therapy with a more cautious privatization. And they will receive a lot of Western help too. Why? Because, to put it crudely, Serbia is seen as small but dangerous. (Russia is dangerous, but too large; Bulgaria is small, but not dangerous enough.) That is one backhandedly helpful legacy of Milošević. A crucial test – this we have learned from other transitions – is whether they can establish the rule of law in a highly criminalized society. That will determine whether Serbia becomes a little Russia or a civilized European country.

Two huge questions remain. First: what country is this? Koštunica greeted 'liberated Serbia', but was then sworn in as president of the Federal Republic of Yugoslavia. Montenegro did not recognize him as such, and he has now suggested changing the state name to Serbia-Montenegro – strongly reminiscent of the 1990 proposal for a hyphenated Czecho-Slovakia, soon followed by their 'velvet divorce'. After the new Serbian elections, the negotiations on a new relationship with Montenegro will begin. Koštunica has made it clear that he would respect the outcome of a referendum in Montenegro – and, for that matter, in Serbia, for the Serbs will not want to stay together with the Montenegrins at any price, in an unequal or sham confederation.

The other question is: what to do about the past? In the West, this is usually reduced to: what to do with Milošević? The Hague? Koštunica has repeatedly ruled out extradition. A trial in Serbia? This is what many people in Serbia want. 'A Dutch prison would be much too good for him' was one comment I heard. 'Let him try a Serbian one.' Or should he just 'spend more time with his family'? 'I really don't care what happens to him,' says Zoran Djindjić. 'We have other priorities now.'

But the problem of the past is far larger and more intricate than just the fate of Milošević. So many people, including a few high in the ranks of the opposition, were formerly servants or supporters of the regime. And then there is the great clash between the one-eyed view of most ordinary Serbs – who see themselves as victims, both of Milošević and of NATO – and the almost equally one-eyed view of many outsiders, who think of 'the Serbs' simply as the villains of

Bosnia and Kosovo. A Serbian truth commission would have a daunting task.

These and many other questions are still open. But already now, two weeks on, we can say a few things with confidence about what has ended, and what has begun.

If the Solidarity revolution in Poland was the beginning of the end of communism, this was the end of the end of communism. It was the last of a twenty-year chain of new-style, central and east European revolutions, each learning from the previous one but also adding new ingredients and variations.[3] And not just in Europe. There are echoes here of the Philippines or Indonesia. And messages, one hopes, for other countries. In a now globalized politics, we have moved beyond the old 1789 and 1917 models of revolution. If it could happen in Serbia, why not in Burma? Why not in Cuba?

Liberation is a big word, particularly for men and women who were semi-free even under Milošević, and still have a lot of the old regime on top of them – both structures and individuals in authority. But they are a great deal more free, and getting more so by the day. 'We just breathe more freely,' one acquaintance told me. Moreover, they can at last plan for the future. One definition of a liberated country is a place that people come back to rather than leave. Serbia will now be such a country.

As the Hungarian revolution of 1956 transformed the image of Hungary in the world, so this Serbian revolution will change that of Serbia. Unlike the Germans in 1945, the Serbs have liberated themselves. If they can go on to address the problem of the past themselves, that reputation will be even better.

This is the end of the Balkan wars. Koštunica cares passionately about the lot of his fellow Serbs in Croatia (the very few that are left there), in Bosnia, in Kosovo (where he wants to see more Serb refugees return), and in Montenegro. But he is a man of peace, and he will pursue Serbian national interests by negotiation. The only people who might possibly want to start a Balkan war now are

23

Albanians in Kosovo and Macedonia; if NATO, with its thousands of troops in Kosovo, cannot prevent that, then it might as well turn itself into a cookery club.

This is also the end of Serbian imperial dreams. I talked in Belgrade to the writer Dobrica Ćosić, who is credited by many with fuelling those dreams in the 1986 Memorandum of the Serbian Academy of Arts and Sciences. Sitting in the headquarters of the Serbian Academy, he told me that the point now was simply to build a modern Serbian nation state. If even the Montenegrins wanted to go their own way – although, he dustily added, Montenegrinness (Montenegrinity? Montenegritude?) was an invention of Stalinist nationalities policy – so be it. Let them go. The Serbs must get on with building their own state.

If that is what happens – and my own hunch is that it will – then we will be close to the end of an even longer and larger story: the two-centuries-old, delayed and long-interrupted process of the for-mation of modern European nation states out of the ruins of the Ottoman Empire.

That, in turn, poses a great challenge to the West, but above all to Europe – and specifically to the European Union. For after the fall of Milošević there is no longer any external obstacle to our building a liberal community not just of fifteen but of thirty democratic nation states. Now we really do have the chance, but also the daunting task, of building that 'Europe whole and free' which George Bush, Senior, memorably invoked in the last twilight of the Cold War.

Quite a lot to have happened between three and seven o'clock one Thursday afternoon.

2000

Serbia's road to democracy and Europe has been predictably bumpy, as has that of the now independent Montenegro. One of the most shocking inci-dents along that road was the assassination of Zoran Djindjić in 2003. For his involvement in the murder of Djindjić, the General 'Legion' mentioned in this essay was subsequently sentenced to forty years' imprisonment by a Serbian court. And Slobodan Milošević did end his days in a prison cell in the Hague.

I join with those who argue that we in Europe should set ourselves the strategic goal of inducting all the states of the western Balkans, including Serbia and Montenegro, as members of the European Union by 28 June 2014, the centenary of the assassination of Archduke Franz Ferdinand in Sarajevo, which lit the fuse for the First World War. Whether today's Europe will prove itself capable of such historical imagination and strategic boldness, we shall see.

'The country summoned me'

It's a freezing winter's night. Standing between the tents of the revolutionary encampment on Kiev's equivalent of Regent Street is Svyatoslav Smolin, a tough-looking, pasty-faced man in a khaki jacket, whose usual job is checking the radiation levels at Chernobyl. He tells me how, on that fateful Monday just over two weeks ago when he heard the news that the opposition candidate had supposedly lost the presidential election, he turned to his wife and said, 'I just have to go.' He came to Kiev, joined the vast protesting crowds on Independence Square and, seeing the tents going up, offered his services. Now he's in charge of the guards in this well-organized section of the 'tent city', which stretches for perhaps half a mile down the broad city boulevard.

Warming himself by one of the braziers of burning timber is Vasil Khorkuda, a stocky, clear-eyed countryman from a rural area near the Carpathian mountains, where he runs a small travel agency. He has never, he says, been active in politics before. But that Monday he, too, decided he simply must go to Kiev. He's been here ever since and he'll stay until 'success', which, he explains, means a president chosen in a free and fair election.

26

Further on, giggling by an all-orange synthetic Christmas tree – this is the Orange Revolution, so even the Christmas tree has to match – is Elena Mayarchuk. Clad in fur and the obligatory orange scarf, she's the owner of a Mary Kay beauty shop in a small town in central Ukraine. Again, the same story: she heard the news; she knew she had to come; she'll stay till the end. And there's Vova, a worker from an industrial city in the north-east, who, striking a heroic pose with both black-gloved, ham-sized hands raised in V-for-victory signs, declares, 'The country summoned me!'

These are the so-called ordinary people who, by their spontaneous reaction on that Monday, 22 November, made history. First it was the Kievans, taking ownership of their own city. Then it was the outsiders. All the well-funded campaign for the opposition candidate, Viktor Yushchenko; all the carefully prepared student activists of the resistance movement Pora ('It's time'); all the Western support for NGOs, exit polls and the like; all the international election monitors; all the telephone calls from Washington or Brussels – none of them would have prevailed over President Kuchma's vicious regime, with its manipulated media, Russian advisers and electoral fraud, were it not for the Svyatoslavs and Vasils, the Elenas and Vovas, coming on to the streets of Kiev in such numbers that they changed everything.

So much is still obscure, corrupt and inauthentic in Ukrainian politics, but at the very heart of this change is something very authentic: human beings hoping to take control of their own destiny. Mere objects of history who become, however briefly, active subjects. Subjects who will be citizens.

Great outside interests are at stake here – Russia and the US struggling for mastery in Eurasia, the shaping of a new European Union – but that is not the story you hear on the streets and the square. Even the most pro-European intellectuals admit that the attractions of turning from a post-Soviet Union towards the European Union played only a small part in the campaign.

No. The story you hear is of a country that was handed independence on a plate in the break-up of the Soviet Union thirteen years ago, but only now is creating the social reality of a sovereign, would-be democratic country. It's the story of a post-communist regime under President Leonid Kuchma which has been so manipulative, bullying and corrupt that even sober analysts describe it as 'gangocracy'. What they call the 'blackmail state' has worked by the president controlling most of the top positions in public life, guaranteeing his placelings' loyalty by holding compromising material – people use the old Soviet secret police term *kompromat* – on their illegal activities. Government by *kompromat*.

If collaborators did step out of line, their businesses were closed down, or they were put in jail, or they were beaten up, or worse. Those monstrous carbuncles on the once-handsome face of Viktor Yushchenko testify to what may well have been a deliberate poisoning. As Yushchenko himself observes: his is the face of Ukraine today.

But not, the power-holders hope, tomorrow. In the end, they overplayed their hand. They proposed for president an apparatchik, Viktor Yanukovych, who as a young man served two prison terms for theft and causing grievous bodily harm. (One of the many jokes circulating in Kiev quips that, unlike the incumbent president, Kuchma, Yanukovych doesn't want a third term.) The lies on the main television channels and the election-rigging became too blatant. And then the Moscow godfather, Vladimir Putin, who presumably holds his own *kompromat* on Kuchma, acted as if Ukraine were still a satrapy of Soviet Russia. That was the last straw.

Probably for the first time in Ukrainian history, the democratic and the national aspirations are marching together. In places such as Bosnia, East Timor or Iraq, Western occupiers talk implausibly of 'nation-building'. Here you see how nations are built, in the solidarity of chanting crowds and the brandishing of new symbols. 'I feel more

Ukrainian now than I did three weeks ago,' says a young man of Russian origin. There, in a single sentence, is the essence of true nation-building. In this still largely Russian-speaking country, just 42 per cent of those asked in a nationwide survey this February identified themselves as 'above all' citizens of Ukraine. (An amazing 13 per cent answered 'Soviet citizen'.) One of the survey's designers bet me that next February it will be 50 per cent or more.

Nation-building includes the invention of tradition. These days, that's done not by bards or historians but by television. Already I see, on the more independent TV channels here, stirring photo-montages of the orange-bedecked demonstrators in the snow, with beautiful girls, crying grandmothers and patriotic music. Oh yes, and that great white-and-gold column on Independence Square, which looks as if it must date back to the early nineteenth century, was erected in 2001.

Now Parliament has cleared the way for the corrupted second round of the election to be repeated on 26 December. I have just returned from hearing Victor Yushchenko declare 'victory' after 'seventeen long days' to a flag-waving crowd beneath that column. 'In these seventeen days,' he said, 'we made this country democratic.' But he hasn't even won the election. There will be many twists and turns ahead. Even if, as seems most likely, he is now elected, disappointment will follow under a president Yushchenko. Touchingly, I see the father of Prague's velvet revolution, ex-president Václav Havel, on Ukrainian television with an orange ribbon in his lapel and warning, precisely, of post-revolutionary disenchantment.

Romantic idealization is certainly not what we should offer here; but clear-sighted respect, yes. Would you leave your job and your family for several weeks to go and live with strangers in a crowded tent on a dirty street, in temperatures plunging to minus 10 degrees? I was so cold after two hours, I had to go back to my hotel for hot tea and first aid. They've been living there for two weeks. These so-called ordinary people, now doing an extraordinary thing, have at least earned the right not to be treated as the objects of outsiders' ideological fantasies or fetid conspiracy theories. Instead, we can simply listen, with critical respect, to their own stories of why they are there.

2004

Orange Revolution in Ukraine

Last autumn, Ukraine imprinted itself on the political consciousness of the world for the first time in its history. In what was christened the 'Orange Revolution', vast crowds wearing orange scarves gathered in sub-zero temperatures in Kiev's Independence Square to demand a fair election for president.*

Observers have placed Ukraine's Orange Revolution in a sequence of peaceful democratic revolutions stretching from the 'velvet revolutions' of 1989 in central Europe, through the Rose Revolution in Georgia in 2003, to what some are already calling the 'Cedar Revolution' in Lebanon. Many Ukrainians are understandably delighted by this attractive labelling, so different from the largely negative or non-existent image they have had in the past. Yet we must look beyond the news headlines to discover how and why this change has come about, and what its consequences may be.

I

The history of Ukraine begins a thousand years ago, when the rulers of a trading state based in Kiev – or Kyiv, to use the Ukrainian spelling

*This essay was written jointly with Timothy Snyder of Yale University, a leading specialist on modern central and east European history.

– converted to Byzantine Christianity. After the Mongol invasions, Kiev and surrounding lands were absorbed by the then combined state of Poland–Lithuania, in which Ukrainians were exposed to the influence of the Renaissance and the Counter-Reformation. As Russian power extended westward, educated Ukrainians offered their services to the Russian empire. The Ukrainian language, related to both Polish and Russian, allowed them to assimilate easily. As nationalism emerged in the nineteenth century, Russians came to see Ukraine as a branch of their own nation. At the same time a Ukrainian national movement began to articulate a distinctive Ukrainian culture.

However, Ukraine failed to achieve independence in 1918. Attempts by Ukrainians to found a state were blocked by Bolshevik and Polish forces. Woodrow Wilson did not think Ukraine was a nation, and the Western powers conceded Ukrainian lands to the Russian White Armies in the hope that they would defeat Bolshevism. In 1921, Ukraine was divided up between the Bolsheviks and Poland.[1] The Bolsheviks granted Ukraine generous space within the new Soviet Union, but the peasantry in Soviet Ukraine was destroyed by the collectivization of agriculture, while the Orthodox Church was subordinated and corrupted, and the intelligentsia was decimated. Among Stalin's worst crimes was the organized famine of 1932–3, which took the lives of at least 3 million people in Soviet Ukraine. His regime was displaced in 1941 by the Nazis, who regarded Ukrainians as racially inferior and brutally treated them as such. Ukraine's Jewish population was all but eliminated in the Holocaust, in which the German occupiers were aided by the collaboration of a minority of Ukrainians. Some Ukrainian nationalists attacked and killed local Poles. Hundreds of thousands of Ukrainian soldiers starved to death in German camps. Yushchenko's father, who survived Auschwitz, was one of the lucky few.

With the return of Soviet power at the end of the war Ukrainian lands were gathered into one political unit. In 1945, Stalin annexed western Ukraine from Poland, thereby bringing people with a different experience of politics into the Soviet Union. Some of them came from Galicia, a part of Austria between 1772 and 1918 that was incorporated into Poland. These Ukrainians were mostly Greek Catholics, their 'uniate' church combining an Eastern liturgy with subordination to the Vatican. Between the two wars the Galicians had been citizens of Poland, which, while an increasingly authoritarian state, generally allowed free expression and accepted the rule of law. After 1945, Nikita Khrushchev, the Communist official in charge of Ukraine, took control of the Soviet pacification of its western part. It was he who added the Crimean peninsula to Soviet Ukraine in 1954, giving the country its present shape.

Soviet power weakened or eliminated in Ukraine those elements of civil society – private farms, churches, the intelligentsia – that had helped to prepare the way for the velvet revolutions in its more fortunate neighbours, such as Poland and Czechoslovakia. Still, when the USSR collapsed in 1991, Ukraine had a name, a capital, a place on the map. But its independence arrived without a major popular movement to shape it.[2] Its foundations were fragile. Many in Russia refused to accept the reality of Ukrainian independence.

During the 1990s, Ukraine was an electoral democracy undergoing a shaky transition to a post-Soviet version of capitalism. Between 1994 and 2004, the regime of President Leonid Kuchma, in which the president appointed almost everybody that mattered, adopted increasingly corrupt, brutal and undemocratic methods. Kuchma pioneered what has been called 'the blackmail state'.[3] Having itself encouraged widespread corruption, his administration blackmailed officials and private citizens by threatening them with evidence of wrongdoing gathered by the secret police – such evidence being known as *kompromat*, the old Soviet term for 'compromising material'. Kuchma also cultivated intimate relations with some of Ukraine's new industrial barons, letting them take over state assets – particularly coal, steel and natural gas – and giving them other favours in return for their political support. The system seemed to work.

After the First World War, the Ukrainian conservative Vyacheslav

Lypyns'kyi had an optimistic thought: even a corrupt Ukrainian state, if it lasted, could create a Ukrainian nation. The rich would adapt to its laws and seek connections with state officials. Those with no cultural attachment to Ukraine would see themselves as citizens of a Ukrainian state if they had a stake in its institutions.[4] The 1990s put these ideas to the test. Agile businessmen and women took over former state assets, created and exploited monopolies, and made lucrative investments. In far-eastern Ukraine, near the Russian border, Rinat Akhmetov, the son of a miner, accumulated a fortune now estimated at more than $3 billion, starting with coal and steel. By financing political parties, these oligarchs – generally Russian speakers from the east – got themselves elected to Parliament. Many of them moved to Kiev and courted favour with President Kuchma. One of them, Viktor Pinchuk, married Kuchma's daughter. Such oligarchs had a vested interest in the survival of Ukraine. In an enlarged Russia, or a restored Soviet Union, they would have been small fish in a big pond, their connections of little value.

Kuchma's Ukraine endorsed the institutions and the symbols of independent statehood. It had embassies, an army, its own police. The national anthem used by the briefly independent Ukrainian People's Republic after the First World War was restored in 1992, and amended in 2003. Every night on television people saw the outline of their country on the weather map. Ukrainian was the state language. Foreign journalists were asked to use the word 'Kyiv' rather than 'Kiev'. Teachers at elite schools used Ukrainian in their classes, and the texts of civil service and university exams were in Ukrainian. Even as much of the political elite continued to speak Russian off camera, the public use of the Ukrainian language became a sign that the state was established.[5] Kuchma himself published a book entitled *Ukraine is Not Russia*.

In 2004, the Kuchma system outdid itself. Viktor Pinchuk and Rinat Akhmetov acquired the privatized Kryvyi Rih steelworks, although their bid was $800 million lower than that of a consortium led by US Steel. One favour deserves another, so Akhmetov helped to finance the presidential campaign of Kuchma's prime minister and handpicked successor, Viktor Yanukovych. Had Yanukovych become president, Ukraine would have remained independent, but its resources would have been even more tightly controlled by a few oligarchs. However, Kuchma's system had two major flaws. First, Ukrainians had the right to vote. Both Kuchma's regime and its candidate, a supremely uncharismatic politician with two criminal convictions in his youth, were unpopular. Second, not everyone with money and political power was satisfied.

Julia Tymoshenko, for example, was an oligarch with a grievance. An economist from the east Ukrainian industrial centre of Dnipropetrovsk, she made her money speculating in natural gas, exploiting loopholes that allowed state-owned firms to pay for energy with goods that could be resold rather than in cash. In this way middlemen (or women) could amass their own fortunes. Tymoshenko was known as the 'gas princess'. Then, as a government minister between 1999 and 2001, she closed those very loopholes, and forced the energy sector to become part of the cash economy. Along with the former central banker Viktor Yushchenko, then prime minister, she worked to reform Ukraine's economy. Kuchma fired them both and put Tymoshenko in prison. Her courage and her refusal to be cowed made her an appealing figure. She was soon freed. However, it was Yushchenko who became the most popular Ukrainian politician. He was able to attract those entrepreneurs who believed they could prosper in an economy where connections with the regime counted for less and the rule of law counted for more.

In November 2000, the headless body of Heorhiy Honhadze, a journalist known for his criticism of Kuchma, was discovered in woods outside Kiev. Audiotapes purportedly leaked by one of Kuchma's bodyguards recorded a voice that sounded like Kuchma's giving orders that Honhadze be done away with. For a few months, Ukrainians took to the streets to demand a 'Ukraine without Kuchma'. Protesting students built a tent city in Kiev. Although their movement failed, this popular mobilization was a new experience for thousands of Ukrainians.

Three years later, Viktor Yushchenko led a candle-lit vigil in memory of the millions of victims of the Stalinist political famine of 1932 and 1933. The presidential campaign was well under way, and many Ukrainians admired the way Yushchenko asked quietly for public remembrance of the national past. But his opponent, the prime minister, Viktor Yanukovych, had Kuchma's support, financial backing from oligarchs and unlimited television coverage. With little access to television, Yushchenko campaigned everywhere in person. He countered televised attacks on him by making personal visits to villages, shaking hands, showing his face.

Last September, several weeks before the election, he was poisoned by a dose of dioxin. The first symptoms appeared after he had dinner with senior secret police officials, although no connection with the poisoning has yet been definitively established. He returned to the campaign with his formerly handsome face horribly ravaged by severe acne and scar tissue. This, he said, 'is the face of Ukraine today'. The Kuchma administration secretly instructed television channels to call the claim of deliberate poisoning a 'bare-faced lie' and a campaign trick.[6] A TV channel owned by Viktor Medvedchuk, an oligarch close to Kuchma, suggested that Yushchenko's illness was caused by questionable personal habits.

2

Despite all these obstacles, Yushchenko won a plurality in the first round of presidential elections on 31 October. On Sunday, 21 November, during the second round, the Kuchma regime coordinated a campaign to falsify the voting results. That evening, it announced a victory for Yanukovych with a margin of about 3 per cent. President Vladimir

Putin hurried to congratulate him. However, independently commissioned and Western-funded exit polls made it clear that Yushchenko had won a decisive victory.

And so the Orange Revolution began – with protests against the rigged election. While the Kuchma regime dominated television, the student movement that called itself Pora[7] – 'It's time' – used the Internet, googling information about the ways other protests had been organized, from Slovakia to Georgia. This use of the Web was something new in the history of east European velvet revolutions. 'I'm not a child of the Internet,' a Belgrade student demonstrator told me in 1997, 'but I'd like to be.'[8] When Ukrainian students started erecting tents on Kiev's main shopping boulevard in the early hours of Monday morning, their website immediately announced this fact to the world, in English, at 02:33:11. They later explained that they had expected the regime to falsify the results of the second round and had therefore prepared their next moves well in advance. That same Monday, many Ukrainian diplomats, both in Kiev and abroad, announced their 'total and unconditional support' for Yushchenko. Their statement was emailed around the world.

What changed everything, however, was the response of ordinary people. At first thousands of Kiev's citizens demonstrated, then hundreds of thousands; soon after, people from the rest of the country answered the call to come to Kiev. One was irresistibly reminded of Prague in 1989 or Poland during the first Solidarity revolution in 1980 and 1981. But where in Poland a quarter-century before it was workers and peasants who were in the vanguard, here it was a fledgling middle class – students, travel agents, the owner of a beauty parlour.

During those revolutionary autumn days, Yushchenko and Tymoshenko usually appeared together on the platform in Independence Square: he a tall, solid, reassuring figure, the horrible pockmarks on his face from the dioxin poisoning now the stigmata of a national hero; she a small, intense woman often in Ukrainian national dress, with her blonde-dyed hair braided in faux-peasant style. The 'gas princess' became the 'goddess of the revolution', though all the time looking more like Marie Antoinette.

The Orange Revolutionaries' first commandment was: never use violence. This is the feature that most plainly distinguishes velvet revolutions from the Jacobin and Bolshevik models of 1789 and 1917. As in several other cases during and since 1989, members of the security forces stepped back from the very brink of using force against the protesters.[9] Yushchenko, Tymoshenko and their allies kept Independence Square full, they maintained peaceful blockades around government buildings, and they waited for the chance to negotiate.

The Supreme Court ordered the central election commission not to make any announcement of victory, pending an investigation of fraud. On 3 December, the Supreme Court found that fraud had indeed taken place and ordered that the second round of elections be repeated by 26 December. Meanwhile, aided by international mediators at a series of 'round table' meetings, Yushchenko made a deal with the outgoing president, Kuchma, who agreed to step aside and to stop supporting Yanukovych. Yushchenko, for his part, agreed to a reduction of presidential power. Parliament passed the appropriate constitutional amendments on 8 December.

Yushchenko won the 26 December repeat of the second round of the elections and was inaugurated as president in January. Tymoshenko was confirmed as prime minister on 4 February.

Oligarchs who originally opposed the newly elected leaders seem to be giving their grudging assent to the new order. Speaking at the World Economic Forum in Davos in January 2005, Pinchuk said that he would support the new power-holders if they do not resort to illegal actions, and he thought that Rinat Akhmetov, the supreme oligarch in eastern Ukraine, would do the same. All they asked for, said Pinchuk, was respect for the law. To anyone who knows their record, this may sound like humbug; but it is useful humbug.

3

Much has been made of a supposedly sharp religious, historical and linguistic division between the Ukrainian western half of the country and the Russian eastern half. The reality is more complicated. Ukraine is a country with a variety of religions, including considerable numbers of Greek Catholics, but Orthodox believers are a large majority, and their votes were split between the two candidates. Culture and history influence today's political outcomes, but they do not dictate them – contrary to the argument of Samuel Huntington's *Clash of Civilizations*. A Ukrainian historian has observed that, after the fall of the Soviet Union, the longer a particular part of Ukraine was ruled by Poland in the past, the more likely were its voters to support candidates emphasizing Ukrainian patriotism. In the first presidential elections in 1991, the candidate of the Rukh independence movement won provinces that had been ruled by Poland for 500 years. In 1994, the pro-Western candidate gained provinces ruled by Poland for 300 years. In 2004, Yushchenko added those ruled by Poland for only 100 years.[10] Western Ukraine keeps expanding eastward.

'The whole country speaks Russian!' said a plainly irritated President Vladimir Putin during the Orange Revolution.[11] In fact, the country is bilingual. Soviet policies ensured that educated Ukrainians spoke Russian, a kindred but quite distinct Slavic language. Today there are young people in western Ukraine who cannot spell in Russian, and there are many Ukrainians and Russians in the south and east who never speak Ukrainian. But most people speak both languages, and many of them shift between the two languages to suit the mood or circumstance – often, disarmingly, in mid-sentence. Political preferences, not language, determined the outcome of the elections. Yushchenko had decisive majorities in provinces where Russian is the major spoken language: in Chernihiv he won 71 per cent of the vote, in Poltava 66 per cent, in Sumy 79 per cent and in Kiev 78 per cent.

Kiev is a Russian-speaking city whose people know when to speak Ukrainian. Kievans always pronounce the name 'Independence Square' in Ukrainian, even when they are speaking Russian. During the campaign, Yushchenko and Tymoshenko spoke in Ukrainian at their public appearances. Declaring victory for the revolution on 8 December, Yushchenko led the crowd in singing the national anthem with his hand on his heart – a habit only recently acquired, apparently from watching US presidents. Across the square, Russian-speaking Kievans put their hands on their hearts and sang it too, or at least tried to sing it, in Ukrainian:

> The glory and freedom of Ukraine live on
> Fate my young brothers will smile upon us yet
> Our enemies shall vanish like dew in the sun
> And we shall rule, brothers, in our own land . . .

Yushchenko and Tymoshenko speak better Ukrainian than Kuchma and Yanukovych do. They also speak better Russian. They are both easterners, proof that Ukrainian identity is not limited to the west. Yet they know that they have to make their case to the miners and steelworkers in the east. Immediately after the revolution each travelled to Donetsk, Akhmetov's eastern bastion, to face the doubters. The 'goddess of the revolution' appeared on Akhmetov's television station. Facing hostile questions in Russian, she held her own. 'The whole country speaks Russian!' – the words may not be as comforting to President Putin as he seemed to believe.

4

Putin's government angrily accused the United States and the European Union of stirring up the Orange Revolution from abroad. Almost daily, the Dutch foreign minister – the Netherlands then held the rotating presidency of the European Union – received angry telephone calls from his Russian counterpart.

Yushchenko leaves no doubt that he wants his country to be part of Europe. In Independence Square, he said, 'The world has seen that Ukraine can already be called European.' Speaking in Davos, he said, 'Our application for EU membership is intended to be filed in the near future.' The EU contributed to the revolution simply by its attractiveness as a club that so many want to join. This is an enduring feature of post-war European politics. Konrad Adenauer, the founding father of the Federal Republic of Germany, spoke as early as the 1950s of Magnet Europa.

Some members of the European Union – Britain and the Netherlands were singled out by one Ukrainian activist – gave significant direct support to election monitors as well as to Ukrainian students, professionals and other groups from civil society. In May 2004, the EU enlarged its membership to take in eight central and east European countries, including the Baltic states, which, like Ukraine, had been Soviet republics until 1991, and neighbouring Poland. This brought the magnet to the Ukrainian border. Under its Dutch presidency, the EU was uncharacteristically sharp in its denunciation of November's electoral fraud. The EU's 'high representative' for foreign policy, Javier Solana, the nearest thing the EU has to a collective foreign minister, then played a leading part at the 'round table' negotiations with Ukrainian leaders in Kiev. Also at the table was the Lithuanian president. However, the informal chair of the talks was Aleksander Kwaśniewski, the president of Poland, the country that in 1989 had pioneered round table talks as a method of achieving regime change.

The Poles came early to the revolution. A large Polish delegation arrived in Independence Square during its first week, to loud cheers, bearing aloft both the red-and-white Polish flag and, significantly, the yellow-on-blue star-spangled banner of the European Union. The Polish presence in Kiev was the latest evidence of a sustained strategy.

In the 1970s, back when Poland was still a Soviet satellite, the influential émigré monthly *Kultura*, based in Paris, proposed a new policy for Poland after the end of communism. Poles should accept the new post-war eastern borders, even though Stalin had seized half of their country. If Poles accepted these borders in advance and did not demand the return of their former lands, they could better cooperate with the democratic opposition movements in the neighbouring Lithuanian, Belarusian and Ukrainian Soviet Republics, and establish friendly relations with them when the Soviet Union collapsed.

These premises were accepted by the anti-communist Polish opposition in the 1980s, and after 1989 they were central to the foreign policy of the Solidarity-led governments of Poland.[12] Warsaw treated Soviet Ukraine as an independent state even before the collapse of the Soviet Union in 1991. Then Poland quickly signed a treaty with independent Ukraine that recognized the current borders and protected national minorities in both countries.

After 1995, Poland's president, Aleksander Kwaśniewski, a former Communist, adopted the strategy developed by *Kultura* and pioneered by Solidarity. Along with President Kuchma, Kwaśniewski jointly commemorated the national tragedies of both Poles and Ukrainians. That he developed a close relationship with Kuchma is one reason Kwaśniewski was an acceptable mediator for both sides in the most critical moments of the revolution. Poland has constantly lobbied for a more generous approach by the EU to Ukraine. In addition to the reluctance of older EU members to accept a relatively poor eastern European country, the main problem was the Kuchma regime. Now Kwaśniewski can speak in bolder tones. Sharing the podium with Yushchenko at Davos, Kwaśniewski delivered a passionate appeal for EU membership for Ukraine, 'this wonderful country . . . a great nation with great leaders'.

What of the American involvement in the election? The US government – and individual American donors – did more to support Ukrainian democrats than western Europeans did. The US State

Department has said it spent $65 million in Ukraine over 2003 and 2004. George Soros's foundation in Ukraine, the International Renaissance Foundation, reported on 20 October 2004 that it had allocated $1,201,904 to non-governmental organizations for 'elections-related projects'. Most of these US dollars (like west and central European funding) went to NGOs, including groups that provided training for student activists and support for an independent press and television, as well as an election-monitoring organization and two independent exit polls. As we have noted, these exit polls played a significant part in helping to start the revolution.

Was all this activity 'intervention in the country's internal affairs', as the old Soviet Union would have put it? It certainly was. So were the very large sums poured into Yanukovych's campaign by Russian sources, which have been estimated in the Russian press to amount to some $300 million. So were the Russian political advisers who helped design the dirty campaign against Yushchenko. So was the summons delivered to Tymoshenko by Russian authorities demanding that she submit to interrogation on criminal charges. (She responded: 'Please do not hinder the struggle for liberation of the Ukrainian nation.'[13]) So were the two campaign appearances in Ukraine by Putin, supporting Yanukovych. The investigation of the poisoning of Yushchenko continues, with the initial evidence suggesting that the toxin most likely came from Russia.

Some 'interventions' by foreigners are justifiable, some are clearly not. There should be an open debate about the ground rules of external, mainly financial intervention to promote democracy, just as there is already a sophisticated debate about the criteria for military intervention on humanitarian or other grounds.[14] But American and European policies in Ukraine were well inside morally defensible limits. The Orange Revolution was not made in Washington, or imposed by Brussels. The West helped citizens of Ukraine to do what they wanted to do for themselves.

After he was elected, Viktor Yushchenko went on holiday in the

Carpathian mountains with Mikheil Saakashvili, who in 2004 became president of Georgia after that country's Rose Revolution. The two issued a Carpathian Declaration, hailing the changes in their two countries as the beginning of 'a new wave of liberation of Europe which will lead to the final victory of freedom and democracy on the European continent'. In an article in the *Financial Times*, President Saakashvili made it clear that this 'third and final wave of the European liberation' should embrace 'the whole post-Soviet region'.[15]

Wishful thinking? Perhaps. Yet some conservatives in Moscow seem to agree. During the Ukrainian events, *Rossiskaia gazeta*, a journal close to the Kremlin, wrote:

> Russia cannot afford to allow defeat in the battle for Ukraine. Besides everything else, defeat would mean velvet revolutions in the next two years, now following the Kiev variant, in Belarus, Moldova, Kazakhstan, Kyrgyzstan and possibly Armenia.[16]

Ukraine's Orange Revolution will also have a direct impact on Putin's increasingly undemocratic state. If nothing else, the free press and television of a large, Russian-speaking neighbour will challenge his regime's control of information. In a poll commissioned by a Russian news service, Russians were asked: 'Do you think a political crisis similar to that in Ukraine is likely to occur in Russia?' Some 42 per cent replied 'never', 35 per cent said 'yes, but not now', and 17 per cent, 'yes, and it will happen soon.'[17] In a conversation in January 2005, Viktor Pinchuk claimed his Russian business partners, his brother oligarchs, were envious of the world esteem being enjoyed by their Ukrainian counterparts. Then he recalled a joke heard recently in Moscow: 'Leonid Kuchma wrote a book called *Ukraine is Not Russia*. Now Putin is writing a book called *Russia is Not Ukraine*.'

2005

Given the optimistic tone of this essay, it is important to acknowledge that things did not go as I had hoped in Ukraine following the Orange

Revolution. Ukraine's trajectory turned out to be very different from those of its central European neighbours. The EU signally and myopically failed to offer Ukraine a clear prospect of membership. Yet even Ukraine's best friends would admit that the Ukrainians sometimes seemed to be their own worst enemies. Corruption and misrule remained rampant; infighting, chronic. As president, Viktor Yushchenko wasted much of his energy fighting his erstwhile Orange ally Julia Tymoshenko. Viktor Yanukovych returned as prime minister in 2006–7, serving notionally under Yushchenko. In an extraordinary turn, Yanukovych then defeated Tymoshenko in the 2010 presidential election.

However, it would be wrong to interpret this simply as 'the wheel coming full circle'. Most international observers concluded that, unlike the election of 2004 which sparked the Orange Revolution, that of 2010 was free and fair. Although Yanukovych promised improved relations with Moscow, no one – least of all the oligarchs backing him – thought the result would or should threaten the long-term independence of Ukraine. Rather the reverse. In his election campaign, Yanukovych described integration into the EU as 'our strategic aim'. Remarkably, his first foreign trip as president was to Brussels.

Meanwhile, we have not (at this writing) seen the spread of velvet revolution across the post-Soviet space, as hoped for by president Saakashvili of Georgia and feared by that Russian analyst. My next chapter notes how an attempted velvet revolution was foiled in Belarus less than two years later. As I observe in the concluding essay of this section, it is not only democrats and would-be revolutionaries who can learn from history. Authoritarian rulers like Belarus's Alexander Lukashenko and Russia's Vladimir Putin can learn as well.

The Revolution That Wasn't

'Nah, still don't give a toss . . .' was the response of someone styled 'thedacs' to my appeal for readers of and posters on the *Guardian's* 'Comment is Free' website to think about Belarus. But the flood of other responses showed that a lot of people do care about what's happening in that frosty pressure point between Russia and the EU. And how they disagree; and how little anyone knows what to do about it.

Obviously we should start from the reality of what's happening on the ground in Belarus. The trouble is that what's happening on the ground in Belarus is a contest over the definition, even the very nature, of that reality. The spokespeople and media of each side claim a certain reality, and their purpose is to create it.

As the post-Sovietologist Andrew Wilson demonstrates in his excellent book *Virtual Politics*, the Belarus of President Alexander Lukashenko is one example of a new type of post-Soviet regime that retains power by what Wilson calls 'faking democracy'. At least as important as the KGB (still so called in Belarus) and the other organs of state power that arrest, intimidate or otherwise get rid of opposition leaders are the so-called 'political technologists', private Russosphere agencies with names such as Nikkolo-M (M for

Machiavelli) and Image-Kontakt. They devise ruthless, Machiavellian election strategies that make Alastair Campbell look like one of the more genteel members of the Mothers' Union. Then a group of election monitors from the former Soviet Union, headed by a former Russian interior minister, declares the resulting elections 'free, open and transparent'. Black is white; or rather, in the post-Soviet version, dark grey is light grey. Anything but orange.

On the other side, opposition leaders, helped by European and American advisers, work to create an inspiring narrative of a nation rising up to free itself from the dictatorial yoke. In the Internet age, you can follow this narrative on websites such as that of the Charter 97 group, founded in conscious tribute to the Czechoslovak Charter 77 movement. On www.charter97.org you have, minute by minute, a story of 'dozens of thousands' of demonstrators defying snow, ice and the police on the Sunday night of a fraudulent election. A '10,000-strong column' has become '40,000' (an estimate far larger than that given by any foreign journalist) by 4.05 on Monday morning. 'Today we are born in a different country – a more courageous and free country,' declares the lead post later that morning, calling for people to reassemble in October Square. 'Call your relatives, friends, colleagues, come with your families. We are the majority, and we shall win!'

But they are not the majority. Most independent observers agreed that these elections were very far from free and fair, and that President Lukashenko is unlikely in reality to have got his claimed 82.6 per cent of the vote on a 92.6 per cent turnout. Yet most also believe that the elusive, contested reality of votes actually cast for him was probably well above 50 per cent. And that's not just the snap impression of visiting journalists. The Belarusian writer Svetlana Alexeyevich, for example, who calls Lukashenko a dictator whose time has passed, also observes: 'A large percentage of people in this society agree with what is taking place in the country. It means they can earn a living somewhere, there is some quota for them in institutions of higher learning, there is still some education and healthcare free of charge.' And an economy apparently flourishing on cheap imported Russian energy.

That said, we cannot know what the majority would have been had opposition leaders had equal access to relatively independent mass media, which they did not. So instead they are trying to create a new kind of 'people power' majority with bodies on the streets, in the spirit of the nineteenth-century American president Andrew Jackson: 'One man with courage makes a majority.' And it takes courage to keep turning out on the streets of Minsk.

As I write this, it looks as if they are not succeeding, unlike their Ukrainian, Georgian and Serbian predecessors. The number of demonstrators seems to have diminished day by day, not grown, Ukrainian orange-style. A couple of hundred protesters are reportedly camping out in October Square, despite police harassment, and the opposition has called for another mass rally next Sunday, but the story in the international media is already 'the revolution that wasn't'. Perhaps it will still happen. Perhaps Lukashenko is crowing too soon that Belarus has resisted 'the virus of colour revolution'. But his statement, too, is about creating reality.

By this stage, some readers who know my earlier work may suspect that I've been infected with a nasty bout of postmodern relativism. Not at all. And there is no moral equivalence between Lukashenko and his opponents. But I insist that precisely those of us who care most about the European spread of freedom must be most careful not to confuse our wishes with reality. When, for example, the website of Radio Free Europe and Radio Liberty (www.rferl.org) reports the Belarus story under a continuing headline 'Overcoming Fear', I must point out that a question mark is missing. We must, above all, insist that, even in such a contest of virtual or potential realities, there's still an underlying bedrock of facts, however difficult to find; and we must stick to those facts. There are so many, and only so many, people locked up. There are so many, and only so many, bodies on the streets.

That's our first duty: to tell it as it is. Then there's interpretation. Three major lines of conflict meet in the Belarusian fulcrum. There's the line between democracy and dictatorship, which post-Soviet political technologists such as Nikkolo-M have made it their business to obscure; the clash of the advancing liberal empires of the West – the EU and American-led NATO – with the retreating empire of Russia; and the ongoing argument about the virtues of more free market or 'neo-liberal' as against more statist, planned economies. These, for reasons of space, I'll return to another time. For beyond the facts, and the interpretation, there's always comrade Lenin's question: what is to be done?

Here, without for a moment confusing wishes with reality, I have an answer. There are many reasons for the different paths followed by Belarus's western and eastern neighbours since the end of the Cold War – the Polish way and the Russian way – but one of the most fundamental is this: that the Poles wanted to join the EU and the EU made it clear the Poles could join if they met certain standards of democracy, the rule of law, market economy and so forth. Now it's the Poles – and Slovaks, Czechs, Lithuanians and other recently self-liberated Europeans – who, as new members of the EU, are saying we must do more to sustain the cause of freedom in places such as Belarus. Besides direct support for independent media, civil society and the democratic opposition, and pressuring the country's leaders, the most important thing we can do is to offer that long-term European perspective.

They are right. This is the corner of Belarus's reality we can directly and legitimately change. So if you do give a toss about Belarus, and you are a citizen of the EU, go blog your government till it hurts. And that includes you, 'thedacs'.

2006

1968 and 1989

During the Velvet revolution of 1989 I spied an improvised poster in a Prague shop window. It showed '68' spun through 180 degrees to make '89', with arrows indicating the rotation. 1968 and 1989: a tale of two revolutions. Or at least, two waves of what many called revolution at the time. A fortieth anniversary this year, a twentieth next. Which of the two will be most memorialized? And which actually changed more?

Nineteen sixty-eight will be hard to beat in the commemoration stakes. Already, more ink has flowed recalling that year than did blood from the guillotines of Paris after 1789. Reportedly more than a hundred books have been published in France alone about the revolutionary theatre of May 68. Germany has had its own beer-fest of the intellectuals; Warsaw and Prague have revisited the bitter-sweet ambiguities of their respective springs; even Britain has managed a retrospective issue of *Prospect* magazine.

The causes of this publicistic orgy are not hard to find. The 68ers are a uniquely well-defined generation all across Europe – probably the best defined since what one might call the 39ers, those shaped for life by their youthful experience of the Second World War. Having been students in 1968, they now – at or around the

age of sixty – occupy the commanding heights of cultural production in most European countries. Think they're going to pass up a
chance to talk about their youth? You must be joking. Not important,
moi?

There is no comparable class of 89. The protagonists in that year
of wonders were more diverse: seasoned dissidents, apparatchiks,
church leaders, middle-aged working men and women standing
patiently on the streets, finally insisting that enough was enough.
Students played a role in a few places and, twenty years on, some of
them are now prominent in their countries' public lives. But the leaders
of 89 were generally older, and many of them were, in fact, 68ers.
Even the Soviet 'heroes of retreat' around Mikhail Gorbachev were
shaped by memories of 1968.

It's a general rule that the events we recall most intensely are those
we experienced when young. The dawn you glimpsed when you were
twenty may turn out to have been a false dawn; the one you witness
at fifty may change the world for ever. But memory, that artful shyster,
will always privilege the first. Moreover, while 1968 happened in both
the western and the eastern halves of Europe, in Paris and in Prague,
1989 only really happened in the eastern half.

Politically, 89 changed far more. The Warsaw and Prague springs
of 1968 ended in defeat; the Paris, Rome and Berlin springs ended
in partial restorations, or only incremental change. Probably the largest
street demo in Paris, on 30 May 1968, was a manifestation of the
political right, which the French electorate then returned to power
for another decade. In West Germany, some of the spirit of 1968
flowed more successfully into Willy Brandt's reformist social democracy. Everywhere in the West, capitalism survived, reformed itself
and prospered. The events of 1989, by contrast, ended communism in
Europe, the Soviet empire, the division of Germany, and an ideological and geopolitical struggle – the Cold War – that had shaped
world politics for half a century. It was, in its geopolitical results, as
big as 1945 or 1914. By comparison, 68 was a molehill.

Revisited today, much of the Marxist, Trotskyite, Maoist or anarcho-liberationist rhetoric of 68 does look ridiculous, childish and morally irresponsible. It was, to quote George Orwell, a kind of playing with fire by people who don't even know that fire is hot. Evoking the beginning of a 'cultural-revolutionary transitional period' – Chairman Mao's brutal Cultural Revolution thus being held up as a model for emulation in Europe – and describing the Vietcong as 'revolutionary forces of liberation' against US imperialism, Rudi Dutschke told the Vietnam congress in West Berlin that these liberating truths had been discovered through 'the specific relationship of production of the student producers'. The production of bullshit, that is. At the London School of Economics they chanted, 'What do we want? Everything. When do we want it? Now.' Narcissus with a red flag.

Those who in 1968 were so harsh on the way some of their parents' generation (the 39ers) had been fellow travellers with the terrors of fascism and Stalinism might wish, on this anniversary, to make a small reckoning of conscience about their own light-hearted fellow-travelling with terror in faraway countries of which they knew little. But many leading representatives of the 68 generation went on to learn from these mistakes and frivolities. They engaged over subsequent decades in a more serious politics of liberal, social democratic or green 'new evolutionism' (to borrow a phrase from the Polish 68er Adam Michnik), including the ending of a slew of European authoritarian regimes, from Portugal to Poland, and the promotion of human rights and democracy in faraway countries of which they learned to know more.

A balance sheet that describes 68 only as frivolous, evanescent and non-consequential, by contrast with a serious and consequential 89, is thus too simplistic. An essential point is made by that archetypical 68er Daniel Cohn-Bendit: 'We have won culturally and socially while, fortunately, losing politically.' Nineteen eighty-nine produced, with an astonishing lack of violence, a transformation of structures of domestic and international politics and economics. Culturally and socially, it has more the character of a restoration, or at least the reproduction or imitation of existing Western consumer societies. Nineteen sixty-eight produced no comparable transformation of political and economic structures, but it did catalyse a profound cultural and social change, in eastern as well as western Europe. ('1968' here really stands for a larger phenomenon, 'the sixties', with the spread of the pill being more important than any demos or barricades.)

No change of this scale is ever only for the better, and we see some negative effects today; but on balance, this was a step forward for human emancipation. In most of our societies, most of the time, the life chances of women, of people from many sorts of minority and from social classes previously held back by stuffy hierarchies are much greater today than they were before 1968. Even critics of 68 such as Nicolas Sarkozy are beneficiaries of this change. (Could the divorced son of migrants have become president in the pre-1968 conservative idyll of his imagining?)

Sharply contrasting though the two movements were, it is the combined effect of the utopian 68 and the anti-utopian 89 which has produced, across most of Europe and much of the world, a socially and culturally liberal, politically social democratic, globalized version of reformed capitalism. Yet in this anniversary year of 68, we are seeing trouble in the engine-room of that reformed capitalism. What if the trouble gets worse next year, just in time for the anniversary of 89? Now, that could be a revolution.

2008

Well, the crisis of capitalism came even sooner than I had anticipated – starting in the second half of 2008 and achieving its maximum force to mark the twentieth anniversary of 1989. Interestingly, we have seen in Poland and the Czech Republic the emergence of what may yet prove to be a class of '09ers. In both countries, a generation of students and young people born in or around 1989 is becoming politically active, in movements like the Polish Krytyka Polityczna *(Political Critique) and the*

Czech Inventura Demokracie *(Inventory of Democracy), and confronting their parents with the real or alleged failures of the older generation. This can be understood as a milder version of what happened in 1968, when young men and women born in or around 1945 revolted against the real or alleged failures of their mothers and (particularly) fathers.*

1989!

Unsurprisingly, the twentieth anniversary of 1989 added to an already groaning shelf of books on the year that ended the short twentieth century. If we extend '1989' to include the unification of Germany and disunification of the Soviet Union in 1990–1991, we should more accurately say the three years that ended the century. The anniversary books include retrospective journalistic chronicles, with some vivid personal glimpses and striking details, essays in historical interpretation, and original scholarly work drawing on archival sources as well as oral history.* I cannot review them individually. Most add something to our knowledge; some add quite a lot. It is no criticism of any of these authors to say that I come away dreaming

---

* This essay discusses the following books: Mary Elise Sarotte, *1989: The Struggle to Create Post–Cold War Europe* (Princeton: Princeton University Press, 2009); Stephen Kotkin, *Uncivil Society: 1989 and the Implosion of the Communist Establishment*, with a contribution by Jan T. Gross (New York: Modern Library, 2009); György Dalos, *Der Vorhang Geht Auf: Das Ende der Diktaturen in Osteuropa* (Munich: C. H. Beck, 2009); Michael Meyer, *The Year That Changed the World: The Untold Story Behind the Fall of the Berlin Wall* (New York: Scribner, 2009); Michael Meyer, *Histoire secrète de la chute du mur de Berlin* (Paris: Odile Jacob, 2009); Victor Sebestyen, *Revolution 1989: The Fall of the Soviet Empire* (New York: Pantheon, 2009); Jeffrey A. Engel (ed.), *The Fall of the Berlin Wall: The Revolutionary Legacy of 1989* (New York: Oxford University Press, 2009); Constantine Pleshakov, *There Is No Freedom Without Bread!: 1989 and the Civil War That Brought Down Communism* (New York: Farrar, Straus and Giroux, 2009); Romesh Ratnesar, *Tear Down This Wall: A City, a President, and the Speech That Ended the Cold War* (New York: Simon and Schuster, 2009).

of another book: the global, synthetic history of 1989 that remains to be written.

I

Over these twenty years, the most interesting new findings have come from Soviet, American and German archives, and, to a lesser extent, from east European, British and French ones. They throw light mainly on the high politics of 1989–1991. Thus, for example, we find that the Soviet Politburo did not even discuss Germany on 9 November 1989, the day the Berlin Wall would come down, but instead heard a panicky report from Prime Minister Nikolai Ryzhkov about preparations for secession in the Baltic states and their possible effects in Ukraine and Russia. 'I smell an overall collapse,' said Ryzhkov.

It is remarkable to read the fulsome welcome Mikhail Gorbachev's adviser Anatoly Chernyaev gives in his diary on 10 November to the fall of the Berlin Wall: 'This is what Gorbachev has done. . . . He has sensed the pace of history and helped history to find a natural channel.' And it is shaming, for an Englishman, to learn how shamelessly Margaret Thatcher seems to have betrayed her public promises to Germany. 'The words written in the NATO communique may sound different, but disregard them,' she told Gorbachev in September 1989, according to a note of their conversation prepared by Chernyaev. 'We do not want the unification of Germany.'

So, in a classic Rankean advance of historical scholarship, we know more than we did at the time about these traditionally documented areas of high politics. By contrast, we have learned little new about the causes and social dynamics of the mass, popular actions that actually gave 1989 a claim to be a revolution, or chain of revolutions.

I spent many hours of my life standing in those crowds, in Warsaw, Budapest, Berlin and Prague; their behaviour was both inspiring and mysterious. What had moved these individual men and women to come out on the streets, especially in the early days, when it was not self-evidently safe to do so? What swayed them as a crowd? Who, in Prague, was the first to take a key ring out of his or her pocket, hold the keys aloft and shake them – an action that, copied by 300,000 people, produced the most amazing sound, like massed Chinese bells?

Historians such as George Rudé, with his pioneering study of the crowd in the French Revolution, E.P. Thompson and Eric Hobsbawm have attempted to understand the underlying dynamics of popular protest in earlier periods. It is surely time for contemporary historians, with better sources at their disposal (hours of television, video and radio footage, for example), to take up the challenge of trying to analyze 1989 from below, and not merely from above.

Every writer on 1989 wrestles with an almost unavoidable human proclivity that psychologists have christened 'hindsight bias' – the tendency, that is, to regard actual historical outcomes as more probable than alternatives that seemed real at the time (for example, a Tiananmen-style crackdown in central Europe). What actually happened looks as if it somehow had to happen. Henri Bergson talked of 'the illusions of retrospective determinism'. Explanations are then offered for what happened. As one scholar commented a few years after 1989, no one foresaw this, but everyone could explain it afterward. Reading these books, I was again reminded of the Polish philosopher Leszek Kołakowski's 'law of the infinite cornucopia', which states that an infinite number of explanations can be found for any given event.

A great virtue of Mary Elise Sarotte's *1989* is that she makes the problem of hindsight bias explicit, and systematically explores the roads not taken. She reminds us, for example, how close East Germany may have come to bloodshed in Leipzig on 9 October 1989: the authorities mobilized a force of eight thousand men, including police, soldiers and Stasi; hospitals were told to prepare beds for possible victims. And she looks at the diplomatic models that were mooted but not executed in the shaping of a new European order in 1990, including that of a pan-European security system built around the continued existence of two separate German states.

Every writer has a professional, geographical or disciplinary bent. Journalists, politicians, diplomats, historians, political scientists, transitologists, scholars of social movements, economists, experts in security studies, civil resistance and international relations – all come to 1989 with their own particular experiences, methods, comparative frames of reference and jargon. Often, they end up saying much the same thing in different ways.

Success has many fathers, and everyone has a favourite. Poles and Catholics like to highlight the role of the Polish pope, particularly in his inspiring visits to Poland in 1979, 1983 and 1987. Germans and Hungarians single out the contribution of Hungarian reform communists who opened the Iron Curtain and let East Germans escape through it. (Michael Meyer, in a book full of vivid personal recollections of events he witnessed as a *Newsweek* correspondent, calls this the 'untold story' of 1989; well, in English perhaps, but in German it has been often told.) Russianists usually give the largest credit to Gorbachev. Germans on the left make the pitch for their version of détente, known as *Ostpolitik;* Americans on the right make it for Ronald Reagan. (Romesh Ratnesar subtitles his dispensable book on Reagan's 1987 'tear down this wall' speech in Berlin 'A City, a President, and the Speech That Ended the Cold War.')

There is nothing wrong with such a plurality of perspectives. Each illuminates a different part of the elephant, or views the whole beast from a different angle. But whenever an author seizes on a single element and says this is *the* explanation, *the* key, you know he is wrong.

Regrettably, Stephen Kotkin, a celebrated historian of the Soviet Union, falls into this trap when he turns his attention to countries he knows less well.[1] *Uncivil Society* contains a lot of meaty, interesting historical explanation of communism's failure, but it is spoiled by a stridently revisionist argument that 1989 was, as the book's subtitle

suggests, little more than an 'implosion of the communist establishment'. This establishment of the party-state, or 'uncivil society' (by
contrast with what he identifies as the imagined or idealized 'civil
society' celebrated by dissident and Western intellectuals at the time),
'brought down its own system'. Except in Poland, 'the focus on the
opposition falls into the realm of fiction.'

His polemic peaks in this line: 'The GDR [East Germany] was a
Ponzi scheme that fell in a bank run.' Now this statement might do
as a provocation in the classroom; as a serious assertion in a book it
is little short of ludicrous. True, thanks to exhaustive research by historians such as Andre Steiner and Jeffrey Kopstein, we now have a clear
understanding of the scale of the GDR's hard currency debt, and the
impact this had on the communist leadership in the autumn of 1989.
On becoming party leader in succession to Erich Honecker, who had
concealed the depth of the problem from most of his colleagues –
and in some sense perhaps even from himself – Egon Krenz asked
for an honest report on the country's economic position. At the end
of October, he was told that the GDR was 'dependent to the greatest
possible extent on capitalistic credit'. But a state is not a bank, let
alone a Ponzi scheme. States can live for long periods with large debt
burdens. States do not simply 'go bankrupt'.

And the GDR was a particular kind of state: it was the Soviet
Zone of Occupation turned into a satellite of the Soviet Union. So
long as that nuclear-armed superpower was prepared to bear the
burden of its satellite states, the GDR could have continued to exist.
But Mikhail Gorbachev and his advisers reckoned that their best
chance of modernizing the Soviet Union lay in large-scale economic
cooperation with the other Germany – the Federal Republic – and
other Western partners. As well as having a strong objection in principle to the use of force, Gorbachev felt it was not worth risking that
prospect of Soviet modernization by supporting repression in the
GDR. If he, or a different Soviet leader, had made a different call,
the GDR could have survived for many years – as a miserable, debt-

ridden, crisis-torn country on the front line of a miserable, crisis-torn empire, to be sure, but that would not be the first such case in history.

The metaphor of the bank run, to which Kotkin often returns, shows what else is defective in his thesis. In a bank run, a mass of individuals, acting in panic, in a wholly uncoordinated fashion, run to a bank to get their personal deposits back. They have no other purpose. They have no organization. They articulate no vision of a better bank, let alone of a different banking system in an alternative polity. This is apparently what Kotkin wants to argue. Always excepting the Polish case, he sees in the crowds in the streets in 1989 only 'social mobilization absent corresponding societal organization'.

And so, referring to the rapid development of Czechoslovakia's Velvet Revolution through mass demonstrations to a nationwide general strike, he writes, 'None of this was inspired or led by dissidents or Civic Forum, which was abolished not long after 1989.' So the general strike somehow called itself. When 300,000 people on Wenceslas Square chanted 'Havel na hrad!' – 'Havel to the Castle!' – this did not mean that Havel's biography, personality or highly visible leadership had anything whatever to do with it. For this was just another 'implosion' of a communist establishment. To anyone who was there, or who simply reads the careful accounts by Czech and Western historians who have studied the Velvet Revolution in detail, this claim is as untenable as the one about the Ponzi scheme. This is revisionism on stilts.

The point about such moments of popular mobilization and civil resistance is that, given certain preexisting conditions (including what may be tiny opposition groups and isolated political prisoners like Havel or Aung San Suu Kyi), forms of societal organization such as Civic Forum – improvised, often chaotic, but nonetheless definitely organization – can emerge with extraordinary speed. This is a phenomenon that historians of 1989 should study more deeply, not deny. To claim that popular and opposition agency in eastern and central Europe had nothing to do with the outcome is as absurd as it would be to claim that 'the people' alone toppled communism and a nuclear-armed empire. As with all historical processes, agency and structure must be understood in a complex interplay.

2

In truth, the essence of 1989 lies in the multiple interactions not merely of a single society and party-state, but of many societies and states, in a series of interconnected three-dimensional chess games. While the French Revolution of 1789 always had foreign dimensions and repercussions, and became an international event with the revolutionary wars, it originated as a domestic development in one large country. The European revolution of 1989 was, from the outset, an international event – and by international I mean not just the diplomatic relations between states but also the interactions of both states and societies across borders. So the lines of causation include the influence of individual states on their own societies, societies on their own states, states on other states, societies on other societies, states on other societies (for example, Gorbachev's direct impact on east-central Europeans) and societies on other states (for example, the knock-on effect on the Soviet Union of popular protest in east-central Europe). These portmanteau notions of state and society have themselves to be disaggregated into groups, factions and individuals, including unique actors such as Pope John Paul II.

The end of communism in Europe brought the most paradoxical realization of a communist dream. Poland in 1980–1981 saw a workers' revolution – but it was against a so-called workers' state. Communists dreamed of proletarian internationalism spreading revolution from country to country; in 1989–1991, revolution did finally spread from country to country, with the effect of dismantling communism. Yet the story is as much one of unintended consequences as it is of deliberate actions – let alone of historical necessity.

So what happened in 1989 can be understood only on the basis of a scrupulous, detailed chronological reconstruction of intended and unintended effects, in multiple directions on multiple stages, day by day and sometimes – as on the evening of 9 November in Berlin – minute by minute. The reporting or misreporting of events, especially by television, is itself a vital part of the causal chain. When a trusted, avuncular presenter on the 10:30pm West German television news declared that 'the gates in the Wall are wide open', they were not yet wide open; but this report helped to make them so, since it increased the flood of East Berliners (who watched and were more inclined to believe West German television) hoping to get through the frontier crossings to the West, and the crowds of West Berliners coming to greet them on the other side. An erroneous report on Radio Free Europe that a student called Martin Šmid had been killed in the suppression of the 17 November 1989 student demonstration in Prague helped to swell the protesting crowds in the first days of the Velvet Revolution in Czechoslovakia. (In what seems to me the best, and certainly the most amusing, of the retrospective chronicles, György Dalos tells how the student came home the next evening to be told by his somewhat agitated father that he was reportedly dead.)

A model of the kind of fine-grained, multinational analysis that we need is the work of the Harvard scholar Mark Kramer on Soviet–east European relations, so far published only in a series of scholarly articles, research papers and book chapters.[2] Basing his work on extensive digging in Soviet and east European archives, plus a wide range of published sources, Kramer demonstrates the full intricacy of the interaction between imperial centre and periphery. He concludes that what he calls the 'spillover' was mainly from the Soviet Union to eastern Europe between 1986 and 1988, in both directions in 1989 and then mainly back from eastern Europe to the Soviet Union in 1990–1991, as the Baltic states, Ukraine and eventually Russia itself were emboldened to follow the east-central European example of self-liberation. If leading academic publishers are not already pursuing Kramer to turn this work into a book, they should start doing so now.

Important though it is, the Soviet–east European interaction is only part of a wider international setting. During the first half of 1989, the new US administration of George H. W. Bush was extremely reticent in its response both to Gorbachev and to the changes being pushed forward by a combination of reform communists and dissidents in Poland and Hungary. What we have learned from the Soviet and east European archives confirms that Washington's assessment was, in fact, far too sceptical. (In one of several excellent scholarly essays in a volume edited by Jeffrey Engel, Melvyn P. Leffler notes how then Defense Secretary Dick Cheney suggested that Gorbachev's policies 'may be a temporary aberration in the behavior of our foremost adversary'.) Nor did Bush set much store by bearded dissidents who looked like something out of Berkeley in the 1960s. Victor Sebestyen, in a book full of sharp snapshots and crisp narrative, has a well-sourced account of the president meeting with the leading Hungarian dissident János Kis in Budapest in July 1989, and subsequently telling aides, 'These really aren't the right guys to be running the place.' Much better to stick with a preppy reform communist.

Yet even though Washington's cautious attitude partly resulted from a misassessment, this was actually the best possible position it could have taken. This time around, unlike in 1956, no one in Moscow could suggest with even a jot of plausibility that the United States was stirring the cauldron in eastern Europe. On the contrary, Bush personally urged General Wojciech Jaruzelski to run for Polish president, as a guarantor of stability, and he was obsessed with doing nothing that could derail Gorbachev. Sarotte suggests that American restraint made it easier for the Soviet Union, too, to step back and let events unfold on the ground in east-central Europe. With some exaggeration, one might say that Washington got it right because it got it wrong.

To give credit where it is due: in the last months of 1989, especially after the fall of the Wall and throughout 1990, this initial super-abundance of caution turned into a combination of entirely deliberate restraint ('don't dance on the Wall!' was the injunction heard in the corridors of the White House and the State Department) and some quite impressive statecraft in support of Helmut Kohl's drive for German unification on Western terms. But for the decisive nine months, from the beginning of Poland's roundtable talks in February to the fall of the Wall in November, the United States' contribution lay mainly in what it did not do.

That is even more true of the other superpower. Kramer argues that at several moments Gorbachev did quietly nudge east European communist leaders in the direction of bolder change. But for the most part, his crucial contribution was to accept changes happening at the periphery of the Soviet Union's outer empire, rather than attempting to slow down or reverse them.

When Helmut Kohl asked him what he thought of the Hungarians' decision to open the Iron Curtain to Austria, he replied, 'The Hungarians are a good people.'[3] Another telling example comes from Poland in August 1989, at a moment when the Solidarity adviser Tadeusz Mazowiecki was trying to form a government led and shaped by non-communists. The last leader of Poland's communist party, Mieczysław Rakowski, records in his diary a telephone conversation with Gorbachev: 'When I [Rakowski] said that one could not alter the situation with the help of a state of emergency, G. said that a new variant of martial law [*stan wojenny*, the Polish term for the martial law imposed by General Jaruzelski in December 1981] is impossible and, however wearisome it would be, we would have to get out of this situation without resorting to such means.' He was, as the German writer Hans Magnus Enzensberger observed, an example of a new kind of hero: the hero of retreat.

Yet Gorbachev's laid-back attitude was based on a much deeper misapprehension than Bush's. He mistakenly believed such changes would stop at the frontier of the Soviet Union, which he saw as a country, not an internal empire. Instead, as Kramer shows, the revolutionary changes in east-central Europe contributed directly to the dissolution of the Soviet Union itself. Robert Conquest, the historian of the Soviet Great Terror and Ukrainian famine, asked Gorbachev many years later whether, if he had known where it would all lead, he would have done the same again. He replied: 'Probably not.'[4]

It is perhaps a characteristic of superpowers that they think they make history. Big events must surely be made by big powers. Yet in the nine months that gave birth to a new world, from February to November 1989, the United States and the Soviet Union were largely passive midwives. They made history by what they did not do. And both giants stood back partly because they underestimated the significance of things being done by little people in little countries.

China also plays an important part. The Tiananmen Square massacre occurred on the very day of Poland's breakthrough in a semifree election, 4 June 1989. I will never forget seeing on a television screen in the makeshift offices of the Polish opposition daily *Gazeta Wyborcza*, amid the excitement of Poland's election day, the first footage of dead or wounded Chinese protesters being carried off Tiananmen Square. 'Tiananmen' happened in Europe, too, in the sense that both opposition and reform communist leaders saw what could happen if it came to a violent confrontation, and redoubled their efforts to avoid it.

To put it another way, the fact that Tiananmen happened in China is one of the reasons it did not happen in Europe. However, an influence then flowed back in the other direction: from the Soviet Union and eastern Europe to China. As David Shambaugh and others have documented, the Chinese Communist Party systematically studied the lessons of the collapse of communism in Europe, to make sure it did not happen to them. Today's China is a result of that learning process.

The year 1989 was one of the best in European history. Indeed, I am hard pushed to think of a better one. It was also a year in which the world looked to Europe – specifically to central Europe, and, at the pivotal moment, to Berlin. World history – using the term in a quasi-Hegelian sense – was made in the heart of the old continent, just down the road from Hegel's old university, now called the Humboldt University. Twenty years later, I am tempted to speculate (while continuing to work with other Europeans in an endeavour to prove this hunch wrong) that this may also have been the last occasion – at least for a very long time – when world history was made in Europe. Today, world history is being made elsewhere. There is now a Café Weltgeist at the Humboldt University, but the Weltgeist itself has moved on. Of Europe's long, starring role on the world stage, future generations may yet say: nothing became her like the leaving of it.

In any case, the longer-term consequences of 1989 are only now beginning to emerge. They, too, belong in the synthetic global history of 1989 that, partly for this reason, could not have been written sooner. But after two decades, the time has come for a brilliant young historian – at home in many languages; capable of empathizing both with powerholders and with so-called ordinary people; a writer of distinction; tenured, but with few teaching obligations; well-funded for extensive research on several continents; Stakhanovite in work habits; monastic in private life – to start writing this necessary, almost impossible masterpiece: a kind of Wagnerian *Gesamtkunstwerk* of modern history. With luck, he or she should have it ready for the thirtieth anniversary, in 2019.

2009

Velvet Revolution in Past and Future

In the autumn of 1989, the term 'velvet revolution' was coined to describe a peaceful, theatrical, negotiated regime change in a small central European state that no longer exists. So far as I have been able to establish, the phrase was first used by Western journalists and subsequently taken up by Václav Havel and other Czech and Slovak opposition leaders.[1] This seductive label was then applied retrospectively, by writers including myself, to the cumulatively epochal events that had unfolded in Poland, Hungary and East Germany, as in 'the velvet revolutions of 1989'.

Twenty years later, in the summer of 2009, the Islamic Republic of Iran staged a show trial of political leaders and thinkers it accused of fomenting *enghelab* -e *makhmali* – that is, precisely, velvet revolution. Across the intervening years, dramatic events in places including Estonia, Latvia, Lithuania, South Africa, Chile, Slovakia, Croatia, Serbia, Georgia, Ukraine, Belarus, Kyrgyzstan, Lebanon and Burma were tagged with variants of adjective + revolution. Thus we have read about singing (Baltic states), peaceful, negotiated (South Africa, Chile), rose (Georgia), orange (Ukraine), colour (widely used, post-orange), cedar (Lebanon), tulip (Kyrgyzstan), electoral (generic), saffron (Burma) and most recently, in Iran, green revolutions. Often, as in the original Czechoslovak case, the catchy labelling has been popularized through the interplay of foreign journalists and political activists in the countries concerned.

These events could, with widely varying degrees of plausibility, be described as attempts – by no means all of them successful – to make a 1989 kind of peaceful, negotiated regime change, including elements of mass protest, social mobilization and nonviolent action. Velvet revolution, it seems, has not just a past but also a present and perhaps a future. Starting as the moniker for a single historical event – *the* velvet revolution in Czechoslovakia in 1989 – it has cast off the definite article to become simply 'velvet revolution': the genus VR.

I

Painting with a deliberately broad brush, one might contrast an ideal type of 1989-style revolution, VR, with an ideal type of 1789-style revolution, as further developed in the Russian Revolution of 1917 and Mao's Chinese revolution. The 1789 ideal type is violent, utopian, professedly class-based and characterized by a progressive radicalization, culminating in terror. A revolution is not a dinner party, Mao Zedong famously observed, and he went on:

> A revolution is an uprising, an act of violence whereby one class overthrows another.... To right a wrong it is necessary to exceed proper limits, and the wrong cannot be righted without the proper limits being exceeded.[2]

The 1989 ideal type, by contrast, is nonviolent, anti-utopian, based not on a single class but on broad social coalitions, and characterized by the application of mass social pressure – 'people power' – to bring the current powerholders to negotiate. It culminates not in terror but in compromise. If the totem of 1789-type revolution is the guillotine, that of 1989 is the round table.[3]

Nonviolent revolution feels to many like a contradiction in terms.

For two hundred years, revolution has been associated with violence. That is one reason people want to qualify these new-style revolutions with a softening adjective. During an internal debate among the leaders of the original velvet revolution, in Prague in autumn 1989, one Czech dissident even queried whether they should use the word 'revolution' at all, since it implied violence.[4] 'Let us refuse any form of terror and violence,' declared the Information Bulletin of the Civic Forum on 2 December 1989. 'Our weapons are love and nonviolence.'[5]

In the case of Pope John Paul II and of Aung San Suu Kyi and other Burmese Buddhists, one can say that the choice of peaceful means was primarily a moral and religious one. 'Defeat evil with good!' was the Polish Pope's often repeated message. In most cases, however, this is a strategic rather than a moral choice – and none the worse for that. Definitionally characteristic of the 1989 type of revolution is a strategic preference for nonviolent action on the part of those who desire change. VR can therefore also be considered as a category of, or overlapping with, another genus: civil resistance.[6]

Trotsky once characterized revolution as 'the forcible entry of the masses into the realm of rulership over their own destiny'.[7] In VR, this happens too, but a vital line is preserved between the forcible and the violent. We speak colloquially of 'the force of numbers', and that is the kind of force we are talking about here. 'If I see 200,000 people, I will resign,' Ukrainian President Leonid Kuchma said dismissively of a relatively small opposition demonstration some years before the 'orange revolution.' In 2004, there were some 500,000 orange-waving protesters on the streets of Kiev – and Kuchma's chosen successor had to resign soon after his fraudulent election victory.[8] These events are characterized by vast turnouts, so that journalistic estimates of numbers become a branch of poetry. How many demonstrators, garlanded in green, filled the streets of Tehran from Revolution (Enqelab) Square to Freedom (Azadi) Square on that unforgettable June 15, 2009?[9] Two million? Three million? No one could know exactly; no one will ever know.

The revolutions of 1789 in France, 1917 in Russia and 1949 in China – all were at some point professedly utopian; all promised a heaven on earth. VR is typically anti-utopian, or at the very least nonutopian. In a given place, it aspires to create political and legal institutions, and social and economic arrangements, that already exist elsewhere (for example, in established liberal democracies) and/or that are claimed (often wrongly, or with much retrospective idealization) to have existed in the same place at an earlier time. François Furet, the historiographer of the French Revolution, doubted if the velvet revolutions of 1989 should properly be called 'revolutions' at all, since they produced 'not a single new idea'.[10] In this sense, they were closer to an earlier, pre-1789 version of revolution, the one that gave the thing its name: a revolution, a revolving, a turning of the wheel back to a real or imagined better past.

Hannah Arendt quotes, as a perfect encapsulation of this idea of revolution-as-restoration, the inscription on the 1651 great seal of Cromwell's Commonwealth, at the height of the English Revolution: 'freedom by God's blessing restored'.[11] Poland in 1989 could have put those very same words on its seal, had it had one. 'The return to Europe', one of the great mottoes of central Europe's 1989, is also a version of the revolution-restoration theme. Most of the subsequent claimants to the title of VR display some such mixture of an idealized national past and a better present located elsewhere. While these movements manifest some unrealistic, idealistic expectations, none of them are decisively shaped by a utopian ideology, a vision of a new heaven on earth. The 'new idea' is the form of revolutionary change itself, not the content of its ideological aspirations.

To say that the 1789–1917–1949 revolutions were class based is of course a gross historical oversimplification, and even misrepresentation. As we know, the Bolshevik Revolution was not actually a heroic mass action of the working class. But it is fair to say that revolutionary leaders such as Lenin and Mao often claimed to be acting in the name of a class or classes – 'workers and peasants', and so on. In VR, the appeals are typically to a whole society, the nation, the people. Nationalism (or patriotism, according to circumstance and interpretation) is often a driving force of these, as it can be of more violent movements. In practice, the strategic key to mass mobilization – to getting those inestimable peaceful crowds out on the streets, to generating 'people power' – often lies precisely in building the broadest possible coalitions between classes, sections of society and interest groups that do not normally cooperate, and among which non-democratic powerholders had previously been able to 'divide and rule'.

In old-style revolution, the angry masses on the street are stirred up by extremist revolutionary leaders – Jacobins, Bolsheviks, Mao – to support radicalization, including violence and terror, in the name of utopia. Bring on the red guards! In new-style revolution, the masses on the street are there to bring the powerholders to the negotiating table. The moment of maximum mass mobilization is the moment of turn to negotiation; that is, to compromise. Or in some cases, to violent repression – at least for the time being. For also characteristic of VR is that it often takes a long time to succeed, after many failed attempts, in the course of which opposition organizers, but also some of those in power, learn from their own mistakes and failures – as, for example, in Poland, Serbia and Ukraine. Protesters 'fail again, fail better', to adopt Samuel Beckett's memorable phrasing. Both sides do it differently next time. Eventually, the moment comes when there are two to tango.

So another name for the genus is 'negotiated revolution'. Exit prospects for the ruling elites are critical. Instead of losing their heads on the guillotine, or ending up hanging from lampposts, transition-ready members of an ancien régime, from a president such as F. W. de Klerk all the way down to local apparatchiks and secret policemen, see a bearable, even a rosier future for themselves under a new dispensation. Not merely will they get away with their lives; not only will they remain at liberty; they will also get to retain some of their social position and wealth, or to convert their former political power into economic power (the 'privatization of the nomenklatura'), which sometimes helps them to make startling returns to political power under more democratic rules (as, for example, have post-communists all over post-communist Europe). In VR, it is not just the Abbé Sieyès who survives. Louis XVI gets to keep a nice little palace in Versailles, and Marie Antoinette starts a successful line in upmarket lingerie.

These uneasy and even morally distasteful compromises with members of the ancien régime are an intrinsic, unavoidable part of velvet revolution. They are, as Ernest Gellner once memorably put it, the price of velvet. They produce, however, their own kinds of post-revolutionary pathology. As the years go by, there is a sense of a missing revolutionary catharsis, suspicious talk of tawdry deals concluded between old and new elites behind closed doors and, among many, a feeling of profound historical injustice. Here I am, a middle-aged shipyard worker in Gdańsk, left unemployed as a result of a painful neoliberal transition to capitalism, while over there, in their high-walled new villas, with their swimming pools full of half-naked girls quaffing champagne, the former communist spokesman and the former secret policeman are whooping it up as millionaires. And their first million came from ripping off the state in the period of negotiated revolution.

There is no perfect answer to this problem, but I will suggest two partial ones. First, absent both the catharsis of revolutionary purging (that orgiastic moment as the king's severed head is held aloft) and retroactive sanctions of criminal justice, it becomes all the more important to make a public, symbolic, honest reckoning with your country's difficult past. This alone can establish a bright line between bad past and better future. That is why I have argued that the essential complement to a velvet revolution is a truth commission. Second, establishing the rule of law as fast as possible is vital to lasting success, and corruption is deeply corrosive of it. 'Speed is more important than accuracy,' the famous motto of the no-holds-barred Czech privatizer and free marketeer Václav Klaus, sacrifices the long-term prospects to the short.

One other feature of some velvet revolutions needs to be mentioned. Traditionally, we would think of a revolution as diametrically counterposed to an election: here, the violent overthrow of a dictatorship; there, the peaceful transfer of power in a democracy. But many examples of VR over the last decade, from Serbia to Ukraine to Iran, had an election as the catalytic moment of the new-style revolution.

In hybrid, semiauthoritarian regimes, the holding of an election – albeit not under fully free conditions, with a key distortion being regime control of television – provides the occasion for an initial mobilization behind an opposition candidate, whether Vojislav Koštunica in Serbia, Viktor Yushchenko in Ukraine or Mir Hussein Moussavi in Iran. Real or alleged rigging of the election by incumbent powerholders is then the spark for a wider social mobilization, with burgeoning demands for change not merely in but *of* the system. The colour symbolic of the opposition candidate – orange in Ukraine, green in Iran – becomes, or at least is now claimed to be, the colour of the whole cheated nation, the colour of the 'colour revolution'. So yet another name for this phenomenon, or a large subset of it, is 'electoral revolution'.

Looking at the recent history of electoral revolutions, a prudent authoritarian ruler might reasonably draw this conclusion: don't risk holding any elections at all! But it is striking how few of them actually do draw this conclusion. Formal democracy, in the sense of holding public ceremonies called elections from time to time, has become established as one of the most widespread international norms. Elections are not just, so to speak, the tribute vice pays to virtue; they also seem to be part of the accepted panoply of legitimation for any self-respecting dictator. And nine times out of ten, authoritarian rulers can emerge victorious from these elections, or 'elections', with some combination of genuine popular support, tribal loyalties, media control, propaganda, bribery, intimidation and outright vote-rigging. In the case of Serbia, for example, Slobodan Milošević did win a series of at least semifree, even three-quarters-free elections, with only some vote-rigging, before losing power in an electoral revolution in 2000. Hubris, based on past successes, helpfully nudges such rulers down the road to nemesis.

2

My purpose here has been to sketch out, schematically and impressionistically, a hypothesis, in order then to qualify and interrogate it – including an indication of conditions under which the hypothesis might, over time, be found more or less persuasive. (More or less persuasive being the historian's qualitative, probabilistic counterparts of the scientist's hard, quantitative proof or disproof.) The hypothesis is that 1989 established a new model of nonviolent revolution that now often supplants, or at least competes with, the older, violent model we associate with 1789.

A first, essential qualification consists in stressing the word 'established', as opposed to 'invented'. Semantically, the Czechoslovak revolution may have been the first to be called 'velvet', but central Europe in 1989 did not spirit this model out of the ether. Relevant earlier history includes not just central Europe's own learning process through the failed emancipation attempts of 1953 (East Germany), 1956 (Hungary), 1968 (Czechoslovakia), and 1970–1971 and 1980–1981 (Poland), but also the mobilization to unseat General Pinochet in Chile, where the 1988 plebiscite preceded central Europe's 1989; the toppling of the Marcoses in the Philippines in 1983–1986, which gave us the wonderful Filipino-English term 'people power'; the 'revolution of the carnations' in Portugal in 1974–1975, arguably the first 'velvet revolution' in postwar Europe; and all the way back to the seminal example of Gandhi in India.

So the suggestion is only that 1989 *established* the model, in the sense that, being such a giant, world-changing event, or set of events, 1989 becomes the major historical reference point for this kind of change; and in the sense that there does seem to have been a lot more new-style revolution around since 1989, and less of the old-fashioned kind. Or so, at least, we are told by those who label these events velvet, colour, peaceful, electoral, negotiated, orange, rose, saffron, cedar, tulip, green, etc., revolutions.

Here a second qualification is overdue. Not everything that is called revolution is, in fact, revolution. Our glossy magazines are full of folderol about 'a revolution' in shoe design, English cooking, retail banking or vacuum cleaners; we all know that this is just hyperbole. Now, over the past twenty years, foreign reporters have been quick to slap the label 'revolution' (plus catchy adjective) on mass street protests that look like, say, Prague in 1989, but in substance may not be. Sometimes those reporters are themselves veterans of earlier revolutions, including 1989; sometimes they may merely wish they had been. And for getting your story on the front page, the word 'revolution' is the next-best thing to actual bloodshed. This, in turn, may be partly because readers and editors still consciously or semiconsciously associate the word 'revolution' with bloodshed. Old stereotypes die hard.[12]

This cautionary remark is, however, complicated by the fact that the external journalistic labelling sometimes helps people involved in an event to characterize, and even to understand in a different way, what they themselves are doing. The foreign journalist's story becomes part of their own story. Framing it as a revolution helps to make it so. There is a spectator-actor-spectator loop.

That said, we do need criteria beyond the naively nominal to determine what properly qualifies as a new-style revolution. The literature on revolutions usefully distinguishes between a revolutionary situation, revolutionary events and a revolutionary outcome. The last is the most demanding. I like the new definition of revolution – or definition of new-style revolution – offered by George Lawson in his valuable book *Negotiated Revolutions*. Revolution, he suggests, is 'the rapid, mass, forceful, systemic transformation of a society's principal institutions and organizations'. (This rightly implies that mass nonviolent action can be 'forceful' without being bloody.)

It will take specialists to apply the Lawson Test to each individual country and region. For most of central and eastern Europe, including the Baltic states, I believe the test is clearly passed, as it is for South Africa. In southeastern Europe, the adjective 'rapid' may often seem less appropriate, but for the most part, there surely has been systemic transformation. In Georgia and Ukraine, very large question marks must be in order. Kyrgyzstan surely does not pass the Lawson Test. And what about Lebanon? There are also cases where (at least for the time being) the movement for rapid, mass, forceful, systemic transformation has clearly been crushed. Burma is one of the plainest examples, but in Europe we should not forget the effective repression of an attempted velvet revolution in Belarus in 2006. And many would argue that the movement of Chinese students and workers whose repression began with the massacre on Tiananmen Square on 4 June 1989 (the very day of Poland's breakthrough semifree election) was the most consequential failure of all.

The largest cohort of definite successes is in just one region of the world – post-communist Europe – and most have so far been within the cultural-historical West, if that is taken (*pace* Samuel Huntington) to include Latin America and the world of Orthodox Christianity. In Asia, there is the strong example of 'people power' in the Philippines, although one should note that the Philippines is a mainly Christian country. Among preponderantly Buddhist or Confucian societies, one might point to South Korea and Taiwan. What of the Muslim world? Whether or not Lebanon's 'cedar revolution' passes the Lawson Test, it took place in a country that is nearly 40 percent Christian. The great significance of the attempted 'green revolution' in Iran is that it has occurred in a very Muslim society, in a self-styled Islamic Republic, and even takes the colour of Islam for its own. Beyond that, one might look to the examples of Indonesia, Mali or Maldives.

There does appear to be a statistical correlation between the choice of nonviolent action and broadly liberal democratic outcomes.[13] However, we must beware the fallacy of confusing correlation with cause. It might be that the kinds of society that adopt nonviolent means are also more likely, and better equipped, to consolidate liberal democracy. Both apparent cause and apparent effect could be symptoms of a deeper cause.

A further question is whether the aspiration to more democracy is also definitionally characteristic of VR – in which case, however, the argument for a link between nonviolence and liberal democracy would risk becoming circular. Could you have a velvet revolution to establish a different kind of dictatorship? Hamas and Hezbollah hardly qualify as nonviolent, although they have done well in elections, but what would emerge from, say, a 'scarab revolution' led by the Muslim Brotherhood in Egypt?

3

What should one conclude from all this? That VR is just a political-journalistic tag? That VR exists, but is really just a type of transition characteristic of what one might call the democratization of the wider West over the thirty-five years since the revolution of the carnations in Portugal in 1974? In which case, since most of the wider West has now been democratized, we would be coming to the end of the line. Or should we rather conclude that, as Zhou Enlai is notoriously supposed to have answered when asked what he thought of the French Revolution, 'it is a little too soon to say'? Twenty years, even thirty-five, is a short time for assessing large-scale historical phenomena. If, over the next two decades, there are many old-style, violent revolutions and few new-style, nonviolent ones, my VR hypothesis will be found wanting. If, however, there are more successful examples of VR in non-Western societies, including Muslim, Confucian and Buddhist ones, then it may seem persuasive.

Yet to say 'we must wait and see' misses a vital point. We – if we mean by that liberal democracies and democrats – are not mere observers in this history. We, like the foreign journalists reporting these stories, are also to some extent actors in them.

It cannot be emphasized too strongly that these movements are born from the conditions and the actions of people in the places concerned. These are not Western plots, as authoritarian rulers from Russia to China to Iran now claim – supported in their paranoia by a few conspiracy-minded Western observers. To be sure, there is often Western involvement, some of it public, some covert, but in no single case can one plausibly claim that it has been decisive. Moreover, the allegations of Western conspiracy are themselves part of the local political game, intended to disqualify opposition leaders in the eyes of an anti-Western public opinion and justify locking them up on the grounds of treason. A classic example is the indictment in the show trial of Iranian reformists, which says at one point:

> The velvet revolution has three arms, intellectual, media, and executive, and each of these has relations to a number of American foundations, and there is a kind of division of labor among them. . . . In this triangle of sedition, each of these American organizations performs a certain function and a number of people cooperate with them. Of these, the most important is an institution called Hooffer [*sic,* i.e., the Hoover Institution] at Stanford, created during the Cold War.[14]

And so on.

What emerges clearly from an international comparative study, however, is that the chances of success or failure depend to a significant degree on external factors – but that these must be understood much, much more broadly than just alleged subversive American plots. The prospects for an attempted velvet revolution depend not just on the nature of the state and society it happens in, but also on the place of that state and society in a wider international setting.[15] Painting once again with a very broad brush, one might suggest that the best chances are to be found in semiauthoritarian states that depend to a significant degree, politically, economically and, so to speak, psychologically, on more democratic ones – and most especially when the foreign states with the most passive influence or active leverage on them are Western democracies. Thus, attempts have failed in large, independent, self-referential states such as China but also in small, isolated, peripheral ones such as Burma, sandwiched as it is between China and India.

As Burma found to its cost in 2007, non-Western democracies such as India have generally been less keen than Western ones to exert active leverage to the benefit of velvet revolutions. Themselves often emerging from a colonial experience, non-Western democracies place a high value on sovereignty, and tend to see even well-intentioned forms of noncoercive external intervention as potentially neocolonial. And, of course, they pursue their own national interests. India, for example, apparently feels that it has an economic, military and geopolitical interest in maintaining good relations with the Burmese military regime. Will this continue to be the case? Or will non-Western democracies in time warm to the (profoundly anti-colonial) enterprise of helping people in less free countries to help themselves? The answer they give may be decisive for the future of VR.

How democrats and democracies can enhance the prospects of VR in other places, if they wish to, is the subject for another essay. So is the question whether they should, even if they can; for some would dispute that this goal is either desirable or legitimate. In any case, it has certainly become more difficult over the last decade, as authoritarian rulers in Russia, China, Iran and elsewhere have identified VR as a hostile Western stratagem, and carefully studied its history so as to nip it in the bud.

In attempting to counter it, they have mimicked some of its techniques: for example, sending their own election monitors and founding their own NGOs (which are in fact, to use a British term, quangos, *quasi*-nongovernmental organizations or even GONGOS, government-organised nongovernmental organisations). Now more than ever, I suspect that the long-term, indirect measures that free societies can take will prove more important and effective than the short-term, direct ones. That is also a lesson from the history of the cold war and its ending.

What we cannot credibly do is sit back and pretend that we are no part of this unfolding history, merely neutral spectators of it. That stance itself has an impact, thus belying its own claim. Whether velvet revolution has a future as well as a past will depend, in the first place, on the will and the skill of people in the places concerned; but it will also depend, in smaller measure, on us.

2009

2.

Europe and Other Headaches

Ghosts in the Machine

On All Saints' Day, the Poles remember their dead. It's an amazing sight. At noon, the centre of Poznań was deserted, like an English town at lunchtime on Christmas Day. But in the main cemetery, amid autumnal woods on the outskirts of the city, vast crowds moved slowly down the paths, each family carrying flowers and special candles in wind-resistant jars to lay at the graves of their loved ones. By lunchtime almost every slab was adorned with fresh flowers and burning candles, a flickering garden as far as the eye could see.

I have witnessed this popular festival of remembrance in Poland several times, and every time it is unforgettable. At dusk, as the frost sets in, 10,000 candles become an archipelago of flame amid the dark silhouettes of tombstones and trees. Somewhere in the distance a choir sings an old patriotic hymn. You can almost see the hovering souls of the dear departed. If, at such a moment, your spine does not tingle, there is something wrong with your spine.

Here is what it means to be a European nation: an imagined community of the dead, the living and the as-yet-unborn, bonded together by a glue called memory. Here is the force that kept the Poles going through nearly two centuries of partition and foreign occupation. According to a poll conducted in 1995, 98 per cent of the

Polish population went to the graves on All Saints' Day. Perhaps the proportion is slightly smaller today, as Poland becomes a more 'normal', contemporary, Western-style nation of consumers. Instead of going to the graves, a young Poznanian may stay at home to watch a DVD or go shopping at the local Tesco. (Tesco is doing well in Poznań.)

Up to a point, this is a healthy kind of normalization; but only up to a point. For if you don't know where you come from, you don't know who you are. Anyone who has seen an elderly relative gradually lose their memory understands that a person without memory is a child. A nation without memory is not a nation. And a Europe without memory will not long remain Europe.

Actually, this is one of Europe's most fundamental problems today; less visible, but no less profound, than our economic difficulties or the crises of our welfare states. What Europe was like sixty years ago remains one of the strongest arguments – perhaps the strongest altogether – for continuing to build a European Union. But if no one remembers what Europe was like sixty years ago, that argument has no force.

Take the stretch of Europe I've travelled over the last few days, from Berlin to Poznań. As you look out of the train window, you see wooden barns, solid brick farmhouses and lovely copses of pine, copper beech and silver birch. On a sunlit autumn day it looks like an idyll. But if you know any history then you know that those trees have their roots in a rich compost of corpses. The corpses of Poles, who died fighting against German occupation. The corpses of Jews, who died trying to escape Nazi transports to the death camps. The corpses of Germans, who died on the flight westward before the advancing Red Army. And, not least, the corpses of hundreds of thousands of young Russian soldiers, killed in the advance to Berlin. Those houses you see have almost all been forcibly transferred from one owner to another. Along the way there was the Berlin Wall (its line now hard to trace), the iron curtain, the Stasi and martial law.

Too much remembering brings its own difficulties. In individual men and women, we call this post-traumatic stress. The past haunts you. But in Poland and Germany, as in the rest of Europe, the larger tendency is to forget. People think only of today's discontents. Some Germans blame Poles for taking their jobs. Some Poles feel exploited by German firms. Germans and Poles in unison blame their politicians for high unemployment, crime and social insecurity. They lack the perspective that only history brings.

So, next to history lessons, we need memorials. In Berlin, my wife and I wandered among the dark-grey concrete slabs, or stele, of the Holocaust memorial, which occupies a whole block just south of the Brandenburg Gate. You have an unsettling sense of menace as the narrow, cobbled walkways take you down between these dark, towering blocks; but then you are cheered up by giggling children dashing around playing hide-and-seek in the maze. And so your thoughts turn from the dead to the living, and then back to the dead.

Yet such public, state-supported memorials also bring their dangers. One of the few major sources of controversy between Germany and Poland today is a plan, originated by the organizations of the Germans driven out of what is now Poland at the end of the Second World War, to have a museum of the expulsions. In every case, the question becomes: why should the state mark this tragedy and not that one? Other nations, religious groups or sexual orientations who see themselves as victims demand recognition of their own 'holocaust(s)'.

In Britain, many people wear poppies as we approach Remembrance Day on 11 November. The central ceremony is a wreath-laying at the Cenotaph in Whitehall, and the traditional understanding has been that this commemorates above all the soldiers, sailors and airmen who died to keep us free. More recently, a grand memorial was erected on Park Lane to commemorate animals that were the victims of war. More recently still, a monument to women who died in the Second World War appeared in Whitehall, just up from the Cenotaph. The order of commemoration seems to me peculiarly British: first the armed forces, then animals, then women.

What often works best of all are the small memorials, relating to a particular local community or even a single house. In a small square in what used to be the Jewish quarter of east Berlin there's a memorial to the deported Jews that is nothing more than a bronze sculpture of a simple kitchen table and two chairs, one of them thrown over on to the floor. In Hamburg they have individual cobblestones on the pavement, inscribed with the names and dates of individual Jews who lived in that particular house.

Nowadays, with just a little virtual digging, you can make your own memorial. I am writing this article in the Hotel Rzymski – that is, the Rome Hotel – in Poznań. Its facade, hall and staircase manifest the kind of flattened neoclassicism that could be 1930s Polish, early 1940s Nazi or late 1940s Stalinist. On the first-floor landing I find some framed plans for the 'Hotel de Rome' in Posen (the German name for Poznań) by the architect Franz Böhmer. They are dated 1941. Sitting at my laptop in the renovated café of the hotel, with its postmodern truncated Roman columns, I use the wireless Internet access to google Franz Böhmer. It turns out he was one of Hitler's architects, also commissioned to convert an imperial palace down the road into the Führer's headquarters for overseeing his eastern territories. My laptop shudders. There is a ghost in this machine.

2005

Are There Moral Foundations of European Power?

When I first came to study history at Oxford, my special interest was the German resistance to Hitler. I had already stood in the grim courtyard of the former Wehrmacht headquarters in Berlin, where Claus Count Stauffenberg and his fellow conspirators were shot, and I had witnessed the thirtieth anniversary commemoration of the bomb plot on 20 July 1974. After studying the history of the Third Reich at Oxford, I went back to Berlin to do my graduate work on that city's travails under the Nazis. I was fascinated by the question of what it was that made one man a resistance fighter, another a collaborator: one a Stauffenberg, another an Albert Speer. The case of Adam von Trott was particularly interesting in this regard because his path to the resistance was as long as it was complex. Trott was tortured by the conflict between love of his country and hatred of the dictator ruling it.*

As it happens, I didn't end up writing about the German resistance to Hitler. I discovered that, just across the Berlin Wall, living people were facing the same dilemmas of resistance or collaboration,

*This essay began life as the Adam von Trott Memorial Lecture, jointly sponsored by Balliol College, Oxford, and Mansfield College, Oxford, and delivered in the chapel of Mansfield College – hence the reference in section 1 to the stained glass in the chapel window.

albeit in a milder form, in communist East Germany. So instead of writing a thesis about Berlin under Hitler I wrote a book about Berlin under Honecker. I went on to study the dissidents in communist-ruled central Europe, and to accompany them along the rocky path to liberation. These dissidents under communism had two things in common with the German resisters to Nazism. One was a deep preoccupation with the relationship between morality and politics. The other was a lasting concern with the moral foundations of any new European order that might emerge after the war – that is, in the case of anti-communist dissidents, after the Cold War.

There is an obvious tension between power and morality. Lord Acton advises us to suspect power more than vice. For that very reason, political theorists through history have given us a rich body of thought on this question – from Aristotle's insistence that virtue is both a cause and an end of good government, right through to contemporary writings in the academic study of International Relations addressing issues like humanitarian intervention, human rights, legality and legitimacy. (I hope philosophers will forgive me if I use the terms morality and ethics more or less interchangeably.)

I shall apply this body of learning and thought to something I call 'European power'. That also requires a word of explanation. By the adjective 'European' I mean here primarily 'of or pertaining to the European Union'. I am well aware that there is a great difference between Europe and the European Union, but in this case I do mean primarily the European Union, both as a unique community of states and as a unique actor in foreign policy. The noun 'power' has been most simply and briefly defined as 'the ability to achieve whatever effect is desired', or to put it another way, the ability to get other people to do what you want them to do.

The question 'What kind of power does Europe have?' is an intriguing one. One answer given by American neoconservatives is 'Not much.' Robert Kagan entitled his famous article about Americans being from Mars and Europeans from Venus 'Power and Weakness'.

American power, European weakness. This position is only tenable if, as many neoconservatives do, you have a one-dimensional definition of power, reducing it to the single dimension of military power. Even then, Europe is not lacking in potential military power. After all, the member states of the European Union have more than a million men and women under arms. The EU is, however, characterized by a lack of deployable, operational military power, and of the willingness to use it. One might add that for many Europeans precisely the *unwillingness* to use military power is one of the moral foundations of European power. Be that as it may, one has to consider also two other dimensions of power: economic power, in which the European Union is in most respects an equal of the United States, and what Joseph Nye has called 'soft power', the power to attract by the allures of your economy, your society, your culture – and perhaps even your universities.

There is, however, also a fourth dimension of European power, which is unique to the European Union. It is what I call the power of induction. This is firstly induction in the sense of magnetic induction: the power to make something happen in an object near to you by magnetic attraction. This the European Union has in considerable degree. But that magnetic power depends on the offer of induction in another sense: at the end of the process, our neighbours will be inducted into membership of the European Union, as one is inducted into a club or society. We see this power of induction currently at work in Turkey and Ukraine. This is a power which the United States does not possess in relation to neighbouring states; it is Europe's fourth dimension.

The claim that there are also moral foundations of its power is made more widely about Europe than about any other political community except the United States, and possibly the United Nations. In advocating European integration in the 1920s, Aristide Briand described his project as 'a moral union of Europe'. This claim is advanced in many different ways, and I propose to examine ten of them. My decalogue will be composed not of commandments but of questions.

I

The first kind of claim is that made in the stained glass windows of the chapel at Mansfield College, Oxford. They represent historical figures ranging from Origen and Augustine, through Aquinas and Anselm, Wycliffe, Luther, Calvin, Zwingli, Grotius and William Penn, all the way to Dr Livingstone. The only one missing is Jean Monnet. In short, this is a claim about the spiritual and intellectual heritage of the European Union. I recently heard the president of the European Commission, José Manuel Barroso, quote Paul Valéry's famous description of the foundations of European power: 'Jerusalem, Athens and Rome.' However, Barroso immediately added, 'we should not forget the Arabic-Islamic contribution, and Slavic and Celtic sources.'

More frequently, reference is made to the Judaeo-Christian tradition. At the Congress of Europe at the Hague in May 1948, Count Richard Nikolaus von Coudenhove-Kalergi, the founding father of the Pan-Europa movement, offered another pairing: 'if Europe is to rise again we must base its future upon the two noblest foundations of its past: on Greek individualism and Christian socialism.' But he also quoted a letter from Senator J. William Fulbright, lavishly praising the European project as a bulwark against the Soviet threat and the contribution of this project to 'the forward march of western Christian civilization'. Not language we often hear these days.

The truth is that claims based on, as it were, the stained glass school of European identity are centrally about Christianity – and specifically about *western* Christendom. Historically, there is no way around it. The first known mention of Europeans, *Europeenses*, is in a chronicle of the battle of Poitiers in 733[1] – a battle fought against the invading Arab Muslims. The very term 'Europe' emerged into wider

90

usage from the pen of Pope Pius II, as a successor to the notion of Christendom. 'Europe' was defined consciously as an answer to the encroaching Turks and the advance of Islam. There is a magnificent letter that Pius II wrote to Sultan Mohammad II, the conqueror of Constantinople. In it he first evokes the powers of Europe: 'Spain so steadfast, Gaulle so warlike, Germany so populous, Britain so strong, Poland so daring, Hungary so active and Italy so rich, high spirited and experienced in the art of war.' Then he says to Mohammad II, in effect: you can't possibly beat us, so join us. 'It is a small thing however that can make you, Mohammad, the greatest and most powerful and most famous man of your time. You ask what it is. It is not difficult to find. It is to be found all over the world. A little water, with which you may be baptized and convert to Christianity.' That was the first message of a newly self-conscious, self-defining Europe.

From the 1460s to the 1960s, this notion of western Christendom – Catholic or Protestant, but not Orthodox – was at the centre of a certain narrative and self-definition of the European project, whether by Christian Democrats or Christian Socialists. However, it clearly will not do today. There is a serious question in what sense Europe is still a Christian continent. In the World Values Survey of 2000 the question was asked, 'Is religion very important to you?' 57 per cent of Americans said yes. For Britain the figure was 13 per cent; for France 11 per cent; for Germany 9 per cent. Europe is now probably the most secular continent on Earth. Of our leaders, Tony Blair is an exception in this respect – which is, I think it is fair to say, one reason he gets on better than others with George W. Bush. The Spanish prime minister, José Luis Zapatero, is perhaps more typical. He was recently quoted as saying that Spaniards would like to see less religion and more sport.

Despite the best efforts of John Paul II, and conservative Catholic Poles, there was no explicit reference to God or Christianity in the preamble to the proposed European constitutional treaty. If we are religious in the sense of religious observance in Europe then it is most likely, nowadays, that we're Muslim rather than Christian. In Berlin, the order of active religious dominations is: first Protestant, second Muslim, third Catholic. There are probably more than 15 million Muslims inside the boundaries of the European Union. With immigration, which we need because of declining birth rates, and with further enlargement of the EU to include countries like Bosnia, Albania and Turkey, Europe will become more Islamic. So a self-definition of Europe as actively embodying the values of western Christendom is, it seems to me, now untenable.

2

A second claim for a moral foundation of European power argues that the key historical foundations of this project are to be found not in western Christendom but in the Enlightenment. If you are a historian of ideas you may immediately ask: which Enlightenment? The British or the French Enlightenment, the German or the Polish one? But certainly there is a more credible fit between the values of any of these Enlightenments and the values that the European Union today proclaims than there is between those of the European Union and those of Pope Pius II. This, however, is something that we have in common with the United States. Ralf Dahrendorf wrote a wonderful book about the United States entitled (in German), 'Applied Enlightenment'. Exactly the same could be said of the European Union. In one respect, however, we are behind and in another beyond the United States. We are 'behind' in the clear separation of Church and State, enshrined in the American constitution and practised there ever since. Britain still has an established church. Sweden, advanced progressive Sweden, had an established church until the year 2000. In Germany you are still invited to pay something called *Kirchensteuer*, 'church tax', on your annual tax return.

On the other hand we are 'beyond' the United States in the spirit of Voltaire's 'écraser l'infâme'. Voltaire would be delighted by much that he would see in today's European society, that is to say rampant secularism: a secularism that is an active, offensive ideology. *Laïcité* is, so to speak, the state religion of France. Indeed a French diplomat was quoted the other day as saying, in connection with the proposed European constitution, 'we don't like God.' And the former Spanish foreign minister, Ana Palacio, added, 'the only banner we have is secularism.'

If you look at the post-9/11 discussion you will see that in Europe, even more than in the United States, some of the European reaction did suggest that the problem in relation to Islamic terrorism was Islam itself – not just perversions of it. The clear implication was that the problem with Islam is not that it is perverted religion, or even the wrong religion, but simply that it is religion.

Does this offensive secularism augment European power? Probably not. On the one hand, young Muslims clearly are attracted to Europe in many ways. On the other hand, when they come to live here they are actively repelled by some of what they find in European society: by its aggressive secularism, atheism, moral relativism and hedonism. It is documented fact that some of those young Muslims were so repelled by the kind of offensive secularism that they encountered precisely in Europe – not in their home countries, not in the United States – that it was here that they became terrorists. That is the case of the Hamburg cell of al-Qaida, which was instrumental in the 9/11 attacks on New York; of the Moroccan bombers who bombed Madrid on 11 March 2003; and of the man who murdered Theo van Gogh in the Netherlands. So one could even argue that the offensive secularism of European society is not an asset but rather a liability for Europe's soft power.

3

Thirdly, one might make a claim in classical form about the legitimacy of the European Union as a foreign policy actor. But then we have to ask: by what right, with what authority, does Javier Solana speak for Europe when he goes to mediate in Ukraine? The answer would seem to be: by the proleptic authority of a constitutional treaty not yet ratified. In practice, what we present to the world is a kind of confused, combined authority. Representing 'Europe' at the round table negotiations in Ukraine during the Orange Revolution there was Solana, the EU's 'high representative' for the common foreign and security policy, but there were also a representative of the Dutch presidency of the EU, the Polish president and the Lithuanian president. Those who have direct democratic legitimacy, as members of national governments, are only indirectly responsible for European foreign policy. Those who are directly responsible for European foreign policy only have an indirect legitimacy.

The conclusion here seems to me clear: in terms of classical legitimacy, European power, as currently represented in EU foreign policy, is less legitimate than that of any democratic nation state, including the United States. If you then ask 'by what authority does the representative of this power claim the right to send young soldiers to risk their lives for a policy?' then the answer in the case of the European Union is even more unclear. Indeed, Javier Solana as a putative foreign minister in the proposed constitutional treaty is not given that authority. As Jan-Werner Müller puts it, in a fine essay on European patriotism, the motto *dulce et decorum est pro Javier mori* doesn't quite convince.

4

Next there is a claim, quite popular in Europe at the moment, about the moral value and indeed superiority of a European 'social model': a set of internal arrangements held to embody qualities of social justice, solidarity and equality superior to those in the United States. Oh, and by the way we don't have the death sentence. Thus, for example, the German chancellor Gerhard Schröder said recently, 'we Europeans rightly understand our social model as a unique civilizational achievement.' Only in Europe, he said, has this specific way of working, of economic production and of living together in solidarity been formed.

This, in turn, is related back to a distinctive set of 'European values'. This is the kind of argument we also saw in the manifesto written by Jürgen Habermas and co-signed by Jacques Derrida at the time of the Iraq crisis. It is a definition of the moral foundations of Europe which puts social justice at the centre of a certain set of values, and defines Europe as the Not-America.

This claim does not hold up to closer empirical investigation. For a start, our social model is not unique, in two respects. First, it is not single: there is in fact an enormous variety of social models in the European Union of (at this writing) twenty-five member states, let alone in the wider Europe. In their marvellous book *Varieties of Capitalism*, Peter Hall and David Soskice identify no fewer than three different varieties of democratic capitalism in the European Union today. They label them 'market', 'coordinated' and 'Mediterranean'. Outsiders who come looking for a European social model, as the Chinese have done, end up realizing there is not one but many. So they take bits and pieces, mix'n'match from the Scandinavian model, the French model, the German model, and so on.

Secondly, it is not unique because it is by no means confined to

Europe. Versions of what we call the European social model can be found in Canada, in New Zealand, in Australia, even in some of the more welfare-oriented states of the United States. Nor do I think it is possible to argue convincingly that the European social model is unambiguously morally superior. It is better in terms of income equality and welfare provision, to be sure, but generally worse in terms of employment and creating jobs. And as Bill Clinton pointed out rather well in an international dialogue about what would come to be called 'the third way', unemployment is itself a form of social inequality. Europe is better in terms of welfare entitlements, which is one reason that we attract so many immigrants. It is worse than the United States in its ability to make immigrants feel at home – and that is partly just because they do receive so many welfare entitlements, which create resentment among the poor, the dispossessed and the unemployed already living in those societies. Certainly our social model can hardly claim a golden record in terms of economic growth in recent years, especially in the 'core' countries of France and Germany. We may be better at redistributing wealth but we are not so good at creating the wealth to be redistributed. The currently popular claim for a moral foundation of European power based on the uniqueness and superiority of our social model is thus highly questionable.

5

Some would assert a unique European contribution to what one might call international social justice: justice, that is, between the rich North and the poor South. Now it is the case that member states of the European Union together give three times more in official development aid than the United States gives. It is the case that we're more attentive to concerns about the environment, the Kyoto Protocol and so on. But this pretension is radically undermined by our extremely poor record on trade protectionism and agricultural subsidies.

Focusing on the issue of trade protectionism, the Oxford-based international charity Oxfam has produced what it calls a Double Standards Index. The European Union is top of the list for double standards, because of our trade interventions and agricultural subsidies. In the year 2000, for example, the average EU subsidy to the average European cow was $913; what we gave in aid for each individual human being in sub-Saharan Africa was $8 per head. $913 for a European cow, $8 for an African person. In the meantime there has been some reform of the Common Agricultural Policy (CAP), and we have the 'Everything But Arms' programme to encourage imports from the developing countries. But the fact remains that in 2003 the CAP was still 46 per cent of the EU's budget, seven times its allocation to aid. According to the World Bank, what the developing countries of the world lost in the exports that they might otherwise have made to developed countries, were it not for the trade barriers and agricultural subsidies, was worth an estimated $100 billion. That is double what the whole OECD gave in development aid. So the claim on the basis of a commitment to international social justice is hard to sustain.

6

European policy in the world is said to be distinguished by its respect for international law and international institutions, including the United Nations. Indeed, the European Union does have a good record in terms of procedural legitimacy, compared to the United States. This is partly for the simple reason that the European Union is itself an international institution, or a set of international institutions, built around a body of supra-national law. So by its very nature it will have a tendency to be more respectful of international institutions and international law. (I leave aside the question of what individual member states do on their own behalf: France, for example, acting unilaterally in its former colonies in Africa.)

The deeper moral question is whether this scrupulous respect for international law and international institutions helped or did not rather hinder us in preventing a genocide happening on our own continent – in Bosnia in the years 1992–5. When we did then intervene to prevent 'another Bosnia' in Kosovo, in 1999, we intervened without explicit authority from the UN Security Council. In a fine report, the independent International Commission on Intervention and State Sovereignty has concluded that the intervention in Kosovo was 'illegal but legitimate'. There are hard and serious questions that Europeans need to address about the circumstances in which such an intervention might be illegal but legitimate.

Here, the memory of Adam von Trott and the 20 July 1944 bomb plot against Hitler may be relevant. Tyrannicide is not explicitly sanctioned in international law. In any case, it would be hard to imagine a tyrannicide authorized in advance by a resolution of the UN Security Council. Yet the attempted tyrannicide of 1944 was a profoundly moral act.

7

The European Union is a model of peaceful international conflict resolution. It brings together states which fought each other for centuries, and which have now decided to resolve their conflicts and differences only by peaceful means. This is what led many former members of the European anti-fascist resistance, in many different European countries, to be among the founding fathers of the European project after 1945. Their motto was 'never again'. Or, as Winston Churchill put it, 'make jaw-jaw not war-war'.

It seems to me that this is the single strongest claim to a moral foundation for European power. If we get tired of those endless nego-tiations and bureaucratic compromises in Brussels, we should remind ourselves that Brussels fudge is the price of peace. One of the prob-lems we have in telling the European story to our younger citizens, in answering their entirely legitimate questions – why Europe? what on earth is the European Union for? – is that the best single answer has to be based on a counterfactual statement about what might happen if the European Union did not exist. That is a difficult argu-ment to make because the case is never provable.

Yet this, it seems to me, much more than the Habermasian claim about our social model, is the respect in which the European Union is genuinely both unique and a model. There is at the moment no other such arrangement of states on earth. NAFTA, MERCOSUR and ASEAN do not compare. This is also an element of Europe's soft power, its power to attract. It is, for example, no accident that the Organization of African States renamed itself the African Union. That was a direct tribute to the European Union, although of course the AU is not comparable to the EU in the way it acts. The attrac-tions of this model extend powerfully to our neighbours, most of whom want to join us not just for economic reasons, and not just to secure their own democracy, but also because the European Union is, in Karl Deutsch's term, a security community.

8

Claim number eight: Europe has developed a model of peaceful regime change. This applies less to the existing members of the European Union than to those, on the continent of Europe but just outside the European Union, who want to become members. The European model of peaceful regime change combines the following elements: first, peaceful social pressure from below, including mass civil disobedience – so called 'people power'. Second, negotiations between government and opposition elites, often at a round table. Third, a supportive international framework. This is a model of velvet revolution which in 1989 supplanted the Jacobin–Bolshevik model of 1789. The model has origins that pre-date 1989. One could reach back to the Portuguese 'revolution of the carnations' in 1974, and to the transformations in Spain and Greece. And it reaches forward to Serbia in 2000 and to Ukraine in 2004.

Here I want to make just two points about this model of peaceful regime change. The first is a moral as well as a political one. In discussing the Polish Solidarity movement's approach to the end of communism, the Polish opposition leader and historian Adam Michnik said the lesson they had learnt from European history is that those who start by storming Bastilles end up building their own Bastilles. Against the Jacobin–Bolshevik principle that 'the end justifies the means', this new European model insists that means also determine ends. For the means you choose can be so corrupting that they ensure that the desired ends are actually never reached. This seems to me a specifically European insight from the twentieth century. It's an insight which could be an important part of the difficult transatlantic conversation about the transformation of the wider Middle East. The wholly valid European contribution to that conversation with the United States is to say: we agree with you entirely about the ends; our problem is with your chosen means.

Secondly, it is no hyperbole to say that over a period of thirty years, from Portugal in 1974 to Ukraine in 2004, the hope of democracy and the hope of Europe have marched hand in hand. Whatever the democratic deficit inside the European Union, to the outside, for its neighbours, the European Union has been a catalyst and a promoter of democracy. The slogan of those peaceful revolutions has been 'the return to Europe'. One democratizes in order to 'return to Europe', and specifically in order to join the European Union. In joining the European Union, you also secure your fragile democracy. Europe and democracy are two sides of the same coin.

9

So Europe is a normative power. In her book on human rights policy towards China, Rosemary Foot characterises the United States and the European Union as the world's two great 'norm entrepreneurs' – creators and exporters of norms. That is another way of describing what the European Union does, drawing on some more or less historically justified claims about what it is to be European. But there is a huge difference between what the European Union does in trying to create linkages between economic relations and respect for human rights in countries not aspiring to membership of the EU, and what it does with respect to countries aspiring to membership – those I call the *europapabile*. In relation to countries further away, the European Union continues to be quite inconsistent. Inconsistent in the different standards applied to Burma on the one hand and China on the other. Inconsistent also in the way we apply those standards, not least because individual EU member states insist on applying their own. One thinks of the contrast between what France does in relations with China and what some Scandinavian countries do. So we have a fragmented, inconsistent, shifting policy.

By contrast, our approach towards those of our neighbours who wish to join the European Union, and who have been accepted as candidates for membership, is formidably effective and intrusive. When we speak of 'intervention' in international relations we tend to think of military intervention, as in Kosovo or Iraq. But the truth is that the European Union has intervened massively in the internal affairs of its neighbours, in central and eastern Europe, and now also in Turkey. From the 'Helsinki Process' to the 'Copenhagen Criteria' for membership of the European Union (and especially the first Copenhagen criterion: democracy, the rule of law and human rights), there has been massive EU involvement in the transformation of the economic, social and political systems of these countries. This transformation has been no less substantive than that which the United States is attempting in the occupation of Iraq – but here, regime change is based on consent. That is Europe's unique power of induction: the fourth dimension of European power.

Arguably the greatest moment of European power – in the sense of EU power – in a given country is in the period shortly before that country joins the European Union. Once you're inside, you can get away with much more. Silvio Berlusconi's near monopoly of terrestrial television in Italy, for example, is something which would be unacceptable in a candidate country. Today's Italy might not qualify to be accepted as a member, but, once you are in, the constraints of European power are much less effective – particularly if you are a larger member state.

In any case, the problem with this power of induction is that it applies only to countries which clearly want to join the European Union and which the Union is prepared to accept as members, or, at least, is prepared to say with a reasonable degree of credibility that it wishes to accept. I think here particularly of Turkey. Our normative power evaporates, or at least is greatly reduced, as soon as that perspective of membership is not there. Even in the so-called 'Barcelona Process' across the Mediterranean, Europe's normative power is drastically diminished.

10

At the Congress of Europe in The Hague in May 1948, Count Coudenhove-Kalergi spoke these memorable words: 'let us never forget, my friends, that Europe is a means and no end.' *Europe is a means and no end.* So, Europe is characterized not just by its own focus on means as well as ends but by the fact that it is itself only a means to a higher end. This insight of a European founding father has been forgotten by many contemporary Europeans. For them, the means has become the end. But European Union, like German unification, is not an end in itself. The European Union should be a building block for a free world, a stepping stone to what Immanuel Kant, in his wonderful essay 'Idee zu einer allgemeinen Geschichte in weltbürgerlicher Absicht', called 'die vollkommene bürgerliche Vereinigung in der Menschengattung' – inadequately translated as 'a complete civil union of the human race'.

If, however, we take seriously a view of the European project as a promoter of universal norms then there is a logic that would lead towards an unending enlargement of the European Union. In this logic, each enlargement leads on to the next. There is already an extraordinary pattern in which countries that were historically each other's fiercest enemies become each other's closest allies in the process of enlargement. Thus Germany was the strongest advocate of Polish membership of the European Union; Greece has become one of the most emphatic advocates of Turkish membership of the European Union; and now Poland is the most vigorous supporter of Ukrainian membership in the European Union. There is, as I say, a powerful logic that leads from one step to the other, assuming always that the Copenhagen Criteria are fulfilled. So that in 2024 we might face the question not just of Ukrainian membership of the European Union but the candidacy of Iraq, Turkey's neighbour. And, of course, Israel. Europe, one might say – flying a little above the ground – is the expanding hard core of world government, of a Kantian *Weltinnenpolitik*.

Why not? Because this core would not be hard. It would be soft, and getting softer by the day. Such an enlargement would end up with a total incoherence of the European Union, a union which would have no sense of solidarity, based – as solidarity between current member states clearly is – on some elements of common culture, common history and common political identity. If Europe is everywhere then it will be nowhere. However, I don't believe that this Kantian imperative, properly understood, necessarily leads to a perspective of infinite enlargement. Rather it should lead us to urgent consideration of what the European Union can do for neighbours who are not candidates for membership, and are not likely to be candidates in any foreseeable future, so that in relation to them Europe cannot exercise its unique power of induction. Secondly, if we think of Europe as a building block for a free world, in the spirit of Count Coudenhove-Kalergi – Europe as a means not an end – then we need to ask ourselves what the relationship should be between this building block of a free world and other building blocks of a free world – starting with the United States, but going on to the other democracies of the English-speaking world, to other liberal democracies altogether, and of course to the United Nations.

Now, you may feel that this conclusion is rapidly approaching what we in English call 'pie in the sky', or what in German is more politely and poetically called *Zukunftsmusik* – the music of the future. For this I make no apology. One lesson we can learn from the German resistance to Hitler, and from the central European dissidents against communism, is that realism is not enough. In the case of Germany in 1944, or of Poland in 1984, or of Ukraine in 2004, the self-styled realists often turn out in the end to be unrealistic, and the idealists turn out to be the better realists. The challenge for thinking and acting at once morally and effectively in international affairs is to find the proper mixture, different from case to case, of idealism and realism. Keeping both feet firmly on the ground we should still reach for the stars.

2004

The Twins' New Poland

Peoples can be luckier than people. People are only young once. They seize their chances or miss them; then they grow old and die. Despite the anthropomorphic similes beloved of romantic nationalists – 'young Italy', 'young Germany' – peoples 'live', in some important sense, for centuries, even millennia, sustained by real or imagined continuities of political geography and collective experience. They can be 'sick' or 'old' for hundreds of years, but then become renewed and youthful.

China today is one example, Spain another and Poland a third. For 200 years, from the end of the eighteenth century, when the first Polish *rzeczpospolita*, or 'republic' (actually an elective monarchy), was divided up like a Christmas turkey between the Prussian, Russian and Austrian empires, to Poland's achievement of full independence (within very different frontiers) at the end of the twentieth century, the Poles had only two decades of fragile self-rule in a single state: their 'second republic' between 1918 and 1939.

Poland's normal condition seemed to be that of occupation, backwardness, frustration and alienation from the foreign-controlled state. The virtues for which it became famous were endurance, cultural vitality and heroic but doomed resistance. Pierced by foreign arrows, its white eagle bled to refresh the national colours of red and white.

Its heroes were martyrs. Even a historian as sympathetic to the Polish cause as Norman Davies could write in 1983 that 'Poland is back in its usual condition of political defeat and economic chaos.'[1]

Anyone looking at Poland today must conclude that the country's basic situation has been transformed. Poland is now a free country. As sovereign as any other European state on a close-knit continent, it has enjoyed unprecedented security in NATO since 1999 and been a full member of the European Union since 1 May 2004. Some analysts already identify Poland as one of the 'big six' inside the EU of twenty-five member states, along with Germany, France, Britain, Italy and Spain. Its gross domestic product has grown by some 50 per cent since it recovered independence in 1990. Young Poles – and more than 40 per cent of the population is under thirty – travel freely throughout the world. Hundreds of thousands of them are now seizing their new opportunities to work in EU states such as Britain. If I step out of my front door in Oxford, I am more than likely to meet a Polish student, either studying here or working in a local café.[2]

When I first travelled to Poland in 1979, the memories of Nazi occupation and Stalinist persecution still haunted the country. I emerged from a restaurant in Warsaw one evening to find that someone had deliberately let the air out of the front tyres of my car. 'Oh, they must think you're a German,' said my host. Among today's teenage Poles, those memories weigh so lightly that the slang phrase for requesting an SMS text message on your mobile phone is 'Send me an SS man.'[3]

I

If you ask when Poland's historic turn for the better began, one answer would be mid-morning on Thursday, 14 August 1980, when a young, unemployed electrician called Lech Wałęsa jumped over the wall of the Lenin Shipyard in the Baltic port of Gdańsk and seized the leadership of an occupation strike that gave birth to a movement called Solidarność. Wałęsa himself gives a different answer: October 1978, when Karol Wojtyła, the cardinal archbishop of Kraków, was elected Pope John Paul II, and the spirit of resistance was strengthened not only in Poland but throughout central Europe. Infuriating Mikhail Gorbachev, Wałęsa attributes the historical credit for the end of communist rule in Europe as follows: 50 per cent, the Polish pope; 30 per cent, Solidarity and other central European liberation movements; 20 per cent, Gorbachev and *perestroika*.

'Kurcze, panie!' (politely translatable as 'Bloody hell, mister!') he tells me, 'I see in those events the hand of God!'[4] If he'd tried to get to the shipyard a few hours earlier on that August morning, at 6am, as he and his mates had originally planned, the secret police would probably have arrested him, but he was late. He can't remember why. Then the strike nearly collapsed, but that was good too, since they ended up with a much better strike committee. He gestures energetically with his whole arm, while emitting his characteristic explosive sigh of wonder. 'And later, in the struggle, what scrapes there were . . . Who on earth could have fixed it like that? . . . Only the hand of God!'

Vigorous, thick-set, ruddy-faced and still sporting his famous walrus moustache, Wałęsa at the age of sixty-two increasingly resembles one of those portly, sabre-wielding eighteenth-century Polish noblemen you see on antique paintings of the country's first experiment in democracy. The former Solidarity leader and former president of Poland still talks non-stop, and his language is, as it ever was, vivid, inimitable and almost untranslatable. Amid the flow there are not just wonderfully comic passages but also flashes of down-to-earth wisdom and shrewd political judgement. They remind you that, at his best, Lech Wałęsa has been a popular leader of rare natural genius.

Whatever the just apportionment of historical credit for the end of communism in Europe, the pioneering contribution of Solidarity in August 1980 was significant enough that twenty-five years later, in

August 2005, planeloads of past and present political leaders disembarked at Lech Wałęsa International Airport in Gdańsk to celebrate the anniversary. Those who came to pay tribute included Václav Havel, the Ukrainian president Viktor Yushchenko, the Georgian president Mikheil Saakashvili, James Baker III (on behalf of two presidents Bush), Zbigniew Brzezinski, the German president, the Serbian president and the European Commission president, José Manuel Barroso.

They spoke in front of a large photo-montage which showed a domino covered with a photo of Lech Wałęsa held aloft by his fellow workers in 1980, knocking down dominoes representing Poland in 1989 (the inauguration of the first non-communist government in the Soviet bloc), the Velvet Revolution in Prague (Václav Havel shaking his keys on Wenceslas Square), the Orange Revolution in Ukraine (Yushchenko), and, finally, a largely concealed domino depicting another revolutionary crowd whose national identity I could not quite make out but may have represented Belarus. Many speakers expressed their solidarity with the oppressed people of Belarus, Europe's last dictatorship, and the hope of a comparable change there.

This 'domino theory' version of the last quarter-century had more than a touch of Polish messianism, as did the accompanying slogan, 'Today was born in Gdańsk.' In truth, the series of successes had many fathers, as Gorbachev and others would point out. Yet, with hindsight, we can justifiably say that the Polish revolution of 1980–81 was the first Velvet Revolution. Despite the martial law imposed by General Wojciech Jaruzelski in December 1981, Solidarity survived – though only just, with many of its leaders arrested – and then revived, through a further wave of strikes in 1988. It came back to give Poland the first of the peaceful central European revolutions of 1989, with the first of their accompanying round tables, at which communist rulers and opposition leaders negotiated a peaceful transition to democracy. Saakashvili and Yushchenko acknowledge the importance of the 1989 example in inspiring the latest wave of what are sometimes called 'colour revolutions', from the toppling of

Milošević in Serbia in 2000, through Georgia's Rose Revolution in 2003, to Ukraine's Orange Revolution in 2004.

So there was much to celebrate in Gdańsk in August 2005. But behind and beyond the celebration, the new Poland has mixed feelings about its recent past, and fears about the future. Wandering away from a triumphal mass near the Gdańsk (no longer Lenin) Shipyard, I made my way back to Gate Number 2, from the top of which Wałęsa used to make his funny, inspiring speeches to the crowd. The blue-grey gate was again decorated with images of John Paul II and the black madonna of Częstochowa, red-and-white flags and flowers, much as I remember it when I arrived in August 1980 to witness the historic strike. But three things were different. To the right of the entrance there was now an ATM machine. Behind the gate there was a vista of decaying buildings, rubble and weeds – for fewer than 3,000 workers are still at work in a shipyard (now owned by a company called EVIP) which in its communist heyday employed more than 15,000. And in front of the gate there stood a large wooden stocks, of the kind used in past times to pillory criminals. Its three head-holes contained straw men wearing dark suits, white shirts and photos as faces. Underneath was written 'Marek Roman, chairman of the EVIP firm – thief', 'Janusz Szlanta, former chairman – thief', 'Jerzy Lewandowski, current chairman – swindler'. In the background, the choir at the triumphal mass sang of peace, forgiveness and love.

2

During the two months following the Solidarity anniversary, the Poles elected a new parliament and a new president. In September 2005, with an electoral turnout barely exceeding 40 per cent, they gave most votes to a centre-right party called Law and Justice, with the more libertarian Civic Platform party coming in second. The Left Democratic Alliance, led mainly by former members of the communist party – known as 'post-communists' since 1989 – had been the dominant party for over ten years; in the September vote its representation in parliament was slashed from 217 MPs to 55. A month later, in the second round of separate elections for president, electoral turnout was just above 50 per cent. A majority of those who did bother to vote chose the candidate of Law and Justice, Lech Kaczyński, over the leader of Civic Platform, Donald Tusk.

These two large parties of the centre-right, Civic Platform and Law and Justice, then failed to agree on a coalition government, which both had previously said they would form. Instead, Law and Justice created a minority government, which will rely for parliamentary support on two parties of the more extreme, populist, Catholic right, the so-called Self-Defence movement and the League of Polish Families, which oppose both economic and social liberalism, and are deeply suspicious of the European Union. The prime minister is a rather sepulchral former schoolteacher called Kazimierz Marcinkiewicz, but everyone knows that the power behind the prime ministerial throne is the leader of Law and Justice, Jarosław Kaczyński – the twin brother of Lech Kaczyński, the new president.

We therefore have the unusual spectacle of a major European country effectively run by twin brothers who look so nearly identical that it's easy to mistake one for the other. (Lech has a distinguishing mole on one side of his nose.) They were born in 1949. Their parents had fought in the anti-Nazi and anti-communist resistance during and immediately after the Second World War and passed that potent heritage of patriotic struggle to their sons. When they were twelve years old, the blond twins starred in a children's film called *Two Who Stole the Moon*. The DVD version has become a bestseller in Poland. I bought a copy when I was in Warsaw, and Jacek and Placek, as they are called in the film, are indeed a charming pair of naughty boys.

Both brothers became seriously engaged in Poland's anti-communist opposition from the 1970s onward. Jarosław, who stayed in Warsaw, participated in one of the leading groups of the democratic opposition, the Committee for the Defence of the Workers, KOR. Lech moved to Gdańsk, where he studied law and became involved with helping workers on the Baltic coast to organize independent trade unions against the communist state. Some friends called him Leszek, to distinguish him from the other Lech in their group – the electrician Lech Wałęsa.

Lech Kaczyński took a doctorate in law, was a Gdańsk activist of Solidarity, and remained active during the years of underground resistance after martial law was imposed in December 1981. I remember him from the strike that took over the Gdańsk shipyard in 1988. This prepared the way for the round table talks of 1989, in which he also participated. After the end of communism, he supported Lech Wałęsa's successful bid for the presidency in 1990, but then split with him in an acrimonious dispute over personalities and positions. Ever since, he and his twin brother have been active on the post-Solidarity right wing of Polish politics, trying to put together a party that could win. 'All their lives they have been working to gain power!' exclaims Wałęsa, with a snort. Now they have succeeded.

Jarosław Kaczyński is forty-five seconds older than Lech, and a skilled, uncompromising, behind-the-scenes political strategist. His younger and generally more conciliatory brother is said to be in awe of him. After being elected president, Lech concluded his acceptance speech by addressing his elder brother and party leader in the style of a soldier's report to a commanding officer. 'Mr Chairman,' he said, 'I report: mission accomplished.'

A wordplay on an abbreviated version of their name, *kaczor*, meaning 'duck' (or, strictly speaking, 'drake'), opens the way to many popular duck jokes, especially among younger, more liberal or left-wing Poles, who circulate them by email, or by 'SS man' text messages on their mobile phones. Poland, one might say, is now in its version of *Duck Soup*. It has gone from Marx to the Marx Brothers. A few commentators in the German press have taken this turn of events less humorously, suggesting that the new president is not just a conservative Catholic nationalist, a strong opponent of both abortion and homosexuality, but is also tainted by anti-Semitism. Jewish friends of mine who have known Lech Kaczyński for thirty years, since his early dissident days, fiercely dismiss the revival of that old anti-Polish stereotype. In Kaczyński's case, they say, it's simply not true. Indeed, they suggest that his embrace of Catholic nationalism is at least as much tactical and strategic – seeing this as the only way to build up an effective right-wing party in Poland – as it is based on any profound personal conviction.

It is fair to say, however, that the new president harbours traditional suspicions of both Germany and Russia, not to mention the European Union. He speaks no foreign languages and was notably reluctant to seek contacts with foreigners during his time as mayor of Warsaw. He is, moreover, much given to conspiracy theories about both domestic and international politics, seeing the hidden hand of security services where others cannot detect it. As the American scholar David Ost observes, adapting a famous analysis by Richard Hofstadter, the Kaczyńskis and their allies represent 'the paranoid style' in Polish politics.[5]

A quarter-century after the 'Polish August' of 1980, Poland is therefore led by twin brothers who are authentic representatives of the right wing of the Solidarity tradition, but who have come to power by exploiting the discontents of those unhappy with what has happened since Solidarity triumphed in 1989. They string these discontents together into a narrative very different from the success story told so eloquently by the post-Solidarity and post-communist liberals who have led Poland for much of the last sixteen years.[6] In fluent English, French or German, people like Bronisław Geremek, the brilliant historian, former Solidarity adviser, and foreign minister from 1997 to 2000, and Aleksander Kwaśniewski, the country's articulate and sure-footed post-communist liberal president for the last ten years, have tirelessly explained to the world how Poland has pioneered the peaceful transformation of communism into liberal democracy and replaced the old command economy with a flourishing free market system, while achieving European standards of respect for human rights. Whatever its omissions, this success story has itself contributed materially to Poland's external successes in joining NATO and the European Union, and in attracting foreign investment.

Yet even the most upbeat Polish liberal must acknowledge that the human cost of the transition to capitalism has been high. The privatization of state enterprises and the introduction of market prices, as well as competition from imported Western goods, resulted in many Poles losing their jobs. Unemployment is now around 18 per cent. Poland has the lowest recorded proportion of people in paid work in the European Union, with just half (51.7 per cent) of those between the ages of fifteen and sixty-four being employed.[7] Among those who have lost most are those who contributed most to Solidarity's victory: the workers. The Polish revolution of 1980–81 was probably the closest thing we have seen to a genuine 'workers' revolution'. In a speech delivered on the anniversary, Bronisław Geremek reflected that while Poland's feuding eighteenth-century nobles destroyed the country's self-made 'noble democracy', its twentieth-century workers dismantled the Soviet-imposed 'workers state'. But if you talk to the workers and unemployed former workers of the Gdańsk shipyard today, most of them are angry and disillusioned.

While some Poles have got richer, many have got poorer. A recent report by the World Bank suggests that growing inequality has contributed to an increase in the number of those below the poverty line.[8] Wałęsa puts it very simply: back then, people had security but no freedom, now they have freedom and hanker after security. Then they had enforced equality, now one person is a millionaire while others are in the gutter. And, he adds, 'that millionaire probably didn't make his money in the cleanest way . . .'

As elsewhere in the post-communist world, today's Polish fortunes often started in the legally unclear period when the communist command economy was dismantled and a variety of ambitious people, some of them post-communists or with good connections to the security services, grabbed for the goods. If the reality was often murky, the perception, especially on the part of the 'losers' from the transition, is even darker. As those neo-medieval wooden stocks ('current chairman – swindler') in front of the Gdańsk shipyard illustrate, it's an article of faith for many ordinary Poles that anyone who is rich must be a thief or a cheat.

This connects with two other popular discontents that the Kaczyński brothers have articulated. The first is a sense that not enough was done after 1989 to make a public reckoning with the communist past, purge the security services, and remove from public life people who took part in repression by the communist regime. Poland had no South African- or Latin American-style 'truth commission'. Its equivalent of Germany's 'Gauck Authority', which gives victims access to their secret police files, only started working about five years ago. Meanwhile, Poland's young democracy has been shaken by charges that senior figures in public life had earlier collaborated with the communist security services. One post-communist prime minister, Józef Oleksy, resigned as a result of such charges.

A second, related, theme is that of a crisis of the Polish state, which is seen to be weak, bloated, inefficient and very prone to corruption. The new prime minister has talked darkly of a 'Bermuda quadrangle' of corrupt politicians, secret police operators, businesspeople and criminals. The main political target here is the post-communists, who, while behaving sensibly and responsibly in foreign relations, were involved in a depressing series of money-for-influence scandals at home. The most notorious is the so-called Rywin Affair, or 'Rywingate', in which a film producer promised that the 'group holding power' (a phrase that has become notorious in Poland) would change a planned law regulating the mass media in return for a $17.5 million bribe.

The Kaczyński brothers and their advisers have deftly combined these popular themes in their calls for a 'moral revolution' in Poland. Lech Kaczyński is a law professor, with a respectable record as minister of justice and head of the national audit office; and the claim implied by the very name of their party – Law and Justice – is that the brothers will restore law to the Polish state and justice to Polish society. In fact, they go a step further. One of their most successful election posters showed Lech Kaczyński as a benign, avuncular, professorial figure, wielding a pen in a book-lined study. Underneath it said 'President of the Fourth Republic'.

This was a brilliant piece of political marketing, but a genuine conservative should have known better. Most Poles describe the sovereign, democratic state that emerged after 1989 as 'the third republic', thus denying the post-1945, communist Polish People's Republic the dignity of being a real Polish *rzeczpospolita* at all. People disagree about when exactly the third republic began. Was it 4 June 1989, when the country's first semi-free elections spelled the effective end of communism in Poland? Was it September 1989, when the Solidarity adviser Tadeusz Mazowiecki formed the country's first non-communist government since 1945? Was it January 1990, when the constitution was changed to restore the old title, Republic of Poland? Was it December 1990, when the new president of the new republic, Lech Wałęsa, chose to receive the insignia of office not from his de facto predecessor, General Wojciech Jaruzelski, the architect of martial law and last president of the Polish People's Republic, but from the president of the London-based government-in-exile, the legal heir to the second republic founded in 1918?

Whatever the exact birth date, a new constitution introduced in 1997, and approved in a national referendum, treats the third republic as something already existing and meant to last. The Kaczyński brothers now want to change that constitution, but there is nothing in their proposed changes, even assuming they can get them through Parliament, to justify the claim that these would create a new republic.

As an election-winning device, however, the slogan of the 'fourth republic' spoke very effectively to a widespread discontent with the entire political system of the third republic, and the 'political class' of people who have been in charge. According to the CBOS polling organization, more than two thirds of those asked say they are dissatisfied with the way democracy is working in Poland. As many as 40 per cent now agree with the statement that 'a strong man in power can be better than democratic governments' – the largest proportion since the recovery of independence.[9] The low electoral turnout also reflects this disillusionment.

One problem for the Kaczyńskis and their political allies is that, for all their claim to be a new broom, they have, from the outset, themselves been part of this discredited political system of Poland's third republic. Their reign has started badly, with failed, ill-tempered coalition talks that exemplify precisely the undignified scramble for power and privilege they claim to be leaving behind. Already the first stories of corruption scandals among their entourage are emerging in the Polish press. Meanwhile, their promised 'moral revolution' is supposedly to be carried out through a purge of the police and security services, the publication of official lists of all collaborators with the communist secret police, and the automatic disbarment of those collaborators from public office for a period of ten years. More trials of senior communists are likely. When I spoke to the now 82-year-old General Jaruzelski, he told me, with weary acidity, that he expects to spend the rest of his life 'in the dock'.[10] In the election, he observed sharply, the Law and Justice party had made promises of material improvement that it could not keep, 'and if the people cannot have bread, they must have circuses.' He expects to be part of the circus.

Another aspect of this 'moral revolution' will seem more familiar to those who know the United States. Polish conservatives heavily emphasize religious and social issues, particularly opposition to abortion and homosexuality. As mayor of Warsaw, Lech Kaczyński banned an 'equality parade' for gays and lesbians, and other mayors have now done the same, provoking protests. The Solidarity trade union organization at the Gdańsk shipyard came out in defence of an 'equality parade' in its city, while in the western Polish city of Poznań a judge ruled that the local ban was illegal. Meanwhile, Polish conservative members of the European Parliament have horrified some of their colleagues with an exhibition in the European Parliament building in Brussels that compares abortion to the killing in Nazi concentration camps.

The United States has its famous divide between 'red' and 'blue' states. On a map of the presidential election, Poland is divided between 'orange' and 'blue' regions. Orange stands for the more liberal parts of the country that preferred Donald Tusk; the more conservative blue areas lean to Kaczyński. The western and northern parts of the country, including Szczecin on the German border and Gdańsk on the Baltic Sea, are mainly orange. With the major exception of the capital, Warsaw, the central, east and south-eastern parts of Poland are largely blue. To some extent this is a socio-economic divide, since the east and south-east are poorer. But historians point out that during the period when Poland was partitioned, the now orange parts of the country were mainly under German rule, while those now mainly blue were under Russia and Austria. Not for the first time in post-communist Europe, very old dividing lines re-emerge on new political maps, as if drawn there in invisible ink.

As with the red–blue division in the United States, the reality is more complex, both geographically and sociologically. But after these elections there is more than ever a sense of 'two Polands': one more liberal, metropolitan, tolerant and open to the outside world, the other more conservative, religious, provincial and inward-looking.

3

What will this third-and-a-bit republic be like under the Kaczyński twins? At best, the twins and their camp could do something to strengthen the state administration and the rule of law. They could clear up the nagging problem of the communist past, if only by demonstrating that not much can be done about it now. They might build from the hodgepodge of unstable right-wing groupings a stable Polish version of a Christian Democratic party, rather as José María Aznar did in the Spanish Partido Popular. At best, they might also enhance the country's economic dynamism with slightly lower taxes, while holding down its outsize budget deficit, and maintain Poland as a realistic and constructive, if socially conservative, member of the European Union.

At worst, they could preside over a weak minority government, rapidly generating a new round of scandals; pursue an unjust witch-hunt instead of a scrupulous reckoning with the communist past; slow down economic growth and deter foreign investment by nationalist protectionism; and ruin Poland's chances of being accepted as one of the 'big six' member states shaping the future of the European Union. Sooner or later, they could go the way of their predecessors in government, battered by defections and then punished by disgruntled voters.

Measured by the standards of the last two centuries of Polish history, these are hardly dramatic alternatives. Even if the Kaczyński twins do their worst, the country's independence, political freedom and security are no more under threat than those of Italy and Spain. Young Poles instinctively understand this, which is why they react with a mixture of protests, moving abroad and duck jokes.

Peoples can be luckier than people. But in a given time, what matters most is the happiness of the individual people who make up a nation. Honesty demands a plain acknowledgement that for millions of Polish men and women, especially among the workers, the poor, the old, and those living in the south and east, the years since 1989 have been painful and disappointing. For them, the reality of freedom has proved very different from the dream.

There is, however, another side to the story. One of the unexpected delights of the Solidarity anniversary reunion was to meet not just old friends and acquaintances but their children – now, like my own, in their early twenties. Back in 1980, my Polish friends and I lived in different worlds. Not just the political possibilities but the life chances, in the broadest sense, of a young Pole were incomparably more limited than those of a young Brit. In the generation of our children, that is no longer true. Today, the life chances of an enterprising young Pole are altogether comparable with those of a young Brit, and by no means only for those from a privileged background, as I see every day among the Polish students and student-workers in Oxford. Something has been won.

2006

The era of twin rule did not last long. Jarosław Kaczyński himself took over as prime minister in the summer of 2006, but his party lost the parliamentary elections in the autumn of 2007. The so-called fourth republic was in fact a continuation of the third. By 2009, Poland could claim to be a more normal European democracy than Silvio Berlusconi's Italy.

Tragically, President Lech Kaczyński, along with 95 others, died in a plane crash at Smolensk on his way to a ceremony to mark the 70th anniversary of the Katyn massacre, in April 2010. Jarosław declared himself a candidate to succeed his brother as president in the election called for summer 2010. As this book went to press, the result was not yet known.

Exchange of Empires

Sitting in a café on Lenin Street, Tiraspol, next to three smartly turned-out female officers in dark green KGB uniforms, I have this wild thought: can the Soviet Union join the European Union?

For the surreal para-state of Transnistria, a breakaway from Moldova on the east bank of the river Dniestr, looks at first glance like a miniature version of the old Soviet Union. In the heart of the capital, a giant redstone Lenin stands proudly before the Supreme Soviet. Across 25 October Street, named for the Russian revolution of 1917, is the obligatory tank on a plinth. In the House of Pioneers, display boards show gnarled, bemedalled Soviet war veterans explaining to eager youths 'How Good It is without War!' Not just on Lenin Street but on Soviet Street, Communist Street and Peace Street every third person seems to be in uniform. The arm badges of those female officers, whose elaborate make-up, brightly dyed hair and high-heeled leather shoes nicely set off their pristine uniforms, proclaim that they belong to the Ministry of State Security (MGB), but informally people still call them KGB. In every government office there is a sullen secretary, a pot plant and a framed portrait of the leader.

It makes me feel almost nostalgic. But look a little more closely and things are not as they seem. In the basement of the House of

Pioneers, the kids are playing Western computer games: Tomb Raider, Tank Racer. The shops on 25 October Street include Adidas and a fast-food restaurant decorated with giant, blown-up photos of American skyscrapers. Up the road, there is a vast new sports complex built by the biggest local company, which is called Sheriff, a tribute to the Wild West frontier marshals of the US. At the Hotel Timoty, the receptionist, Tania, is dressed in a stretchy white tracksuit, emblazoned Dolce e Gabbana. Not the genuine article, of course. She explains to me that the hotel's name – Timoty – in the Russian version, stands for TIraspol-MOscow-TIraspol, signalling the heavy involvement of Russian capital.

Even the tank on the plinth tells a new story. It commemorates not the Soviet Union's great patriotic war of 1941–5 but the heroic 'war' of 1992, in which the local forces of this heavily Sovietized, largely Russian-speaking strip of land, aided by the Russian 14th Army, won their de facto autonomy from the authorities of Moldova, who had adopted the Latin rather than Cyrillic script for their Moldovan/Romanian state language, and were tentatively reorienting the territory west of the river Dniestr towards Romania, Europe and the West. Since then, the entity which in English is most conveniently called Transnistria (that is, across the Dniestr, seen from the west) and which in Russian styles itself, literally translated, the On-the-Dniestrian Moldovan Republic, has equipped itself with its own flag, crest (with hammer-and-sickle), anthem, president, parliament, uniformed border guards, security service, police, courts, schools, university, constitution – most of the attributes of statehood, except international recognition.

Its president, Igor Smirnov, who looks like a cross between Dr Faustus and a provincial dentist, runs a repressive, corrupt regime, sustained by virtually free energy supplies from the Russian Gazprom, the presence of a small number of Russian troops, some local industry – including arms factories – and, by most accounts, a good dose of illegal trafficking in arms and people. While a recent offer to undercover *Sunday Times* reporters to sell them a post-Soviet Alazan missile with a 'dirty bomb' warhead may have been a con job, Western experts in the area believe that weapons supplies to rogue regimes and potential terrorists do come from, or through, Transnistria.

Now, however, the Smirnov regime is under pressure. To its west, the president of the internationally recognized Moldovan state, though himself a communist, is trying to get closer to the European Union and the United States. On its other three sides is Ukraine, where the Orange Revolution has produced a more pro-Western president with a greater interest in closing this black hole. The EU and the US are again looking at possible negotiated solutions. Smirnov also faces some opposition at home, which is partly supported by the mighty Sheriff oligarchs. Even in Transnistria, there is just the faintest smell of orange.

Sitting in the bare, cold offices of his foundation for the defence of human rights, Alexander Radchenko tells me that Smirnov 'has the powers that Stalin had, or Saddam Hussein'. He and other parliamentarians want to change the constitution to allow them to impeach the president, strengthen the constitutional court, and so on. He has received threatening phone calls: 'You can end up in the Dniestr.' Yet on closer questioning it emerges that what Radchenko, a stocky former political commissar in the Red Army, would really like is less a 'return to Europe' than a return to the Soviet Union. 'Of course!' he exclaims, flashing several gold teeth as he smiles, 'in the Soviet Union there was peace, friendship among the people, and welfare. There was no unemployment, no homelessness, no drug addicts, no prostitutes, no people-trafficking.' The rot set in, he says, soon after Stalin died. This is orange Transnistrian-style.

What does Transnistria matter to anyone who is not, as I am, a lover of the Tintinesque and a connoisseur of obscure east European conflicts? Perhaps not much – except to the people who live there, to the women who are brutally trafficked from there, and to those who are killed by the weapons coming out of there. Yet it also highlights a historical development, only half perceived by most of us, which has driven so many of the changes we have witnessed in Europe over the last quarter-century, and is still driving change in Europe today.

That development is the decline and fall of the Russian empire. At first, it was possible to believe that this was just the fall of the Soviet empire, not the Russian one. When you reach Georgia, Ukraine and Transnistria, that is no longer possible. In the centre of Tiraspol is a giant statue of Field Marshal Alexander Suvorov. It marks the conquest of this territory and the founding of this city by the great tsarist general, at the end of the eighteenth century. Here, it's not just the Soviet but the tsarist empire that is crumbling.

We Europeans now have three choices. We can leave such territories as black holes. We can allow the US to become the new imperial power. Or we can decide that the European Union, in a security partnership with the United States, should gradually expand to bring more freedom, respect for human rights and a long-term prospect of prosperity, even to such parts of the former Soviet Union. Provided, of course, the people living there want it to.

Yet the EU is the most reluctant empire in the history of humankind. The enlargement that we have done thus far is already fuelling the no vote in core countries like France. If the EU does not expand to take in more parts of the former Soviet Union, places like Transnistria will remain black holes. If it does, the European Union risks itself going the way of the former Soviet Union. That is the dilemma we see illuminated, as by a Red Army rocket flare, on the left bank of the river Dniestr.

2005

Why Britain is in Europe

The question 'why is country "X" in Europe?' will be answered in very different ways according to the history, intellectual tradition and language of the country concerned. If we ask why France is in Europe, a French intellectual might, for example, reply 'parce que la France sans l'Europe n'est pas la France – et l'Europe sans la France n'est pas l'Europe!' Now, this answer might not seem entirely satisfactory to us, but if it seems satisfactory to him, and to a sufficient number of his compatriots, then in a very important sense it is a satisfactory, even a sufficient, answer to the question posed. If we ask why Germany is in Europe, someone might answer, as did Wolfgang Bergsdorf, an adviser to Helmut Kohl, 'The raison d'état of a united Germany is its integration into Europe.' Or as the veteran German foreign minister Hans-Dietrich Genscher once observed, 'Our foreign policy is the more national, the more European it is.' These may seem slightly vertiginous formulations, but once again, if they are convincing to a sufficient number of Germans, then they are, in an important sense, satisfactory and sufficient answers. As for the question why Poland is in Europe, the answer has to come – this being Poland – in poetry. In the words of the great romantic poet Juliusz Słowacki: 'If Europe is a nymph, then Naples is the nymph's bright, blue eye; Warsaw is her heart.' It is one thing for John Major to tell us that Britain should be at the heart of Europe; quite another to have one of your great romantic poets explain that you *are* the heart of Europe.

In short, there is no such thing as an objective, scientific or even fully rational answer to such a question. There must be national answers which are rooted in national histories, experiences and, not least, languages. So the answers we seek to the question 'Why is Britain in Europe?' must be British answers, rooted in our national experience, our intellectual traditions and history. In this essay, I explore four possible kinds of answer: from geography; from history, or more accurately from the historiography of our pre-1945 history; from contemporary history, specifically the history of Britain's coming to join – and decide in a referendum to stay in – what is now the European Union, between 1945 and 1975; and, finally, politics, posing the question whether it is good for us today and why are we still there.*

I

First, geography, or more precisely historical cartography. One obvious British answer to the question why we're in Europe is: we're here because we're here. Or, as many British people would perhaps say: we're there because we're there. This can be seen on any number of maps, starting with the map from the Philips school atlas that the young Margaret Thatcher, Margaret Hilda Roberts, would almost certainly have used when she was at school in 1939 and 1940. However we look at the world, whether upside down or the other way up, Britain is in Europe. If we look at it from China, Britain is in Europe. I recently bought an Iranian map of Europe at a kind of stall outside the birthplace of Ayatollah Khomeini, in the town of Khomein. Again,

*This essay started life as the inaugural Ben Pimlott Memorial Lecture, delivered in 2005. The original lecture was illustrated with slides of the maps mentioned.

Britain is firmly part of Europe – unlike Turkey, which is half in and half out. I took the trouble to ask the Map Librarian at the British Library whether he knows of any significant historical map of Europe which does not contain the British Isles, in one form or another. His answer was no.

Maps are not just expressions of physical realities. They are ways of seeing, expressions of mentalities, products of human classification and human imagination. But this particular human classification is remarkably old and enduring. The distinction between Europe and Asia is by far the oldest continuous geopolitical distinction in the world. It goes back to the ancient Greeks, of course, and in cartography at least to the second century BC. If we take a cartographic reconstruction of the world according to Eratosthenes, the ancient Greek geographer who lived in Alexandria between the third and second centuries BC, we find that Europe, although rather an odd shape, is recognizably where it is today – and the large island top left is Britannia.

In the many medieval reconstructions of Ptolemy's geography, Britain is very firmly part of Europe. In fact, in Ptolemy's geography the first section is always Europe, and the first map in that section is always Britain. Then there are the medieval 'T and O' maps, with their famous tripartite division of the world. There is Europe, and in it there is Britannia. In historical cartography, the place of Turkey in Europe – or not in Europe – is hotly contested; the place of Russia is contested; that of the Maghreb is contested. But through twenty-three centuries, and viewed today from any other part of the world, Britain is part of Europe.

Of course, there are also other ways of seeing expressed through maps. For example, on what's called an Elementary Map, an early nineteenth-century map of the elements of physical geography, we have the familiar Island as an element of geography, counterposed to the Continent, or Mainland. And we have the map of Empire, with Britain at the centre and Europe virtually ceasing to exist. On one map of Empire, in a recent and very serious history of the British Empire, when you look at continental Europe all the inscription says is 'French Empire'. That is perhaps a rather characteristically British view of Europe.

So mental maps vary considerably. In 2003 I had the interesting experience of participating in a debate in London on the motion 'The Channel is Wider than the Atlantic'. On the proposing side was, among others, the Conservative Eurosceptic John Redwood. The motion was decisively carried. A majority of that well-heeled London audience thought that the Channel is wider than the Atlantic. With such mental maps we move from geography to history, for these perceptions of relative distance are shaped by historiography.

2

How do we view our pre-1945 history? Towards the end of his *General Theory*, John Maynard Keynes has a famous passage in which he writes: 'practical men, who believe themselves to be quite exempt from any intellectual influences, are usually the slaves of some defunct economist. Madmen in authority who hear voices in the air are distilling their frenzy from some academic scribbler of a few years back.' And practical men are even more the slaves of some defunct historian. As are practical women, such as Margaret Thatcher, who, speaking at the Centre for Policy Studies in 1999, said, 'God separated Britain from mainland Europe, and it was for a purpose.' Here is a wonderful condensation of a nationalist historiography, which projects history forwards from geography, or backwards into geography.

Behind that single sentence lies a whole narrative, originally Victorian, of British history marching forward from Island to Empire, advancing teleologically towards the goal of spreading freedom. The classic statement is to be found in John Seeley's Cambridge lectures, published in 1883 as *The Expansion of England*. 'What,' asked John

Seeley, 'is the general drift or goal of English history?' (Perhaps only in England could 'drift' and 'goal' be used as synonyms.) And he answers himself, 'the words which jump to our lips in answer are liberty, democracy.' Then he tells the story of the expansion of England, first, to cover the British Isles, to become Great Britain, which he regarded as a kind of internal Empire, and then to what he called Greater Britain, the Empire overseas.

A still more influential version of that grand narrative is H. E. Marshall's children's book *Our Island Story*. The preface to this book is entitled 'How This Book Came to be Written' and datelined Melbourne, Australia, 1905. It begins thus:

'What a funny letter, Daddy,' said Spen, as he looked at the narrow envelope which had just arrived, and listened to the crackle of the thin paper.

'Do you think so?' said Daddy. 'It is from home'.

'From home!' said Spen, laughing, 'why, Daddy, this is home.'

'I mean from the old country, Spen.'

'The old country, Daddy?' said Veda, leaving her dolls and coming to lean against her father's knee, 'the old country? What do you mean?'

'I mean the little island in the west, to which we belong and where I used to live', said Daddy.

'But this is an island, a great big one, Mother says [meaning Australia]. So how can we belong to a little island?' asked Spen.

'Well, we do – at least, the big island and the little island belong to each other'.

'Oh, Daddy, do 'splain yourself. You are not 'splaining yourself at all,' said Veda.

'Well', said Daddy with a sigh, 'long, long ago . . .'

'Oh!' said Spen, 'it's a story', and he settled himself to listen.

'Yes,' said Daddy, 'It's a story. And a very long one, too. I think I must ask someone else to tell it to you.'

And that someone is Mrs H. E. Marshall. This preface summarizes perfectly where that narrative was coming from, namely from the experience of Empire – in this case, specifically, from Australia.

H. A. L. Fisher's *History of Europe*, published in 1935, describes the English lamenting the loss of their French territories in the four-teenth and fifteenth centuries, not realizing that 'A good fairy was preparing to place their remote island in the centre of the habitable globe.' Mental geography again: 'in the centre of the habitable globe'.

This famous narrative acquired a huge boost during the Second World War, and particularly in the formative moment of 1940: Britain standing alone – as in the David Low cartoon of the British soldier standing defiantly on a shore nearly engulfed by waves, and shaking his fist at a sky full of Nazi planes – 'Very well, alone!' says the soldier. One of the great authors and popularizers in that period was G. M. Trevelyan, of whom David Cannadine has written an illuminating biography. Trevelyan's *English Social History* was first published in Britain in 1944, and had sold nearly 400,000 copies by 1949; it was, as J. H. Plumb commented, not just a social history but a social phenomenon. There Trevelyan wrote that after the Hundred Years War 'England was left as a strange island, anchored off the conti-nent.' Going on to explore English exceptionalism, he added, 'If the French noblesse had been capable of playing cricket with their peas-ants, their chateaux would never have been burned.' And so on to Arthur Bryant, the poor man's Trevelyan, with his tedious wartime volumes *The Years of Endurance* and *Years of Victory*, describing what he called 'Freedom's own island . . . set in a silver sea'.

It needs to be emphasized that this powerful and evocative grand narrative remained enormously influential well into our own time. It continued to be written by some; for example, by Paul Johnson. His *The Offshore Islanders: England's People from Roman Occupation to European Entry* was published in 1972 with, on its dust jacket, the famous remark of Hugh Gaitskell, from 1962 – the time of the first British application to join the EEC – that this would be 'the end of a thousand years of history'. But above all, this 'Island Story' narrative was influential because of what I call 'textbook time-lag'. It normally takes a number of years until the conventional historiographical wisdom filters down into textbooks. Those textbooks then stay in classrooms for a considerable number of years – or, in the case of children's books like *Our Island Story*, in the home, where parents often like to read to their children the stories they themselves enjoyed. And the history you read as a child is often the history that has the greatest impact on you, remaining engraved on your memory. So that the textbook time-lag can easily be a period of forty or fifty years. Keynes observed that people are the slave of some academic scribbler 'of a few years back' – but it can be of quite a few decades back.

It is not surprising that Lady Thatcher, at school in 1939 and 1940, imbibed and made her own that version of history. It is perhaps a little more surprising that our own very modern and liberal Archbishop of Canterbury could mention the other day, after a discussion of the public role of history, that *Our Island Story* had been one of his favourite childhood books. That grand narrative was the narrative that people of my generation, who went to school in the 1950s and 1960s, grew up with. It was the narrative that Tony Blair imbibed, to the extent that he studied any history at all, at prep and public school, and you find traces of it in the speeches that he has given about Europe. For example, in a speech delivered in Warsaw in 2000, where he describes Britain thus: 'Britain, the victor in the Second World War, the main ally of the United States, a proud and independent-minded island race (though with much European blood flowing in our veins)'. 'Island race' – Arthur Bryant, thou shouldst be living at this hour! And this is the version of history that seeps down and is regurgitated endlessly in the pages of our tabloid newspapers, as in a memorable front page of the *Sun*, prompted by the proposed European constitutional treaty: '1588: We saw off the Spanish, 1805: We saw off the French, 1940: We saw off the Germans, 2003: Blair surrenders Britain to Europe.'

Professional historians, unlike *Sun* journalists, have done some significant work in revising this historiography in the period since Britain joined the European Community. First, they have done what one could call the historiography of historiography. They have showed us how national identities are constructed, how traditions are invented, to recall the famous title of a book edited by Eric Hobsbawm and Terence Ranger. Linda Colley quotes in her influential book *Britons* a judgement that Britain is 'an invented nation, not so much older than the United States'. Invented, of course, in contradistinction to France in what, in the dread jargon of identity studies, I have heard called the 'othering' of France. 'Britain,' wrote Seamus Deane, 'in order to define its own sense of what it was, had to create in France its opposite.' That creation of the French 'other' was enormously effective, so that, for example, Margaret Thatcher's father, Alderman Alfred Roberts, viewed the French as 'corrupt from top to bottom'.

This historiography of historiography has been part of a wider comparative international exercise, in which many European countries have critically examined their own historiographies. These have usually also been shaped by claims of national exceptionalisms. Take, for example, the post-war German historiography of the so-called *Sonderweg*, Germany's 'special path' through modern history. Wolfgang Mommsen has observed that, to a significant degree, the historiography of the *Sonderweg* depended on a counterfactual model, which was a kind of idealized version of Britain's progress towards liberal democracy. So the definition of German exceptionalism was produced by taking what the British have considered to be British exceptionalism and treating it as a benchmark of modern Western normality – as, if you will, the European norm. Our national exceptionalism became their benchmark of European normality.

Moreover, what professional historians have done in the last thirty years, and particularly in the last fifteen, is to help us to see British history altogether in a much wider international context, notably by emphasizing not what divides us from other European countries but what we have in common. The classic example here is Norman Davies's book *The Isles*, which helpfully gives us the names of all our kings in their original languages, but which also has as its first map Britain in about 8000 BC – that is, before the emergence of the strip of water that would become 'the English Channel', when we really were 'a piece of the continent, a part of the main'. What relevance that has to modern history is not clear, but it is significant that this is the first map in a book that is trying to give us a sense of being part of Europe.

Other historians have explored the way in which what is now Britain was, for much of its history, part of a trans-Channel polity. They have argued that, across the great ruptures of the sixteenth and seventeenth centuries, from the Henrician Reformation to the revolutions of the seventeenth century, there was much more continuity than had previously been thought. They have also explored what British history continued to have in common with other parts of what has been called the Anglosphere. So this new historiography does not merely replace the claim that Britain was an exceptional island that created an empire with a claim that Britain was just another European country. Rather, it describes what Jeremy Black has rightly called the 'duality of ocean and continent' which has defined our history. Britain is a European country, but not just a European country.

Finally, what professional historians have done over the last thirty years, in the context first of our debates about devolution, and then of the reality of devolution, is to remind us that it is totally absurd to talk as Trevelyan did about an island called England. We have to talk about the isles, which are home to four nations. Hugh Kearney's book is called *The Isles: The History of Four Nations*. If you include the histories of Scotland, Wales and Ireland, then you have a great deal more commonality and interchange with the histories of continental Europe. It is no accident that many Scots drive around Britain with the name of their country given on their cars in French, *Écosse*.

So there is a large body of professional historiography on which to draw. But how has this affected what, to use Macaulay's famous phrase, every schoolboy knows? The truth is, I'm afraid, that the impact on what every schoolchild knows has been minimal. We have gone from a necessary, and healthy, deconstruction of the nationalist historiography of 'Our Island Story' to another extreme, which is the dismantling of any sense of a continuous national history in our school curricula. What most British children now experience at school is what Gordon Marsden has called the Yo! Sushi school of historical instruction – as in the Yo! Sushi bars, with the little plastic plates of sushi coming round on the conveyor belt. First you get a little bit of Hitler, then you get a little bit of Stalin – everybody gets a bit of Hitler and Stalin. Then you may get a tiny bite of the Industrial Revolution, and perhaps a morsel of the Tudors and Stuarts. You end up with absolutely no sense of the continuity of British history, however critically examined. We have gone from a simplistic, misleading mythical story – 'Our Island Story' – to a condition where we have no story at all.

3

My third avenue of exploration is that of contemporary history, particularly concerning the period 1945 to 1975. Here the question why Britain is in Europe becomes more narrowly the question why Britain joined and decided to stay in what is now the EU; more precisely still, why Britain's ruling elites chose to apply to join not once but three times, under three different governments, and then sold that decision to public opinion. Here we have an extraordinary richness of sources: private and public papers, witnesses who have been systematically interviewed, starting with the pioneering work of Michael Charlton and continuing with the oral history done by the Institute of Contemporary British History. We have a rich smorgasbord of analysis by historians, political scientists and journalists such as Alan

Milward, David Reynolds, Ben Pimlott, Peter Hennessy, John Young, Hugo Young, Andrew Geddes, Anne Deighton, Stephen George and Piers Ludlow – to mention just a few.

In this historiography, there are, so far as I can see, no major controversies: the picture is rather well known, and broadly agreed. I want to single out just a few salient points from this impressive body of work. For a start, those applications to join were, without question, a reaction to both the perception and the reality of decline. David Reynolds summarizes the argument of his book about British foreign policy in the twentieth century, *Britannia Overruled*, in four words: 'Britain has lost power.' This was a reaction also to a perceived economic decline, where the economic performance of the original six members of the European Economic Community (EEC) outstripped that of the United Kingdom, and trade grew much faster between the industrialized states of Europe than it did inside the Commonwealth. But if we look back to the debates of that time, what is striking is how prominent the political as well as the economic arguments were, and especially the argument that a stable and cohesive western Europe was a vital British national interest in the context of the Cold War. If you read the speeches in the House of Commons in 1971 and during the 1975 referendum, speakers again and again revert to the issue of security – the security of western Europe vis-à-vis the Soviet bloc. Correspondingly, a vital factor was that our closest ally, the United States, was consistently urging us to get into the EEC.

Above all, what is striking about the debates of this time, both public and private, is that they centred around the notion of Britain's world role. Paul Sharp rightly insists that the argument that we must, so to speak, keep the Great in Britain, that we must preserve a world role, had itself become a core part of the definition of the national interest by British elites. A former Permanent Under Secretary of the Foreign Office, for example, looking back on the decision to apply, said the thinking was: 'If we don't take this opportunity, we shall be of no more account than a small peripheral European country. We went in', he reflected, 'to prevent our being kicked down to a really lower league.'

That post-imperial angst which you hear already in Tennyson's poetry in the late nineteenth century – without the Empire, Tennyson wrote, we should be 'some third rate isle half lost amongst our northern seas' – is the constant leitmotif of these debates. Interestingly, one of the main reasons that we decided not to go in at the beginning in the 1950s is the same reason that we decided to go in, or attempt to get in, from the early 1960s. In 1950, Ernest Bevin protested to American supporters of European integration that 'Britain was not part of Europe, she was not simply a Luxembourg.' Anthony Eden, reflecting on what we would be without the Empire and Commonwealth, said, 'We should be no more than some millions of people living on an island off the coast of Europe, in which nobody wants to take any particular interest.' It is precisely that concern that drove us into the European community in the 1960s and 1970s. The goal is the same; only the means have changed. This is reflected very clearly in the 1971 White Paper, which averred that, if we did not enter the EEC, 'in a single generation we should have renounced an imperial past and rejected a European future.' This notion of the world role is closely bound up with a constant British obsession, the notion of 'leadership', which you find again and again in the speeches of Tony Blair – the idea that Britain must lead in Europe. This is a view expressed almost parodically in a remark that Willy Brandt recalls the then foreign secretary, George Brown, making to him in 1967: 'Willy, you must get us in so we can take the lead.'

'We' is, of course, always the elites. This leads to my last observation on contemporary history. In all this process of analysis and reflection and decision, public opinion was hardly considered at all; until it was seen to be becoming a problem. The Cabinet Minutes for September 1962 record that 'public opinion was getting dangerously sceptical, and needed correction'. 'Correction' – like penal correction. And so there was a little propaganda blitz, and then public opinion was forgotten again. The same happened in the early 1970s, when Gallup surveys showed there was a majority for withdrawal. In January 1975 there was a much larger and more effective campaign, the government got the 'yes' vote it wanted, and then public opinion was once again forgotten. No systematic attempt was made to inform, let alone to persuade, British public opinion about the case for Britain being in Europe. This is a constant feature of British European policy. So that, if we ask what every schoolchild knows today about this superbly documented history of Britain's relations with Europe in the years 1945 to 1975, the answer is: nothing at all.

4

This leads me directly to my final area: contemporary politics. If we ask why Britain is still in the EU, whether EU membership has been good for Britain and what are the reasons today for staying in, then the remarkable fact is that, although we have an endless thing called a British 'European debate'– in a fashion reminiscent of *Groundhog Day* you wake up to hear yet another ding-dong row between a Europhile and a Europhobe on the *Today* programme on BBC Radio 4, repeating all the same arguments that we have all heard a million times – nonetheless we are ill placed to make any reasonably informed judgement on these questions. The British themselves say in answers to opinion polls that they don't know much about the European Union; that they trust neither European institutions nor the British press to tell them about European institutions; and that they don't care, anyway. Don't know, don't trust, don't care.

Surprisingly, it is hard to find an unbiased, analytical balance sheet of whether EU membership has been good for Britain, and what the costs and benefits are. The last serious attempt I know was made in a volume edited by Simon Bulmer and published in 1992. Even the basic facts are disputed: for example, the so-called fact that 3 million British jobs depend on our trade with Europe.

What is more, even the basic criteria for judging whether it is good for us to remain in the European Union are disputed. For example, it makes a huge difference whether you consider it important that Britain should have a world role or not. That is one of the decisive considerations for those, from Tony Blair to most senior officials, who are in favour of staying in: so we can 'make a difference', so we can influence the global agenda on climate change, or on Africa, or on weapons of mass destruction. But there is a perfectly coherent position which says, 'Why should we?' A leading Eurosceptic, Charles Moore of the *Daily Telegraph*, once said to me, 'You know, all this talk of a world role – that's Foreign Office talk. We don't need to have a role. All that matters is that this country should be rich and free.' An offshore Switzerland? Why not?

Unless you make up your mind what the criteria should be for judging the balance sheet, you have no chance of making a proper judgement. Moreover, if you look more closely at the key arguments, what you find is that they depend on counterfactuals. The key counterfactual for advocates of the European Union is: what would Europe be like without the European Union? That is, of course, strictly unknowable. Would it still have the largest single market in the world? Would the great majority of countries in Europe still be democracies? Would there be peace in most of Europe? Yet these are core arguments in favour of the European Union. The key counterfactual for radical British Eurosceptics, those who want to get out, is: what if Britain were outside the EU? Again, the answer is strictly unknowable. The only examples we have to draw on are states such as Norway and Switzerland, countries much smaller than Britain and with a very different history – and the facts of their position are also disputed.

The European Union has clearly changed out of all recognition between the referendum we had in 1975 and the referendum we did not have in 2006. And the British debate is at least ten years, if not more, behind the reality of today's European Union. The very subject of the phrase 'Britain in Europe' has changed in the meantime. This is not the same Britain, because of devolution. There is no longer a Cold War, so that compelling argument from the requirements of west European security has fallen away – at least in terms of security against the Soviet Union. A corollary is that the United States is no longer an enthusiastic supporter of European integration, or of Britain being part of it.* The economic relationship between France and Germany, on the one hand, and Britain on the other, has more or less reversed; it is now they who are struggling more than us. An EU which is enlarged to twenty-five and soon twenty-seven or more member states has no possibility of ever becoming a federal superstate. Indeed, after the French 'no' to the European constitutional treaty, one leading French thinker, Alain Duhamel, commented that the date of the referendum, Sunday, 9 May 2005, might prove to be the birthday of *l'Europe anglaise*, an English or British Europe: large, loose, free-trading, open, deeply un-French. That is a perception widely shared by many people on the continent. It contributed substantially to the 'no' votes, particularly in France. Yet it is a perception most people in this country have hardly even noticed, because we do not have the necessary levels either of historical knowledge (the fault of our schools) or of contemporary reporting and analysis (the fault of our media).

5

In addressing the question why Britain is in Europe we have taken a short walk down four avenues of exploration: geography, historiography, contemporary history and politics. We have found in all of them that the area of solid, undisputed, well-established fact is much

---

*This was written during the Bush administration, and was particularly true of George W. Bush's first term.

smaller than you might think; a much larger area is a matter of selection, interpretation and counterfactuals, of ways of seeing (including maps), ways of thinking, ways of feeling, and, above all, of conscious and unconscious choices. Before we even begin to answer the question why Britain is in Europe, we have first to ask: what kind of people do we think we are? Who do we want to be? What story do we want to tell? What role, if any, do we want the United Kingdom to play in the wider world? It is really not possible even to pose the question, let alone to answer it, without this prior exploration, which simply does not happen in our public debates.

Alas, this is now even less likely to happen than it was five, or ten, or fifteen years ago. In the 1990s, during the government of John Major, the run-up to Blair's election in 1997 and the early Blair years, there was a real posing of the question. The matter of Britain was understood to be in significant measure the matter of Britain in Europe. In the last paragraph of his *Hope and Glory: Britain 1900–1990*, published in 1996, the historian Peter Clarke wrote that increasingly all the difficult issues of British politics revolved around our relationship with the European Union: 'issues,' he wrote, 'which could hardly remain unresolved into the twenty-first century'. Well, here we are, well into the twenty-first century. Those issues are still unresolved, and my guess is that they are going to remain so for a good time to come.

Absent the referendum on the EU's constitutional treaty, which was the one way we were, willy-nilly, going to get that debate about the question 'Why is Britain in Europe?', we are not going to have it. The last thing Tony Blair is going to do is to try and lead us into that debate without the referendum. Gordon Brown is, if anything, more wary of the EU and more fascinated by the United States than Tony Blair; he certainly won't take us there. David Cameron is a liberal modernizer in many other respects, but a liberal modernizer for whom the European project is something slightly old-fashioned – and one who secured his selection as party leader by making promises to his Eurosceptic colleagues. None of them is going to be interested in putting this issue at the centre of British public debate. Apart from anything else, to do so would risk dividing their own parties. And therefore it seems unlikely to be put squarely to the British public for many years to come, as it has not been put since that one brief moment in 1975. Jean-Paul Sartre is said to have observed that not to decide is also to decide. Whether or not that is true, this is the only kind of decision Britain is likely to make for the foreseeable future.

2005

I wish I could add here that in the intervening years something has changed in Britain's attitude to Europe. In fact, with the revival of the Conservative Party, the ambivalence has become more acute. So our interim verdict must be: the same, only more so.

Europe's New Story

Europe has lost the plot. As we celebrate the fiftieth birthday of the European Economic Community that became the European Union, Europe no longer knows what story it wants to tell. A shared political narrative sustained the post-war project of (west) European integration for three generations, but it has fallen apart since the end of the Cold War. Most Europeans now have little idea where we're coming from; nor do we share a vision of where we want to go to. We don't know why we have an EU or what it's good for. So we urgently need a new narrative.

On this fiftieth anniversary of the Treaty of Rome, I propose that our new story should be woven from six strands, each of which represents a shared European goal. The strands are freedom, peace, law, prosperity, diversity and solidarity. None of these goals are unique to Europe, but most Europeans would agree that it is characteristic of contemporary Europe to aspire to them. Our performance, however, often falls a long way short of the aspiration. That falling short is itself part of our new story and must be spelled out. For today's Europe should also have a capacity for constant self-criticism.

In this proposal, our identity will not be constructed in the fashion of the historic European nation, once humorously defined as a group of people united by a common hatred of their neighbours and a shared misunderstanding of their own past. We should not even attempt to retell European history as the kind of teleological mythology characteristic of nineteenth-century nation-building. No good will come of such a mythopoeic falsification of our history ('From Charlemagne to the euro'), and it won't work anyway. The nation was brilliantly analysed by the historian Ernest Renan as a community of shared memory and shared forgetting; but what one nation wishes to forget another wishes to remember. The more nations there are in the EU, the more diverse the family of national memories, the more difficult it is to construct shared myths about a common past.

Nor should our sense of European togetherness be achieved by the negative stereotyping of an enemy or 'other' (in the jargon of identity studies), as Britishness, for example, was constructed in the eighteenth and nineteenth centuries by contrast with a stereotyped France. After the collapse of the Soviet communist 'east', against which western Europe defined itself from the late 1940s until 1989, some politicians and intellectuals now attempt to find Europe's 'other' in either the US or Islam. These attempts are foolish and self-defeating. They divide Europeans rather than uniting them. Both the negative stereotyping of others and the mythmaking about our own collective past are typical of what I call Euronationalism – an attempt to replicate nationalist methods of building political identity at the European level.

In this proposal, Europe's only defining 'other' is its own previous self: more specifically, the unhappy, self-destructive, at times downright barbaric chapters in the history of European civilization. With the wars of the Yugoslav succession and the attempted genocide in Kosovo, that unhappy history stretches into the very last year of the last century. This is no distant past. Historical knowledge and consciousness play a vital role here, but it must be honest history, showing all the wrinkles, and not *mythistoire*.

By contrast with much traditional EU-ropean discourse, neither unity nor power is treated here as a defining goal of the European project. Unity, whether national or continental, is not an end in itself, merely a means to higher ends. So is power. The EU does need more capacity to project its power, especially in foreign policy, so as to protect our interests and realize some benign goals. But to regard European power, *l'Europe puissance*, as an end in itself, or desirable simply to match the power of the US, is Euronationalism not European patriotism.

So our new narrative is an honest, self-critical account of progress (very imperfect progress, but progress nonetheless) from different pasts towards shared goals which could constitute a common future. By their nature, these goals cannot fully be attained (there is no perfect peace or freedom, on earth at least), but a shared striving towards them can itself bind together a political community. What follows are notes towards the formulation of such a story, with built-in criticism. This is a rough first draft, for others to criticize and rework. If something along these lines does not appeal to a sufficient number of Europeans, there's no point in continuing with it. If it does, perhaps there is.

FREEDOM

Europe's history over the last sixty-five years is a story of the spread of freedom. In 1942, there were only four perilously free countries in Europe: Britain, Switzerland, Sweden, Ireland. By 1962 most of western Europe was free, except for Spain and Portugal. In 1982 the Iberian peninsula had joined the free, as had Greece, but most of what we then called eastern Europe was under communist dictatorship. Today, among countries that may definitely be accounted European, there is only one nasty little authoritarian regime left – Belarus. Most Europeans now live in liberal democracies. That has never before been the case; not in 2,500 years. It's worth celebrating.

A majority of the EU's current member states were dictatorships within living memory. Italy's president, Giorgio Napolitano, has a vivid recollection of Mussolini's fascist regime. The president of the European commission, José Manuel Barroso, grew up under Salazar's dictatorship in Portugal. The EU's foreign policy chief, Javier Solana, remembers dodging General Franco's police. Eleven of the twenty-seven heads of government gathered round the table at the spring 2007 European council, including the German chancellor, Angela Merkel, were subjects of communist dictatorships less than twenty years ago. They know what freedom is because they know what unfreedom is.

To be sure, people living under dictatorships wanted to be free mainly because they wanted to be free, not because they wanted to be EU-ropean. But the prospect of joining what is now the EU has encouraged country after country, from Spain and Portugal thirty years ago to Croatia and Turkey today, to transform its domestic politics, economy, law, media and society. The EU is one of the most successful engines of peaceful regime change ever. For decades, the struggle for freedom and what is emotively called the 'return to Europe' have gone arm in arm.

Shortcomings

Closer examination shows that many of Europe's newer democracies are seriously flawed, with high levels of corruption – especially, but by no means only, in south-eastern Europe. Money also speaks too loudly in the politics, legal systems and media of our established democracies, as it does in the US. Whatever the theory, in practice rich Europeans are more free than poor ones. The EU is a great catalyst of democracy but it is not itself very democratic. EU regulations are justified in the name of the treaty of Rome's 'four freedoms' – the free movement of goods, people, services and capital – but these regulations can themselves be infringements of individual freedom. Anyway, the EU can't claim all the credit: the US, NATO and the Organization for Security and Cooperation in Europe have also played a major part in securing Europeans' freedoms. Until recently, the defence of individual human rights and civil liberties has been more the province of the Council of Europe and its European Court of Human Rights than of the EU.

PEACE

For centuries, Europe was a theatre of war. Now it is a theatre of peace. Instead of trying out our national strengths on the battlefield, we do it on the football field. Disputes between European nations are resolved in endless negotiations in Brussels, not by armed conflict. The EU is a system of permanent, institutionalized conflict resolution. If you get tired of Brussels waffle and fudge, contemplate the alternative. It may seem to you unthinkable that French and Germans would ever fight each other again, but Serbs and Albanians were killing each other only the day before yesterday. You cannot simply rely on goodwill to keep the peace in Europe. This may be an old, familiar argument for European integration but that does not make it less true. Sometimes the old arguments are still the best.

Shortcomings

We cannot prove that it was European integration that kept the peace in western Europe after 1945. Others would claim that it was NATO and the hegemonic system of the Cold War, with the US functioning as 'Europe's pacifier'; others again would cite the fact that western Europe became a zone of liberal democracies, and liberal democracies don't go to war with each other. Several things happened at once and historians can argue about their relative weight. Anyway, central and eastern Europe did not live at peace after 1945: witness the Soviet tanks rolling into East Berlin, Budapest and Prague, and the 'state of war' declared in Poland in 1981. Moreover, Europe – in the sense of the EU and, more broadly, the established democracies of Europe – failed to prevent war returning to the continent after the end of the

Cold War. Twice it took US intervention to stop war in the Balkans. So what are we so proud of?

LAW

Most Europeans, most of the time, live under the rule of law. We enjoy codified human and civil rights and we can go to court to protect those rights. If we don't receive satisfaction in local and national courts, we have recourse to European ones – including the European Court of Human Rights. Men and women, rich and poor, black and white, heterosexual and homosexual, are equal before the law. By and large, we can assume that the police are there to defend us, rather than advancing the interests of those in power, doing the bidding of the local mafia or lining their own pockets. We forget how unusual this is. For most of European history, most Europeans did not live under the rule of law. At least two thirds of humankind still does not today. 'I have a gun, so I decide what the law is,' an African officer at a roadblock told a journalist of my acquaintance, before pocketing an arbitrary 'fine'.

The EU is a community of law. The Treaty of Rome and succeeding treaties have been turned into a kind of cumulative constitution by the work of European courts. One scholar has described the European Court of Justice as 'the most effective supranational judicial body in the history of the world'. EU law takes priority over national law. Even the strongest governments and corporations must eventually yield to the rulings of European judges. Why are the leading European football teams full of players from other countries? Because of a 1995 ruling of the European Court of Justice. It is thanks to the judicial enforcement of European laws on the 'four freedoms' that most Europeans can now travel, shop, live and work wherever they like in most of Europe.

Shortcomings

In practice, some are more equal than others. Look at Silvio Berlusconi. And there are still large areas of lawlessness, especially in eastern and south-eastern Europe. In established democracies, security powers, including detention without trial, have been stepped up, violating civil liberties in the name of the 'war on terror'. And the primacy of European law and the power of judges is, of course, precisely what Eurosceptics – especially in Britain – hate. They see it as stripping power from the democratically elected parliaments of sovereign states.

PROSPERITY

Most Europeans are better off than their parents, and much better off than their grandparents. They live in more comfortable, warmer, safer accommodation; eat richer, more varied food; have larger disposable incomes; enjoy more interesting holidays. We have never had it so good. Look at Henri Cartier-Bresson's wonderful book of photographs *Europeans* and you will be reminded just how poor many Europeans still were in the 1950s. If you represent the countries of the world on a map according to the size of their gross domestic product, and shade them according to GDP per head, you can see that Europe is one of the richest blocs in the world.

Shortcomings

Bond Street and the Kurfürstendamm are not typical of Europe. There are still pockets of shaming poverty, even in Europe's richest countries, and there are some very poor countries in Europe's east. It is also very hard to establish how much of this prosperity is due to the existence of the EU. In his book *Europe Reborn*, the economic historian Harold James reproduces a graph that shows how GDP per capita in France, Germany and Britain grew throughout the twentieth century, with large dips in the two world wars from which we recovered with rapid post-war growth. Overall, prosperity grew at roughly the same rate in the first half of the century, when we didn't have the European Economic Community, as in the second half, when we did. The main reason for this steady growth, James suggests, is the development and application of technology.

The EU's single market and competition policy have almost certainly enhanced our prosperity; policies like the Common Agricultural Policy, and extra costs due to EU regulations and social policy, have almost certainly not. Countries like Switzerland and Norway have done well outside the EU. In any case, the glory days of European growth are far behind us. In the last decade, the more advanced European economies have grown more slowly than the US, and far more slowly than the emerging giants of Asia.

DIVERSITY

In an essay entitled 'Among the Euroweenies', the American humorist P. J. O'Rourke once complained about Europe's proliferation of 'dopey little countries'. 'Even the languages are itty-bitty,' he groaned. 'Sometimes you need two or three just to get you through till lunch.' But that's just what I love about Europe. You can enjoy one culture, cityscape, media and cuisine in the morning, and then, with a short hop by plane or train, enjoy another that same evening. And yet another the next day. When I say 'you', I don't just mean a tiny elite. Students travelling with easyJet and Polish plumbers on overnight coaches can appreciate it too.

Europe is an intricate, multicoloured patchwork. Every national (and sub-national) culture has its own specialities and beauties. Each itty-bitty language reveals a subtly different way of life and thought, ripened over centuries. The British say, 'What on earth does that mean?'; the Germans, 'What in heaven should that mean?' ('Was im Himmel soll das bedeuten?'): philosophical empiricism and idealism captured in one everyday phrase. *Awantura* in Polish means a big, loud, yet secretly rather enjoyable quarrel. *Bella figura* in Italian is an untranslatable notion of how a man or woman should wish to be in the company of other men and women.

This is not just diversity; it is peaceful, managed and nurtured diversity. America has riches and Africa has variety, but only Europe combines such riches and such variety in so compact a space.

Shortcomings

This is the strand on which I can see the least credible criticism. Eurosceptics decry the EU as a homogenizing force, driving out old-fashioned national specialities like handmade Italian cheese (with delicious added hand-grime) or British beef and beer measured in imperial pounds and pints. But the examples are not so numerous, and for every element of old-fashioned diversity closed down by EU regulation there are two new ones opened up, from the Caffè Nero on a British high street to the cheap weekend trip to Prague. Europeanization is generally a less homogenizing version of globalization than is Americanization.

SOLIDARITY

Isn't this the most characteristic value of today's Europe? We believe that economic growth should be seasoned with social justice, free enterprise balanced by social security – and we have European laws and national welfare states to make it so. Europe's social democrats and Christian democrats agree that a market economy should not mean a market society. There must be no American-style, social Darwinian capitalist jungle here, with the poor and weak left to die in the gutter.

We also believe in solidarity between richer and poorer countries and regions inside the EU, hence the EU funds from which countries like Ireland and Portugal have benefited so visibly over the last two decades. And we believe in solidarity between the world's rich North and its poor South; hence our generous national and EU aid budgets and our commitment to slow down global warming, which will disproportionately hurt some of the world's poorest.

Shortcomings

This is the strand where Europe's reality falls painfully short of its aspiration. There is a significant degree of social solidarity, mediated by the state, in the richer European countries, but even in our most prosperous cities we still have beggars and homeless people sleeping rough. In the poorer countries of eastern Europe, the welfare state exists mainly on paper. To be poor, old and sick in Europe's wild east is no more pleasant than it is to be poor, old and sick in America's wild west. Yes, there were big financial transfers to countries like Portugal, Ireland and Greece, but those to the new member states of the EU today are much meaner. In the years 2004 to 2006, the 'old' fifteen member states contributed an average of €26 per citizen per year into the EU budget for enlargement – so our trans-European solidarity amounted to the price of a cup of coffee each month. As for solidarity with the rest of the world: our agricultural protectionism is as bad as anyone's and the EU is responsible, with the US, for the shameful stalling of the Doha round of world trade talks.

These are, I repeat, merely notes towards a new European story. Perhaps we need to add or subtract a theme or two. The flesh then has to be put on the bare bones. Popular attachment, let alone enthusiasm, will not be generated by a list of six abstract nouns. Everything depends on the personalities, events and anecdotes that give life and colour to narrative. These will vary from place to place. The stories of European freedom, peace or diversity can and should be told differently in Warsaw and Madrid, on the left and on the right. There need be no single one-size-fits-all version of our story – no narrative equivalent of the eurozone interest rate. Indeed, to impose uniformity in the praise of diversity would be a contradiction. Nonetheless, given the same bone structure, the fleshed-out stories told in Finnish, Italian,

Swedish or French will have a strong family likeness, just as European cities do.

Woven together, the six strands will add up to an account of where we have come from and a vision of where we want to go. Different strands will, however, appeal more strongly to different people. For me, the most inspiring stories are those of freedom and diversity. I acknowledge the others with my head but those are the two that quicken my heart. They are the reason I can say, without hyperbole, that I love Europe. Not in the same sense that I love my family, of course; nothing compares with that. Not even in the sense that I love England, although on a rainy day Europe runs it close. But there is a meaningful sense in which I can say that I love Europe – in other words, that I am a European patriot.

Our new European story will never generate the kind of fiery allegiances that were characteristic of the pre-1914 nation state. Today's Europe is not like that – fortunately. Our enterprise does not need or even want that kind of emotional fire. Europeanness remains a secondary, cooler identity. Europeans today are not called upon to die for Europe. Most of us are not even called upon to live for Europe. All that is required is that we should let Europe live.

2007

National Anthems

On a wintry Monday in 2008, Placido Domingo was supposed to stand up in Madrid and sing some proposed new words for the Spanish national anthem. The winner of a competition organized by the Spanish Olympic Committee, they are, at least in the English translation, of irredeemable banality:

> Long live Spain!
> From the green valleys
> To the wide sea,
> A hymn of brotherhood

etc., etc. But in a country whose inhabitants can't agree how many nations they are, the leaking of this anodyne text provoked a wave of controversy. 'It's absolute drivel,' said a leading commentator. Anyway, shouldn't it be sung in Basque and Catalan as well? Or perhaps in a medley of five languages, like the South African anthem? Wouldn't it be wiser, after all, to leave the historic Royal March as a song without words – as it has been ever since the words, approved by General Franco, were abandoned when Spain moved to democracy? And so, just five days beforehand, the Spanish Olympic

Committee suddenly withdrew this proposal, although insisting that the hunt for new words goes on.

Meanwhile, in another corner of Europe, a Committee for the Selection of a Kosovo National Anthem is reportedly at work, preparatory to an expected declaration of independence. The international community would appreciate it if the new statelet did not adopt exactly the same flag and anthem as neighbouring Albania. Ibrahim Rugova, Kosovo's former president, once tried his own hand at a new anthem: 'When the war-cry descends on Kosovo'. War-cry! Just what we need. But since there are still a few Serbs living in Kosovo, shouldn't part of the new anthem be in Serbian? Maybe, in the true spirit of radical multiculturalism ('You have your culture, we have ours'), it could have an Albanian verse vowing death to their (unspecified, but clearly Serb) enemies, followed by a Serbian one vowing death to their enemies (unspecified, but clearly Albanian).

The history of national anthems is a history of embarrassment. They show up, like an X-ray, all the weaknesses and fracture lines in the body of a state. As a general rule, when a nation doesn't sing its anthem, that's a sure sign of trouble. For some two decades after Stalin's death and disgrace, the Soviet Union did not sing the words of its anthem, since they declared (in Paul Robeson's catchy rendition):

> And Stalin our leader with faith in the people
> Inspired us to build up the land that we love.

East Germany anticipated its own demise by banning the words of its anthem, because they celebrated 'Germany, united fatherland'. (When the text was written in the 1940s, the idea was that the fatherland would be united under communist rule.) More recently, Bosnia's constitutional court declared unconstitutional the old Serbian nationalist anthem adopted by the so-called Serb Republic inside Bosnia.

Rare and happy is the country which has an agreed anthem, in a single language, that is (a) tuneful, (b) uncontroversial and (c) non-banal. In the banality stakes, those short-lived Spanish words face stiff international competition. I remember, for example, the tones of hooting derision in which a young Australian sang to my family, as we walked the streets of Sydney, the lyrics of 'Advance Australia Fair'. But the Bahamas surely take the biscuit:

> Lift up your head to the rising sun, Bahamaland;
> March on to glory your bright banners waving high.
> See how the world marks the manner of your bearing!

Frankly, the first verse of 'God Save the Queen' is quite dreary too. It only really gets going in the second verse:

> Scatter her enemies,
> And make them fall.
> Confound their politics,
> Frustrate their knavish tricks

Now that's worth singing; but usually we don't.

Yet even the banal national anthems can produce moments of collective emotion which have those proverbial hairs standing on the nape of your neck. How much more so when it's one of the few great ones. A South African friend described how moved he was the first time he saw a white South African rugby team singing 'Nkosi Sikelel' iAfrika'. One barely dares to mention the Jews of Europe singing the 'Hatikvah' in the shadow of the Nazi extermination camps, so tragic was the circumstance.

'The Star-Spangled Banner' must also be counted among the greats, but the greatest of them all is 'La Marseillaise'. There are several good reasons to want to be French; singing 'La Marseillaise' is among the best. If you ask, 'What does it mean to be a nation?', this is what philosophers would call an ostensive definition. Everyone knows the scene in *Casablanca* when the resistance hero Victor Laszlo tells the orchestra in Rick's Bar to play 'La Marseillaise', so as to drown out the Germans singing 'Die Wacht am Rhein'.

I have long been convinced that the screenwriters of *Casablanca* stole the idea from what is, in my opinion, an even greater film, Jean Renoir's *La Grande Illusion* – made five years earlier. Here, French prisoners of war are performing a revue, some dressed in women's clothes, before an audience of their comrades and some German officers, when one of the performers interrupts to say, 'We've recaptured Douaumont.' The orchestra instantly strikes up the tune, the 'women' tear off their wigs and stand to attention, and the whole company of French prisoners belts out 'Aux armes, citoyens / Formez vos bataillons'– and, staring at their captors, on to the passage where it demands that the 'impure blood' of the invaders should soak the furrows of France's fields.

National anthems are not just tokens of statehood; at best, they are part of the nervous system of a living political community. In which regard, it's striking how few successful international anthems there are. The Madrid experiment is apparently prompted by the Beijing Olympics. The Olympic movement actually has its own anthem, but few people know it and the words are purest candyfloss. What people actually wait for at the Olympics – not to mention at football matches, or at war – is their national tune.

The EU has a great tune, the music to Beethoven's 'Ode to Joy', but no official words. The UN has neither. The unofficial protest song 'We Shall Overcome' enjoys a certain international currency, but probably the most successful international anthem in modern history (leaving aside religious ones) was global communism's rallying song, the 'Internationale'. Even those who hated the reality of communism could sometimes enjoy singing it. There were stirring versions in many languages. And why did it come closest to competing with the great national anthems? Because it is martial, bloodthirsty and presents a heroic 'us' trumpeting defiance at an evil 'them'.

The conclusion is plain. If the world is to have the anthem it deserves, we need a big fat common enemy. I'm afraid inanimate challenges like climate change, Aids or meteors won't do the trick. What we need is some really nasty aggressor to be repulsed. When the Martians invade, the world will get its 'Marseillaise'.

2008

'O Chink, where is thy Wall?'

Remember, remember, the 9th of November. But who does? Just seeing that date, would you instantly have known that I refer to the night the Berlin Wall came down in 1989? Dates age faster than we do, said the poet Robert Lowell, and most of the time that is true.

For an older generation of central Europeans, 9 November meant the *Kristallnacht*, the 'night of broken glass' in 1938, when Nazi thugs left the streets of Berlin strewn with the smashed glass of Jewish shopkeepers' windows. For those still older, it recalled Hitler's attempted putsch on 8–9 November 1923. Each 9 November supplants the last. Perhaps – heaven forbid – in a few years' time there will be an attempted terrorist attack in Berlin on a 9 November and Germans will have to work out whether to call it 9/11, European style, or 11/9, American style.

Earlier this week, I spent an afternoon with a long-time East German friend showing my younger son, who was three years old in 1989, the places where the wall used to be. There's not much left: a few stretches of old concrete and raked sand (once the 'death strip' where would-be escapers from the former East Germany were shot), grainy museum photos, a stark and rusty memorial. The ruins of Persepolis are more vivid. For those of us who were there, the experience – both the taste of our friends' long imprisonment and the magical moment of liberation – is unforgettable, life-transforming; to explain it to someone who was not there requires a novelist's effort of evocation. 'To feel how it was' ('Fühlen, wie es war') a local newspaper captions a picture of children stretching out their fingers to touch an internally illuminated, multicoloured plastic replica of the wall, erected by a Korean artist in front of the Brandenburg Gate. Or rather, how it wasn't.

This remoteness is not merely a function of age or physical distance. Over dinner, I asked my East German friend's eldest son, who as a 21-year-old escaped through the perforated Iron Curtain from Hungary to Austria in the summer of 1989, and is now a priest in west Berlin, what his parishioners would make of it if this Sunday he preached a sermon based on his experience. Not much, he said. The west Berlin congregation would probably think: there he goes again, bothering us with his eastern reminiscences. Like the bored family when Dad starts retelling for the umpteenth time his veteran's tales of Vietnam or the Second World War.

But imagine the case of a young woman born on the morning of 9 November 1989, here in East Berlin, and therefore eighteen this Friday. How would she celebrate and reflect on her coming of age? 'Just like someone in Spain or Britain,' say my friends. Spain is probably a better comparison. There is a general sense that there was a dark and gloomy past somewhere back there, before one was born, like the shadow of the Franco dictatorship for a young woman in Madrid. But it's only marginally relevant to your own life.

So why has this epochal event, considered by many historians to mark the end of the 'short twentieth century' (1914–91), faded so rapidly from lived experience? Perhaps because, unlike, say, the 4th of July, it did not start a big new thing that is still with us (for example, the United States). It was more a great ending than a great beginning.

On the morning after, there were huge questions in the air. Could (and should) Germany be peacefully united? Could (and should) communism, which had abolished virtually all private property, emasculated the rule of law and supplanted democracy with the 'dictatorship of the proletariat', be transformed back into capitalism? As the joke went at the time: we know that you can turn an aquarium into fish soup, but can you turn fish soup back into an aquarium? Eighteen years on, these questions have been answered. Yes, you can. Driving into the centre of east Berlin, I noticed an alternative, hippy-style shop which had on its door a parody of the famous Cold War Berlin signs that used to say: 'You are now leaving the American sector' (of West Berlin, that is, crossing into the Soviet sector, or East Berlin). This parodic notice read: 'You are now leaving the capitalist sector.' But it isn't true. Even among the incense and beads behind that alternative shop door, capitalism rules, OK.

The ultimate proof of the triumph of capitalism is to be seen in a striking full-colour advertisement that has appeared in the pages of the *Economist* and the *Financial Times* in recent weeks. It shows a thoughtful-looking Mikhail Gorbachev, sitting in the back of a car through whose rear window you can clearly see one of the few remaining stretches of the Berlin Wall. Beside him is a leather bag by Louis Vuitton, for which luxury goods manufacturer this world historical figure and hero of our time is now serving as an advertisement. Eighteen years on, that seems to me a perfect icon of the age we're in.

What, then, is left of that incredible November night, when the people made their own history as they danced through the wall? 'Was bleibt?' ('What remains?'), as the East German novelist Christa Wolf mournfully asked. Apart from our fading memories, there is, I believe, at least one thing that survives with a future. The fall of the Wall is perhaps the world's most famous image of the triumph of what we call in English 'civil resistance' – that is, popular non-violent action. It followed massive peaceful demonstrations in Leipzig and other East German cities. As one East German worker told me at the time,

'You see, it shows Lenin was wrong. Lenin said a revolution could succeed only with violence, but this was a peaceful revolution.'

The East German 'revolution of the candles', as some dubbed it at the time, had predecessors, from the non-violent campaigns of Gandhi and Martin Luther King to Poland's Solidarity. It has also had many successors, from the Velvet Revolution in Prague, which followed within a matter of days, to South Africa, Slovakia, Serbia, Ukraine and, most recently, the protests led by Buddhist monks in Burma – too hastily tagged the 'saffron revolution' – and those of lawyers in Pakistan today. (Expect a 'lawyers' revolution' tag, assuming some journalist hasn't reached for it already.)

I am involved in a research project, led by my Oxford colleague Adam Roberts, which is looking at many of these cases of the use of civil resistance and trying to work out why some succeeded and others failed.[1] Courage, imagination and skilled organization of peaceful protest is not enough, if other factors of power – the army and police, a colonial power, neighbouring states, international media, economic forces – are not sufficiently present, benign or amenable. You need your Gorbachev, your Helmut Kohl, your Western TV cameras and, not least, your party leaders who give up without a shot fired in anger. But you also need the citizens on the streets, with their candles, banners, chants and the sheer peaceful force of numbers. Without them, there is no revolution. With them, you can change the course of world history, even in the face of a nuclear-armed superpower. So the date may fade, but the example lives on.

2007

The Perfect EU Member

Driving through Toronto I saw a shiny black 4x4 with an English flag sticking out of one side window and a German flag out of the other. Presumably a Canadian family of mixed English and German origin, so rooting for both teams in the World Cup. A little later I saw a car with the Portuguese flag on one side and the Italian on the other. It occurred to me that this pretty much sums up what we've been trying to achieve in Europe since the Second World War. Welcome to the European Union – in Canada.

In fact, why doesn't the European Union invite Canada to join at once? In most respects it would be a much easier fit than Ukraine, let alone Turkey. It effortlessly meets the EU's so-called Copenhagen Criteria for membership, including democratic government, the rule of law, a well-regulated market economy and respect for minority rights. Canada is rich, so would be a much-needed net contributor to the European budget, at a time when the EU has been taking in lots of poorer states. One of Europe's besetting weaknesses is disagreement between the British and the French, but on this the two historic rivals would instantly agree. English-speaking Canada would strengthen the Anglophone group in the EU, Quebec the Francophone.

Take the list of things that many Europeans consider to be most characteristic of us – by contrast with the United States. We Europeans believe that the free market should be tamed by values of social justice, solidarity and inclusiveness, realized through a strong welfare state. We don't have capital punishment. We believe that military force should only be used as a last resort and with the sanction of international law. We support international organizations. We love multilateralism and abhor unilateralism. We tend to think that men and women should be able to live more or less as they please with whomever they please, irrespective of gender and sexual orientation. We pride ourselves on our diversity. Check, check, check. Welcome to Canada.

Look a little closer at the opinion surveys and there are a few distinguishing marks. Canadians still tend to place a little more store by self-reliance and the woodsman frontier spirit than most Europeans. Canadians tend to be a bit more religious than most Europeans – though not more than the Poles or Ukrainians. Most important, their attitude to immigration and ethnic minorities is more positive than that of most Europeans. But these differences in attitudes could easily be accommodated within the wide spectrum of today's EU, while a Canadian-style embrace of immigration and ethnic minorities would do Europe a power of good.

OK, I know it's not going to happen. After saying yes to Turkey, the EU is having difficulty finding clear and consistent grounds for saying no to other, still more remote candidates – but being in the general vicinity of Europe does seem to be a continuing requirement. Now I guess an agile Canadian Inuk could traverse the melting ice floes to Greenland, which belonged to the EU for twelve years and now has a special treaty relationship with it. From there it's a relatively short boat trip to Iceland, which is generally considered to be a European country.

But it would be hard to argue, with a straight face, that Canada is in Europe. Moreover, with some 85 per cent of its exports going to the United States, and so many of its business, energy and human links running north–south across the border, Canada is increasingly integrated into the US economy. The price the EU demands for opening its internal borders to new members is that they should tighten up their external border with non-EU neighbours. That would be a tall order for Canada, along the longest frontier on earth, with the most powerful neighbour on earth.

This mildly amusing thought experiment – Canada as EU member – has a serious point. To look at Canada and its values is to understand how foolish it is to try to define Europe by reference to an allegedly unique set of 'European values'. Values matter, but these European values are shared by most Canadians more than they are by many Europeans. And many of these values are also shared by Americans in the liberal blue states of the US.

Yet another thing Canadians and Europeans have in common is an obsession with the United States, and with distinguishing themselves from it, often by crude stereotyping. A Canadian writer observes that his compatriots 'love to yell about how modest we are'. Just like today's Europeans. Canadians and Europeans enjoy wallowing in a sense of moral superiority towards the imperial hyperpower, while doing rather little to improve the world outside their borders. Canada's defence spending, at around 1.2 per cent of GDP, is low even by European standards. (Among NATO members, only Luxembourg and Iceland spend less.) So is its foreign-aid budget, a mere 0.27 per cent of GDP in 2004 – despite the fact that it was the Canadian statesman Lester Pearson who more than thirty years ago proposed what has become the UN target of developed countries spending 0.7 per cent of GDP on foreign aid. There is the arrogance of power, but there is also the arrogance of impotence.

Yet this impotence is self-imposed. The potential power – military, economic and soft – of the established liberal democracies outside the US is enormous. The three largest sets are the democracies of Europe, most but not all of them gathered in the EU; the

Anglosphere/Commonwealth democracies, including Australia, New Zealand, Canada (intersecting with the Francosphere), South Africa and India (the world's largest democracy); and the Hispanosphere and Lusosphere democracies of Latin America. Between us, we have a combined GDP much larger than that of the US, as well as natural resources and specific strengths that the hyperpower cannot match. Instead of sitting round like a bunch of poor cousins, complaining all the time about the behaviour of the rich American uncle, we should be thinking what we ourselves can do to make a difference beyond our shores.

Canada, for example, has a tradition of peacekeeping that it is now controversially extending to more combative peacemaking in Afghanistan. With its profusion of natural riches, and its outsize share of the world's ice and snow, it has a unique contribution to make in crafting international environmental policies and in the battle against the effects of climate change.

With its carefully balanced federal model, securing the rights of a multicultural society in a bilingual framework, it has unique constitutional experience to offer the many multi-ethnic countries around the world that are struggling to avoid a fledgling democracy becoming a tyranny of the majority – and hence a catalyst for renewed ethnic conflict. Why not share this experience, in a distinctive Canadian version of democracy promotion? Or do we think the promotion of democracy should be left entirely to the Bush administration, while we sit on the sidelines and jeer?

So, in this respect at least, I return from Toronto wishing Canadians would be just a little less European. But then, in this respect, I also wish Europeans would be a little less Canadian.

2006

3.

Islam, Terror and Freedom

La Alhambra

'I am your choice, your decision: yes, I am Spain.' Thus the poet W. H. Auden, responding to the Spanish Civil War in 1937. A lifetime later, Spain is the theatre of another war that affects every European, every citizen of any democracy. This is a war that won't be won by men with guns and bombers from the air. It's a war to avoid another war.

On one side of a broad city street, here in Madrid, you can view Picasso's *Guernica* at the Queen Sofia Art Centre. Probably the single most famous artistic image of war in the modern world, this commemoration of a town bombed during the Spanish Civil War shows, in giant angular segments of black, grey and white, distorted and dismembered body parts – legs, arms and, most of all, heads, with each mouth open in a howl of pain. Just a few metres away, on the other side of the street, is the Atocha railway station. Here, on the morning of 11 March last year, *Guernica* was repeated. In the space of a few seconds, living, breathing men and women – mothers, wives, fathers and sons – were torn into dismembered body parts by the impact of bombs planted on suburban commuter trains. We must imagine their mouths still open in a last howl of pain.

The memorial to the victims in Atocha station is no Picasso. At first glance, it could be two self-service ticket machines. On closer examination, these turn out to house metal keyboards on which you can type a message of commemoration or solidarity, linked to a scanned image of your hand. Between the two memory machines hang large white cylinders on which people can write whatever they like. 'Never again' features several times. 'Aznar, Bush and Blair are the assassins.' And a voice of touchingly ungrammatical Polish optimism: 'Don't stay in hopeless. Polska.'

The Atocha memorial lacks any hint of artistic grandeur. Yet its very banality is also somehow appropriate – for this war will be won or lost not in some grand showdown but in a trillion tiny everyday encounters, like those of commuters pouring off a suburban train.

You can understand this better if you walk back up past the *Guernica* museum to the Lavapiés neighbourhood, where many north African immigrants live and several of the 11 March Islamist bombers used to hang out. Here, in Tribulete Street, you can view the bolted metal door of one of the small telephone shops, called *locutorios*, from which immigrants can make cheap calls home. But the owner of this *locutorio*, Jamal Zougam, used his telecommunications expertise to prepare the mobile phones that detonated the train bombs by remote control. His premises are now up for rent, but the door still bears the legend New Century Locutorio. New century indeed.

Lavapiés does not feel like a ghetto. In its narrow streets, Spanish and north African shops are still mixed up together. So are the people. But I have the sense of a community which could go either way: the strengthening of peaceful coexistence or a downward spiral to low-level urban civil war.

Perhaps the most impressive thing the Spanish people have done in the year since the '11-M' attacks is the thing they haven't done. They have not struck back, scapegoating Moroccans or Muslims of any nationality. A recent report by Human Rights Watch pays this cautious tribute: 'To our knowledge, there have not been any clearly documented cases of racist violence that can be attributed directly to the March 11 bombings.' It goes on to quote the president of the association of Moroccan workers and immigrants in Spain: 'The reaction has overall been exemplary, that of a society that knows how to distinguish between a few terrorists and a community.'

Nonetheless, talking to people in Lavapiés you glimpse a society close to some tipping-point. A Spanish bar-owner, his voice quivering with anger and alcohol, tells me how he hates people like his former neighbour Zougam, the mobile phone bomber. 'If I had had a gun on 11 March,' he says, 'I would have shot them here myself.' Muhammad Said, a nineteen-year-old Moroccan in hand-painted sneakers, complains about increased police harassment since the bombings. Why, only three days ago the police roughed up a friend of his and confiscated his mobile phone, just because it showed a photo of Osama bin Laden! So was bin Laden a hero to this friend of his? Yes, of course. But Said himself is training to be a plumber and says he's been kindly treated by his teachers. A man on the cusp, then, between integration and alienation.

I ask another Muhammad ('just call me Muhammad'), a voluble sixteen-year-old, about last year's bombings just down the road, at the Atocha station. Well, he says, he doesn't like to see people dying 'even if they are Christians and Jews'. But in this case, because of what Aznar did in the Iraq war . . .

Later, in a heavily guarded conference centre on the outskirts of the city, I sit with an illustrious galaxy of politicians, international officials and thinkers, at a memorial summit convened to discuss 'democracy, terrorism and security'. The central idea of this intelligently conceived conference is that 'democratic government is the only legitimate – and still the only effective – way of fighting terrorism.' It aims to produce, in a Madrid Agenda, the most comprehensive plan of action yet seen for a democratic response to terrorism.

I look forward to studying the result. What states and international organizations do next will plainly matter a great deal, from coordinated police and intelligence work to immigration policies, from competing strategies for the democratization of the wider Middle East to preventing the proliferation of weapons of mass destruction. The resulting policies have a direct impact on our own Arab streets, as both Muhammads' comments make clear.

But this war to avoid a larger war will only be won if ordinary citizens across Europe are consciously engaged in it, through millions of commonplace interactions with people of different colour and faith. These are the experiences that determine whether the Muslim immigrants who already live among us in such large numbers will turn towards or away from Islamist extremism, and eventually terrorism. This is not the 'war on terror', in which the mighty armies and security apparatuses of powerful states are repeatedly outmanoeuvred by a few technically ingenious people who are prepared to sacrifice their own lives. It's a war to prevent such people wanting to become terrorists in the first place.

A great French historian once said that a nation is 'a plebiscite on every day'. So is this peaceful war to prevent the emergence of terrorism in the alienated minds of ordinary men and women. It's a war of small things, of tiny, everyday acts.

Back in Tribulete Street, there is an Arab restaurant called La Alhambra, which people charged with involvement in the 11 March bombing used to frequent. When I went there, I met two Spanish women who were studying Arabic and getting acquainted with their neighbours' culture. Although they were Spanish women without headscarves, they were greeted warmly by the Arab restaurant-owner. That, too, is the Madrid Agenda.

2005

Islam in Europe

On a bright summer's day in 2006, I visited the famous basilica of Saint-Denis, on the outskirts of Paris. I admired the magnificent tombs and funerary monuments of the kings and queens of France, including that of Charles Martel ('the Hammer'), whose victory over the invading Muslim armies near Poitiers in AD 733 is traditionally held to have halted the Islamization of Europe.[1] Stepping out of the basilica, I walked a hundred yards across the Place Victor Hugo to the main commercial street, which was thronged with local shoppers of Arab and African origin, including many women wearing the *hijab*. I caught myself thinking: so the Muslims have won the Battle of Poitiers after all! Won it not by force of arms, but by peaceful immigration and fertility.

Just down the road from the basilica of the kings, in the discreet backyard offices of the Tawhid association, I met Abdelaziz Eljaouhari, the son of Berber Moroccan immigrants and an eloquent Muslim political activist. He talked with fluent passion, in perfect French, about the misery of the impoverished housing estates around Paris – which, as we spoke, were again wracked by protests – and the chronic social discrimination against immigrants and their descendants. France's so-called 'Republican model', he said furiously, means in practice 'I speak French, am called Jean-Daniel, and have blue eyes and blond hair.' If you are called Abdelaziz, have a darker skin, and are Muslim to boot, the French Republic does not practise what it preaches. 'What *égalité* is there for us?' he asked. 'What *liberté?* What *fraternité?*' And then he delivered his personal message to Nicolas Sarkozy, the hard-line interior minister and leading right-wing candidate to succeed Jacques Chirac as French president, in words that I will never forget. 'Moi,' said Abdelaziz Eljaouhari, in a ringing voice, 'moi, je suis la France!'

And, he might have added, *l'Europe.* For the profound alienation of many Muslims – especially the second and third generations of immigrant families, young men and women themselves born in Europe – is one of the most vexing problems facing the continent today. If things continue to go as badly as they are at the moment, this alienation, and the way it both feeds and is fed by the resentments of mainly white, Christian or post-Christian Europeans, could tear apart the civic fabric of Europe's most established democracies. It has already catalysed the rise of populist anti-immigrant parties and contributed very directly to the terrorist attacks on the United States on 11 September 2001 (hijackers such as Mohamed Atta were radicalized during their time in Europe), the Madrid bombings of 11 March 2004, the murder of the Dutch filmmaker Theo van Gogh on 2 November 2004, the London bombings of 7 July 2005, and the planned attempt to blow up several passenger planes flying from Britain to the US, foiled by the British authorities on 10 August 2006.

Europe's difficulties with its Muslims are also the subject of hysterical oversimplification, especially in the United States, where stereotypes of a spineless, anti-American, anti-Semitic 'Eurabia', increasingly in thrall to Arab/Islamic domination, seem to be gaining strength.[2] As an inhabitant of Eurabia, I must insist on a few elementary distinctions. For a start, are we talking about Islam, Muslims, Islamists, Arabs, immigrants, darker-skinned people or terrorists? These are seven different things.

Where I live – in Oxford, Eurabia – I come into contact with British Muslims almost every day. Their family origins lie in Pakistan, India or Bangladesh. They are more peaceful, law-abiding and industrious British citizens than many a true-born native Englishman of my acquaintance. As the authors of an excellent new study of Islam in France point out, most French Muslims are relatively well integrated into French society.[3] Much of the discrimination Abdelaziz Eljaouhari complains about, which exists in different forms and degrees in most European countries, applies equally to non-Muslims of immigrant origin. It is, so to speak, indiscriminate discrimination against people with darker skins and foreign names or accents; plain, old-fashioned racism or xenophobia, rather than the more specific prejudice that is now tagged Islamophobia.

Across the continent of Europe, there are a number of very different, albeit overlapping, issues concerning Islam. The Russian Federation has more than 14 million people – at least 10 per cent of its rapidly shrinking population – who may plausibly be identified as Muslim, but most Europeans don't consider them as part of Europe's problem.[4] In the case of Turkey, by contrast, a country of nearly 70 million Muslims living in a secular state, Europeans hotly debate whether such a large, mainly Muslim country, which has not been considered part of Europe in most traditional cultural, historical and geographical definitions, should become a member of the European Union. In the Balkans, there are centuries-old communities of European Muslims, more than 7 million in all, including one largely Muslim country, Albania, another entity, Kosovo, which will sooner or later be a state with a Muslim majority, and Bosnia, a fragile state with a Muslim plurality, as well as significant minorities in Macedonia, Bulgaria, Serbia and Montenegro.

These Balkan Muslims are old Europeans and not immigrants to Europe. However, like the Turks, they do form part of the Muslim immigrant minorities in west European countries such as Germany, France and Holland. Within a decade, most Balkan Muslims will probably be citizens of the European Union, either because their own states have joined the EU or because they have acquired citizenship in another EU member state. The shameful feebleness of western Europe's response to Serbian and, to a lesser degree, Croatian persecution of Bosnian Muslims in the 1990s has fed into a broader sense of Muslim victimhood in Europe. That west Europeans (and the US) intervened militarily in Kosovo to prevent an attempted genocide of Muslim Albanians by Christian Serbs is less often remembered.

When people talk loosely about 'Europe's Muslim problem', what they are usually thinking of is the more than 15 million Muslims from families of immigrant origin who now live in the west, north and south European member states of the EU, as well as in Switzerland and Norway. (The numbers in the new central and east European EU member states, such as Poland, are tiny.) Although counting is complicated by the fact that the French Republic, being in theory blind to colour, religion and ethnic origins, does not keep realistic statistics, there are probably somewhere around 5 million Muslims in France – upward of 8 per cent of the total population. There are perhaps 4 million – mainly Turks – in Germany and nearly one million, more than 5 per cent of the total population, in Holland.

Most of them live in cities, and generally in particular areas of cities, such as the administrative region around Saint-Denis, which contains some of the most notorious housing estates on the outskirts of Paris. An estimated one out of every four residents of Marseilles is Muslim. In his fascinating new book, *Murder in Amsterdam*, Ian Buruma cites an official statistic that in 1999 some 45 per cent of the population of Amsterdam was of foreign origin, a figure projected to rise to 52 per cent by 2015, with the majority of those people being Muslim. And Muslim immigrants generally have higher birth rates than the 'native' European population. According to one estimate, more than 15 per cent of the French population between sixteen and twenty-five years old is Muslim.[5]

So with further immigration, high relative birth rates, and the prospect of EU enlargement to the Balkans and perhaps Turkey, more and more citizens of the EU are going to be Muslim. In some urban neighbourhoods of Britain, France, Germany, Italy, Spain and Holland they will make up anywhere between 20 and 90 per cent of the population. Most of them will be young; far too many will be poor, ill educated, underemployed, alienated – feeling at home neither in the place they live nor in the lands from which their parents came – and tempted by drugs, crime, or political and religious extremism.

If we, the – for want of a better word – traditional Europeans, manage to reverse the current trend and enable people like Abdelaziz and his children to feel at home as new Muslim Europeans, they could be a source of cultural enrichment and economic dynamism, helping to compensate for the downward drag of Europe's rapidly ageing population. If we fail, we shall face many more explosions.

I

Ian Buruma – half Dutch, half British and wholly cosmopolitan – has had the excellent idea of returning to his native Holland to explore the causes and implications of the murder on 2 November 2004 of Theo van Gogh, a filmmaker and provocative critic of Muslim culture, by a 26-year-old Moroccan Dutchman named Mohammed Bouyeri. Arriving on a bicycle, Bouyeri shot van Gogh several times on a public street, then pulled out a machete and cut his throat – 'as though slashing a tyre', according to one witness. He used another knife to pin to van Gogh's chest a long, rambling note, calling for a holy war against all unbelievers and the deaths of a number of people he abhorred, starting with the Somali-born Dutch politician Ayaan Hirsi Ali, to whom the note was addressed. Van Gogh and Hirsi Ali had together made the short film *Submission*, which dramatizes the oppression of women in some Muslim families by projecting quotations from the Koran on to the half-naked bodies of young women, as they intone personal stories of abuse. Bouyeri's murder note concluded:

I know for sure that you, Oh America, will go down
I know for sure that you, Oh Europe, will go down
I know for sure that you, Oh Netherlands, will go down
I know for sure that you, Oh Hirsi Ali, will go down
I know for sure that you, Oh unbelieving fundamentalist,
  will go down

One question that preoccupies Buruma in *Murder in Amsterdam*, a characteristically vivid and astute combination of essay and reportage, is: whatever happened to the tolerant, civilized country that I remember from my childhood? (He left Holland in 1975, at the age of twenty-three.) What's become of the land of Spinoza and Johan Huizinga, who claimed in an essay of 1934 that if the Dutch ever became extremist, theirs would be a moderate extremism? Van Gogh's murder was, Buruma writes, 'the end of a sweet dream of tolerance and light in the most progressive little enclave of Europe'. Yet part of his answer seems to be that the reality always differed from the myth of Dutch tolerance – if one looks, for example, at wartime and post-war attitudes towards the Jews. And he quotes a remarkable statement by Frits Bolkestein, a leading Dutch politician and former European commissioner: 'One must never underestimate the degree of hatred that Dutch people feel for Moroccan and Turkish immigrants.' Not 'Muslims', note, but immigrants from particular places.

Now Buruma revisits the verdant suburbs of his childhood (the words 'verdant' and 'leafy' recur), talking to intellectuals and those he ironically calls Friends of Theo, hearing their accounts of how the Dutch model of multiculturalism, with separate 'pillars' for each culture, broke down. Too many immigrants were allowed in too fast, and they were not sufficiently integrated into Dutch society, linguistically, culturally or socially. The parents were brought to Holland to work as what the Germans call *Gastarbeiter*, 'guest workers', but their children are mainly left unemployed.

As for Dutch attitudes towards Islam, Buruma suggests that people like the anti-immigrant populist politician Pim Fortuyn were so angry with the Muslim reintroduction of religion into public discourse because they had just 'painfully wrested themselves free from the strictures of their own religions', meaning Catholic or Protestant Christianity. Not to mention Muslim attitudes towards homosexuals – Fortuyn was gay – and women. Questioned about his hostility to Islam, Fortuyn said, 'I have no desire to have to go through the emancipation of women and homosexuals all over again.' Like van Gogh, Fortuyn was also murdered, Dutch-style, by a man arriving on a bicycle, though his assassin was not a Muslim. Van Gogh was fascinated by Fortuyn; in fact, Buruma writes, the filmmaker was making a 'Hitchcockian thriller' about Fortuyn's assassination when he was himself killed by Bouyeri.

The responses of people like Fortuyn and van Gogh are the more accessible part of this story for us non-Muslim Europeans, or more generally Westerners. What we really need to understand is the other part: the experience of the Muslim immigrants and their descendants. Was the killer Mohammed Bouyeri a lone madman or the symptom of a larger malaise? The answer is not reassuring. Bouyeri comes from what I call the Inbetween People: those who feel at home neither in the European countries where they live nor in the countries from which their parents came. They inhabit 'dish cities', connected to the lands of their parents' birth by satellite dishes bringing in Moroccan or Turkish television channels, by the Internet and by mobile phones. Unlike most Muslim immigrants to the US, many of them physically go 'home' every summer, to Morocco, Algeria, Turkey or other countries in Europe's near abroad, sometimes for months at a time. In their European homes, the second generation often speaks the local language – Dutch, French, English – with their brothers or sisters and the native language – Berber, Arabic, Turkish – with their parents: '50–50', as one Berber-Moroccan Dutchman tells Buruma. Buruma asks which soccer team this man would support. Morocco! Which passport would he rather have? Dutch!

Almost all the young people I met in the riot-prone housing projects around Paris told similar stories of a life between: of idyllic summers spent at their grandparents' farms in Algeria and Tunisia; of divided loyalties, crystallized by the question 'Which soccer team do you support?' 'Algeria!' those of Algerian descent told me – and a 2001 match between Algeria and France famously degenerated into a nasty riot. But when the Algerian-French Zinedine Zidane led the French team in the World Cup, they supported France.[6] 'In Morocco I'm an émigré, in France, I'm an immigré,' said Abdelaziz Eljaouhari.

Culturally, they are split personalities. And the disorientation is not just cultural. Buruma meets a psychiatrist specializing in the mental problems of immigrants. Apparently women, and the first generation of immigrant men, tend to suffer from depression; second-generation men, from schizophrenia. According to his research, a second-generation Moroccan male is ten times more likely to be schizophrenic than a native Dutchman from a similar economic background.

Mohammed Bouyeri was one of those second-generation Berber-Moroccan Dutchmen, torn this way and that. He attended a Dutch high school named after the painter Piet Mondrian, spoke Dutch, drank alcohol, smoked dope, had an affair with a half-Dutch, half-Tunisian girl. He was attracted to Western girls, but furious when his sister found a boyfriend, Abdu. Sex before marriage was fine for himself, but not for her. The traditionally all-important family honour was thought to be irreparably stained in the eyes of his Moroccan Muslim community by a daughter or sister having sex before marriage. Bouyeri attacked Abdu with a knife and went to jail for a spell. His mother died of breast cancer. Mohammed turned his back on what he now increasingly saw as decadent European ways. He grew a beard, took to wearing a Moroccan *djellaba* and prayer hat, and came under the influence of a radical Takfiri preacher from Syria. He posted Islamist tracts on the Web and watched videos of foreign infidels in the Middle East having their throats cut by holy warriors. According to a Dutch source cited by Buruma, Bouyeri's friend Nouredine passed his wedding night with his bride on a mattress in the future assassin's apartment, watching infidels being slaughtered.

On 1 November 2004, Mohammed Bouyeri spent a quiet evening with friends. They went out for a stroll, listening to Koranic prayers through headphones attached to digital music players. Mohammed remarked how beautiful the night sky looked. Next morning he rose at 5.30am, prayed to Allah, and then bicycled off to butcher van Gogh. He apparently intended to get killed himself in the ensuing gunfight with police.

Bouyeri's story has striking similarities with those of some of the London and Madrid bombers, and members of the Hamburg cell of al-Qaida who were central to the 11 September 2001 attacks on New York. There's the same initial embrace and then angry rejection of modern European secular culture, whether in its Dutch, German, Spanish or British variant, with its common temptations of sexual licence, drugs, drink and racy entertainment; the pain of being torn between two home countries, neither of which is fully home; the influence of a radical imam, and of Islamist material from the Internet, audiotapes, or videocassettes and DVDs; a sense of global Muslim victimhood, exacerbated by horror stories from Bosnia, Chechnya, Palestine, Afghanistan and Iraq; the groupthink of a small circle of friends, stiffening one's resolve; and the tranquil confidence with which many of these young men seem to have approached martyrdom. Such suicide killers are obviously not representative of the great majority of Muslims living peacefully in Europe; but they are, without question, extreme and exceptional symptoms of a much broader alien-ation of the children of Muslim immigrants to Europe. Their sickness of mind and heart reveals, in an extreme form, the pathology of the Inbetween People.

2

Buruma devotes a chapter to Ayaan Hirsi Ali and *Submission*, the film she made with Theo van Gogh showing the mistreatment of Muslim women. Hirsi Ali's own story has been told in countless profiles and interviews. In fact, she is irresistible copy for journalists, being a tall, strikingly beautiful, exotic, brave, outspoken woman with a remarkable life story, now living under permanent threat of being slaughtered like van Gogh. Among the many awards listed on the back cover of her new book of essays, *The Caged Virgin*, next to the Moral Courage Award, the International Network of Liberal Women Freedom Prize, Dutchman [*sic*] of the Year 2004, the Coq d'Honneur 2004 and the Danish Freedom Prize, is *Glamour* magazine's Hero of the Month Award. That's how we like our heroes – glamorous. It's no disrespect to Ms Hirsi Ali to suggest that if she had been short, squat and squinting, her story and views might not be so closely attended to.

While both books under review were at the press, a further scandal erupted around her. The hard-line Dutch immigration minister, Rita Verdonk, revoked Hirsi Ali's Dutch citizenship, after a Dutch television report had 'revealed' that she had given false details when applying for asylum in the Netherlands in 1992. (In fact, Hirsi Ali had already told the story herself many times; when Buruma suggested to her that she was, in a phrase often used by the British tabloid press, a bogus asylum-seeker, she replied, 'Yes, a very bogus asylum-seeker.') The minister's harsh decision provoked a storm of protest in the Dutch Parliament, where Ayaan Hirsi Ali was a representative of Verdonk's own party. Verdonk was compelled to revoke her revocation, and the coalition forming the Dutch government fell apart as a result. But the damage had been done. Hirsi Ali announced her resignation from the Dutch Parliament and her intention to move to the American Enterprise Institute in Washington.

Having read many interviews with her, and spent an evening in London talking to her both onstage and offstage, I have enormous respect for her courage, her sincerity and her clarity. This does not mean one must agree with all her views. *The Caged Virgin* is subtitled, in its American edition, *An Emancipation Proclamation for Women and Islam*. It would be more accurate to call it a manifesto for the emancipation of women from Islam. She tells horrifying, true stories of the oppression and abuse of young women in some Muslim immigrant families in Europe, based on her experience first as an interpreter and then as a politician. Some of these young women are forced to marry people they don't want to marry – she uses the term 'arranged rape'. Others are abused by husbands, fathers or uncles. If they try to leave, or take up with a boyfriend, they are intimidated, beaten and even murdered in 'honour killings'. Hirsi Ali writes that there were eleven such killings of Muslim girls in just two police districts of Holland in the space of seven months in 2004 and 2005.

Young girls from countries like Somalia are submitted to what is euphemistically called 'female circumcision' – a procedure she describes as involving 'the cutting away of the girl's clitoris, the outer and inner labia, as well as the scraping of the walls of her vagina with a sharp object – a fragment of glass, a razor blade or a potato knife, and then the binding together of her legs, so that the walls of the vagina can grow together'. Hirsi Ali rightly describes this not as 'female circumcision' but as 'genital mutilation'. (She herself was subjected to this horrifying procedure, at the behest of her Somali grandmother.) And she writes a moving and very practical text entitled 'Ten Tips for Muslim Women Who Want to Leave' – preparing them for the shock, pain and possible danger of leaving a Muslim family.

Hirsi Ali performs a great service in drawing our attention to these horrors, which are the dark underside of a supposedly tolerant 'multiculturalism'. However, some Muslim women object to the way in which she blames their oppression on the religion of Islam, rather than on the specific national, regional and tribal cultures from which they come. (Hirsi Ali herself acknowledges that genital mutilation is not prescribed in the Koran.) Buruma reports a televised meeting she had with women in a Dutch shelter for abused housewives and battered daughters, several of whom objected strongly to the film *Submission*. 'You're just insulting us,' one cried. 'My faith is what strengthened me.' According to Buruma, she dismissed their objections with a lofty wave of her hand.

Submission was always meant to be a provocation. Muslim culture, Hirsi Ali writes, needs something like Monty Python's *Life of Brian*, directed by an Arabic Theo van Gogh, with a Muhammad figure in the main lead. (This sentence was probably written before van Gogh's murder; the Dutch edition of this book appeared in 2004.) She recalls that a decisive moment in her own experience was reading a book called *The Atheist Manifesto*. She also drew inspiration from John Stuart Mill's essay 'On the Subjection of Women'. 'I ask that we do question the fundamental principles' of Islam, she says. And on the last page of her book she concludes that 'the first victims of Muhammad are the minds of Muslims themselves. They are imprisoned in the fear of hell and so also fear the very natural pursuit of life, liberty, and happiness.'

Having in her youth been tempted by Islamist fundamentalism, under the influence of an inspiring schoolteacher, Ayaan Hirsi Ali is now a brave, outspoken, slightly simplistic Enlightenment fundamentalist. In a pattern familiar to historians of political intellectuals, she has gone from one extreme to the other, with an emotional energy perfectly summed up by Shakespeare:

> '... as the heresies that men do leave
> Are hated most of those they did deceive.'

This is precisely why she is a heroine to many secular European intellectuals, who are themselves Enlightenment fundamentalists. They believe that not just Islam but all religion is insulting to the intelligence and crippling to the human spirit. Most of them believe that a Europe based entirely on secular humanism would be a better Europe. Maybe they are right. (Some of my best friends are Enlightenment fundamentalists.) Maybe they are wrong. But let's not pretend this is anything other than a frontal challenge to Islam. In his crazed diatribe, Mohammed Bouyeri was not altogether mistaken to identify as his generic European enemy the 'unbelieving fundamentalist'.

Now every man and woman in Europe must self-evidently be free to advance such atheist or agnostic views, without fear of persecution, intimidation or censorship. I regard it as a profound shame for Holland and Europe that we Europeans could not keep among us someone like Ayaan Hirsi Ali, whose intention was to fight for a better Holland and a better Europe. But I do not believe that she is showing the way forward for most Muslims in Europe, at least not for many years to come. A policy based on the expectation that millions of Muslims will so suddenly abandon the faith of their fathers and mothers is simply not realistic. If the message they hear from us is that the necessary condition for being European is to abandon their religion, then they will choose not to be European. For secular Europeans to demand that Muslims adopt their faith – secular humanism – would be almost as intolerant as the Islamist jihadist demand that we should adopt theirs. But, the Enlightenment fundamentalist will protest, our faith is based on reason! Well, they reply, ours is based on truth!

3

The very Dutch stories of Theo van Gogh, Ayaan Hirsi Ali and Mohammed Bouyeri fill only a small corner of the vast, complex tapestry of Europe and Islam. If we ask 'What is to be done?' the answer is: many different things in different places. We must be foxes, not hedgehogs, to recall Isaiah Berlin's famous use of a fragment of

Archilochus: 'The fox knows many things but the hedgehog knows one big thing.' Against the strident hedgehogs of Fox News we must continue to insist that this is not all just one big War on Terror, to be won by the Good Guys eliminating the Bad Guys.

Buruma rightly emphasizes the cultural diversity of Muslim immigrants: Berbers from the Rif mountains are not quite like Moroccans from the lowlands; Turks have different patterns of adaptation from Somalians, let alone Pakistanis in Britain. In the nineteenth century, European imperialists studied the ethnography of their colonies. In the twenty-first century, we need a new ethnography of our own cities. Since European countries tend to have concentrations of immigrants from their former colonies, the new ethnography can even draw on the old. At the same time, the British, French, Dutch and German ways of integration – or non-integration – vary enormously, with contrasting strengths and weaknesses. What works for, say, Pakistani Kashmiris in Bradford may not work for Berber Moroccans in Amsterdam, and vice versa.

We have to decide what is essential in our European way of life and what is negotiable. For example, I regard it as both morally indefensible and politically foolish for the French state to insist that grown women may not wear the *hijab* in any official institution – a source of additional grievance to French Muslims, as I heard repeatedly from women in the housing projects near Saint-Denis. It seems to me as objectionable that the French Republic forbids adult women to wear the *hijab* as it is that the Islamic Republic of Iran compels them to wear the *hijab*, and on the same principle: in a free and modern society, grown men and women should be able to wear what they want.[7] More practically, France surely has enough difficulties in its relations with its Muslim population without creating this additional one for itself.

On the other hand, freedom of expression is essential. It is now threatened by people like Mohammed Bouyeri, whose message to people like Ayaan Hirsi Ali is: 'If you say that, I will kill you.' Indeed, Buruma tells us that Bouyeri explained to the court that divine law did not permit him 'to live in this country or in any country where free speech is allowed'. (In which case, why not go back to Morocco?) But free speech is also threatened by the appeasement policies of frightened European governments, which attempt to introduce censorship in the name of intercommunal harmony. A worrying example was the British government's original proposal for a law against incitement to religious hatred. This is a version of multiculturalism which goes, 'You respect my taboo and I'll respect yours.' But if you put together all the taboos of all the cultures in the world, you're not left with much you can speak freely about.

Skilled police and intelligence work to catch would-be terrorists before they act (as the British police and security services appear to have done in August 2006) is essential not just to save the lives of potential victims. It's also vital because every terrorist atrocity committed in the name of Allah hastens the downward spiral of mutual distrust between Muslim and non-Muslim Europeans. One young Moroccan-Dutch woman tells Buruma that before the September 11 attacks on New York, 'I was just Nora. Then, all of a sudden, I was a Muslim.' Heading off this danger will also mean closer surveillance of the militant Islamist imams whom we repeatedly find radicalizing disaffected young European Muslim men.

From another angle, European economies need to create more jobs and make sure Muslims have a fair crack at getting them. A recent Pew poll found that the top concern among Muslims in Britain, France, Germany and Spain was unemployment. In view of the historic sluggishness of job creation in Europe, fierce competition from low-cost skilled labour in Asia, and the reflexes of xenophobic discrimination in many European countries, this is easier said than done. Housing conditions are another major source of grievance. However, to try to remedy that through public expenditure will strain already stretched budgets; if it is seen to be done at the expense of the 'native' population living nearby, it could also translate into more votes for populist anti-immigrant parties.

Europe's problem with its Muslims of immigrant origin, the pathology of the Inbetween People, would exist even if there were an independent, flourishing Palestinian state, and if the United States, Britain and some other European countries had not invaded Iraq. But there's no doubt that the Palestinian issue and the Iraq war have fed into European Muslims' sense of global victimhood. This is made amply clear by the personal stories of the Madrid and London bombers. In a recent poll for Britain's Channel 4 television, nearly a third of young British Muslim respondents agreed with the suggestion that 'the July bombings [of London] were justified because of British support for the war on terror.'[8] Establishing a workable Palestinian state and withdrawing Western troops from Iraq would, at the very least, remove two additional sources of grievance. An attack on another Muslim country, such as Iran, would exacerbate it.

In the relationship with Islam as a religion, it makes sense to encourage those versions of Islam that are compatible with the fundamentals of a modern, liberal and democratic Europe. That they can be found is the promise of Islamic reformers such as Tariq Ramadan – another controversial figure, deeply distrusted by Ayaan Hirsi Ali, the French left and the American right, but an inspiration to many young European Muslims. Ramadan insists that Islam, properly interpreted, need not conflict with a democratic Europe. Where the Eurabianists imply that 'more Muslim Europeans means more terrorists', Ramadan suggests that the more Muslim Europeans there are, the less likely they are to become terrorists. Muslim Europeans, that is, in the sense of people who believe – unlike Mohammed Bouyeri, Theo van Gogh and, I suspect, Ayaan Hirsi Ali – that you can be both a good Muslim and a good European.[9]

Ultimately, this is a challenge as much for European societies as for European governments. Much of the discrimination in France, for example, is the result of decisions by individual employers, who are going against the grain of public policy and the law of the land. It's the personal attitudes and behaviour of hundreds of millions of non-Muslim Europeans, in countless small, everyday interactions, that will determine whether their Muslim fellow citizens begin to feel at home in Europe or not. Together, of course, with the personal choices of millions of individual Muslims, and the example given by their spiritual and political leaders.

Is it likely that Europeans will rise to this challenge? I fear not. Is it still possible? Yes. But it's already five minutes to midnight – and we are drinking in the last chance saloon.

2006

This essay, and the work by Ian Buruma it discusses, provoked a controversy, often based on misunderstanding and sometimes on wilful misrepresentation. I have not replied systematically to all the points raised, and to do so here would break the bounds of this book. For those who followed that debate, I would point out that I no longer use the term 'Enlightenment fundamentalist', since it gives rise to the misunderstanding that some symmetry is suggested with 'Islamic fundamentalist' – a label now used almost synonymously with 'terrorist'. However, I stand by most of the analysis and conclusions of this essay. There remains an important set of questions about which version of the Enlightenment we need now, and another about the nature and limits of Islamic reformism – of which Tariq Ramadan is a very problematic example. The essays that follow in this section give a clear idea of the kind of liberal secularism for which I argue.

The Invisible Front Line

To return from the United States to Europe is to travel from a country that thinks it is on the front line of the struggle against jihadist terrorism, but is not, to a continent which is on the front line but still has not fully woken up to the fact. On the front line at home, I mean; abroad is another matter. Only a fool would rule out the possibility of another terrorist assault on what is now styled the American homeland, but the fact is that in the six years since 11 September 2001 there have been several major attacks (Madrid, London) and foiled plots in Europe. In the United States there have been no major attacks and, so far as we know, just a few averted conspiracies. All the evidence shows that American Muslims are better integrated than those in western Europe. Last week's arrest of a group apparently planning a September 11 anniversary attack in Germany suggests that the threat to the *Heimat* is greater than that to the 'homeland'.

An invisible front line runs through the quiet streets of many a European city. Like it or not, whether you live in London or Oxford, Berlin or Neu-Ulm, Madrid or Rotterdam, you are on that front line – much more than you ever were during the Cold War. This struggle is partly about intelligence and police work to prevent those who have already become fanatical, violent jihadists from blowing us up at St Pancras or the Gare du Nord. Ordinary non-Muslim Europeans can only do a little to help this work, as well as worrying about the curtailment of civil liberties. Ordinary, peaceful, law-abiding Muslim Europeans can do a little more.

The larger part of this struggle, and the more important in the longer term, is the battle for the hearts and minds of young European Muslims – usually men – who are not yet fanatical violent jihadists, but could become so. All over our continent, and around its edges, there are hundreds of thousands of young Muslim men who could go either way. They could become tomorrow's bombers or they could become tomorrow's Europeans: good citizens, funders of our faltering state pension schemes, committed internationalists.

The chemistry here can be understood a little better by thinking back to the last wave of youth terrorism, in the 'German autumn' of thirty years ago and Italy's Red Brigades. When I lived in Berlin in the late 1970s I met quite a few people who told me, 'You know, there was a moment when I could have gone either way.' They could have slunk away to join the Red Army Faction, like those acquaintances of their acquaintances, Horst and Ulrike. Instead, they became journalists, academics or lawyers, and are now pillars of a society under attack from another, potentially more destructive wave of terrorism.

Of course we cannot take the comparison too far, but one basic feature is the same: beside the hard core of fanatics there is a penumbra of people who could go either way. In Germany, they were (and are) called the *Sympathisanten*, the 'sympathizers'. Among European Muslims, they might very roughly be correlated with those who, in surveys, refuse to condemn suicide bombings, although that figure is inflated by attitudes to Palestine. One analyst estimates that while the hard core may comprise 1 per cent of British Muslims, the penumbra of *Sympathisanten*, the could-go-either-way group, is perhaps 10 per cent.

If you look at the biographies of actual jihadist assassins over the last six years, from the September 11 bomber Mohamed Atta, radicalized in Hamburg, to Mohammed Bouyeri, murderer of Theo van Gogh, you find again and again the same story: young men who were first attracted to a modern, Western way of life, quite different from that of their parents, but then angrily rejected it in favour of a violent, extremist version of political Islam. Fortunately, there are also people who travel the other way. Read Ed Husain's book *The Islamist* for an illuminating account of how one young British man was sucked into extremist Islamism, but then turned away from it, while still remaining a Muslim. So much now depends on whether the 10 per cent veer towards the barbaric 1 per cent, or, like Husain, rejoin the civilized majority. (This is not a clash of civilizations; it is a clash between civilization and decivilization.)

The recent defection of a former senior member of Hizb ut-Tahrir in Britain, Maajid Nawaz, is another very encouraging sign. As once Europe had a formidable cohort of ex-communists, so soon we may have a strong group of ex-Islamists. No one knows better how to fight the disease than those who have cured themselves of it.

Iraq is a sideshow in this larger struggle. President Bush may still claim that Iraq is the front line in the war on terror ('if we don't stop them there, they'll come for us here'), but even some of his senior commanders don't believe that. To be sure, there is now an al-Qaida in Iraq, where there wasn't before the invasion. The Iraq war has become an added grievance for disaffected Muslims everywhere – it was cited by the London bombers – although note that Germany's non-participation in the Iraq war did not keep it safe. Nor should we avert our eyes from the further uncomfortable truth that an American withdrawal from Iraq will be celebrated by violent jihadists as a victory for bin Laden.

But the larger truth is that a British soldier returning from Basra to Bradford will be coming from one front line to another. This invisible front line is not a military but a cultural-political one, and it will ultimately be more decisive in defeating the lure of the jihadist way of death. The returning soldier may do more to reduce the threat of terrorism in Britain by his off-duty attitude to British Muslims in his home town than by anything he did, gun in hand, in Basra.

Afghanistan is a different matter. Rooting out al-Qaida and beating back the renascent Taliban is an integral part of combating jihadist terrorism. So is trying to change the poisonous mixture of radical religion and politics in Pakistan and Saudi Arabia. The man who seems to have been a ringleader of the German group, a convert to Islam called Fritz Gelowicz, was radicalized in the Multi-Kultur-Haus (another blow to the good name of multiculturalism) in Neu-Ulm by instructors from the toxic Wahhabi sect of Islam, based in and funded by that great American ally, Saudi Arabia. He then reportedly went for Arabic language training in Syria and terrorist training in the border regions of Pakistan, in a camp run by the Islamic Jihad Union, originally an Uzbek group. According to German sources, the instruction to launch the anniversary attack came by email from Pakistan. So in its pathology, the threat we face is both international and intranational, global and local. Death comes to you out of Neu-Ulm by way of Waziristan. The invisible front line runs 5,000 miles away – and right in front of your nose.

If we are calm, clear-sighted and resolute, we will eventually win this struggle and remain free. A continent that has rid itself of the horrors of imperialism, fascism and communism will see off this lesser menace too. But it will take many years and we had better shape up to it.

2007

Against Taboos

What a magnificent blow for truth, justice and humanity the French national assembly has struck. Last week it voted for a bill that would make it a crime to deny that the Turks committed genocide against the Armenians during the First World War. *Bravo! Chapeau bas! Vive la France!* But let this be only a beginning in a brave new chapter of European history. Let the British parliament now make it a crime to deny that it was Russians who murdered Polish officers at Katyn in 1940. Let the Turkish parliament make it a crime to deny that France used torture against insurgents in Algeria.

Let the German parliament pass a bill making it a crime to deny the existence of the Soviet Gulag. Let the Irish parliament criminalize denial of the horrors of the Spanish Inquisition. Let the Spanish parliament mandate a minimum of ten years' imprisonment for anyone who claims that the Serbs did not attempt genocide against Albanians in Kosovo. And the European Parliament should immediately pass into European law a bill making it obligatory to describe as genocide the American colonists' treatment of Native Americans. The only pity is that we, in the European Union, can't impose the death sentence for these heinous thought crimes. But perhaps, with time, we may change that too.

Oh brave new Europe! It is entirely beyond me how anyone in their right mind – apart, of course, from a French-Armenian lobbyist – can regard this draft bill, which in any case will almost certainly be voted down in the upper house of the French parliament, as a progressive and enlightened step. What right has the parliament of France to prescribe by law the correct historical terminology to characterize what another nation did to a third nation ninety years ago? If the French parliament passed a law making it a crime to deny the complicity of Vichy France in the deportation to the death camps of French Jews, I would still argue that this was a mistake, but I could respect the self-critical moral impulse behind it.

This bill, by contrast, has no more moral or historical justification than any of the other suggestions I have just made. Yes, there are some half a million French citizens of Armenian origin – including Charles Aznavour, who was once Varinag Aznavourian – and they have been pressing for it. There are at least that number of British citizens of Polish origin, so there would be precisely the same justification for a British bill on Katyn. Step forward Mr Denis MacShane, a British MP of Polish origin, to propose it. Or how about British MPs of Pakistani and Indian origin proposing rival bills on the history of Kashmir?

In a leading article the *Guardian* averred that 'supporters of the law are doubtless motivated by a sincere desire to redress a 90-year-old injustice.' I wish that I could be so confident. Currying favour with French-Armenian voters and putting another obstacle in the way of Turkey joining the European Union might be suggested as other motives; but speculation about motives is a mug's game.

It will be obvious to every intelligent reader that my argument has nothing to do with questioning the suffering of the Armenians who were massacred, expelled or felt impelled to flee in fear of their lives during and after the First World War. Their fate at the hands of the Turks was terrible and has been too little recalled in the mainstream of European memory. Reputable historians and writers have made a strong case that those events deserve the label of genocide, as it has been defined since 1945. In fact, Orhan Pamuk – this year's winner of the Nobel Prize in literature – and other Turkish writers have been prosecuted under the notorious article 301 of the Turkish penal code for daring to suggest exactly that. That is significantly worse than the intended effects of the French bill. But two wrongs don't make a right.

No one can legislate historical truth. In so far as historical truth can be established at all, it must be found by unfettered historical research, with historians arguing over the evidence and the facts, testing and disputing each other's claims without fear of prosecution or persecution.

In the tense ideological politics of our time, this proposed bill is a step in exactly the wrong direction. How can we credibly criticize Turkey, Egypt or other states for curbing free speech, through the legislated protection of historical, national or religious shibboleths, if we are doing ever more of it ourselves? This weekend in Venice I once again heard a distinguished Muslim scholar rail against our double standards. We ask them to accept insults to Muslim taboos, he said, but would the Jews accept that someone should be free to deny the Holocaust?

Far from creating new legally enforced taboos about history, national identity and religion, we should be dismantling those that still remain on our statute books. Those European countries that have them should repeal not only their blasphemy laws but also their laws on Holocaust denial. Otherwise the charge of double standards is impossible to refute. What's sauce for the goose must be sauce for the gander.

I recently heard the French philosopher Alain Finkielkraut going through some impressive intellectual contortions to explain why he opposed any laws restricting criticism of religion but supported those on Holocaust denial. It was one thing, he argued, to question a religious belief, quite another to deny a historical fact. But this won't wash. Historical facts are established precisely by their being disputed and tested against the evidence. Without that process of contention – up to and including the revisionist extreme of outright denial – we would never discover which facts are truly hard.

Such consistency requires painful decisions. For example, I have nothing but abhorrence for some of David Irving's recorded views about Nazi Germany's attempted extermination of the Jews – but I am quite certain that he should not be sitting in an Austrian prison as a result of them. You may riposte that the falsehood of some of his claims was actually established by a trial in a British court. Yes, but that was not the British state prosecuting him for Holocaust denial. It was Irving himself going to court to sue another historian who suggested he was a Holocaust denier. He was trying to curb free and fair historical debate; the British court defended it.

Today, if we want to defend free speech in our own countries and to encourage it in places where it is currently denied, we should be calling for David Irving to be released from his Austrian prison. The Austrian law on Holocaust denial is far more historically understandable and morally respectable than the proposed French one – at least the Austrians are facing up to their own difficult past, rather than pointing the finger at somebody else's – but in the larger European interest we should encourage the Austrians to repeal it.

Only when we are prepared to allow our own most sacred cows to be poked in the eye can we credibly demand that Islamists, Turks and others do the same. This is a time not for erecting taboos but for dismantling them. We must practise what we preach.

2006

Respect?

Last weekend I went and sang a lot of words that I don't believe. Do I think an angel appeared to a woman called Mary roughly 2007 years ago and told her she had become pregnant without sleeping with Joseph? I don't. Do I think Good King Wenceslas tramped out into the snow to bring 'yonder peasant' food and wine? Not likely. Yet the words were beautiful and familiar, the medieval church was candlelit, my family was with me, and I was moved.

In the next few days, hundreds of millions of people will, like me, go to sing, often with gusto and delight, lines they do not believe or, at best, only half believe. According to a recent Harris opinion poll for the *Financial Times*, only one in three people in Britain say they are 'a believer'. In France, it's less than one in three; even in Italy, it's less than two thirds; only in the United States does the figure exceed three quarters. And it would be interesting to know what proportion of that minority of true believers in Britain and France are Muslims.

That set me thinking – in this extended festive season of Bodhi Day, Hanukah, Christmas, Eid-ul-Adha, Oshogatsu, Guru Gobind Singh's birthday and Makar Sankranti – about what it means to say that we respect someone else's religion in a multicultural society. It seems to me that the biggest problem many post-Christian or nominally Christian Europeans have with the Muslims living amongst them is not that those Muslims are believers in a different religion from Christianity but that they are believers in a religion at all.

This baffles the intellectually significant minority of Europeans who are, so to speak, devout atheists, proselytizing believers in the truths discovered by science. For them the issue is not any particular religious superstition, but superstition itself. It is also what worries the much larger number of Europeans who themselves have some vague, lukewarm religious beliefs, or are mildly agnostic, but put other things first. If only the Muslims wouldn't take their Islam so seriously! And, many Europeans would add, if only the Americans wouldn't take their Christianity so seriously!

Now one can argue about whether the world would be a better place if everyone became convinced of the atheistic truths of natural science, or at least took their religion as lightly as most part-time, demi-Christian Europeans do. (Myself, I'm agnostic on that point.) But clearly this can't be the premise on which we build a multicultural society in a free country. That would be just as intolerant as the practice of those majority Muslim countries where no other faiths than Islam are allowed.

On the contrary, in free countries every faith must be allowed – and every faith must be allowed to be questioned, fundamentally, outspokenly, even intemperately and offensively, without fear of reprisal. Richard Dawkins, the Oxford scientist, must be free to say that God is a delusion and Alistair McGrath, the Oxford theologian, must be free to retort that Dawkins is deluded; a conservative journalist must be free to write that the Prophet Muhammad was a paedophile and a Muslim scholar must be free to brand that journalist an ignorant Islamophobe. That's the deal in a free country: freedom of religion and freedom of expression as two sides of the same coin. We must live and let live – a demand that is not as minimal as it sounds, when one thinks of the death threats against Salman Rushdie and the Danish cartoonists. The fence that secures this space is the law of the land.

The interesting question is whether there is a kind of respect that goes beyond this minimal law-fenced live-and-let-live yet stops short of either a hypocritical pretence of intellectual respect for the other's beliefs (the currency of much inter-faith polylogue) or unbounded relativism. I think there is. In fact, I would claim that I know there is – and most of us practise it without even thinking about it. We live and work every day with people who hold, in the temples of their hearts, beliefs that we consider certifiably bonkers. If they seem to us good partners, friends, colleagues, we respect them as such – irrespective of their private and perhaps deepest convictions. If they are close to us, we may not merely respect but love them. We love them, while all the time remaining firmly convinced that in some corner of their minds they cling to a load of nonsense.

Routinely, almost instinctively, we distinguish between the belief and the believer. To be sure, it's easier to do that with some beliefs than it is with others. If someone is convinced that $2 + 2 = 5$ and the earth is made of cheese, that will impede everyday coexistence a little more. Yet it's amazing what diverse and even wacky beliefs we do, in practice, coexist with quite happily. (The widespread popular faith in astrology is a good example.) That said, the conduct of the believers can affect our judgement of the belief irrespective of its scientific truth-content. For example, I do not believe there is a God and therefore assume that some 2007 years ago a couple called Joseph and Mary just had a baby. But what a man he turned out to be! Like the great Swiss historian Jacob Burckhardt, I can't get anywhere with Christ as God, but as a human being Jesus Christ seems to me a constant and wonderful inspiration – perhaps even, as Burckhardt put it, 'the most beautiful figure in world history'. And some of his later imitators didn't do so badly either.

My quarrel with the Dawkins school of atheists is not anything they say about the non-existence of God but what they say about

Christians and the history of Christianity – much of which is true, but leaves out the other, positive half of the story. And, as the old Yiddish saying goes, a half-truth is a whole lie. In my judgement as a historian of modern Europe, the positive side is larger than the negative. It seems to me self-evident that we would not have the European civilization we have today without the heritage of Christianity, Judaism and (in a smaller measure, mainly in the Middle Ages) Islam, which legacy also paved the way, albeit unwittingly and unwillingly, for the Enlightenment. Moreover, some of the most impressive human beings I have met in my own lifetime have been Christians.

There is a respect that flows from the present conduct of the believers, irrespective of the scientific plausibility of the original belief. A multicultural society can, at best, be an open, friendly competition between Christians, Sikhs, Muslims, Jews, atheists and, indeed, two-plus-two-equals-fivers, to impress us with their character and good works. 'By their fruits ye shall know them.'

2006

Secularism or Atheism?

A great debate of our time concerns how people with different religions, ethnicities and values can live together as full citizens of free societies. Here's the common thread that runs through half a dozen news stories every day. Yesterday, for example: a schoolteacher arrested and charged in Sudan for allowing children to call a teddy bear Muhammad; the poor, ethnically mixed housing estates around Paris going up in smoke again; Israel–Palestine peace talks, with their implications for relations between Muslims and non-Muslims everywhere; a Jewish school in London criticized for insisting that for a child to qualify for admission the applicant's mother had to be born Jewish; angry scenes in Oxford as a student debating society offers a platform to a Holocaust denier.

A large part of this debate is about the position of Muslims in Europe, but it's important to remember that the issues are much wider. Recently, discussion of Muslims in Europe has crystallized around a few personalities, including some views attributed to me. Such a personalization of the issues helps to dramatize them, but it also risks disappearing down obscure polemical back alleys of the 'who did or did not say what about whom' variety. It's probably more useful to put personalities aside for the moment and restate some of the basics of the secular liberal position that I propose.

Muslims start from Islam. Liberals start from liberalism. I'm a liberal, so I start from liberalism – not in the parody version propagated by the American right, but liberalism properly understood as a quest for the greatest possible measure of individual human freedom, compatible with the freedom of others. I believe that, faced with the challenges of growing diversity, we, the citizens, need to agree and spell out more clearly the essentials of a free society. A charter of citizens' rights and duties, as proposed by Gordon Brown, would be one way to take this forward.

Among the essentials is freedom of expression, which has been eroded to an alarming degree, both by death threats from extremists and by misconceived pre-emptive appeasement on the part of the state and private bodies. Freedom of expression necessarily includes the right to offend; not the duty, but the right. We must, in particular, be free to say what we like about historical figures, be they Moses, Jesus, Muhammad, Churchill, Hitler or Gandhi (and then let our claims be tested against the evidence). We may not agree with what controversialists say about these figures but we must defend to the death their right to say it. There should, for obvious reasons, be limits to what we are free to say about living people, but these limits must be very tightly drawn.

Among the liberal essentials is equality before the law, including equal rights for men and women. Among the essentials is also freedom of religion. Since a core liberal notion is that we must be free not just pursue our own version of the good life but also to question and revise it, it follows that we must be free to propagate, question, change or abandon our religion. In a free society, proselytization, heresy and apostasy are not crimes. This – and apostasy in particular – is not accepted in many versions of Islam, but it is a liberal essential on which there can be no compromise.

In order to secure these freedoms, we need a secular public sphere. But what exactly do we mean by that? To say 'Enlightenment values' is not enough. Which Enlightenment? The Enlightenment of John

Locke, which claimed freedom for religion, or that of Voltaire, which aspired rather to freedom from religion? (I deliberately simplify a complex history.) A liberal order in which the devotees of all Gods are free to try their hand in the public square, on an equal footing with those who insist – correctly, in my view – that there is no God? Or a liberal order in which all gods are kept as far as possible out of the public square? (The French republican understanding of *laïcité* is closer to the latter, the United States' first amendment tradition to the former.) I'm more of a Lockean myself, but I don't think this debate is best pursued at the abstract, theoretical level of 'which Enlightenment?' Better to tackle specific issues: faith schools, new mosques, the teaching of evolution, the *hijab*, Muhammad cartoons and so on.

We do, however, need to be clearer about the difference between secularism and atheism. Secularism, in my view, should be an argument about arrangements for a shared public and social life; atheism is an argument about scientific truth, individual liberation and the nature of the good life. Today's debate around Islam is bedevilled by a confusion between the two. Atheists must be free to say to Muslims, Christians or Jews: 'Your mind would be much more free if you gave up your ridiculous belief in God.' Believers must be free to argue back: 'You would have a more profound sense of personal freedom if you did believe.' But neither is entitled to demand that of the other as a condition for participating as a citizen in a free society. The public policy argument about freedom for religion and the private conviction argument about freedom from or in religion should operate on different levels.

That distinction would, of course, no longer hold if being a devout Muslim were in fact incompatible with being a full citizen of a free society. I feel this is what quite a few participants in the current debate, both atheist and Christian, really believe, while seldom spelling it out so clearly. Yet the thought keeps peeping through, for example in the formula 'Islam is incompatible with democracy.' But what

Muslims say and do in the name of Islam has varied enormously through history, and varies enormously today. Yes, of course, there are the Koran and the Hadith, just as there is the Bible. But, as in all great religions, these are complex texts, subject to diverse interpretations.

When a Muslim letter-writer to the *Guardian* tells us, with the aid of Koranic references, that Islam, properly understood, supports 'the vital principle of freedom of speech', what possible interest have we non-Muslim liberals in arguing against him? If a Christian supports the rule of law, as we understand it in a twenty-first-century secular liberal state, we don't cry, 'But your Old Testament says "life for life, eye for eye, tooth for tooth"!' Unless, of course, an atheist agenda – to show that religion is not just nonsense but dangerous nonsense – trumps the secular liberal agenda, which is to find the ways in which people with different beliefs can live together peacefully in freedom.

2007

No Ifs and No Buts

Salman Rushdie, with a little help from Her Majesty, has again clarified the battlelines on which we stand. Because Britain is honouring him for what he has written, he is again being threatened with death. An Iranian organization has offered a reward of some £80,000 for his murder. Pakistan's religious affairs minister, Muhammad Ijaz ul-Haq – the son of the former military dictator Zia ul-Haq – told his country's national assembly that a suicide bombing could be justified as a response. Almost as grotesque was the reaction of a British Muslim peer, Lord Ahmed of Rotherham, who expressed his outrage at 'honouring the man who has blood on his hands'. White-is-black thinking of an almost Orwellian kind, this turns the victim into the murderer.

The issue here is not whether Rushdie's writing merits a knighthood, nor whether left-wing, cosmopolitan writers should accept honours from Her Majesty. (My answers, by the way, are 'Yes' and 'Why not?') The issue is whether people should be killed, or face a serious threat of being killed, for what they say or write; and whether a sovereign, democratic state should censor its recognition of its citizens in the face of such intimidation. On this there can be no compromise, no ifs or buts. All our individual solidarity, all the necessary resources of the state, are called for at such a moment. Although this did not seem uppermost in the minds of the committee that recommended the award, when the Queen taps Mr Rushdie on the shoulder with her ceremonial sword and says 'Arise, Sir Salman', she will now be striking a regal blow for free speech.

The right to free speech is not unlimited. In determining its limits, context matters. The American judge Wendell Holmes famously observed that a man should not be free to shout a false alarm of 'Fire!' in a crowded theatre. Now the fact is that even if a secular liberal intellectual were to say 'Mad Mullah X deserves to be shot', the likelihood of someone shooting Mullah X as a result is close to zero. So far as we know, there are no al-Darwinia brigades making bombs in secret laboratories in north Oxford, awaiting an order from their beloved Imam Dawkins to assassinate Mullah X. If, however, a Muslim cleric or intellectual says, 'Salman Rushdie deserves to be shot', there are people who may take it literally. Remember that Rushdie's Japanese translator was murdered, his Italian translator stabbed and his Norwegian publisher shot because Ayatollah Khomeini had called for everyone involved in publishing *The Satanic Verses* to be punished.

Because of this explosive context, Muslim speakers need to exercise a particular care in their choice of words. But we non-Muslims need, in return, to be generously clear about the distinction between what a free society requires of them and what we merely desire. We may desire that they abandon what we regard as outmoded superstitions, 'see reason', become modern, liberal, secular. But, in a free society, nobody should require that of them. The toleration of widely differing opinions and beliefs is precisely what distinguishes a free society from the ideological regimes of the Middle East. Rushdie wrote a fiction that was deeply offensive to many Muslims. Muslims have the right to be deeply offensive back. All that a free society requires of them – as of every citizen – is that they conduct this argument peacefully and obey the law of the land.

I note with appreciation and respect how a growing number of British Muslims, including some who burned Rushdie's books back in 1989, are now standing firmly on this line. I will be the first to defend their right to articulate their beliefs in ways that may be as offensive to an atheist as Rushdie's novel was to them. In a free society, we don't have to agree. We only have to agree on how we disagree.

2007

4.
USA! USA!

Mr President

One afternoon in the early summer of 2001, I received a surprising telephone call at my office in Oxford. A girlish American voice, claiming to speak 'from the White House', asked if I would come to a meeting with the president, next Thursday, between 1.40 and 4.10pm, to prepare him for his first official trip to Europe. The National Security Council, she said, could pay a coach class airfare.

Having established that this was not a student hoax, I replied that I did have a lunch that day but would try to move it. Normally, I'm wary of such meetings. I think people who write about politicians should not get too close to them. On the other hand, I see no reason not to share your expertise with democratically elected leaders of any stripe, and I have, on isolated occasions, done so with politicians as diverse as Margaret Thatcher, Tony Blair and Gerhard Schröder. Anyway, this was just too intriguing to pass up.

At the appointed hour on Thursday, 31 May, we assembled for a briefing in the Roosevelt Room, with Teddy Roosevelt peering down from horseback at one end and Franklin D. from his desk at the other. From there, we moved to the Map Room. I was absorbed in studying the last military map seen by FDR before his death in April 1945 – a map of the final phase of the war in Europe, marked here and there with a 'pocket' or 'likely pocket' of German resistance – when suddenly the forty-third President of the United States, George W. Bush, was amongst us. 'Quite tall. Square-set, tanned. Dark suit. Quite formal greetings. Clipped style,' I recorded in my notebook, when I wrote up my recollections of the meeting a few hours later, while waiting at National airport for my plane home.

The president led us upstairs and into a whistlestop tour. Here was the Lincoln Bedroom that had been used, he observed, 'for . . . many things'. (The Clintons had been accused of misusing it for fund-raising purposes.) The Queens' Bedroom – oddly, for a republic. ('Yes, we got rid of them,' someone in the entourage joked. But there was Barbara Bush.) And the Truman Balcony, looking south over the gardens. What I remember most from there – my memory now transformed irreversibly by the 11 September 2001 attacks – is the planes taking off from National airport and climbing directly over the White House. Back then, in May 2001, it did not even occur to me that these were potential weapons of mass destruction flying overhead. Back then, they were just planes.

We settled down to work in a large, yellow-painted drawing room called the Yellow Oval Room (not to be confused with the Oval Office), which gives directly on to the Truman Balcony. On one side sat, in throne-like chairs, the president and the vice-president, a lowering Dick Cheney. On the other sat the national security adviser, Condi Rice – whom I had come to know and like as a colleague at Stanford University – and her deputy, Stephen Hadley, with some officials behind them. The invited guests were placed on two large sofas, completing a kind of open square: myself, Lionel Barber, then US editor of the *Financial Times*, and Felix Rohatyn, financial legend and former US ambassador to France, on one sofa, tasked with talking about Europe; facing us Michael McFaul, also of Stanford, and his fellow Russian expert Thomas Graham, primed to talk about Russia. A phalanx of soft drinks was arrayed on a large low table, at an uncomfortable distance from both sofas. So far as I can recall, in the more than two hours of our conversation, only the president dared to reach for a beverage.

'I sit before you, an unvarnished Texan,' said Bush, in a characteristically self-deprecating opening.[1] He wanted to know more before this important trip, he explained. He came to it with a certain feeling that 'our great country' was tied down by all these international commitments. He did not use Jefferson's phrase 'entangling alliances', but that was very much the spirit of his remark.

His suspicion of most forms of liberal internationalism was a recurrent theme. Later in the afternoon, he complained that there had been far too many half-baked US military interventions. My notes have him exclaiming, 'What would we be doing in Rwanda.' Lionel Barber's have him saying, 'I ain't going to get into no Somalia.' American troops, he insisted, should not be used as 'cross-walk soldiers'. He did not look best pleased when I observed – did I add 'with respect, Mr President'? – that 'Macedonia is not Somalia.'[2]

He looked even less pleased when Lionel said that Europeans feared the US might be moving 'from mindless multilateralism to mindless unilateralism'. Truth to tell, the president did not seem altogether familiar with the word multilateralism, let alone the thing. When he came back to it later, he turned to Barber and said something like 'so that's your multiculturalism ... or multinationalism ...' We both had the impression that he meant multilateralism. Multibloodysomethingism anyway.

'Do we want the European Union to succeed?' he asked at one point. When Lionel and I replied, rather emphatically, that as British Europeans we certainly wanted the EU to succeed, and we thought the United States should too, he pulled back, saying, 'That was a provocation!' Yet his administration's subsequent preference for dealing with individual European powers, a.k.a. divide and rule, suggested that this was a genuine question – to which some present, such as the lowering Cheney, would answer no. When Felix Rohatyn told him the Germans had 'a federalist project' for Europe, the president interjected: 'Can you define federalist project?' 'I mean, like the US,' explained Rohatyn.

On most issues relating to Europe he seemed to have an open, not to say an empty mind. He responded quite favourably to the suggestion, made first by me and strongly supported by Mike McFaul, that a stable, liberal, democratic Russia should in the long run be offered membership in NATO. But on two matters his mind was entirely made up. One was missile defence. 'I'm absolutely committed to the concept,' he said. This was 'not Star Wars'. It was directed against many threats, not only Russia. Iranian missiles were mentioned. He felt that in his upcoming meeting with Vladimir Putin he could persuade the Russian president to join him in this historic undertaking: 'My object is to make him feel recognized as a great power.' Sure, the GDP of Russia was less than that of Texas, 'but I'm not going to tell him that'. Instead, he wanted to convince Putin that together they could make a deal 'for the defence of the world'. 'For the defence of the world' . . . who but the president of the United States could seriously utter such a phrase? But defence against whom?

The other subject on which he had a firm view, expressed at length, was climate change. Where he came from, he said, in west Texas, they talk about One World Government – 'Well, I've found it! It's the international environmental lobby.' In prescribing energy emission limits in the Kyoto treaty, which did not even include the giant emerging economies of Asia, he thought the Europeans were trying to steal a competitive edge over the US: 'They were trying to screw us.' According to my notes, a long spiel about the folly of the Greens ended in this verdict: 'Kyoto is mush.' However, he did recognize that his administration hadn't handled the Kyoto issue very well ('Agreed,' said Condi crisply) and he promised they'd try to come up with something new before the European trip.

His judgements on individual countries seemed inseparable from those on their current leaders. He liked Tony Blair – 'easy to deal with . . . supports missile defence' – and he liked the bonhomous

Jacques Chirac, but he 'had some problems with Germany'. When I asked what problems, his answer was all about Chancellor Gerhard Schröder and his foreign minister, Joschka Fischer. He suspected (not without reason, as it later turned out) that Schröder might want to play Russia against the US. As for Fischer, the man had a radical left-wing past and, worst of all, he was a Green. He, Bush, had teased Fischer – 'I like teasing, you know' – by saying that he had told the German chancellor that his government had too many Greens in it, and then he had winked at Fischer, to show he was teasing. To which that humourless German had irritably responded: 'Well, the trouble is there are not enough Greens in yours.' (Joschka might not have been good at taking a joke, but history would prove him disastrously right.)

This confusion between the country and its current leaders seems to be a professional deformation among early twenty-first-century world leaders, who meet each other frequently at bilateral and multi-lateral summits. The less they know of each other's countries, the more their judgement is influenced by the personalities. Thus, for example, I found at a now notorious 'Chequers seminar' with Margaret Thatcher, held to discuss the prospect of German unification in early 1990, that her view of Germany was shaped by her personal dislike of Helmut Kohl, and her sense that he had bullied her at summit meetings of European leaders.[3] Worse still, he had success-fully bullied her. On the other hand, her generally negative view of France was softened by a certain feminine fascination with François Mitterrand. Bush and Blair, too, both misjudged their relationship with France because they were charmed by the genial Jacques Chirac. (What is it about these Frenchmen?) The country/leader fallacy is perfectly captured in his minor gem of Bushspeak about Putin: 'My object is to make him feel recognized as a great power.' When he met Putin for the first time, just a few weeks after our White House meeting, he famously said that he 'looked the man in the eye' and found him 'very straightforward and trustworthy'. More, he had 'got a sense of his soul'. And with that soul-searching, Bush got Russia, as he got so much else, wrong.

Our discussion of Russia yielded one other telling insight. In the long run, he said, Russia would have no alternative but to join forces with Europe and the West. For, east of the Urals, they faced a rising China: 'That's a subject for another session.' I felt this was a president still searching for his central foreign policy narrative, but, to the extent that he had developed any overall geopolitical view, it did seem that he saw China replacing the Soviet Union as the United States' great global competitor, and prospective enemy.

When he wound up at the end, he looked directly at me: 'And, by the way, I don't think Macedonia is Somalia. I had the Macedonian president in here the other day and, as the only two Methodist world leaders, we prayed together . . .'4

With that bizarre coda, it was farewell time – and off to the airport in a battered old Washington taxi. Reflecting on the man, I found him a strange, uneven and unstable mixture: rather stiff, conservative East Coast gentleman and shoot-from-the-hip, cowboy Texican; a quick, businesslike intelligence and alarming ignorance; America First nationalism and yearning to be a statesman like his dad; a self-deprecating charm, that suggested a centred, rooted personality, and hints of a deep insecurity.

At one moment, apropos of nothing in particular, he veered off into an anecdote about a summit of North and South American leaders at which, after 'articulating and articulating', as Condi had instructed him to do, he decided to stay silent on a significant issue. Then the chairman turned to him and said, 'But Mr President, you are the most powerful man on earth.' And, Bush told us, 'I thought to myself, hmmm . . . Yeah . . . it takes a little time to grow into this job.' But would he? Somewhere deep down, he obviously had some doubts whether he would. So did I.

Sixteen weeks later, those planes became weapons of mass destruction, and the world changed. The Bush administration found its defining narrative: the Global War on Terror. World War IV. Where FDR defeated Hitler, Bush would defeat Osama bin Laden. Or, when they couldn't find bin Laden, Saddam Hussein. China, from being the prospective enemy, became a valued partner in this global struggle. In these dramatically testing circumstances, the world learned the answer to George W. Bush's innermost question. No, he would not be up to the job. He would, in fact, turn out to be one of the worst presidents in modern American history. He would do great damage to the world, both by what he did and, even more, by what he failed to do on global challenges like climate change. And the eight years of his presidency would bring great harm to his own country: to its economy, to its power, to its good name.

But we didn't know all that then. One of the most difficult – strictly speaking, impossible – things for historians to recapture is a sense of what people did *not* know at the time. We all fall into a trap that the French philosopher Henri Bergson labelled 'the illusions of retrospective determinism'.

As I squeezed myself into my coach class seat at the back of a crowded plane, I discovered that the man sitting next to me was of that particular American type that combines, for fellow passengers on a long-haul flight, two major disadvantages: exceedingly fat and exceedingly friendly. Launching into what was obviously meant to be a five-hour rolling conversation, he asked me what I had been doing in Washington. I hesitated for a moment, measured the prospect ahead, and replied: 'Oh, I've just been seeing a couple of people in the administration.'

2009

9/11

Where were you when you heard the news that Kennedy had been shot? That the Berlin Wall was coming down? And now: that the World Trade Center was under attack? This was one of those defining moments of global experience and emotion, shared through television. You walk down the street and you know that everyone around you is thinking of the same thing. And hundreds of millions with them, across the world.

But the big question is: which kind of global event will it be? Will it be like the Kennedy assassination – shocking, unforgettable, but ultimately of little import for the course of history? Or will it be more like the fall of the Wall, an event that does change the course of history, with consequences that are played out over many decades and all the continents?

My hunch is that it will prove to be closer to the latter – for two reasons. First, because this was a catastrophe foretold. For years now, security experts have been warning us that, after the end of the Cold War, the greatest threat to the security of our prosperous capitalist democracies – the West or the North, according to your point of view – might come from terrorist attack. Most people did not quite believe it. Yes, there have been horrific bombings, but there has been no really large defining moment – no Berlin blockade or Cuban missile crisis of the new age – to impress it upon every mind. Well, here it is: images of the most famous cityscape in the world wreathed in smoke and changed utterly. So, far from being a one-off freak occurrence, this is the worst-case realization of deeper trends already charted and foreseen.

Second, I think that it will change the course of history because what happens in the world at the start of the twenty-first century depends more than ever before on the conduct of a single country, the United States, and this attack seems likely to have an incalculable impact on the psychology of that country. So much of the great and largely benign continuity of American foreign policy since 1945 has depended on the outside world not impacting directly on the lives of most Americans.

Anyone who has spent time in America will know what I mean. People grumbled in small-town bars about entangling alliances. Congressmen and commentators in Washington made threatening noises about isolation or retribution. But most of the people, most of the time, really didn't care that much what happened in the rest of the world, one way or the other.

On that solid foundation of deep popular indifference the soaring steel towers of American foreign policy were erected by elite architects. With the most significant external attack on the heart of the American homeland since British forces burned Washington in 1814, that paradoxically solid foundation will be shaken. It may seem odd to fear the moment when ordinary Americans really start to care about the outside world, but we may yet find ourselves longing nostalgically for the old, self-contained indifference that has so often annoyed the foreign visitor.

There are many things that public opinion has prevented American leaders doing in the world. Since Vietnam, for example, there has been the phobia about risking the lives of American soldiers for fear that they would come back in bodybags.

Hence the bombing of Kosovo from a safe altitude of 15,000 feet. But there were very few things that public opinion actively compelled leaders to do in foreign policy. The Manhattan horror seems to have changed that – for the time being, anyway. Suddenly, the cry goes up from throats half-choked with debris and dust, and from millions across America: revenge! Get the bastards who did this, preferably with smart weapons and no casualties, of course, but if not, if it means some bodybags – well, so be it.

So what happens now, in the post-September 11 world? Here, to concentrate the mind, are three scenarios:

SCENARIO ONE

The United States starts behaving more like Israel. Feeling itself embattled and besieged, but with a manifest destiny, it lashes out with its hi-tech military at anyone who might even seem to want to attack it. Any terrorist attack provokes instant retaliation, without waiting for proof that the attack actually came from that source. An eye for an eye, a tooth for a tooth – and never mind exactly whose eye or tooth it is. This is the course being urged on America by Ehud Barak, the former Israeli prime minister. America, he says, should go to war against terrorism – all known terrorists.

One should never underestimate the influence, not so much of Israel directly, but of the example of Israel on the Republican right in the US. In the 1980s, for example, there were curious but strong connections between the ruthlessness that Israel was showing in Lebanon and the toughness that the Reagan administration chose to demonstrate in Central America.

Many of the first reactions in Washington seem to point in this direction. Colin Powell, the US secretary of state, says that, whatever the legal position, most Americans feel their country is at war – and he feels that way too. Everyone talks of Pearl Harbor, and of swift and certain retribution. Against whom? 'I have no doubt in my mind that it's Osama bin Laden,' says Senator John Kerry, of Massachusetts. Now Osama bin Laden, the Saudi billionaire terrorist, is protected in Afghanistan by the ruling Taliban. And President Bush himself says that 'we will make no distinction between the terrorists who committed these acts and those who harbour them.'

So, bombs away over Afghanistan, innocents are killed along with the guilty, and more waves of anger roll towards the United States from parts of the Arab and Islamic worlds? The US as Greater Israel.

SCENARIO TWO

The West versus the rest. With countries like Britain standing 'shoulder to shoulder' with the United States, as Tony Blair has promised, the Bush administration takes a more considered approach. Instead of America wreaking unilateral vengeance, a strategy is put together in conjunction with America's Western allies. But the coalition does not extend much beyond the NATO allies and a few other traditional friends of the West.

This larger West itself becomes embattled. Britain finds itself in the front line, with British landmarks such as Canary Wharf enduring the same fierce security as will doubtless now apply to the office towers of Manhattan. There is, for years to come, an ongoing battle with the diverse and constantly shifting forces of terrorism. The terrorists find shelter in states that we describe as 'rogue', but which see themselves as brothers in Islam, brothers in anti-Zionism or simply brothers in the great alignment of the world's poor against the world's rich. They in turn are tacitly supported by greater powers, such as China, that seek allies or clients in their own global game.

SCENARIO THREE

The United Nations against the terrorists. Displaying the patience and restraint that he showed in handling the crisis earlier this year when an American spy plane was brought down in China, President Bush allows the time needed to establish with a reasonable degree of probability who was actually responsible for these attacks. Direct American armed reprisals are limited to them. At the same time, he works with and through the UN to establish a coalition for action against terrorism that is wider than the West. In particular, it includes Russia and China. At moments, it has seemed as if the Bush administration has seen the world entering into a new version of the Cold War, with China in the role of the new Soviet Union. But it is not China that has struck at the heart of America.

Such painfully coordinated international action may be less effective at stopping particular terrorists in the short term, but its longer-term effect is to pull together disparate states with the most powerful glue of all: a common enemy. Instead of Samuel Huntington's 'clash of civilizations', there is the defence of civilization – in the singular. And the bedrock of civilization includes the human rights of all, and international law applied equally to all.

These three scenarios start from the immediate response to what President Bush accurately described as 'mass murder'. But the implications stretch far beyond. Ever since George Bush was elected, we have been speculating how far he is prepared for the United States to 'go it alone'. In the jargon: will he be unilateralist or still act multilaterally? Now, in the most extreme circumstances, we shall find out.

It may seem wild to suggest that how the US responds to a terrorist attack, however large and horrific that attack, will shape the whole international system. It may yet be true. If the fall of the Berlin Wall was the true end of the short twentieth century, there is a good case for arguing that the demolition of the World Trade Center was the true beginning of the twenty-first. Welcome to another brave new world.

2001

The reader must judge this prognosis, written just a few days after 11 September 2001. I would say we got something between Scenarios One and Two, but sadly not Three.

Anti-Europeanism in America

This year, especially if the United States goes to war against Iraq, you will doubtless see more articles in the American press on 'Anti-Americanism in Europe'. But what about anti-Europeanism in the United States? Consider this:

> To the list of polities destined to slip down the Eurinal of history, we must add the European Union and France's Fifth Republic. The only question is how messy their disintegration will be.[1]

And:

> Even the phrase 'cheese-eating surrender monkeys' is used [to describe the French] as often as the French say 'screw the Jews'. Oops, sorry, that's a different popular French expression.[2]

Or, from a rather different corner:

> 'You want to know what I really think of the Europeans?' asked the senior State Department official. 'I think they have been

wrong on just about every major international issue for the past 20 years.'[3]

Statements such as these recently brought me to the United States – to Boston, New York, Washington, and the Bible-belt states of Kansas and Missouri – to look at changing American attitudes towards Europe in the shadow of a possible second Gulf war. Virtually everyone I spoke to on the East Coast agreed that there is a level of irritation with Europe and Europeans higher even than at the last memorable peak, in the early 1980s.

Pens are dipped in acid and lips curled to pillory 'the Europeans', also known as 'the Euros', 'the Euroids', 'the 'peens' or 'the Euroweenies'. Richard Perle, now chairman of the Defence Policy Board, says Europe has lost its 'moral compass' and France its 'moral fibre'.[4] This irritation extends to the highest levels of the Bush administration. In conversations with senior administration officials I found that the phrase 'our friends in Europe' was closely followed by 'a pain in the butt'.

The current stereotype of Europeans is easily summarized. Europeans are wimps. They are weak, petulant, hypocritical, disunited, duplicitous, sometimes anti-Semitic and often anti-American appeasers. In a word: 'Euroweenies'.[5] Their values and their spines have dissolved in a lukewarm bath of multilateral, transnational, secular and postmodern fudge. They spend their euros on wine, holidays and bloated welfare states instead of on defence. Then they jeer from the sidelines while the United States does the hard and dirty business of keeping the world safe for Europeans. Americans, by contrast, are strong, principled defenders of freedom, standing tall in the patriotic service of the world's last truly sovereign nation state.

A study should be written on the sexual imagery of these stereotypes. If anti-American Europeans see 'the Americans' as bullying cowboys, anti-European Americans see 'the Europeans' as limp-wristed pansies. The American is a virile, heterosexual male; the

European is female, impotent or castrated. Militarily, Europeans can't get it up. (After all, they have fewer than twenty 'heavy lift' transport planes, compared with the United States' more than 200.) Following a lecture I gave in Boston an aged American tottered to the microphone to inquire why Europe 'lacks animal vigour'. The word 'eunuchs' is, I discovered, used in the form 'EU-nuchs'. The sexual imagery even creeps into a more sophisticated account of American–European differences, in an already influential *Policy Review* article by Robert Kagan of the Carnegie Endowment for Peace entitled 'Power and Weakness'.[6] 'Americans are from Mars,' writes Kagan approvingly, 'and Europeans are from Venus' – echoing that famous book about relations between men and women, *Men are from Mars, Women are from Venus*.

Not all Europeans are equally bad. The British tend to be regarded as somewhat different and sometimes better. American conservatives often spare the British the opprobrium of being 'Europeans' at all – a view with which most British conservatives, still mentally led by Margaret Thatcher, would heartily agree. And Tony Blair, like Thatcher before him, and Churchill before her, is cited in Washington as a shining exception to the European rule.

The worst abuse is reserved for the French – who, of course, give at least as good as they get. I had not realized how widespread in American popular culture is the old English pastime of French-bashing. 'You know, France, we've saved their butt twice and they never do anything for us,' Verlin 'Bud' Atkinson, a Second World War veteran, informed me at the Ameristar casino in Kansas City. Talking to high school and college students in Missouri and Kansas, I encountered a strange folk prejudice: the French, it seems, don't wash. 'I felt very dirty a lot,' said one college student, recalling her trip to France. 'But you were still cleaner than French guys,' added another.

Two prominent American journalists, Thomas Friedman of the *New York Times* and Joe Klein of the *New Yorker*, back from extensive book tours around the United States, separately told me that wherever they went they found anti-French sentiment – you would always get a laugh if you made a dig at the French. The *National Review Online* editor and self-proclaimed conservative 'frog-basher' Jonah Goldberg, who also can be seen on television, has popularized the epithet quoted above, 'cheese-eating surrender monkeys', which first appeared in an episode of *The Simpsons*. Goldberg told me that when he started writing anti-French pieces for *National Review* in 1998 he found 'there was a market for it.' French-bashing became, he said, 'a shtick'.

I

Clearly it will not do to throw together neoconservative polemics, Kansas City high school students' prejudices against French bathroom behaviour, remarks of a senior State Department official and senior administration officials, and then label the whole bag 'anti-Europeanism'. As a European writer, I would not want to treat American 'anti-Europeanism' in the way American writers often treat European 'anti-Americanism'.

We have to distinguish between legitimate, informed criticism of the EU or current European attitudes and some deeper, more settled hostility to Europe and Europeans as such. Just as American writers should, but often don't, distinguish between legitimate, informed European criticism of the Bush administration and anti-Americanism, or between legitimate, informed European criticism of the Sharon government and anti-Semitism. The difficult question in each case, one on which knowledgeable people may reasonably disagree, is: where's the dividing line?

We also need to keep a sense of humour. One reason Europeans like to laugh at President George W. Bush is that some of the things he has said – or is alleged to have said – are funny. For example: 'The problem with the French is that they don't have a word for entre-preneur.'[7] One reason Americans like to laugh at the French is that there is a long Anglo-Saxon tradition – going back at least to Shakespeare – of laughing at the French. But there's also a trap here. Conservative writers such as Jonah Goldberg and Mark Steyn make outrageous statements, some of them obviously humorous, some semi-serious, some quite serious. If you object to one of the serious ones, they can always reply, 'But of course I was only joking!' Humour works by exaggeration and playing with stereotypes. But if a European writer were to describe 'the Jews' as 'matzo-eating surrender monkeys' would that be understood as humorous banter? Of course the context is very different: there has been no genocide of the French in the United States. Yet the thought experiment might give our humorists pause.

Anti-Europeanism is not symmetrical with anti-Americanism. The emotional leitmotifs of anti-Americanism are resentment mingled with envy; those of anti-Europeanism are irritation mixed with contempt. Anti-Americanism is a real obsession for entire countries – notably for France, as Jean-François Revel has argued.[8] Anti-Europeanism is very far from being an American obsession. In fact, the predominant American popular attitude towards Europe is mildly benign indifference, mixed with impressive ignorance. I travelled around Kansas for two days asking people I met, 'If I say "Europe" what do you think of?' Many reacted with a long, stunned silence, sometimes punctuated by giggles. Then they said things like 'Well, I guess they don't have much huntin' down there' (Vernon Masqua, a carpenter in McLouth); 'Well, it's a long way from home' (Richard Souza, whose parents came from France and Portugal); or, after a very long pause for thought, 'Well, it's quite a ways across the pond' (Jack Weishaar, an elderly farmer of German descent). If you said 'America' to a farmer or carpenter in even the remotest village of Andalusia or Ruthenia, he would, you may be sure, have a whole lot more to say on the subject.

In Boston, New York and Washington – 'the Bos-Wash corridor' – I was repeatedly told that even people who know the continent well have become increasingly indifferent towards Europe since the end of the Cold War. Europe is seen neither as a potent ally nor as a serious potential rival, like China. 'It's an old people's home!' said an American friend who attended both school and university in England. As the conservative pundit Tucker Carlson remarked in an exchange on CNN's Crossfire: 'Who cares what the Europeans think. The EU spends all of its time making sure that British bologna is sold in kilos not pounds. The whole continent is increasingly irrelevant to American interests.'[9] When I asked a senior administration official what would happen if Europeans went on criticizing the US from a position of military weakness, the gist of his response was: 'Well, does it matter?'

Yet I felt this claim of indifference was also overstated. Certainly, my interlocutors took a lot of time and passion to tell me how little they cared. And the point about the outspoken American critics of Europe is that they are generally not ignorant of or indifferent to Europe. They know Europe – half of them seem to have studied at Oxford or in Paris – and are quick to mention their European friends. Just as most European critics of the United States fiercely deny that they are anti-American ('Don't get me wrong, I love the country and the people'), so they will almost invariably insist that they are not anti-European.[10]

Anti-Americanism and anti-Europeanism are at opposite ends of the political scale. European anti-Americanism is mainly to be found on the left, American anti-Europeanism on the right. The most outspoken American Euro-bashers are neoconservatives using the same sort of combative rhetoric they have habitually deployed against American liberals. In fact, as Jonah Goldberg himself acknowledged to me, 'the Europeans' are also a stalking-horse for liberals. So, I asked him, was Bill Clinton a European? 'Yes,' said Goldberg, 'or at least, Clinton thinks like a European.'

There is some evidence that the left–right divide characterizes popular attitudes as well. In early December 2002, the Ipsos–Reid polling group included in their regular survey of US opinion a few questions formulated for the purposes of this essay.[11] Asked to choose one of four statements about American versus European approaches to diplomacy and war, 30 per cent of Democratic voters but only 6 per cent of Republican voters chose 'The Europeans seem to prefer diplomatic solutions over war and that is a positive value Americans could learn from.' By contrast only 13 per cent of Democrats but 35 per cent of Republicans (the largest single group) chose 'The Europeans are too willing to seek compromise rather than to stand up for freedom even if it means war, and that is a negative thing.'

The divide was even clearer when respondents were asked to pick between two statements about 'the way in which the war on Iraq should be conducted'. Fifty-nine per cent of Republicans as opposed to just 33 per cent of Democrats chose 'The US must remain in control of all operations and prevent its European allies from limiting the States' room to manoeuvre.' By contrast, 55 per cent of Democrats and just 34 per cent of Republicans chose 'It is imperative that the United States allies itself with European countries, even if it limits its ability to make its own decisions.' It seems a hypothesis worth investigating that actually it's Republicans who are from Mars and Democrats who are from Venus.

For some conservatives, the State Department is also an outpost of Venus. William Kristol, one of America's hereditary neoconservatives, writes of 'an axis of appeasement – stretching from Riyadh to Brussels to Foggy Bottom'.[12] Down the Bos-Wash corridor, I was several times told of two groups competing for President Bush's ear over Iraq: the 'Cheney–Rumsfeld group' and the 'Powell–Blair group'. It is rather curious for a British citizen to discover that our prime minister has become a senior member of the State Department.

Atlanticist Europeans should not take too much comfort here, for even among lifelong liberal State Department Europeanists there is an acerbic edge of disillusionment with the Europeans. A key episode in their disillusionment was Europe's failure to prevent the genocide of a quarter of a million Bosnian Muslims in Europe's own back-yard.[13] Since then, there has been Europe's continued inability to 'get its act together' in foreign and security policy, so that even a dispute between Spain and Morocco over a tiny, uninhabited island off the Moroccan coast has to be resolved by Colin Powell.

'They are not serious' was the lapidary verdict on 'the Europeans' delivered to me by George F. Will over a stately breakfast in a Washington hotel. Though Will is very far from being a State Department liberal, many in the department would agree. Historically, the tables are turned. For what was Charles de Gaulle's verdict on the Americans? 'Ils ne sont pas sérieux.'

2

So there is, in significant quarters of American life, a disillusionment and irritation with Europe, a growing contempt for and even hostility towards 'the Europeans', which, at the extreme, merits the label 'anti-Europeanism'. Why has this come about?

Some possible explanations have emerged already; to explore them all would take a book. Here I can only indicate a few more places to look. For a start, there has always been a strong strain of anti-Europeanism in the United States. 'America was created as an antidote to Europe,' Michael Kelly, the former editor of the *Atlantic Monthly*, has observed. 'Why,' asked George Washington, in his Farewell Address, 'by interweaving our destiny with that of any part of Europe, entangle our peace and prosperity in the toils of European ambition, rivalship, interest, humour or caprice?' For millions of Americans, in the nineteenth and twentieth centuries, Europe was the place you escaped from.

Yet there was also an enduring fascination with Europe, famously exemplified by Henry James; a desire in many respects to emulate, and then outdo, two European countries above all, England and France. Arthur Schlesinger Jr quoted to me the old line 'When Americans die, they go to Paris.' 'Every man has two countries,' said Thomas Jefferson, 'his own and France.' When was it that American attitudes towards England and France diverged so sharply? Was it 1940, the year of France's 'strange defeat' and England's 'finest hour'? Thereafter De Gaulle recovered French self-esteem in opposition to the Americans while Churchill conjured a 'special relationship' between his parents' two nations. (To understand the approaches of Chirac and Blair to the US today the key names are still de Gaulle and Churchill.)

For fifty years, from 1941 to 1991, the United States and a growing fellowship of Europeans were engaged in a joint war against a common enemy: first Nazism, then Soviet communism. This was the heyday of the geopolitical 'West'. There were, of course, repeated transatlantic strains throughout the Cold War. Some of today's stereotypes can be found fully formed in the controversies of the early 1980s about the deployment of cruise and Pershing missiles, and American foreign policy towards Central America and Israel.[14] They were formed in the minds of some of the same people: Richard Perle, for example, then widely known for his hard-line views as 'the prince of darkness'. These transatlantic arguments were often about how to deal with the Soviet Union, but they were also finally constrained by that clear and common enemy.

Now no longer. So perhaps we are witnessing what the Australian writer Owen Harries foresaw in an article nearly ten years ago in *Foreign Affairs*: the decline of 'the West' as a solid geopolitical axis, owing to the disappearance of that clear and common enemy.[15] Europe was the main theatre of the Second World War and the Cold War; it is not the centre of the 'war against terrorism'. The gap in relative power has grown wider. The United States is not just the world's only superpower; it is a hyperpower, whose military expenditure will soon equal that of the next fifteen most powerful states combined. The EU has not translated its comparable economic strength – fast approaching the US $10 trillion economy – into comparable military power or diplomatic influence. But the differences are also about the uses of power.

Robert Kagan argues that Europe has moved into a Kantian world of 'laws and rules and transnational negotiation and cooperation', while the United States remains in a Hobbesian world where military power is still the key to achieving international goals (even liberal ones). The first and obvious question must be: is this true? I think that Kagan, in what he admits is a 'caricature', is actually too kind to Europe, in the sense that he elevates to a deliberate, coherent approach what is, in fact, a story of muddled seeking and national differences. But a second, less obvious question is: do Europeans and Americans wish this to be true? The answer seems to be yes. Quite a lot of American policymakers like the idea that they are from Mars – on the understanding that this makes them martial rather than Martian – while quite a lot of European policymakers like to think they are, indeed, programmatic Venusians. So the reception of Kagan's thesis is a part of its own story.

As a soon-to-be-enlarged European Union searches for a clearer identity, there is a strong temptation for Europe to define itself against the United States. Europe clarifies its self-image by listing the ways in which it differs from America. In the dread jargon of identity studies, America becomes the 'other'. Americans don't like being 'othered'. (Who does?) The impact of the September 11 terrorist attacks increases their own readiness to accept a martial and missionary account of America's role in the world.

Stanley Hoffmann has observed that France and the United States are both nations that see themselves as having a universalizing, civilizing mission. Now there is a European, rather than a merely French, version of the *mission civilisatrice*, a 'EU-topia' of transnational, law-based integration, and it clashes most acutely with the latest, conservative version of an American mission.[16] Thus, for example, Jonah Goldberg quotes with irritation the claim by the veteran German Atlanticist Karl Kaiser that 'Europeans have done something that no one has ever done before: create a zone of peace where war is ruled out, absolutely out. Europeans are convinced that this model is valid for other parts of the world.'

Each side thinks its model is better. This applies not only to the rival models of international behaviour, but also to those of democratic capitalism: the different mix of free market and welfare state, of individual freedom and social solidarity, and so on.[17] For the political scientist Charles A. Kupchan, the author of the recent book *The End of the American Era*, this presages nothing less than a coming 'clash of civilizations' between Europe and America. Where Kagan thinks Europe is characterized by enduring weakness, Kupchan sees it, not China, as the United States' next great rival.[18] Many Europeans would love to believe this, but in the United States I found Kupchan almost alone in his view.

There is, I think, one other, deeper trend in the US. I've mentioned already that for most of the nineteenth and twentieth centuries American suspicion of things European was mixed with admiration and fascination. There was, to put it bluntly, an American cultural inferiority complex. This has gradually faded. Its fading has been accelerated, in ways that are not easy to pin down, by the end of the Cold War and the United States' consequent rise to a unique preeminence. The new Rome no longer feels in awe of the old Greeks. 'When I first went to Europe in the 1940s and 1950s, Europe was superior to us,' a retired American diplomat with long European experience wrote to me recently. 'The superiority was not personal – I never felt demeaned even by condescending people – but civilizational.' Not any more. America, he wrote, 'is no longer abashed'.[19]

3

All these trends were somewhat obscured for eight years after the end of the Cold War by the presence in the White House of an honorary European, Bill Clinton. In 2001, George W. Bush, a walking gift to every European anti-American caricaturist, arrived in the White House with a unilateralist agenda, ready to jettison several international agreements. After September 11, he defined his new presidency as a war presidency. I found that the post-September 11 sense that America is at war persists more strongly in Washington than anywhere else in America, including New York.[20] It persists, above all, in the heart of the Bush administration. The 'war against terrorism' strengthened an existing tendency among the Republican elite to believe in what Robert Kaplan has called 'Warrior Politics', with a strong seasoning of fundamentalist Christianity – something conspicuously absent in highly secularized Europe. As Walter Russell Mead of the Council on Foreign Relations put it in his book *Special Providence*, it brought back the 'Jacksonian' tendency in American foreign policy.[21] Al-Qaida terrorists were the new Creek Indians.

The American question to Europeans then became, as the conservative columnist Charles Krauthammer put it to me, 'Are you in the trenches with us or not?' At first, the answer was a resounding yes. Everyone quotes the *Le Monde* headline: 'Nous sommes tous des Américains.' But a year and a half later, the only European leader who most Americans think is in the trenches with them is Tony Blair.[22] Many in Washington feel that the French have reverted to their old anti-American attitudes, and that the German chancellor, Gerhard Schröder, won his re-election last September by cynically exploiting anti-Americanism.

When and where did European and American sentiment start diverging again? In early 2002, with the escalation of the Israeli–Palestinian conflict in the Middle East. The Middle East is both a source and a catalyst of what threatens to become a downward spiral of burgeoning European anti-Americanism and nascent American anti-Europeanism, each reinforcing the other. Anti-Semitism in Europe, and its alleged connection to European criticism of the Sharon government, has been the subject of the most acid anti-European commentaries from conservative American columnists and politicians. Some of these critics are themselves not just strongly pro-Israel but also 'natural Likudites', one liberal Jewish commentator explained to me. In a recent article Stanley Hoffmann writes that they seem to believe in an 'identity of interests between the Jewish state and the United States'.[23] Pro-Palestinian Europeans, infuriated by the way criticism of Sharon is labelled anti-Semitism, talk about the power of a 'Jewish lobby' in the US, which then confirms American Likudites' worst suspicions of European anti-Semitism, and so it goes on, and on.

Beside this hopeless tangle of mutually reinforcing prejudice – difficult for a non-Jewish European to write about without contributing to the malaise one is trying to analyse – there are, of course, real European–American differences in approaches to the Middle East. For example, European policymakers tend to think that a negotiated settlement of the Israeli–Palestinian conflict would be a bigger contribution to the long-term success of the 'war against terrorism' than a war on Iraq. The larger point, for our purposes, is that where the Cold War against communism in Middle Europe brought America and Europe together, the 'war against terrorism' in the Middle East is pulling them apart. The Soviet Union united the West, the Middle East divides it.

Coolly examined, such a division is extremely stupid. Europe, just next door and with a large and growing Islamic population, has an even more direct vital interest in a peaceful, prosperous and democratic Middle East than the United States does. Moreover, I found two senior administration officials in Washington quite receptive to the argument – which is beginning to be made by some American commentators – that the democratization of the greater Middle East should be the big new transatlantic project for a revitalized West.[24] But that's not how it looks at the moment.

At the moment it seems that a second Gulf war will only widen the gulf between Europe and America. Even if there is not a war on Iraq, the Middle East can still provide the vortex in which real or alleged European anti-Americanism fuels real or alleged American anti-Europeanism, which in turn fuels more anti-Americanism, both being aggravated by sweeping charges of European anti-Semitism. A change might come through a major conscious effort on both sides of the Atlantic, or with a new administration arriving in Washington in 2005 or 2009. Yet a lot of damage can be done in the meantime, and the current transatlantic estrangement is also an expression of the deeper historical trends I have mentioned.

You might say that to highlight 'American anti-Europeanism', as I have done in this essay, will itself contribute to the downward spiral of mutual distrust. But writers are not diplomats. American anti-Europeanism exists; and its carriers may be the first swallows of a long, bad summer.

2003

I treated the themes of this essay in much greater depth in my book Free World: America, Europe and the Surprising Future of the West. *The change in transatlantic attitudes that I envisaged 'with a new adminis-tration arriving in Washington in 2005 or 2009' did come with the advent of Barack Obama in 2009 (see the essays that follow in this section); but some of the underlying shifts remain.*

In Defence of the Fence

After watching Colin Powell's riveting performance at the UN Security Council, with its crackling phone intercepts, satellite photos and carefully crafted televisual moments, I asked myself: what does this change in your view of the Iraq war? The answer is: not much. I remain unconvinced by the case for – and doubtful of the case against.

'He has the fence firmly stuck up his arse,' a friend recently remarked of the poet laureate's position on Iraq. 'Fence-sitter' is rarely a compliment.

Most people admire decisiveness and despise vacillation. Adversarial party politics demands the immediate taking of stands and the exaggeration of minor difference. The media, fiercely competing for viewers, listeners and readers, cry out for strong, polarized positions: Bush v Saddam, Benn v Thatcher, Hitchens (C) v Hitchens (P). It makes better television, you see.

But on Iraq, I would still like to defend a position of tortured liberal ambivalence. Being liberal doesn't mean you always dither in the middle on the hard questions. I was strongly against the Soviet invasions of Czechoslovakia and Afghanistan, against the American interventions in Nicaragua and El Salvador, for military intervention in Bosnia and Kosovo, and for the war against al-Qaida in Afghanistan, all on good liberal grounds. Iraq is different and more difficult. I see four strong arguments on each side.

FOR

1. Saddam's regime is one of the nastiest in the world today. He has committed genocide against the Kurds and holds his own people in terror. To remove him would be a blessing for his country and the region. However messy post-war Iraq became – and it surely would be messy, like post-war Bosnia, Kosovo and Afghanistan – it could hardly be worse.

2. Saddam has twice attacked neighbouring countries. He has, as Powell documented, stockpiled large quantities of horrifying chemical and biological weapons, and is hiding what remains of them. He is still trying to get nuclear ones. If he ever got an effective, deliverable nuclear weapon, this would be a major disaster for the world – as it would be in North Korea, but rather more so, because of who Saddam is and where he is. I support CNDD: the Campaign for the Nuclear Disarmament of Dictators.

3. He has flouted sixteen UN resolutions over twelve years. He clearly does not want to disarm or to cooperate fully with the UN inspectors. (What self-respecting sovereign dictator would?) The justification in international law for military action is stronger in this case than over Kosovo. A second UN resolution would give the 'proper authority' required by 'just war' theory.

4. Consequences (optimistic). This could be a catalyst for democratic change in the Middle East. A peaceful, prosperous, reconstructed Iraq – an 'Iraqi West Germany' – could be a model for the whole region. Next stops, Saudi Arabia and Iran. The spread of freedom might eventually transform the regional context for solving the Israel–Palestine problem, as

the democratization of eastern Europe finally brought the solution to the division of Germany.

AGAINST

1. War should always be a last resort. However magically precise the new American hi-tech bombs are, innocent Iraqis will be killed. Couldn't Saddam be kept in check for years to come by the current combination of deterrence and containment?
2. 'Just war' theory asks for 'right intention'. On balance, I think Blair has the right intentions. I'm not convinced about the Bush administration. Different people there have different agendas, of course, and human motives are always mixed. As a crude indication, I'd put the motives index something like this:

   • A feeling that this is part of a broader 'war against terrorism', which since September 11 is a fight for the homeland security of the US: 20 per cent.
   • A genuine conviction that Saddam with weapons of mass destruction poses a major threat to the free world: 20 per cent.
   • Frustration at not being able to get Osama bin Laden or wrap up al-Qaida, coupled with the conviction that you can at least use your vast military power to defeat Saddam: 15 per cent.
   • A sense of unfinished business from the first Gulf War, plus George Bush's personal anger at 'the guy who tried to kill my dad': 15 per cent.
   • An initial calculation by Bush's political adviser Karl Rove, perhaps now regretted, of domestic political advantage: 10 per cent.
   • A sense that there's no way back. How can Bush go into the next presidential election with Saddam still in power? 10 per cent.

- That hope of transforming the Middle East, also to the long-term advantage of Israel: 5 per cent.
- Oil: 5 per cent.

You can vary the percentages according to taste, but, whichever way you turn it, this does not add up to a majority set of good liberal reasons.

3. Saddam's links to al-Qaida are marginal. All the evidence that Colin Powell could muster showed little more. It just will not do to claim that war on Iraq is the continuation of an enlightened struggle against 'Islamic fascism' that began on September 11. Osama bin Laden regards Saddam's regime as apostate. They are two very bad things, but they are also two very different things.

4. Consequences (pessimistic). Even if Islamicist terror bombers hate Saddam, an American–British 'imperial' invasion of Iraq will increase the chances of Arab terror attacks in Europe and America. If you want to democratize the Middle East, an imperial war is not the best way to start. Supporting a velvet revolution in Iran, fostering democratic reform in Saudi Arabia and knocking together the fat heads of Sharon and Arafat to advance an Israeli–Palestinian settlement would all be better. Anyway, the model occupation-born democracies of West Germany and Japan are historical exceptions. We're as likely to see an 'Iraqi Yugoslavia', torn between Kurd, Shia and Sunni. Bush's America has no stomach for 'nation-building', and the acronym-soup international administrations of Bosnia, Kosovo, Afghanistan, etc. are hardly encouraging examples. Altogether, the regional consequences are more likely to be bad than good.

My hunch is that if you injected Tony Blair with a truth serum in the dark reaches of the night, he would confess to most of this liberal ambivalence. I don't believe that he has secret intelligence of a kind that would convince us all if only we could be allowed to see it. And the Foreign Office is constantly whispering warnings in his ear. But in public, he is full of passionate, even missionary conviction. Why? Because of who he is, of course – a Gladstonian Christian liberal interventionist. Perhaps because he thinks that maintaining British solidarity and influence with the US is more important even than the probable negative consequences of a war with Iraq. But also because he's prime minister, not a writer or commentator. He has to decide. He has to lead. He has to convince a sceptical public and resentful party.

That doesn't mean we all have to do the same, putting just one side of a complex dilemma with passionate, simplistic conviction. Even if it does make better television.

2001

Note how all but two halves of two of my arguments for *the Iraq war (the brutality of Saddam's regime and his flouting of numerous UN resolutions) have subsequently collapsed. On weapons of mass destruction, we were misled by Tony Blair, Colin Powell and others. The failure to plan for a difficult occupation vitiated the 'just war' claim about consequences. I guessed that 'however messy post-war Iraq became . . . it could hardly be worse', but in the bloodiest period of anarchy, many Iraqis told pollsters and journalists that things* were *worse than under Saddam. All four arguments* against, *by contrast, hold up very well. I still defend the right of the commentator not always to take sides, but in this case I got it wrong. Next time, I shall need a great deal more convincing. I'm not alone in that.*

Zorba the Bush

What an amazing bloody catastrophe. The Bush administration's policy towards the Middle East over the five years since 9/11 is culminating in a multiple train crash. Never in the field of human conflict was so little achieved by so great a country at such vast expense. In every vital area of the wider Middle East, American policy over the last five years has taken a bad situation and made it worse.

If the consequences were not so serious, one would have to laugh at a failure of such heroic proportions – rather in the spirit of Zorba the Greek who, contemplating the splintered ruins of his great project, memorably exclaimed, 'Did you ever see a more splendiferous crash?' But the reckless incompetence of Zorba the Bush has resulted in the death, maiming, uprooting or impoverishment of hundreds of thousands of men, women and children – mainly Muslim Arabs but also Christian Lebanese, Israelis, and American and British soldiers. By contributing to a broader alienation of Muslims it has also helped to make a world in which, as we walk the streets of London, Madrid, Jerusalem, New York or Sydney, we are all, each and every one of us, less safe. Laugh if you dare.

In the beginning, there were the 9/11 attacks. It's important to stress that no one can fairly blame George Bush for them. The invasion of

Afghanistan was a justified response to those attacks, which were initiated by al-Qaida from its bases in a rogue state under the tyranny of the Taliban. But if Afghanistan had to be done, it had to be done properly. It wasn't. Creating a half-way civilized order in one of the most rugged, inhospitable and tribally recalcitrant places on the planet was always going to be a huge challenge. If the available resources of the world's democracies, including those of a new, enlarged NATO, had been dedicated to that task over the last five years, we might at least have one partial success to report today.

Instead Bush, Cheney and Rumsfeld drove us on to Iraq, aided and abetted by Tony Blair, leaving the job in Afghanistan less than half done. Today Osama bin Laden and his henchmen are probably still holed up in the mountains of Waziristan, just across the Afghan frontier in northern Pakistan, while the Taliban is back in force and the whole country is a bloody mess. Instead of one partial success, following a legitimate intervention, we have two burgeoning disasters, in Afghanistan and in Iraq.

The United States and Britain invaded Iraq under false pretences, without proper legal authority or international legitimacy. If Saddam Hussein, a dangerous tyrant and certified international aggressor, had in fact possessed secret stockpiles of weapons of mass destruction, the intervention might have been justified; as he didn't, it wasn't. Then, through the breathtaking incompetence of the civilian armchair warriors in the Pentagon and the White House, we transformed a totalitarian state into a state of anarchy. Claiming to move Iraq forward towards Lockean liberty, we hurled it back to a Hobbesian state of nature. Iraqis – those who have not been killed – increasingly say things are worse than they were before. Who are we to tell them they are wrong?

Now we are preparing to get out. After working through Basra in Operation Sinbad, a reduced number of British troops will draw back to their base at Basra airfield. We will sit in a desert and call it peace. If the White House follows the Baker–Hamilton commission's advice,

US troops will do something similar, leaving embedded advisers with Iraqi forces. Three decades ago, American retreat was cloaked by 'Vietnamization'; now it will be cloaked by Iraqization. Meanwhile, Iraqis can go on killing each other all around, until perhaps, in the end, they cut some rough-and-ready political deals between themselves – or not, as the case may be.

The theocratic dictatorship of Iran is the great winner. Five years ago, the Islamic republic had a reformist president, a substantial democratic opposition, and straitened finances because of low oil prices. The mullahs were running scared. Now the prospects of democratization are dwindling, the regime is riding high on oil at more than $60 a barrel, and it has huge influence through its Shia brethren in Iraq and Lebanon. The likelihood of it developing nuclear weapons is correspondingly greater. We toppled the Iraqi dictator, who did not have weapons of mass destruction, and thereby increased the chances of Iran's dictators acquiring weapons of mass destruction. And this week Iran's President Ahmadinejad once again called for the destruction of the state of Israel. Those American neocons who set out to make the Middle East safe for Israel have ended up making it more dangerous for Israel.

We did not need an Iraq Study Group to tell us that resolving the Arab–Israeli conflict through a two-state solution for Israel and Palestine is crucial. In its last months the Clinton administration came close to clinching the deal. Under Bush, things have gone backwards. Even the Bush-backed Ariel Sharon scenario of separation through faits accomplis has receded, with the summer war in Lebanon, Hamas ascendancy in Palestine (itself partly a by-product of the Bush-led rush to elections), and a growing disillusionment of the Israeli public.

Having scored an apparent success with the Cedar Revolution in Lebanon and the withdrawal of Syrian troops, the Bush administration, by its tacit support of sustained yet ineffective Israeli military action in the summer of 2006, undermined the very Lebanese government it was claiming to support. Now Hizbullah is challenging the country's Western-backed velvet revolutionaries at their own game: after the Cedar Revolution, welcome to the Cedar Counter-Revolution. In Egypt, supposedly a showcase for the United States' support for peaceful democratization in the Bush second term, electoral success for Islamists (as in Palestine and Lebanon) seems to have frightened Washington away from its fresh-minted policy before the ink was even dry. On the credit side, all we have to show is Libya's renunciation of weapons of mass destruction, and a few tentative reforms in some smaller Arab states.

So here's the scoresheet for Afghanistan, Iraq, Iran, Israel, Palestine, Lebanon and Egypt: worse, worse, worse, worse, worse, worse and worse. With James Baker, the United States may revert from the sins of the son to the sins of the father. After all, it was Baker and George Bush Sr who left those they had encouraged to rise up against Saddam to be killed in Iraq at the end of the first Gulf War – not to mention enthusiastically continuing Washington's long-running Faustian pact with petro-autocracies such as Saudi Arabia. I'm told that Condoleezza Rice, no less, has observed that the word democracy hardly features in the Baker–Hamilton report.

Many a time, over these years, I have warned against reflex Bush-bashing and knee-jerk anti-Americanism. The United States is by no means the only culprit. Changing the Middle East for the better is one of the most difficult challenges in world politics. The people of the region bear much responsibility for their own plight. So do we Europeans, for past sins of commission and current sins of omission. But Bush must take the lion's share of the blame. There are few examples in recent history of such a comprehensive failure. Congratulations, Mr President; you have made one hell of a disaster.

2006

Four years on, this verdict stands.

Warsaw, Missouri

In Warsaw, Missouri, there's a ghost who keeps talking to me through the mouths of strangers. He is the ghost of slavery past, and he casts a long shadow, even across the streets of this cheerful little lakeside town on a sunny autumn day. A local Obama campaign volunteer tells me about a woman she had canvassed who said she personally would vote for Barack but that her daughter wouldn't – and then the mother lowered her voice – 'because he's black'. Nor would her son: 'he's even more racist.' How horrible to feel impelled to say that of your own children. The jokey-scary commercial paraphernalia of Halloween is all around, but here are America's real ghosts and witches.

Missouri matters. It is a national weathervane. Located bang in the middle of the American heartland, where east meets west and north meets south, over the past hundred years it has chosen the winner in every presidential race except one. In the opinion polls, it's among the few states that are still too close to call. That's why Obama was here speaking to massive rallies a fortnight ago, and why both he and Joe Biden are back here again this Thursday. That's why the Obama organization in Missouri plans to use its 25,000 volunteers to knock on some 1.3 million doors during the last four days of the campaign.

Most of those key swing voters are in the sprawling, laundered suburbs of St Louis and Kansas City, but every vote from these rural areas, whose native sons include one of the greatest Democratic presidents, Harry Truman, will count too. And I'm in the heart of the rural heartland: beautiful, gently rolling country, with dawn mist rising from cattle ponds, trees turning every impressionist's shade of autumn russet, yellow and red, cows picturesquely munching lush grass, and roadside signs proclaiming 'Dirt for Sale' and 'Jesus is Lord'.

On the corner of Van Buren and Kosciusko street (Tadeusz Kościuszko, that is, the Polish freedom fighter who inspired the town's name), I notice a neat, white-painted house with a sign in the window saying 'This House Protected by God'. Out front, a guard dog barks. (A dog called God?) And there's another sign on the lawn: 'For Sale'. The Lord may provide, but people have housing and money worries here as everywhere. And they don't just hunt for the sport. A good shot can put a nourishing turkey or quail on the table for dinner. So the Republicans claim Obama wants to take away your gun. A McCain advertisement on the local country music radio station declares, in a deep countryman's voice, 'We love our God and we love our guns' – and you can almost hear a second capital G. And, it goes on, 'liberals' want to take them away, being 'out of touch with our America'.

I had expected race to be an issue here, but I'm struck by how close to the surface the old wounds and prejudices are. I don't even have to ask; it just keeps coming up. At the local headquarters of the McCain campaign, four warmly hospitable local ladies tell me about their enthusiasm for Sarah Palin. When the talk turns to the inevitable subject, one of them says people are afraid of being thought racist if they come out against Obama. Another recalls how in her childhood, not so far from here, the Ku Klux Klan was still active, and there were roads a black man could not safely walk. They add that nineteenth-century Warsaw was a slave town, but Cole Camp, founded by German Lutherans just a few miles to the north in the same county, was not. So Missourians fought about it during the Civil War, in the course of which Warsaw was several times burned and razed to the ground.

Up the road in Sedalia a former army officer, for many years a staunch Republican, tells me he will vote for Obama. He's disgusted at the way the Bush administration lied to them about Iraq. But it would be easier if Obama were white. In fact, he would find it difficult to vote for him if he were really African-American. 'That's black slave American,' he helpfully explains to this foreigner. Those people are so 'mad' inside, he says, using the word in the colloquial American sense. Fortunately, Obama's not really an African-American, just an American with an African father; but he still feels 'queasy' about it.

Now don't get me wrong. I'm emphatically not here as a condescending urban liberal, hell-bent on sneering at these sad, backwoods rednecks and maligning them as racists. Far from it. These were decent, honest, warm-hearted people I met, and they were frankly acknowledging and wrestling with the problem of residual racism, not propagating it. Nor am I leaping to any conclusion so simplistic as 'Race will decide this presidential race.' Mine was a wholly unscientific sample of about 1 per cent of the population (2,070, according to the road sign) of one small town in the conservative rural area of one swing state.

Because of the extraordinary Obama and his extraordinary neighbour-to-neighbour campaign, this election has become a vast national conversation, not only about America's future but also about its difficult past. The map of Missouri is weirdly strewn with old European names: Warsaw, Dresden, Windsor, Odessa, Versailles (correct pronunciation: Ver-sails). Old European cities with a lot of history, including much bloodshed and ethnic conflict. Yet I doubt that in any of them today, perhaps not even in Warsaw, Poland, the wounds of old wrongs still go as deep or throb as hard as they do in their quiet Missourian homonyms, where nice middle-aged Republican ladies can tell you at once who did what to whom nearly 150 years ago.

The Obama campaign may prefer to concentrate on the future, but this difficult conversation about America's past is itself also about its future. It's painful and may even be a little risky, but it brings the possibility of healing, especially if enough Americans overcome their secret doubts, their 'queasiness', and follow Obama's intriguingly worded appeal to 'come together as one nation, one people, and once more choose our better history.'

2008

Dancing with History

To join that ebullient crowd in front of the White House shortly after midnight on Tuesday, 4 November 2008, was to dance with history. 'Bush out now!' and 'Goodbye, na na na na', they chanted, to the sound of drums. 'Obama! Obama!' Car horns honked. A saxophone blared from the passenger window of a bright red pick-up truck. A young man beat a saucepan with a metal spoon. 'This is the biggest housewarming party I've ever been to,' an African-American woman with a stars-and-stripes headscarf dreamily confided, as she shimmied across 16th Street. And, this being our time, everyone both yapped and photo-snapped on their mobile phones.

Most of all, though, these mainly young revellers chanted the slogan that Obama had just made the leitmotif of his acceptance speech in Chicago: 'Yes We Can! Yes We Can!' Even the car horns took up the three-stroke rhythm: beep-beep-beep. When I went to bed, well into the early hours, I could still hear the chants reverberating up to my hotel window. Yes-We-Can! Yes-We-Can!

But can they? Can he? Can we?

To say that he is the first black president in American history is more to write the last lines of the last chapter than the start of a new one. That chapter of pain is both remarkably ancient and shockingly recent. I observed people voting in a downtown polling station located in a church of the African Methodist Episcopal denomination, which, a sign records, was established to protest against segregated worship in 1787. Across the Anacostia river, in a poor neighbourhood where mine was almost the only white face, an election supervisor – a Baptist preacher in everyday life – told me how African-Americans, often voting for the first time, had brought their children to witness the moment of which Dr King had dreamed. Only by listening to their voices can you fully appreciate what will be the impact of the mere sight of a black family occupying that white house.

But Obama is much more than just black American. Like a growing number of citizens of our mixed-up world he is, as the columnist Michael Kinsley nicely puts it, 'a one-man ethnic stew'. This qualifies him to represent all those Americans, of every hue and mix, that I saw in the long queues of people waiting to vote in downtown Washington, and in that crowd before the White House. 'Where are you from?' I asked a man who I guessed might be of north African origin. He stopped dancing for a moment, looked at me and said, 'From my mother.' A wonderful answer, also a rebuke, and minted for the age of Obama.

For Obama is simultaneously the first post-ethnic president. To reduce this story to the black–white dichotomy is as useful as a black-and-white photograph of a colourful scene. John McCain may have singled out Joe the plumber to represent an old-fashioned, putative 'silent majority' of white working-class Americans, but actually they now constitute a (not so) silent minority. And José the plumber voted for Obama. In fact, Obama's vote benefited from almost every aspect of America's growing demographic diversity. Introducing him in Florida during the campaign, Bill Clinton highlighted this new diversity, saying that both Florida and Obama represent 'the world's present and America's future'. That seems to me the wrong way round: it's America's present and the world's future. Where once America lagged, it now leads.

Mark carefully, however, what the Obama model is. It deploys civic nationalism to transcend ethnic diversity. Many of Tuesday's revellers were waving the stars and stripes or sporting it on some part of their dress. No right-wing Republican could insist more than Obama does on American uniqueness, exceptionalism, manifest destiny. His proclaimed purpose is 'to make this century the next American century'. If George W. Bush said that, we from the rest of the world might regard it as rank nationalist arrogance. Because it's Obama, we somehow accept it.

Now comes the test. As he acknowledged in his sober acceptance speech, America has a huge mountain to climb. The very circumstances that ensured his victory make it more difficult for him to succeed. One can argue about 'what would have happened if . . .', but it's indisputable that the campaign turned decisively in his favour after September's financial meltdown. Now the crisis is really hitting the real economy, on his chosen terrain of jobs, homes, savings and healthcare for ordinary Americans. He inherits a soaring national debt from Bush, who presided over a massive redistribution of wealth from future generations to the present one. The country faces two wars, in Iraq and Afghanistan, and a host of other challenges around the world.

Meanwhile, America itself is still divided. The gulf between red and blue may even be more difficult to bridge than that between black and white. Many Americans are still irrationally suspicious of Barack Hussein Obama, but an entirely rational observer could conclude that his instincts are more socially and culturally liberal than those of a cultural-conservative Republican, and less economically liberal than those of a libertarian Republican. To overcome those concerns, he would have to govern from the centre or even centre-right, disappointing his own supporters and taking on some triumphalist Democrats in Congress.

Has he got what it takes: in himself, his team and the power resources at his disposal? I spent the days before the vote talking to not a few Washington insiders, including some well placed in his campaign. Their unanimous refrain was: we don't know. We don't know which of the many policy options he'll plump for; we don't know who he'll choose for the key posts; we don't know what he'll be like on the job. Few presidential candidates have had less of an executive or legislative track record from which to guess their future performance in a job like no other.

On one thing all agree: if he can run the country the way he has run his campaign – one of the most effective ever – then America will be in good hands. But a country is not a campaign. He is, in every sense of that overused word, cool. He barely looked excited even as he accepted the presidency before an ecstatic crowd. As president, his hard-power resources may be somewhat diminished, but no one in the world currently has more soft power. Where the Bush administration used military 'shock and awe' to hunt down weapons of mass destruction that turned out not even to be there, Obama is himself a weapon of mass attraction.

And he can appeal to what is perhaps America's greatest power resource: the can-do spirit of innovation, enterprise and hard work, mixed with civic patriotism, which this country invites everyone to embrace, wherever they come from. This is the promise summed up in what Obama called in his acceptance speech 'that American creed: Yes We Can'. The American creed they were chanting outside the White House on that unforgettable Tuesday night.

If you ask me whether all this will be enough to surmount all the obstacles America now faces, I must in all honesty reply that, on a sober assessment, I doubt it. But we can again hope, and hope we must.

2008

Liberalism

Government and markets both have their place in a decent society, President Barack Obama suggested in his Inaugural Address, but can become a force for ill if they are without restraint. Missing from his address was only the proper name of the political philosophy, coded into the constitutional DNA of the United States, that proposes this and other balances: liberalism.

Like many of Obama's speeches, the Inaugural presented, in substance, a blend of classical constitutional and modern egalitarian liberalism. The thing, but never the word. Anyone who knows anything about contemporary political discourse in the United States understands why.

Just over twenty years ago, a group of leading American intellectuals, gathered by the historian Fritz Stern, placed an advertisement in the *New York Times* trying to defend the word 'liberalism' against its abuse by Ronald Reagan and others on the American right. It was in vain. Over the last two decades a truly eccentric usage has triumphed in American public debate. Liberalism has become a pejorative term denoting – to put the matter a tad frivolously – some unholy marriage of big government and fornication.

This weird usage leads, at the extreme, to book titles like *Deliver Us from Evil: Defeating Terrorism, Despotism, and Liberalism* – a work of the Fox News presenter Sean Hannity. But it infects the mainstream too. Asked during a primary debate to define 'liberal', and say if she was one, Hillary Clinton replied that a word originally associated with a belief in freedom had unfortunately come to mean favouring big government. So, she concluded, 'I prefer the word progressive, which has a real American meaning.' This implies that the meaning of 'liberal' must be unreal, un-American, or possibly both.

The United States is not the only place where 'liberalism' is fiercely contested. At a conference held at Oxford University shortly before Obama's inauguration in January 2009, speakers from the Americas, Europe, India, Japan and China explored what the organizers (of whom I was one) deliberately called 'Liberalisms'. Interestingly, what is furiously attacked as 'liberalism' in France, and in much of central and eastern Europe, is precisely what is most beloved of the libertarian or 'fiscal conservative' strand of the American right. When French leftists and Polish populists denounce 'liberalism', they mean Anglo-Saxon-style, unregulated free market capitalism. (Occasionally the prefix neo- or ultra- is added to make this clear.)

One Chinese intellectual told us that in his country 'Liberalism means everything the government doesn't like.' The term is used in China as a political instrument to attack, in particular, advocates of further market-oriented economic reform. Standards of what counts as socially or culturally liberal also vary widely. An Indian speaker wryly observed that in India a 'liberal' father is one who allows his children to choose whom they want to marry.

Faced with this worldwide conceptual cacophony, some at the conference argued that we should abandon the term, or at least dismantle it into component parts with plainer meanings. But combinations and balances belong to liberalism's defining essence, and the whole is greater than the sum of its parts. As the Oxford political theorist Michael Freeden observed, if just one of the necessary components – for example, the free market – dominates, then the result can be illiberalism. The vital, never-ending debate over liberalism is not just over its indispensable ingredients, but also over their form, proportion and relation to one another.

A plausible minimum list of ingredients for twenty-first-century liberalism would include liberty under law, limited and accountable government, markets, tolerance, some version of individualism and universalism, and some notion of human equality, reason and progress. The mix of ingredients differs from place to place. Whether some distant cousin really belongs to the extended family of liberalisms is a matter of healthy dispute. But somewhere in this contested, evolving combination there is a thing of enduring value.

This has been an American argument, some would say the American argument, for more than 200 years. In fact, the United States is still full of liberals, both progressive or left liberals and, I would insist, conservative or right liberals. Most of them just don't use the word. Liberalism is America's love that dare not speak its name.

For obvious reasons, we are now witnessing worldwide criticism of a version of pure free market liberalism, a.k.a neo-liberalism, charged with having led us into our current economic mess. Yet, our Chinese and European colleagues agreed that markets remain an indispensable condition of liberty. One leading Chinese economic reformer even suggested that there is less income inequality in those Chinese provinces where the market plays a larger role.

I don't expect President Obama to use that word any time soon. But those of us who believe in the universal, enduring value of liberalism are happy to see him start by vigorously restoring more of the thing. He has decisively reasserted the importance of equal liberty under the rule of law, not least by ordering the closing of Guantánamo Bay prison. Seeking a more just and efficient balance between government and markets is at the heart of his domestic agenda. He has also found ways to present the traditional liberal value of tolerance in new language that speaks to our increasingly mixed-up world.

Then, perhaps in his second term, he might even dare to rescue the word.

2009

5.
Beyond the West

Beauty and the Beast in Burma

First of all, there is this difficulty: to identify the people I talked with in Burma could send them back to prison. The leaders of this grotesque army-state are officially titled, as in some schoolboy version of Orwellian dystopia, 'Secretary-1', 'Secretary-2', 'Secretary-3'. So in my notebook, later smuggled out, I refer to their victims and my interlocutors as U-1, U-2, Daw-1, Daw-2, and so on – 'U' and 'Daw' being, in Burmese, the respectful forms of 'Mr' and 'Mrs'. In what I write here, I must further disguise identities and omit telling detail, because, precisely, it will tell.

I

'I'm a vegetarian,' says U-5. 'I became a vegetarian after being in prison. You see – I'm sorry to have to tell you this – we ate rats.' But how did they cook them? 'We couldn't. We just dried them in the sun and ate them raw.' From the balcony of a good Chinese restaurant we look across to the great royal fort of Mandalay, its broad moat shimmering in the twilight. A tourist's delight. U-5 tells me that the embankment of the moat was recently rebuilt by forced labour. His own family was compelled to work on it. Earlier, from the top of Mandalay Hill, he pointed first to a landmark that the tourist guides never mention: the large, semicircular prison where he, like many others, spent years in solitary confinement for his part in the pro-democracy protests of 1988. The rat house.

U-13 describes the thick blue hood his interrogators put over his head. The hood was filthy with the sweat, mucus and blood of previous captives. He could scarcely breathe as the interrogators attached electrodes to four points on his body. They charged the electrodes from a small, primitive, hand-cranked generator. Each time he heard the cranking sound, he knew that another electric shock was coming.

I find an everyday fear that is worse than in Ceauşescu's Romania. And desperate everyday want. In poorer parts of the countryside, peasants ask each other, 'Fingers or spoon?' 'Fingers' is better: it means you have enough solid rice in your bowl to eat with your fingers. 'Spoon' indicates a few grains of rice in a watery soup. Increasingly, the answer is 'spoon'.

A hundred years ago, Burma exported more than 2 million tons of rice in a year. It was called the rice basket of India. Forty years ago, it still exported one million tons. In 1999, the figure was less than 70,000 tons. As the country's exports of rice have declined, its illicit export of drugs has soared. From being the rice basket of India, Burma has become the opium bowl of the world.

Tales of misery and horror ten years after the citizens of Burma voted overwhelmingly, on 27 May 1990, for the National League for Democracy, led by Aung San Suu Kyi, and, in the large swathes of the country inhabited by ethnic minorities, for other opposition parties. Denied what they voted for, they've had a decade of this.

Yet, perversely, the images that linger in my memory are all of heartrending beauty. Early one morning, I set out with a friend to drive across the Irrawaddy delta. As the sun rose, a magical landscape emerged through the morning mist: bamboo houses, raised on stilts amid the endless green and emerald patchwork of paddy fields; farmers in broad hats bicycling silently along the raised river bank; brilliant white pagodas with gilded conical spires, dotting the landscape like so many whitewashed anthills; ox-drawn wooden ploughs, slowly turning the underwater mud.

I dozed, and woke again, and saw, at the side of the road, outlined against the dawn, the most lovely girl in the world. She was dressed from head to toe in pink and white, and she held out, with an exquisite elegance of posture, sensual yet demure, a large silver offering bowl. A shy smile flashed from under a large, conical bamboo hat. A moment, and she was gone. Had I been dreaming? When we returned along the same road seven hours later, she was still there, still looking cool and fresh. What's more, she had collected 2,500 kyats (about $8 at the free market exchange rate) for the local monastery.

Then: the old wooden junks slowly drifting down the broad, muddy river, carrying bags of rice from the antiquated rice mills of Bassein; the shaven Buddhist boy-monks in crimson robes, walking barefoot with their mesmerically regular stride, keeping 'the mind mindful' as they collect rice and curry from the households of the faithful.

In Rangoon, there was the unending wonder of the Shwedagon pagoda, its vast, banded golden spire subtly changing shade with the movement of the light. On my first evening in Burma, I walked up to the Shwedagon at about nine o'clock and found myself the only foreigner in the entire temple complex. All around me were Burmese, men as well as women wearing the traditional *longyi*, an ankle-length, skirt-like garment. Some prayed devoutly to one of the many Buddhas; others sat smoking a cheroot or idly chatting in the warm, scented air. I marvelled at the tranquillity of a national shrine that seemed still authentically part of a traditional culture – something unthinkable, lost for ever, at St Peter's, or St Paul's, or the Taj Mahal, let alone in the temples of Bangkok, where you can't walk two yards without stumbling into a German tourist, praying with clasped video camera to the great god Sony.

I have rarely seen a more beautiful country, or a more ugly regime.

The connection between this beauty and that beast is complicated. It's tempting to say simply that the country is beautiful in spite of its politics. But that is too easy. For these gentle allures of an older world are also a result of the isolation and economic regression enforced by forty years of bad politics. This is the beauty of backwardness. Travelling to communist-ruled eastern Europe had the same bittersweet charm, and for much the same reason. I call it the paradox of revolutionary conservation. Not all revolutions have this oddly conservative effect – Mao's Cultural Revolution certainly did not – but some do.

However, the result is always a debased and corrupted version of the old. Burma may still look like Rudyard Kipling's 'beautiful lazy land full of very pretty girls and very bad cheroots'. What is more, those who live here may genuinely find deeper pleasures and satisfactions in a slower, more traditional way of life, in the seasonal round, the pagoda festival, the leisurely, raucous, bawdy *pwe* (a kind of folk theatre performance), and in the sempiternal consolations of unquestioned religion. The recipe for individual human happiness is mysterious, and cannot be obtained from Wal-Mart.

Yet there is also, most definitely, a hard, corrosive reality of worsening poverty, malnutrition and infant mortality; of more than 3 million people driven from their homes, some of them now living in barely human conditions in the jungle; of forced labour, rampant corruption, banditry, sexual exploitation, and the closely linked plagues of drug abuse and AIDS, with an estimated half-million people in Burma being HIV-positive.

Meanwhile, amid the archaic beauty that charms the privileged Western visitor, you glimpse a pathetic craving for even the cheapest totems of the West. Young men proudly sport baseball caps above the otherwise universal national dress of flip-flops, *longyi*, and cotton shirt or blouse. A few already wear their baseball caps reversed: globalization's moronic meme. The cheroot is abandoned for a cheap Rothmans cigarette called 'London', garishly advertised everywhere.

Even the monks possess, hidden away in an old wooden cupboard, a television – and they all seem to be football fans.

'Aya Shiya!' a friendly young monk urged upon me, as I sat on the steps of a pagoda. 'Aya Shiya!' What timeless oriental wisdom was this? Finally, I recognized the name of Alan Shearer, the Newcastle United striker.

2

Military intelligence, says one of the oldest jokes in the world, is a contradiction in terms. Burma is a country ruled by military intelligence. Military Intelligence, now formally entitled the Directorate of Defence Services Intelligence, is the backbone of this regime. Its boss, Lieutenant General Khin Nyunt, though not formally head of the junta, is Secretary-1. But military intelligence, in the broader sense, has been ruining the golden land through four decades.

In 1962 a wildly superstitious former postal clerk, born Shu Maung but now known to the world as General Ne Win ('Brilliant like the sun'), organized an army takeover, arguing that the country's feeble multiparty democracy was incapable of keeping the Union of Burma together against communist and ethnic minority rebels. Ne Win led Burma down what he called 'the Burmese Way to Socialism', into twenty-six years of surreal isolation. His 'socialism' was actually more like Japanese national socialism of the early 1940s (when the imperial Japanese trained the original Burma Independence Army), mixed with post-colonial nationalism, attempted autarky, vulgar Buddhism, astrology and a brutal war against the insurgents. His Asian Albania was so non-aligned that it even resigned from the Non-Aligned Movement. Eighty-nine this May, Ne Win still lives in Rangoon, just across the Inya Lake from Aung San Suu Kyi. He is thought to wield continued shadowy influence over the regime, but no longer to run it from day to day.

In fact, the old despot's announcement of his retirement in July 1988 was a major catalyst of the nationwide protests on the supposedly auspicious date of '8.8.88'. Crushing those protests with great brutality – estimates of the number who died in the ensuing orgy of repression range from 3,000 to 10,000 – the army formed a State Law and Order Restoration Council, or SLORC. It even sounds like a beast. A few years ago, apparently advised by a PR firm that this name played badly in the West, the generals changed it to State Peace and Development Council. From the Tolkienesque to the Orwellian.[1] However, the regime's opponents continue to call it 'The Slorc', and so shall I.

The Slorc is not simply a military dictatorship. Rather, it is an army-state, as communist countries were party-states. Army officers shadow or control all functions of the state and most of the activities of everyday social life. Even the Red Cross is a paramilitary organization. The military is estimated to consume a staggering 40 per cent of the national budget. Even according to official figures, expenditure on defence is sixteen times that on healthcare. Since 1988, the army has grown in size from some 200,000 to more than 400,000. You see soldiers everywhere.

The country displays all the familiar pockmarks of dictatorship: high grey walls, barbed wire, armed guards, bureaucracy, crude paper forms in quadruplicate, propaganda, censorship, inefficiency and fear. Under the heading 'People's Desire', faded red billboards proclaim, 'Oppose those relying on external elements, acting as stooges, holding negative views.' Just occasionally, as if to compensate, there is a green billboard saying, 'Please provide assistance to international travellers.' Well, thank you, Slorc.

I had hoped that I would never in my life have to read a newspaper more boring than the East German communist party daily, *Neues Deutschland*. I had not seen *The New Light of Myanmar*. ('Myanmar' is another Slorc renaming, casting off the supposedly imperialist 'Burma' in favour of another Burmese word for Burma.)

In leaden prose, *New Light* records how Secretary-1 (usually on page 1), Secretary-2 (page 2) or Secretary-3 visit another flourishing school, hospital or factory, greeted by ever-smiling pupils, doctors, workers. But instead of Marxism as the official ideology, we have Buddhism. No issue is complete without some account of a general making gifts to a Buddhist monastery: 'In conclusion, the Secretary-1 expressed his wishes, "May I be able to attain Nirvana due to merits gained for building and donating the centre, may I be a worthy son who can promote Buddhist Sasana in case I go round the circle of rebirth . . ."' Otherwise, I suppose, he would be in danger of coming back as a rat. Elsewhere, New Light tells you about the Tatmadaw Golf Tournament. The Burmese military learned national socialism from the Japanese; from the British, golf. The game is, apparently, one of the great passions of the high command.

Experienced observers say the top commanders see themselves as heirs to Burma's absolute monarchs, from the medieval Anawrahta of Bagan to the hapless King Thibaw, whom the British peremptorily expelled from the Mandalay palace in 1885. At a recent reception for the diplomatic corps, the generals had laid on an 'abasement dance' that used to be reserved for homage to the king.

Since this is an army-state, the economy is also directly run by the military, with disastrous results for the country, although not for the generals. The post-1988 military leaders have denationalized many companies – and given them to themselves. A share of the spoils has gone to foreign investors, especially from China, Singapore, Taiwan and Japan, as well as British, French and American oil companies. But in almost every joint venture, the Burmese partner is either military, ex-military or related to the military. Corruption is endemic. Someone who worked for a foreign tobacco company described to me how a generous present – an expensive new set of golf clubs, for example – had to be sent around to the responsible general's home, before he would even receive the supplicant businessman. As a result, senior officers live in large, luxurious houses, while junior officers and other ranks share the general poverty. According to a recent World Bank report, the economy is locked in a steep downward spiral.

The end that supposedly justifies all the Slorc's means is 'non-disintegration of the Union'. *A Brief History of the Myanmar Army*, sold at the vast, empty armed forces museum, manages not to mention the 1990 election while explaining that the Slorc saved the country from 'the kind of anarchy experienced in the (former) Soviet Union, Yugoslavia, and Indonesia'. The generals' one substantial achievement has been to negotiate ceasefire agreements with most, though not all, of the ethnic rebels. These agreements typically leave the rebel leaders in far-reaching control of their own areas, often with private armies and free to do much as they please. In several cases, this includes very direct involvement in the large-scale production and export of heroin and amphetamines. In return, drug barons like the notorious Khun Sa, who now lives unhindered in Rangoon, launder their profits through investments in the Burmese economy. Secretary-1 last year graced with his presence the opening of another infamous drug dealer's headquarters.

Yet these ceasefires are only temporary, pending the new constitution which the regime has spent seven years not producing. The Slorc's constitutional proposals envisage a distinction between 'national' politics, where the 'leading role of the armed forces' would be secured, as it used to be in Suharto's Indonesia, and 'party' politics, where Aung San Suu Kyi's National League for Democracy (NLD) could compete with all the rest. In the meantime, however, the Indonesian model has gone down the drain, to be replaced by a fragile new democracy. And the NLD has refused to have anything to do with this unequal negotiation since, in 1995, Aung San Suu Kyi emerged from six years of house arrest in her mother's villa on University Avenue, across the Inya Lake from the old tyrant Ne Win.

3

Of course I had come to see Suu. I say 'Suu' in this familiar fashion because I had been talking about her as Suu for years with her husband, Michael Aris, a dear friend and colleague of mine at Oxford. Michael died tragically of cancer in March 1999, cruelly prevented by the Slorc from ever seeing his wife again. He had told me of her close interest in the way dissidents prepared peaceful change in central Europe, and we had long been plotting my trip to Burma. I had also learned of Suu from other mutual friends who knew her well during her more than twenty years as student, budding cultural historian, hard-up housewife and devoted mother in north Oxford.

Five thousand miles away, in her homeland, she is an uncrowned queen, respectfully referred to even by close acquaintances as 'Daw Suu', and known to millions of Burmese simply as 'The Lady'. She is this legend because she is the daughter of the father of the nation, Aung San, the architect of Burmese independence, assassinated in 1947, when she was two; because of the extraordinary, charismatic style in which she joined what she called 'Burma's second struggle for independence', with a speech before hundreds of thousands at the Shwedagon on 26 August 1988, and has led it ever since; and because of the Mandela-like mystique that comes from the combination of long captivity, international fame – including, in her case, the 1991 Nobel Peace Prize – and daily vituperation by the regime. Wherever I went, people asked me, 'How is she? Is she in good health?' Popular imagination endows her with almost supernatural powers. There is something even painful in the way so much depends on this one human being.

The Lady is no longer formally under house arrest, but the stretch of University Avenue running past her home is blocked off, and military intelligence allows only foreign diplomats, UN officials and a few close associates to enter. She herself has limited freedom of movement within Rangoon. We met at the house of a friendly diplomat.

She is – first things first – quite as delicately beautiful as in the photographs, reproduced like icons around the world. She looks much younger than fifty-four, with fine, upright posture, and a sophisticated version of Burmese traditional dress: fresh flowers in her hair, long, dark red *longyi*, and blue velveteen sandals. Every inch the lady. Indeed, she is ladylike with the slightly old-fashioned gentility of the Anglo-Indian school – she was 'finished' at Lady Sri Ram College in New Delhi, where her mother was Burmese ambassador. So there's refined small talk, with a hint of genteel primness, but happily subverted by an informal wit and still-girlish laugh.

Fragile, then? Yes, but also quick, decisive, very consciously her father's daughter. A leader. Crisp, highly disciplined, tough – even harsh in her judgements on former allies who have not come back, after their years in prison, to go on fighting with the NLD. But she is still tougher on herself. In his introduction to *Freedom from Fear*, a collection of her writings, Michael Aris recalled how she went on hunger strike in 1989 to demand that she should be allowed to join her followers in the appalling conditions of Insein prison. For her decision to join her people's struggle she has paid a huge personal price, in years of separation from her children. She spends most of her time in the large, run-down villa on the lakeside, with a strict routine of exercise, meditation, writing, reading and conducting party business.

One of her passions is literature. We talked of Jane Austen, Dickens and, inevitably, of Kipling – who, with the infuriating casualness of genius, unforgettably captured the spirit of this place in his ballad 'Mandalay', although he only spent a few days in Burma and never even went to Mandalay. I had been told by someone in, as it happens, Mandalay, that she had translated Kipling's 'If' into Burmese. She said this was not true, but she had used and interpreted an existing translation at her rallies, and the text, with her comments, had been published as a pamphlet. For her, the poem that in England is often dismissed as the epitome of imperialist bombast is 'a great poem for dissidents'.

She and Michael named their youngest son Kim, after the hero of Kipling's novel. She asked me if I could find the full version of the poem that provides the epigraph to the last chapter of *Kim*:

Drawbridge let fall – He's the Lord of us all –
The Dreamer whose dream came true.

The lines, she said, had always meant much to her.

Most of the time we talked politics, for her life is now the struggle. Like Václav Havel, who nominated her for the Nobel Peace Prize, she insists that she had politics thrust upon her. However, even as a dissident playwright, Havel was a natural politician. Talking to him in the 1980s, I always had a strong sense of a political strategy. I did not have this impression with her. She has a firm grasp of what new political system Burma needs; a much less clear idea of how to achieve it. But then, does anyone else?

Her critics – both inside Burma and in the exile community – say she is inflexible and intransigent. Yet she left me in no doubt that she sees the need for compromise if one wants a non-violent transition – and to a devout Buddhist, non-violence is a categorical imperative. The starting point of any new political opening must be a recognition by the regime of the results of the May 1990 election; but there should then be a negotiation about arrangements for a transition. The top military would not have to fear for their lives. 'Those I've talked to know I wouldn't be nasty to them,' she says, speaking of her jailers like a headmistress discussing a bunch of naughty children. In the interests of a peaceful transition, it might even prove necessary to leave them 'some of their ill-gotten gains'. A truth commission, rather than kangaroo courts, would be her chosen instrument of dealing with the dreadful past.

However, she judges that the time for such compromise has not yet come. Now is the time for more pressure, not less, so as to bring the generals to the negotiating table. When she is not conducting a shadow foreign policy, she is busy with the National League for Democracy – which the regime still formally accepts as a legal political party, while harassing and imprisoning its members. She suspects the generals released her in 1995 because they thought the NLD was finished. But, she insists, it's not. Particularly important is a committee they have established, together with some ethnic minority parties, to represent the parliament that should have been constituted following the May 1990 election.

Next day, I came to give a lecture at the NLD headquarters. Hastening from my car to the entrance – for there is a heavy military intelligence presence outside – I found a narrow, two-storey house, bedecked with the movement's red flags, stifling hot and bursting with activity. I spoke to what was literally a packed house of some 200 people – perhaps half of them under thirty, since this was the office's regular 'youth' day. Suu chaired the meeting, translated my talk into Burmese, and added her own pithy comments. To either side of us sat, like a Greek chorus, the men she calls her 'uncles' – elderly party members, several of them former army officers, on whose support and advice she relies heavily.

I talked about the transitions to democracy in Central Europe, South Africa and elsewhere. Although there were undoubtedly regime spies present, people asked questions freely – and seemed never to want to stop. Many were quite well informed, especially about recent changes in Indonesia and Malaysia. (Here, as once in communist-ruled eastern Europe, Western radio stations broadcasting in the native language are a vital lifeline.) They loved the idea of their generals sweating before a truth commission. 'How does one make a truth commission?' asked an earnest-looking girl in the front row, pen poised over notebook. From the back, a man wondered if this procedure necessarily involved amnesty, as in South Africa, and seemed relieved to hear that it did not.

'You see!' said Suu afterward. 'It's not so bad, is it?' Then she went off to talk to a delegation from the Irrawaddy delta youth wing while I was driven to the airport, where 'customs officials' minutely searched my luggage and ripped the film out of my camera.

4

How might peaceful change come about in Burma? What chance for a Silken Revolution? One must start by saying that the best chance was probably missed ten years ago. In May 1990, the regime was stunned by the NLD's election victory. If, before the eyes of the world's press and television, then present in Rangoon, the NLD had immediately organized a mass march to University Avenue and freed Aung San Suu Kyi from house arrest, the country might look very different today. But the 'uncles' then running the NLD, too fearful of risking violence and perhaps also too trustful of their former army colleagues, failed to seize the moment. This was the turning point at which history failed to turn.

Ten years later, the heart of the Burmese problem is that Suu has all the legitimacy and the Slorc has all the power. If the NLD had a little more real power, and the Slorc had a little more legitimacy, a negotiated transition would be easier to imagine. There's no doubt that Suu and the NLD still have huge potential support. The pertinent question asked by a British support group, 'Why are 400,000 men so afraid of one woman?', is easily answered. Given an election tomorrow, the opposition would almost certainly win another landslide victory.

The trouble is, the generals know this. For all their firepower, they, too, live in fear. I was told by a reliable source that many of the top Tatmadaw commanders actually sleep in their offices or barracks. Nothing could better illustrate their siege mentality. If they feared popular retribution ten years ago, how much more must they fear it now. As with every dictatorship in history, optimistic interpreters – not Sovietologists but Tatmadawlogists – think 'reformers' lurk behind the closed doors. Secretary-1 is even billed as a Slorc Andropov. But the generals show no outward sign of any serious readiness to deal.

Meanwhile, although the NLD's potential power is huge, its actual, effective presence is very limited. That Rangoon office is the signal exception. More typical is the NLD secretary in a provincial town who told me, 'We can do nothing.' His wife had just lost her job because of the NLD connection. Suu's brightest political advisers are imprisoned or exiled. For now, the regime has quite effectively corralled her and the 'uncles' in a small, semi-private space, albeit with a vast international audience.

Those I spoke to recognize the importance of what dissidents in Poland called 'the self-organization of society'. But 'it's impossible here' was their common refrain. Talking to one Rangoon writer, I asked, 'What about civil society?' He laughed, and gestured around the tiny, bare room, where two disconsolate colleagues sat beside a small pile of magazines: 'This is our civil society!' Those magazines are what is left of independent debate, but they are subject to fierce censorship. I was shown a recent issue of one journal in which even references to 'people concerned for the future' and 'those interested in the new' had been excised. At another editorial office, I was told that an article about the plague of mosquitoes in Rangoon had been banned. The censors apparently suspected a political allegory.

Students could be a more potent force. This is something of a Burmese tradition: Aung San started his political career as a student leader; in the 1960s, the most courageous urban opposition to Ne Win came from the universities; it was students who initiated and led the 1988 protests. Again, the Slorc knows this. That's why a student activist recently received a fifty-two-year prison sentence, and most of the country's universities are closed. Rather than risk their own power, the military bosses sacrifice the higher education of a generation and hence the future of their country. A few university departments have reopened, often carefully relocated outside the main cities. Young people who can afford them take private courses in English, computing or business studies. Meanwhile, the military have medical and engineering colleges to make sure their own children don't suffer.[2]

Another important social group are the Buddhist monks. I heard quite contradictory views on the question of whether Theravada Buddhism encourages resistance to dictatorship and support for democracy, but there is no doubt that the monks have significant potential as both protesters and mediators. Last November, the abbot of one of the largest monasteries in the country wrote public letters to General Than Shwe, the head of Slorc, to Aung San Suu Kyi and to Ne Win, appealing for dialogue between 'the sons and daughters of the nation'. I had hoped to meet him, but was told that he was under close surveillance and my visit 'would not be good for him or you'. However, I sat barefooted before another venerable sage. While a choir of mosquitoes made a leisurely meal of my feet, he sadly explained to me how the Slorc had bought off the institutionalized Buddhist hierarchy, the so-called Sangha Council, with donations, televisions, cars, and a judicious mixture of intimidation and flattery.

Nonetheless, the sage continued, ordinary monks shared the suffering and frustration of the society from which they came. In 1988, monks had been in the forefront of demonstrations, especially in Mandalay. Now they were again waiting for the call. Some estimates suggest that there are as many as 400,000 monks in Burma: one for every soldier.

Finally, further economic decline might provoke spontaneous popular protest. But this is not an industrialized economy, in which economic crisis produces large concentrations of angry workers, capable of concerted action. More than 70 per cent of the people still live on the land, and a dispersed rural population is always easier to repress. In a pre-emptive action, the generals have moved many of the urban poor out of Rangoon into settlements beyond rivers. The bridges over those rivers are heavily guarded and, as Ne Win famously remarked in 1988, 'When the army shoots, it shoots to hit.'

Even a whistle-stop tour of possible forces for change must also mention the ethnic minorities, and what might be called the semi-external and external actors. For Burmese politics are anything but a simple fairy-tale confrontation between Suu and Slorc, beauty and the beast. I did not witness, and cannot begin to encompass, the fiendishly complex mixtures of ethnic discontent, insurgency and drug trade, varying widely between the country's numerous ethnic groups – Shan, Karenni, Mon, Wa, Chin, Kachin and so on.[3] Altogether, these minorities make up roughly a third of the country's population: a dangerous proportion, as all students of nationalism know. They have been crucial to shaping Burmese politics for half a century, and in any negotiated transition ethnic minority leaders will immediately demand their place at the table.

By 'semi-external' actors I mean people like the thousands of students and other political activists who fled to Thailand after the bloody repression of 1988, some of whom still move in and out across that porous frontier, and the government-in-exile, which works in sometimes ill-coordinated tandem with the NLD. These in turn are closely linked to the remarkable profusion of foreign support groups concerned with Burma. For Burma has become one of the great symbolic causes of our time. There are now more than a hundred unofficial Burma websites. The idealism and energy of those involved will be a great asset when freedom comes, but the current impact of this virtual Burma on the real one is small. One analyst dryly observes that the much-heralded anti-Slorc protests planned for '9.9.99' – widely held by superstitious Burmese to be another especially auspicious date for action – were more of an event outside Burma than they were inside.

Coordinated action by states might have more direct influence on the regime than this 'international civil society'. Burma enjoys the rare distinction of being annually condemned by UN resolution. In an unprecedented step, the International Labour Organization (ILO) has come close to expelling Burma for its continued use of forced labour. The UN secretary general has just appointed a new special representative for Burma, Razali Ismail, a Malaysian who, it is hoped, will be more active than the last.

Beyond this, however, the countries with an interest in Burma are lamentably divided. Britain and America support a policy of pressure and selective sanctions: the approach favoured by Aung San Suu Kyi and the NLD. US sanctions, in particular, have denied Burma major foreign investment and international development loans. A milder version of this Anglo-American policy is the agreed position of the European Union, although Germany and France are more inclined to pursue détente with Burma. Japan, South Korea and several ASEAN countries have followed a much softer policy of 'private diplomacy' and economic engagement. Burma was accepted into ASEAN in 1997, against the wishes of the NLD. All this is reminiscent of Cold War debates about the merits of 'megaphone diplomacy' versus 'constructive engagement', but here there is the added dimension of allegedly 'Asian' versus 'Western' approaches. In March, a secret meeting of major interested powers tried to narrow the differences. Much to the Slorc's annoyance, it took place in Seoul and was attended by ASEAN members such as Thailand and Malaysia.

Yet even if these 'Asian' and 'Western' policies converge, the Slorc can still rely on the largest Asian power: China. For all the differences in official ideology, Burma is now almost a client state of communist China. A flourishing trade goes up and down the old Burma road, to and from the province of Yunnan, on very favourable terms for the Chinese. Mandalay is increasingly a Chinatown where Chinese businessmen live like lords, in houses bigger even than those of the generals. Burma's other large Asian neighbour, India, claims that the Slorc has given its Chinese allies strategic access to the Indian Ocean. The arrival of a Chinese Gorbachev in Beijing could really change the international constellation around Burma. Alas, it hardly seems imminent.

Only a fool would predict the future of such an immensely complex witches' brew. My own melancholy hunch, based on the views of many I talked to, is that explosion is more likely than negotiation. Several people pointed out to me that Burma's long-suffering Buddhist gentleness has alternated, historically, with short periods of violent protest. No one can know what the spark will be, although the death and funeral of Ne Win is mentioned as one potential risky moment for the regime. An explosion, particularly if it took the form of a peasants' revolt, might initially be suppressed by the well-prepared army, with more bloodshed. Such a crisis would also have an important international consequence, for it could see the West arrayed on one side and China on the other. After Taiwan, Burma!

The hope must be that, as in Indonesia and Malaysia, such violence would eventually be the midwife of negotiation. We would then have to look for four miracles – as if reaching this point were not already miracle enough. First, that the opposition and the Slorc could negotiate an orderly transition to democracy. Second, that the country would not fall apart in this most dangerous period for all multi-ethnic polities: when dictatorship is dying and democracy is still unborn. Ten years ago, the main political representatives of the ethnic minorities were ready to work within the framework of a new democratic federation. It is less clear that they would do so now. Third, that, with the help of the outside world, the new government could begin to tackle an appalling list of problems: poverty, malnutrition, banditry, an over-mighty army, corruption, poor education, decayed or non-existent infrastructure, drugs, ethnic insurgency, ethnic insurgent drug lords with private armies, AIDS – you name it, Burma has it.

Finally, and I fear most unrealistically, I would hope against hope for a fourth miracle: that something of the tranquil beauty of an isolated, traditional culture, almost unique in today's world, could survive the necessary and longed-for tempest of modernity. But the armies of global capitalism are waiting at the frontier, engines revving up, with their container-loads of tawdry goods, their ready-made life-style packages, sex shops, reversed baseball caps, and state-of-the-art software for the unceasing manufacture of new consumer desires. These armies are more irresistible than any Tatmadaw or People's Army, because they are truly welcomed as liberators. If so few of the good things of an older world have survived in central Europe, where conditions were so much more favourable, how could they be saved here?

5

On my last evening, as on my first, I went to the Shwedagon. Again, there was a quiet glory. As I sat gazing up at the golden winking wonder, outlined against a black velvet sky, I thought of all that I had seen – and of Michael, and of Suu.

Suddenly I was accosted by a fat woman, expensively dressed, with a smart leather shoulder bag and a curiously expressionless face: 'Where you from?' In broken English she told me of her great love for the Lord Booodah and how she had come to pray for her husband who was born on a Tuesday. 'Burma people help foreigners,' she said, 'only a few not-good people not help.' Her sons, she added, were at university – one was studying medicine. And her husband who was born on a Tuesday? Well, he was a major general in the Burmese air force. On her stubby fingers she wore four of the largest, most heavily gem-encrusted rings I have ever seen. Ostentatious wealth – and easily portable in case of trouble. What was the phrase Suu had used? 'Ill-gotten gains.' Then the general's wife waddled off, with two servants scuttling behind her.

I stayed awhile, and sent up a secular prayer: that all my pessimistic analysis should be proved quite wrong; that the four miracles should follow; and that Aung San Suu Kyi should, herself, be 'The Dreamer whose dream came true'.

2000

Soldiers of the Hidden Imam

Carved high in the towering rock of Naqsh-e Rostam, gazing out across the desert, are the tombs of the great Persian emperors from two and a half millennia ago: Darius, Xerxes, Artaxerxes. Lower down the cliff face of this imperial Mount Rushmore you see a dramatic stone relief, shimmering in the heat. It shows a later Shah of all the Shahs, Shapur I, accepting the surrender of the Roman emperor Valerian, in the year AD 260 according to the Christian calendar. The conqueror, on horseback and gloriously accoutred, towers over the unmounted, swordless, vanquished Caesar.

'What happened to Valerian?' I asked my Iranian companion.

'Oh, he was killed, of course.'

I

In the autumn of 2005, as today's Iranian rulers defied the new Rome by pressing ahead with their nuclear programme, I travelled for two weeks through what is now the Islamic Republic of Iran. In the year of their Lord 1384, I talked to mullahs armed with laptops, regime supporters in the religious hotbed of Qom, and Islamic philosophers highly critical of the regime. I met intellectuals of all stripes, artists, farmers, politicians and business people. Most memorably, I had long, intense conversations with some of the young Iranians who make up the majority of the country's population. I see their earnest faces before me as I write, especially those of the women, framed in the compulsory Islamic head scarf, the *hijab*, which they somehow manage to convert into an accessory of grace and quiet allure.

At a rooftop restaurant in the wondrous city of Esfahan, I witnessed the continuity of Persian culture, with a singer chanting verses from the fourteenth-century poet Hafez while local diners peered up at the blue, cream and turquoise dome of the Sheikh Lotfallah mosque, illuminated against the night sky. (You do not often hear verses from Chaucer being sung in an English pub.) More typically, I was plunging through the heat, dust, eye-stinging pollution and kamikaze traffic of Tehran, that anarchic city of 12 million people, whose drivers treat every roundabout as an invitation to play the American game of chicken, only swerving to avoid one another's bumpers with milli-metres to spare. Or sometimes not swerving.

I also got a taste of life behind the high garden walls of the houses of the middle and upper class, where the *hijab* immediately comes off and opinions are scathingly contemptuous of the ageing revolu-tionary Islamic zeal of the country's new president, Mahmoud Ahmadinejad. Within minutes of my arrival at one such house, bikini-clad women were teasingly inviting me to come naked into the swimming pool, while the men offered me a drink from a bottle marked 'Ethanol 98 per cent proof'.

These encounters illustrated a trait, apparently of long pedigree, to which my Iranian interlocutors constantly drew my attention: the contrast between what Iranians say outside and what they say inside those high walls. Double-talk as a way of life. I have never been in a country where so many people told me I should not believe what people said. (Taken strictly, a self-defeating proposition.) Again and again they pointed to the Shiite custom of *taghiye*, by which believers are entitled to lie in defence of their faith. Today's non-believers have their own *taghiye*.

Iranians also warned me that theirs is a country rich in superstition – sometimes conveyed by very modern means. In the middle of a Tehran traffic jam, my driver received a text message on his mobile phone. It asked him urgently to pray for the return of the hidden imam, the Shiites' twelfth imam or mahdi, who supposedly went into hiding some 1127 years ago. A secular intellectual wondered aloud whether a society so rife with mendacity and superstition is at all susceptible to understanding through reason.

Amid this wild medley of ancient and modern, I sought answers to one crucial question: how might Iran's post-revolutionary Islamic regime be transformed, whether gradually or suddenly, by social and political forces inside that country? And I added a second: how might the policies of Europe and the United States, which fortunately do not at the moment include an Iraq-style attempt to impose 'regime change' by military occupation, affect those domestic forces?

2

The political system of the Islamic Republic of Iran is at once fiendishly complex and extremely simple. Most of the Iranians I met preferred to stress the complexity. The country has at least two governments at any one time: a semi-democratic formal state structure, now headed by President Mahmoud Ahmadinejad, and a religious-ideological command structure headed by the Supreme Leader, Ayatollah Ali Khamenei. There are numerous shifting formal and informal power centres, including political parties in Parliament, ministries, rich religious foundations, the Revolutionary Guards, and the multimillion-man Basij militia, whose mobilization helped Ahmadinejad to get elected. There are also backroom ethnic or regional mafias, and numerous competing intelligence, security and police agencies –

eighteen of them according to one recent count. No wonder Iranian political scientists reach for terms like 'polyarchy', 'elective oligarchy', 'semi-democracy' or 'neopatrimonialism'.

Yet the longer I was there, the more strongly I felt that the essence of this regime remains quite simple. At its core, the Islamic Republic is still an ideological dictatorship. Its central organizing principle can be summarized in four sentences: (1) There is only one God and Muhammad is his Prophet. (2) God knows best what is good for men and women. (3) The Islamic clergy, and especially the most learned among them, the jurists qualified to interpret Islamic law, know best what God wants. (4) In case of dispute among learned jurists, the Supreme Leader decides.

This is the system which its inventor, Grand Ayatollah Ruhollah Khomeini, justified by radically reinterpreting the Islamic concept of *velayat-e faqih*, usually translated as the 'Guardianship of the Jurist'. This system is not Islam; it is Khomeinism. It would not exist without that one old man, whose grim portrait still stares out at you everywhere in Iran, though now usually flanked by the bespectacled figure of his successor and epigone, the current Supreme Leader, Ayatollah Khamenei. If you ever doubted the importance of the individual in history, consider the story of Khomeini.

I visited his childhood home in the provincial market town of Khomein – ayatollahs generally take an honorific name from their home town, so Khomeini means 'of Khomein'. It's a substantial, rather handsome, yellow-brick house, with the traditional outer and inner courtyards, and an inscription celebrating the 'birthplace of the Sun of Khomein'. His father was murdered when he was four months old, his mother died when he was fifteen, and he was given over to the theological schools that trained him to be a cleric. If even one of his parents had lived, might this have been a different story? Outside, a billboard describes him, justly enough, as 'the revivor of religious government in [the] contemporary world'.

Khomeini was both the Lenin and the Stalin of Iran's Islamic revolution. The system he created has some similarities with a communist party-state. In Khomeinism, the Guardianship of the Jurist is an all-embracing political principle that is the functional equivalent of communism's Leading Role of the Party. Here, too, you have parallel hierarchies of ideological and state power, with the former always ultimately trumping the latter. The Islamic Republic's ideological half is almost entirely undemocratic: the Supreme Leader is assisted by a Guardian Council, an Islamic judiciary and an Assembly of Experts. All of them are dominated by conservative clerics. The state institutions are more democratic, with a genuine if limited competition for power. However, the Guardian Council arbitrarily disqualifies thousands of would-be candidates for Parliament, the regime controls the all-important state television channels, and security forces like the Basij militia can both mobilize and intimidate voters, so one cannot seriously talk of free and fair elections.

As in communist party-states, there is intense factional struggle, which Western observers sometimes mistake for pluralism. Unlike in communist party-states, factions actually appeal to voters to strengthen their position. Thus Ahmadinejad successfully presented himself to voters as a kind of plain man's puritan outsider to the system, yet he is now wholly of it, working closely with Khamenei and the Guardian Council. His rival in the second-round presidential run-off, former president Hashemi Rafsanjani, was discredited as being too much part of the resented group of mullahs in control: 'A stick would have won against Rafsanjani,' an Iranian politician told me. Rafsanjani now tactically criticizes Ahmedinejad's Islamic revolutionary-style speech to the United Nations as being undiplomatic. Yet he himself remains head of the powerful Expediency Council, which mediates between the undemocratic ideological hierarchy and the semi-democratic Parliament. It was Rafsanjani who this summer declared that 'the system [*nazam*] has decided' on the resumption of uranium reprocessing. When leaders use that specific term *nazam*, 'the system', everyone knows they mean the ideological

command hierarchy right up to the Supreme Leader – God's representative on earth.

In a communist party-state, the party line was to be found in the
pages of *Pravda* or *Neues Deutschland*. In the Islamic mullah-state,
the 'imam line' is handed down through Friday prayers, two sessions
of which I attended, first at the gorgeous Pattern-of-the-World
mosque in Esfahan and, the next week, in a closely policed compound
at Tehran University. In both places a high-ranking Islamic clergyman
– the chair of the Guardian Council, at my Tehran session – delivered a fulminating political homily, denouncing in particular America
and Britain. The political message was sandwiched between conventional Muslim prayers, like a kebab wrapped in nan bread. In Tehran,
the final prayers ended with an orchestrated crowd chant, 'Down with
America! Down with Israel! Down with the enemies of the
Guardianship of the Jurist!'

3

How can such a regime be transformed, or, as many still prefer to
say, reformed? I heard the word 'reform' innumerable times as I travelled around Iran. I soon realized that it meant several different things.
First, there's an ideological debate among Islamic intellectuals, turning
on what in the communist world used to be called 'revisionism' – that
is, attempts to revise the ideology on which the state is built. As the
views of revisionists in, say, 1950s Poland were also part of a wider
debate about international communism, so the views of these Iranian
revisionists have significant implications for international Islam.

I was impressed by the liveliness of this debate. While many Iranians
are clearly fed up with Islam being stuffed down their throats as a
state religion, I found no sense that Islamic ideology is a dead issue,
as, for example, communist ideology had become a dead issue in
central Europe by the 1980s. Far from it. In Khomeini's theological

capital of Qom, now home to some 200 Islamic think tanks and institutions of higher education, I met with a research group on Islamic political philosophy. Why should Islam not be compatible with a secular, liberal democratic state, I asked, as is increasingly the case in Turkey? 'Turkey is not Qom,' said Mohsen Rezvani, a young philosopher wearing the robes and turban of a mullah, to laughter around the table. Islam, Rezvani said, is 'anthropologically, theologically, and epistemologically' incompatible with liberal democracy. Anthropologically, because liberal democracy is based on liberal individualism; theologically, because it excludes God from the public sphere; and epistemologically, because it is based on reason not faith. Then they handed me an issue of the *Political Science Quarterly* – not the American journal but their own Qom-made version. Here I read an English-language abstract of an admiring article by Rezvani about Leo Strauss.

'So you're a neoconservative!' I teased him.

Oh no, he replied, the American neoconservatives don't properly understand Leo Strauss.

I could see at once, even before I had the full article translated for me, what a conservative Iranian mullah would find to admire in Strauss: the insistence that there is a single truth in a classic text, and that the intentions of the author (for example, God, in the case of the Koran) are best interpreted by a neo-Platonic intellectual vanguard (for the Koran, the Islamic jurists whose ranks Rezvani aspires to join). Yet this Wolfowitz of Qom was immediately contradicted by others at the table, citing Islamic modernists such as Abdolkarim Soroush who maintain that Islam is compatible with a secular state.

Back in Tehran, I met a most impressive Islamic revisionist, Professor Mohsen Kadivar, a smiling, learned and courageous mullah. One reason the Iranian Islamic debate is so lively is that the Shiite tradition not only permits but encourages spirited disagreement between the followers of rival grand ayatollahs of the highest category, those who have earned the title *marja-i taqlid*, or 'source of imitation'. Professor Kadivar is a disciple of the Grand Ayatollah

Hossein-Ali Montazeri, who was to have been Khomeini's successor as Supreme Leader until the father of the revolution disinherited him and put him under house arrest in Qom.

A few years ago, Kadivar took the bold step of arguing that the Guardianship of the Jurist has no sound basis in the Koran or mainstream Islamic thought, and is incompatible with the essence of a true republic. He also questioned the Islamic rectitude of condemning people (for example, Salman Rushdie) to death in their absence, and suggested in a newspaper interview that today's Iran reproduces characteristics of the Shah's monarchic rule: 'People made the revolution so that they could make decisions, not so that decisions would be made for them.' He paid for his intellectual honesty with eighteen months in prison.

So that's what the regime's cheerleaders mean when they chant at Friday prayers, 'Down with the enemies of the Guardianship of the Jurist!' Direct criticism of the Guardianship of the Jurist, and of the 'sultanic' rule of the Supreme Leader, is also the unforgivable offence of the country's most prominent political prisoner, the journalist Akbar Ganji – once, like Kadivar, an enthusiastic supporter of the Islamic revolution.

I quoted to Kadivar the observation of the Polish philosopher Leszek Kołakowski, himself a former communist revisionist, that the idea of democratic communism is like fried snowballs. 'Exactly!' cried Kadivar. Democratic Khomeinism is like fried snowballs.

That is emphatically denied by another group, also known as 'Islamic reformists', who used to be Kadivar's comrades in the revolution. What we might call 'in-system' reformers have been in government for the last eight years, under the state president Mohammad Khatami. Their hope was precisely that they could reform and partially democratize the Islamic Republic, while leaving unchallenged the central pillars of Khomeinism. They failed. Many people who supported President Khatami and his fellow reformists in the late 1990s told me they are bitterly disappointed.

I talked to one of the in-system reformers' most influential strategists, Saeed Hajjarian, a former head of counterintelligence who in 2000 was shot through the neck, probably by an assassin from a competing secret service connected to the Revolutionary Guards. We met in his spartan, neon-lit office-cum-sickroom in a dreary, stale-smelling, unmarked building, which turned out to belong to the intelligence service of the state presidency. On his bare office wall was an image of Ayatollah Khomeini – Imam Khomeini, as he is officially called in the Islamic Republic – hovering miraculously above his own tomb. On the desk below was a large pile of photocopied articles from Western academic journals, analysing transitions to democracy.

Perhaps only in Iran could you sit inside a secret service building with a mystical image of the Ayatollah Khomeini gazing down on a pile of Western articles about transitions to democracy. But how on earth would these elements combine? As a result of the assassination attempt, Hajjarian, a frail, yellow-faced figure in a fawn-coloured tracksuit, can barely move his body and his speech is slurred. Yet his pithy answers conveyed a sharp political intelligence. He spoke, until he grew tired, of how the reformists could recover, rebuilding popular support through more professional organization and better use of the press and television. They should, he suggested, raise more funds from business and appeal to ordinary people's everyday material concerns, as Ahmadinejad successfully had in his campaign. But I came away from this encounter feeling that the prospects of a full recovery for the in-system Islamic reformists are little better than Hajjarian's own.

4

That scepticism is shared by the outspoken journalist Emadeddin Baghi, a former Islamic reformist who was jailed for more than two years because of his critical writing. Sitting in the neat, modern office of the non-governmental organization that he has founded for the defence of prisoners' rights, Baghi, a dark-bearded, courteous man in early middle age, told me that what is needed now is not reform from above, within the mullah-state – as Hajjarian still advocates – but organization from below, in civil society. I was reminded of central European dissidents after the failure of the Prague Spring and Dubček's 'socialism with a human face'. Like them, Baghi believes that the way forward is not ideological revisionism or in-system reform – former President Khatami's failed Khomeinism with a human face – but people organizing themselves in society independently of the state.

Although I found his general argument convincing, it struck me that Baghi, who still has a one-year suspended prison sentence hanging over his head, was talking about very modest attempts at social organization. He said plainly that such efforts should be confined to what the mullah-state would not find politically threatening. He knows very well that even prominent activists like himself and, more recently, close colleagues of the Nobel Peace Prize winner Shirin Ebadi can be locked up at any moment. And he knows that critical journals and newspapers are often simply shut down, as his own newspaper was.

Almost everyone I have mentioned thus far – from top officials of the current regime like President Ahmadinejad, through critics such as Hajjarian, Kadivar and Baghi, to political prisoners like Akbar Ganji – was once an active participant in the Islamic revolution. They are the children of the revolution. However, there are also many secular leftists and liberals who opposed the Shah but never participated in the Islamic revolution, and now work in NGOs, in publishing, in the universities or in cultural life, including the country's often electrifying moviemakers. One secular liberal especially well known in the West is Dr Ramin Jahanbegloo, the author of a book of conversations with Isaiah Berlin, who has brought thinkers such as Jürgen Habermas, Richard Rorty and Antonio Negri to lecture to passionately interested audiences of up to 2,000 people in Tehran.

Yet whether secular or Islamic, the room for manoeuvre of those working in what they like to call 'civil society' is quite limited. All NGOs, for example, have to be officially registered, and their permits renewed each year. Galley proofs of books have to be submitted for censorship by the Ministry for Culture and Islamic Guidance, and the censored pages must then be typeset again so that readers cannot tell where something has been excised. Universities are tightly controlled. Theoretical discussion of the merits of democracy is possible; practical criticism of the Guardianship of the Jurist is definitely not.

The very fact that the system has several centres of power adds an extra element of uncertainty. For example, I talked to one dissident student who was released by the official state security service only to be rearrested a few months later by the Revolutionary Guards. No one knows exactly where the limits are. As a result, there is both a remarkable freedom of intellectual debate and a permanent undercurrent of fear.

For someone who has studied the ways post-totalitarian or authoritarian dictatorships, whether in Europe, Latin America or South Africa, have gradually become less oppressive states, and eventually democracies, the main question about Iran is therefore this: what forces inside its society might help to increase peaceful social pressure for gradual regime change?

Industrial workers in Iran have so far shown no signs of organizing themselves, as Poland's did in the Solidarity movement twenty-five years ago. Among farmers there is much rural unemployment and some discontent. In a sun-baked mountain village, I talked to shepherds who told me that half their fellow villagers were unemployed. Many came out to the fields at night to take drugs. Yet the main response to rural misery is to migrate to the towns. There they swell the numbers of the urban poor who, rather than contributing to a political opposition, are more likely to be recruited as thugs or mobilized in the streets by the regime's Basij militia.

What of the rich, Westernized business leaders? The ones I talked to are witheringly critical of the regime in private, but dependent on it for their businesses. Some have formed commercial partnerships with leading mullahs. They would probably be willing to support an opposition movement at the moment of decisive change, like the oligarchs in Serbia and Ukraine, but not before. Anyway, they themselves point out that most of the Iranian economy is still in the hands of the traditional merchants of the country's teeming bazaars, the *bazaaris*, who range from tiny stallholders to big-time export–import operators. In Iran, the *bazaaris* have traditionally been allies of the Islamic clergy, the *ulama*, and so far there are few signs of their changing sides.

Meanwhile, the regime has major assets for preserving its power. With oil at more than $60 a barrel as I write, its oil revenues have within six months covered the entire state budget for the current accounting year. The government can generously subsidize basic foodstuffs – bread, tea, sugar, rice – and keep the price of fuel extremely low for the country's manic drivers. When I was there, petrol cost an astonishing 35 cents a gallon. A quarter of the workforce are state employees, dependent on the authorities for their jobs. The numerous security services are well provided for. Less than thirty years after an initially peaceful revolution that turned violent and oppressive, most people old enough to remember have little appetite for another revolution. And if the United States and Britain, the Great Satan and Perfidious Albion, try to increase the pressure from outside, Iran can make life more difficult for the foreign occupiers in the Shiite parts of Iraq, where the influence of the Islamic Republic continues to grow.

What, then, has this regime to fear? Only one thing, I conclude, but that a very big one: its own young people, the grandchildren of the revolution.

5

Iran is a remarkably old country, with some 2,500 years of continuous history. It is also a remarkably young country. Two thirds of its 70 million people are under thirty years of age. This is at least partly the result of deliberate policy: in the 1980s, the first decade after the revolution, the mullahs encouraged a baby boom, denouncing the decadent Western practice of birth control and calling for mass procreation to replace the country's million martyrs in the Iran–Iraq war. Patriotic couples who produced five or more infants were given a free building plot. The regime's propaganda called these children 'soldiers of the hidden imam'.

To turn these young people into good Islamic citizens, the mullahs opened a nationwide network of new universities, called the Islamic Free University, complementing the existing ones. According to the Iranian statistical yearbook for 1382 (that is, 2003–4), there are some 2 million students currently enrolled in higher education across Iran, roughly half of them women. And one should add to the brew more millions of recent graduates.

So now you see them everywhere, these 'soldiers of the hidden imam', talking on their mobile phones or flirting in the parks, the girls' *hijab*s a diaphanous pink or green, pushed well back to reveal some alluring curls of hair, while their rolled-up jeans deliberately show bare ankles above smart, pointed leather shoes. In the cities, the supposedly figure-concealing long black jackets that were previously required have often been replaced by skimpy, figure-hugging white or pink versions. In a teahouse under the arches of a seventeenth-century brick bridge in Esfahan, I met a beautiful young woman, heavily made up and wearing perfume, who was flaunting a good four inches of bare calf above ankles decorated with costume pearl bracelets. Yes, she giggled, there's a rumour that under the new government they'll be introducing a fine of 25,000 tomans (about

$15) for each centimetre of exposed flesh – but she didn't care. Even in the provincial birthplace of the Sun of Khomein, young women were wearing Western-style jeans and shoes under their close-fitting jackets.

The clothes worn by men have a less familiar symbolic language. A law student came to see me dressed in a dark suit and tie. At first, I thought he must be a young fogey. I could not have been more wrong. Because the regime's regulation dress for men is strictly tie-less (as was President Ahmadinejad when he addressed the UN), to wear a suit and tie is a mark of brave nonconformity. Another student, who had been imprisoned several times for dissident activity, told me, 'The tie is a sign of protest!'

Often, their protest takes unpolitical forms. Many want to emigrate and join the millions of Iranians already living abroad. I was repeatedly told of this generation's hedonism; of wild parties behind the high walls of apartment buildings in prosperous north Tehran, with Western pop music, alcohol, drugs and sexual play. One T-shirt I spotted in the Tehran bazaar said, 'Wanted: Meaningless Overnight Relationship'. If they can afford it, they slip over to Dubai for a few days, where the young women can tear off the *hijab* and jive as they please.

Yet for long and memorable hours I met with many serious-minded, impressive young people, most of them well informed about their own country and keen to improve it. They can learn a lot from the local press, if they read carefully. They listen to Western radio stations (the BBC's Persian service or the US-backed Radio Farda), and they watch satellite television, which, though officially prohibited, is accessible to an estimated one in four Iranians. They use the Internet very inventively. Some politically or morally suspect websites are blocked on Iranian servers – that of the dissenting Grand Ayatollah Hossein-Ali Montazeri (montazeri.com), for example, or, rather curiously, that of the University of Virginia. (The experienced Iranian Web surfer who alerted me to this suggests that the Islamic censors' automatic search engines must have detected the word 'virgin' in Virginia.) But they have ways of getting around the blocks.

Iran also has at least 50,000 bloggers. One student explained that since these blogs are often anonymous, people can speak their minds freely, in a way they generally don't dare to even in circles of student friends, since among those friends might be a regime spy. Alluding to the regime's own euphemistic description of its intelligence agents as 'unknown soldiers of the hidden imam', students call them, with heavy irony, 'soldiers of the hidden imam'. Which is, of course, what they themselves were supposed to be.

The regime has spent twenty-five years trying to make these young Iranians deeply pro-Islamic, anti-American, anti-Western and anti-Israeli. As a result, most of them are resentful of Islam (at least in its current, state-imposed form) and rather pro-American, and have a friendly curiosity about Israel. One scholar, himself an Islamic reformist, suggested that Iran is now – under the *hijab*, so to speak – the most secular society in the Islamic world. Many also dream of life in America, sporting baseball caps that say, for example, 'Harward [*sic*] Engineering School'. Quite a few young Iranians even welcomed the invasion of Iraq, hoping it would bring freedom and democracy closer to them. Seeing how the US invasion has benefited the Shiites in southern Iraq, they joke that President George W. Bush is 'the thirteenth imam'.

These 45 million young people are the best hope there is of peaceful regime change in the Islamic Republic of Iran. Their 'soft power' could be more effective than forty-five divisions of the US Marines. One positive legacy of the eight years of Khatami's reformist presidency is that this generation has grown up with less fear than its predecessors. The students at Tehran University launched a large-scale protest in summer 1999. They will never forgive Khatami for allowing it to be suppressed. Each year since, a small number of them have tried to mark the anniversary with demonstrations, which have been broken up by the police. Repression is fierce: as I write, a well-known student leader has just been condemned to six years in prison. Yet the impression I got from those I talked to is that they intend to struggle on, perhaps with subtler and more inventive forms of protest.

The potential of what I came to think of as Young Persia is huge. These young Iranians are educated, angry, disillusioned, impatient, and when they leave college most of them will not find jobs appropriate to their training. Given time and the right external circumstances, they could take the lead in exerting the kind of organized social pressure that would allow – and require – the advocates of reform, even of transformation, to gain the upper hand inside the dual state.

The United States would, however, be making a huge mistake if it concluded that these young Iranians are automatic allies of the West – and, so to speak, soldiers of the thirteenth imam. Their political attitudes towards the West are complex, often deeply confused and volatile. Unlike in neighbouring Turkey, even the most outspoken would-be democratizers don't envisage their country becoming part of the West. They seek a specifically Iranian version of modern society. If they see their ancient civilization in a wider regional setting at all, they call it the Middle East or Asia. 'We Oriental people,' one student activist prefaced his remarks. Moreover, they are as ill informed about Western policies and realities as they are well informed about Iran's.

What of Iran's nuclear programme? That was not a pressing concern for the young people I met. None of them raised the issue in conversation with me. When I asked them about it, they fell into two groups. The first group felt that Iran, a proud but insecure nation flanked by neighbours already possessing nuclear weapons, has a right not just to civilian nuclear power but also to nuclear weapons. The second felt that a democratic Iran should undoubtedly have such a right, but they would rather this repressive regime did not obtain nuclear weapons. Yet both insisted with equal vehemence that an American or Israeli bombing of nuclear installations, let alone an Iraq-style invasion, would be a wholly unacceptable response to Iran's nuclear ambitions.

'I love George Bush,' said one thoughtful and well-educated young woman, as we sat in the Tehran Kentucky Chicken restaurant, 'but I would hate him if he bombed my country.' She would oppose even a significant tightening of economic sanctions on those grounds. A perceptive local analyst reinforced the point. Who or what, he asked, could give this regime renewed popular support, especially among the young? 'Only the United States!'

If, however, Europe and the United States can avoid that trap; if whatever we do to slow down the nuclearization of Iran does not end up merely slowing down the democratization of Iran; and if, at the same time, we can find policies that help the gradual social emancipation and eventual self-liberation of Young Persia, then the long-term prospects are good. The Islamic revolution, like the French and Russian revolutions before it, has been busy devouring its own children. One day, its grandchildren will devour the revolution.

2005

In the 'Green Movement' of sustained mass protest in 2009, the grand-children of the revolution showed what they were prepared to do. The movement was crushed, for now, as such non-violent movements often are at the first attempt. But I stand by my prediction.

East Meets West

Kangaroos, I read in the *South China Morning Post*, originally came from China. The paper's source is Australia's Centre of Excellence for Kangaroo Genomics, so it must be true. Whatever next. Pandas originating in France? Kiwis from Costa Rica?

The time is out of joint. The skies are full of portents. Yesterday's financial titans are reduced to dust, while General Motors has become a beggar at the door of government. The world is being reshaped before our eyes, and in Hong Kong some of the world's sharpest traders quietly mark the shifts.

Seen from Hong Kong, this unique meeting point of East and West, a first and obvious shift is from West to East. More specifically: the strengthening of China's hand and the weakening of America's. As one navigates around Hong Kong's archipelago of skyscrapers, connected by overhead walkways, one now looks with some concern at the AIG Tower and perhaps with a little more respect at the dark-glass cutting edge of I. M. Pei's Bank of China tower – although Norman Foster's HSBC still seems to be holding up well. On television, one flicks between the all-American footballer turned treasury secretary Hank Paulson uncharacteristically losing his cool before a congressional committee, as his bail-out seems to need bailing out, and Hu Jintao advancing serenely with a 600-strong delegation to the Asia–Pacific summit in Peru, where the Chinese president will sign a bilateral trade deal that could see China overtake the US as Peru's leading trading partner.

Interviewed on a regional channel, the Indian finance minister notes with satisfaction that the Washington financial summit was of the G20, not just of the G8. That's how it should be, he says, and how it should remain. The Chinese leadership's rictus of developmental modesty ('A superpower? What, us?') slips for a moment as Jin Liqun, who chairs the supervisory board of China's sovereign wealth fund, says developed countries should seek help from developing countries such as China 'with humility'. Referring to the request for an additional capital injection into the IMF, he comments, 'Nobody is going to play with you if you want China to spend money amid the deepening financial crisis while still giving us little voting power.'

Will an ideological shift accompany the power shift? It's plainly true that American-style free market economics are under something of a cloud, even in such a hothouse of free market trading as Hong Kong – while the mainland Chinese mix of a more statist market economy, with huge accumulated reserves to draw on in such a crisis, looks rather brighter. I'm told some Chinese Hongkongers do read it that way, even with a tinge of national pride. But they are also far too familiar with all the weaknesses of the Chinese system, as experienced by their mainland relatives and friends – the inequality, the corruption, the insecurity and, yes, the inefficiency – to fall for any simplistic notion of a shining Chinese model.

In fact, the story I'm told here is a much more interesting and subtle one. It's the story of a great, pragmatic debate across the whole of China, one in which Hong Kong Chinese intellectuals and civil society activists can and do participate. How does a Chinese society combine the efficiency of a market economy, tapping a native entrepreneurial spirit comparable to America's, with some degree of equity, social cohesion or even 'harmony'? Behind those big, round words is an often desperate and unstable social reality that has citizens of the People's Republic frequently going on the streets to protest – the Ministry of Public Security recorded some 74,000 'mass incidents' in 2004 – and even, as happened in November 2008 in Gansu province, to battle riot police and trash government buildings. How do you make this thing work? All suggestions welcome. Well, almost all.

To be sure, the ideological framing remains significant. President Hu is not going to pursue something he calls 'democratic capitalism', and soon to be ex-president George Bush will not embrace 'socialism with American characteristics'. But underneath the big labels, the realities are often surprising. For example, most people would think of the United States as the land of small government and China as a land of big government. But the Chinese scholar Wang Shaoguang estimates that in China today central and local government together still only redistribute some 20 per cent of GDP. In the US, the figure is much higher; how high depends on which federal state you live in, but government certainly redistributes more in blue America than it does in red China.

What really matters is what works. Some people here extend this complex pragmatism even to the political system. It's not just democracy or no democracy, they say, white or black. There are many shades of democracy. The intriguing suggestion is made that the system Hong Kong uses to 'elect' its chief executive – which combines an election committee composed mainly of nominated representatives of so-called functional constituencies (different sectors of the economy, religious groups, even twenty members representing Chinese medicine) with the ultimate say-so of the authorities – is one model the Chinese leadership is looking at, as it considers how to extend what it calls democracy in its own system.

If true, that's fascinating, and would be progress. But the impression of the 2008 American presidential election is still too fresh in my mind to buy the claim that this is all democracy. Yes, there are many variations between outright tyranny and liberal democracy, but

somewhere along the way there is a bright line; and it's not that difficult to find. Here's the test: if you don't know who's going to win the
election, you're probably in a democracy. We weren't sure Obama was
going to win – remember? Who will succeed Hu is not a choice the
Chinese people will make. The line is clear, and fundamental.

When it comes to the socio-economic system, however – to the
complex negotiations between growth, social cohesion and environmental sustainability, or between the roles of the public and private
sector – then I do believe that, within the universe of market
economies, there is no longer any simple clear line, no black and
white. Just as mainland China, Hong Kong and even Taiwan are in
a complex and sometimes indirect conversation about how you do
this in a Chinese society, so it would be entirely meaningful for
Chinese policymakers to sit down with the leaders of India or Brazil
and say: so how do you handle this issue there? This is how we're
trying to do it here.

Rudyard Kipling, the poet of British Empire who naturally visited
Hong Kong, wrote a famous poem called 'The Ballad of East and
West': 'Oh, East is East, and West is West, and never the twain shall
meet . . .' No longer true, if it ever was. They meet and mingle all
the time. The poem goes on: ' . . . there is neither East nor West
. . . / When two strong men stand face to face . . .' These days, it's
more a matter of: there is neither East nor West when weak governments try to meet the demands of restless peoples, on an overheating
planet.

2008

The Brotherhood against Pharaoh

In front of the towering golden sandstone entrance to the temple of Edfu stands an imposing granite statue of a falcon, some 12 feet tall, representing Horus, a premier league Egyptian god. Sculpted into his chest is a small figure of one of the Greek rulers of Egypt at the time when the temple was built. To buttress his political legitimacy, the alien neo-pharaoh had not merely wrapped himself in the flag but carved himself into the stone of a powerful god. The rulers of Egypt have been playing this game for thousands of years – and they are at it again today.

More than three millennia before the birth of Christ, when ancient Britons were still wandering the primal forests in skins, behaving like proleptic football thugs, the first dynasty of the pharaohs had already built a unified kingdom down the valley of the Nile, and they were treated as demi-gods. Later they presented themselves as children and intimates of the sun-god Ra, of Isis and Osiris, and of their divine offspring, the falcon-headed god Horus.

Gods were great for keeping you in power, but they were also fungible. Over the centuries, as the politics changed, there were god-mergers and corporate god-takeovers. Luxor luminary Amun and sun-god Ra merged to become Amun-Ra, a strong new brand. The

Ptolemaic successors of Alexander the Great promoted Serapis, a deliberate blending of Greek and Egyptian gods. At the Graeco-Roman temple of Philae, you see a mother and child image sculpted on the walls of the sanctuary, but the face of the mother has been chiselled away. In a Christian time, Isis was thus crudely rebranded Mary, turning the falcon-god Horus into Jesus.

Later, there was Allah, of course, and his messenger Muhammad. For the nineteenth-century Albanian-born Muhammad Ali Pasha, the new divinity was European-style modernity. For Napoleon and Lord Cromer there were the Western gods of progress and civilization, carried by the bayonet and the Gatling gun. For Nasser, the architect of post-colonial Egypt, there was pan-Arabism but also socialism, with added Islam.

Now they're changing gods again at the pharaoh's palace. Twenty-six years into the reign of President Mubarak, amendments are proposed to the constitution. Article 1, instead of reading 'the Arab Republic of Egypt is a democratic, socialist state based on an alliance of the working forces of the people', is to say simply 'the Arab Republic of Egypt is a democratic state, based on citizenship . . .'. Socialism is being excised like the face of Isis at Philae. References to it are to be removed from nine other articles of the constitution.

Despite the opposition of secular and Coptic Christian politicians, article 2 will continue to describe sharia as 'the principal source' for Egyptian legislation. At the same time, by banning both political parties based on religion and independent candidates in presidential elections, the president's ruling National Democratic party aims to keep its principal enemy, the outlawed but popular Muslim Brotherhood, out of any future competition for legal political power. So it tries to embrace Islam while fighting Islamism.

Politics, seen from this perspective of 5,000 years of Egyptian history, is something very different from what you find in US civics textbooks. It's not about the installation of this or that logically and legally constructed political system, based on this or that ideology.

It's about rulers borrowing, bending and merging gods, ideologies and legal systems, adapting to internal and external forces, mixing coercion and patronage, sharing some of the spoils where necessary, but always with the goal of maximizing your own power and wealth, and hanging on to it for as long as possible – for yourself, and your children, and your children's children. Those who take the legitimating religion or ideology too seriously – be it Osirisism or socialism – are missing the point. The gods come and go; what endures over the millennia is men's lust for power and wealth, and their vain quest for immortality.

Which brings us back to the regime of President Hosni Mubarak, who is seventy-eight years old. Although he has been re-elected until 2011, a succession crisis – that bane of all authoritarian regimes – is looming. One thing that brought people on to the streets in the Kifaya ('Enough!') protest movement, during the run-up to the presidential election in 2005, was the prospect that he might be grooming his son, Gamal Mubarak, to succeed him. 'Despite the police, no to extension, no to succession!' chanted the veteran left-wing activist Kamal Khalil. 'Oh, Egypt,' he continued, 'you still have a palace, you still have slums, tell those who live on Orouba [a boulevard in a neighbourhood with many grand houses, including the president's residence] that we live ten to one room.'

For now, President Mubarak has seen off the Kifaya movement and he has also seen off the short-lived US pressure for rapid democratization. The military, police and security service foundations of his rule seem as solid as the mighty pylons of the temple at Karnak. (They also render valuable services to the Pentagon, including extensive overflight facilities and the dirty business of extraordinary rendition.) He has a rather impressive prime minister, Dr Ahmed Nazif, a computer scientist by education, who described to me his government's push to integrate Egypt into the global economy. They are lowering barriers to trade and investment, and achieved growth of more than 5 per cent last year. Gamal Mubarak, who has an MBA and used to work for the Bank of America, is one of the driving forces behind the government's new free market agenda. But the economic benefits will only trickle down to the poor, if at all, in the longer term, while the costs will be felt sooner – for example, in the reduction of state subsidies for petrol and household fuel.

For many of those who live ten to one room in the poorer quarters of Cairo, the great myth remains that of the Muslim Brotherhood, with its brilliantly simple slogan 'Islam is the solution'. So long as it is banned, the Brotherhood does not need to demonstrate how exactly Islam is the solution. It can hardly be expected to produce detailed, specific policies, let alone to deliver on them. In fact, the Mubarak regime is performing the Brotherhood a great service by continuing to persecute it. Trying to strangle Islamism, it feeds its growth. And the secular left-wing and Coptic Christian oppositionists, to whom I have talked, feel themselves caught between the devil and the deep green sea. (Green as in the colour of Islam.) On many cultural issues, including women's rights, they actually regard the Mubarak regime as the lesser evil.

Whatever happens in the transition from Hosni Mubarak over the next decade – whether we get President Mubarak II, or a candidate supported by the military, or someone else – I would bet on one thing: the Islamic component in the legitimating god-mix of Egyptian politics is likely to grow stronger, not weaker. If you find that worrying, I can suggest only one faint consolation: in time, it will pass. The process may take decades, but one day Islamism, too, will join the 5,000-year line of the gods that failed.

2007

Cities of No God

They generally start working in the drug gangs at thirteen or fourteen. The oldest are about twenty-one. What happens afterwards? 'Most of them are dead.' They are killed in gunfights with other criminals and the police, or murdered in the city's hellish prisons. I'm standing in one of the twisting mud alleys of the shantytown in Royal Park. All around, just a few hundred metres away, I can see the apartment blocks of one of the richer residential districts of São Paulo, each smartly painted block surrounded by high walls and electric fences. Rich kids from the private school across the road drop into the shantytown for their fix of dope or crack. 'It's a kind of drive-through,' says my guide, a university graduate who has chosen to live here and work on a community project.

How do mothers react if their sons join the drug gang? 'They go to church.' Emerging from a narrow alley, we find one of the neo-Pentecostal churches that are so popular among Brazil's poor – actually little more than a shabby, breeze-block house, with a hand-painted sign. In front of the church stands a group of teenagers in smart tracksuits and sneakers. 'No photographs,' snaps my guide. They are the dealers. These kids prefer a short, exciting life in a drug gang to the prospect of weary years spent as a gardener, car washer or dog-walker for the surrounding rich. It beats school any day. Even as a rookie look-out, you earn more than your teacher does. Why bother with education?

Returning at dusk along a street of small shack-like stores and bars, we meet a guy with dreadlocks, introduced as 'Cocoa'. He's a hip-hop artist, stage-name 'MC Magus'. Does he sing about their everyday life? Sure he does. Right there in the dusty street he begins to rap: 'Identical days that are hard to bear, a people locked in drudgery / chained by norms, proposals and homicides.' (It sounds better with Portuguese rhymes and a hip-hop beat.) He sings of oppression, hope-lessness and a discrimination which is also racial – for the majority of the people here, as in most of the shantytowns, are black. Afterwards his girlfriend prints me a copy of this song – 'Walking in the Darkness' – from her aged computer in their tiny, breeze-block house; and we talk. In some ways, things have got better since the drug gangs took over, says MC Magus. At least they keep the peace inside the shanty-town. And the police? He laughs. They only drop in to collect their cut of the drug money.

Of the more than 19 million people who inhabit the vast urban sprawl of Greater São Paulo, an estimated 2.5 million live in the shantytowns, or *favelas*. The one in Royal Park is among the best. 'Oh, that's the Chelsea of the *favelas*,' a local expert on urban violence tells me, with a smile.

To see worse you have to drive out for at least an hour to some-where like São Bernardo, the borough where the country's President Lula grew up in extreme poverty and made his name as a car workers' union leader. Here the shanty hovels crawl across the landscape for as far as the eye can see. For those who live there, my hour by car translates into four hours by bus and on foot to get to work (if they are lucky) as a domestic servant in one of the leafy neighbourhoods. 'My maid' is the characteristic opening of the descriptions of the urban poor that one receives from the good left-liberals of São Paulo, over an excellent lunch in one of the city's outstanding restaurants.

As in: 'My maid has to get up at four in the morning to be at my apartment by eight.'

Brazil is, next to India and the United States, one of the world's largest democracies. It has been a serious democracy for just under twenty years and has passed the test of peaceful transfer of power between rival parties and presidents. This young democracy has survived economic crises, a creakingly complex federal system and recurrent corruption scandals. It has a vibrant, combative free press. The military, which used to run the place, now takes a back seat. It is, in many ways, an inspiring experiment. But the question Brazil poses is how long you can sustain a liberal democracy with such extremes of inequality, poverty, social exclusion, crime, drugs and lawlessness. Next door, in Hugo Chávez's Venezuela, you see the ever-present populist temptation.

Indeed, there is a question how far you can really call this a liberal democracy, given such extremes. The Brazilian legal scholar Oscar Vilhena Vieira argues that you can't properly talk of the rule of law – one of the essentials of liberal as opposed to merely electoral democracy – when there is no basic equality before the law. Here, the privileged few are above the law (a Brazilian Paris Hilton would not find herself behind bars) and the impoverished many are beneath it. The rich enjoy virtual immunity from the local police, and the local police enjoy virtual immunity for anything they might do to the poor, who also happen mainly to be black. In the *favelas*, most murders go not merely unpunished but uninvestigated. In a state school in São Bernardo, I'm invited to take over an English language class for a few minutes. What would the children like to be when they grow up, I ask. 'A policeman!' shouts one eleven-year-old boy. And why would he like to be a policeman? 'So I can kill people.' He makes shooting gestures with his hands. Bang bang.

I tell this just as it happened. I did not ask a deliberately leading question. And I double-checked the translation of what the kid said. To stumble so easily into a world that, in its essentials, closely resembles the poverty, drug-driven violence and police corruption portrayed in Fernando Meirelles's riveting film *City of God* – minus the pulsating music and glorious Technicolor – is quite shocking.

But one must avoid the trap of journalistic cliché and not ignore the other side of the story. MC Magus told me he didn't like Meirelles's film because it only showed the bad stuff. Most people here tried to pursue decent, working lives, despite the awful conditions. He himself works long hours doing pizza delivery on his motorbike. Only yesterday they had a great street party to celebrate a popular saint's day. In the *favelas*, there is a small but growing number of small businesses and entrepreneurs. Impressive NGO activists, like my guide, try to open people's horizons, with computers, theatre, sport or hip-hop.

Under two successive presidents, Lula and his predecessor Fernando Henrique Cardoso, governments have tried to expand job opportunities, professional training and, above all, basic schooling. Some two thirds of the children in the school where I was briefly a guest teacher are there partly because their families receive cash benefits on condition that the child attends school 85 per cent of the time. (The money is paid directly to the mother.) 'The kids with benefits show up,' said the school's director. How much they learn is another question, given that they come in three shifts, morning, afternoon and evening, with forty-five to a class and desperately underpaid, overworked teachers. But at least some wish to learn.

'I want to be a doctor,' said a girl in the third row, following the would-be policeman. Why? 'I want to save lives.' The future of liberal democracy in Brazil will depend on which of these two children is better able to realize their childhood dreams.

2007

Beyond Race

Some time ago, Brazil's census takers asked people to describe their skin colour. Brazilians came up with 134 terms, including *alva-rosada* (white with pink highlights), *branca-sardenta* (white with brown spots), *café com leite* (coffee with milk), *morena-canelada* (cinnamon-like brunette), *polaca* (Polish), *quase-negra* (almost black) and *tostada* (toasted). This often light-hearted poetry of self-description reflects a reality you see with your own eyes, especially in the poorer parts of Brazil's great cities.

Walking through the City of God, a poor housing estate just outside Rio de Janeiro – and the setting for the film of that name – I saw every possible tint and variety of facial feature, sometimes in the same household. Alba Zaluar, a distinguished anthropologist who has worked for years among the people of the district, told me they make jokes about it between themselves: 'You little whitey', 'You little brownie', and so on. And those features, with their diversity and admixture, are often beautiful.

Brazil is a country where people celebrate, as a national attribute, the richness of miscegenation, giving a positive meaning to what is, in its origins, an ugly North American misnomer. There is, however, a nasty underside to this story. 'Racial democracy' is an established, early twentieth-century Brazilian self-image, by contrast with a then still racially segregated United States. Yet the reality even today is that most non-whites are worse off economically, socially and educationally than most whites. And part of this inequality is due to racial discrimination.

I went to Brazil asking questions about poverty, social exclusion and inequality. Within minutes, my interlocutors were talking about race. This happened, too, in a conversation with the impressive former president, Fernando Henrique Cardoso. In a vivid memoir, *The Accidental President of Brazil*, he recalls his own research as a young sociologist in the shantytowns. Noting the extensive blending of the races, he nonetheless concluded that 'in general terms, to be black was to be poor in Brazil.'

To address this problem his government initiated affirmative action programmes, and these have grown under President Lula. Many universities now have quotas both for applicants from state schools and for black undergraduates. Those for black students are the object of fierce controversy. First, there are objections of principle. Maria-Tereza Moreira de Jesus, a black poet and writer, has said, 'Racism exists, from how one is treated in a shop to being interviewed for a job, but basing entrance on race is another form of racism.' MC Magus told me he thought such quotas were a bad idea. 'We are all equal,' he said.

There is also a practical difficulty. In such a mixed society, how do you decide who is black? The problem was graphically illustrated by the case of identical twins, Alex and Alan Teixeira da Cunha, who both applied to the University of Brasilia under its quota scheme. Alan was accepted as black, Alex rejected as not black. The university actually has a commission that determines race on the basis of photographs of the candidates, using phenotypes including hair, skin colour and facial features. The person who first told me about this was Jewish. 'You can imagine what I think of it,' he said.

Some of the country's very active black movements prefer the term

'Afro-descendant'. But a recent scientific study of mitochondrial and nuclear DNA estimates that upwards of 85 per cent of the population – including tens of millions of Brazilians who regard themselves as white – have a more than 10 per cent African contribution to their genome. Those early Portuguese settlers usually didn't bring their wives with them.

That leaves the subjective self-definition Brazil has traditionally used. Recent figures from the official institute for geography and statistics suggest that some 50 per cent of Brazilians classify themselves as 'white', a little more than 40 per cent as 'brown', just over 6 per cent as 'black', and less than 1 per cent as 'indigenous' or 'yellow' – that is, of Asian, especially Japanese, descent. These are direct translations of the five categories offered. In a bold move, representatives of the black movements, some of them supported by North American foundations, have proposed that the whole non-white population should be classed as black. Then everything would be simple – black and white.

Others cry in horror that this would be to import the worst of American-style racial classification and to deny the whole Brazilian specificity of miscegenation. If there really have to be university admission quotas by colour – something courts in the US have declared to be discriminatory – let them at least be based on the traditional Brazilian method of self-identification. In the past, people have tended to define themselves as being towards the lighter end of the spectrum, especially as they became more prosperous. 'Money whitens,' a sociologist dryly observes. If quotas were to result in a few more people preferring to be black, so be it. After so many centuries when it was more advantageous to be white – slavery was only abolished in Brazil in 1888 – there's a case for stacking the cards just a little the other way. And if that means that one day a girl most people would consider to be white applies to university as black, well, good luck to her.

As a non-Brazilian, I am in no position to adjudicate on this argument. I can see the powerful case against colour quotas; I can also see the tough, inherited reality of discrimination that must be addressed. Brazilians will decide this themselves. But I would say with all my heart that I hope Brazil moves closer to making a reality of its old myth of 'racial democracy', rather than retreating to anachronistic racial pigeonholing and the reduction of complex identities to a single attribute. For what I discovered in Brazil is also an anticipation of all our futures, in a world where peoples will be increasingly mixed up together.

I realize, of course, the danger of seeming like an affluent, white outsider – well, not so much white as *alva-rosada* – who sallies into the shantytowns for a few days and exclaims, 'How beautiful these people are!' I could write the satire myself. Yet I will say it. What I glimpsed in Brazil, even amidst the poverty and drug-driven violence of the City of God, was the beauty of miscegenation. I learned to celebrate it from Brazilians themselves.

It is precisely this mixing that has helped to make Brazilians among the most handsome human beings on earth. What is foreshadowed here – but I repeat, only if Brazil can correct its dreadful social and economic imbalances, including a heritage of discrimination – is the possibility of a world in which skin colour is nothing more than a physical attribute, like the colour of your eyes or the shape of your nose, to be admired, calmly noted or joked about. And a world in which the only race that matters is the human race.

2007

6.
Writers and Facts

The Brown Grass of Memory

Granted: he was a member of the Waffen-SS. But suppose that revelation had not overshadowed the publication of Günter Grass's memoir, like a mushroom cloud. What should we have made of *Peeling the Onion*? We should, I believe, have said that this is a wonderful book, a return to classic Grass territory and style, after long years of disappointing, wooden and sometimes insufferably hectoring works from his tireless pen, and a perfect pendant to his great 'Danzig trilogy' of novels, starting with *The Tin Drum*. That is what we should still say, first and last.

An account of his life from the outbreak of the Second World War in September 1939, when as an eleven-year-old war-enthusiast he collected fragments of shrapnel from the first fighting in his native Danzig, to the publication of *The Tin Drum* in 1959, *Peeling the Onion* repeatedly surprises, delights and moves with passages of great descriptive power. He enables us not merely to see but to hear, touch and smell life in the tiny, two-room apartment in Danzig where he grew up, with a shared lavatory on the staircase – 'a stink-cell, the walls of which fingers had smeared'.[1] From this suffocating narrowness the teenager longed to escape into what he saw as the romantic, heroic world of service in the Führer's armed forces. So at the age of fifteen he volunteered to fight on a U-boat, but his offer was not accepted.

No writer is better at evoking smell – that literary Cinderella among the senses. Few novelists have written more lovingly about food, celebrating hearty German sausage and coldwater fish. Everything of the earth earthy, of the flesh fleshly, belongs naturally to Grassland. His characteristic, deeply realistic mixing of the public and private is both touching and funny. For the adolescent him, he recalls, the flow and, increasingly, ebb of the German armies on the eastern front, though worrying, was of far less pressing concern than the unpredictable ebb and flow of his own penis. This he detailed, at length, to his father-confessor.

When he is drafted into the armed forces at the age of sixteen, in the autumn of 1944, and finds himself in a unit of the Waffen-SS, his reaction to the hardships of training is to stop in a quiet corner of the woods through which he has been ordered to carry a daily pot of coffee to his company's *Unterscharführer* and *Hauptscharführer* – and to piss into their coffee. He does this repeatedly, 'my regular morning act of revenge', and speculates that it helped him to keep going, to survive even the most sadistic treatment 'with an inner grin', unlike the poor fellow in a neighbouring company who hangs himself on the strap of his gas mask.

The account of his tank unit's desperate action in April 1945, almost surrounded by advancing Russian troops, is one of the most vivid descriptions of the experience of war that I have read: Tolstoy crossed with Vonnegut. He hides under a tank from the rockets of one of the Red Army's so-called 'Stalin organs' and wets his pants from fear. In the silence after the rockets stop, he distinctly hears beside him a loud, sustained chattering of teeth. The chattering teeth, he discovers when he crawls out from under the tank, belong to a senior officer of the Waffen-SS. The young enthusiast's image of the Teutonic hero begins to crumble. On the ground around them, 'body parts were to be found.'

He gets lost behind Russian lines. Wandering in the woods,

exhausted, hungry and afraid, he hears someone nearby. Friend or foe? Nervously he intones the beginning of a German folk song about little Hans wandering out 'into the wide world' alone, 'Hänschen klein ging allein . . .' To his immeasurable relief the hidden stranger responds with the rest of the line, ' . . . in die weite Welt hinein'. Had the other man been a Russian, we would probably have no *Tin Drum*. Instead, he's an avuncular German corporal, who advises the now seventeen-year-old Grass to take off his Waffen-SS jacket. If he is captured, the Russians won't take kindly to those double runes.

There's a beautifully evoked moment of calm, as they wolf down potato soup from a field canteen in the spring sunshine. Through his descriptive powers, you can smell that soup, hear the sudden silence, feel the warmth of the sun on his face. Then all hell breaks loose again. The corporal has his legs shredded by shrapnel. In the ambulance, he asks Grass to feel down the top of his trousers and check that his cock and balls are still there. They are; but his legs will soon be amputated. Here is the human reality of war, whether at Austerlitz, Kursk or in Baghdad today. (Grass still has a shrapnel splinter in his left shoulder from that attack.)

There are other unforgettable passages. The portrait of his loving, aspirational mother, and her death of cancer, several years after the war, in a shabby, windowless hospital back room: 'Lenchen . . . mein Lenchen,' stammers the desolated husband. How his mother and sister refused to talk about what the Russian soldiers did to them at the moment of 'liberation', but how he finally gathers, from one remark his sister makes, that the mother had offered herself in the daughter's place – as the object, we understand, of serial rape. The evocation of his solitary wanderings through the ruined cities of post-war Germany, including a spell working in the coal mines where, over lunch down the shaft, old communists and old Nazis still argued furiously.

Fear and hunger are the twin sensations that permeate these pages. His chapter about seeing action with the Waffen-SS is entitled 'How

I Learned Fear'. His hunger is threefold. First, hunger for food, especially in American prisoner-of-war camps. Second, hunger for sex, described in a kind of lingering, amused physical detail that reminds me of the work of the English poet Craig Raine, whose poem 'The Onion, Memory' anticipates Grass's book-long metaphor.

Food and sex are united in a key Grass word, *Fleisch*, which in German means both meat, as in beef or pork, and the flesh, as in 'the spirit is willing but the flesh is weak.' Describing a wildly drunken four-in-the-bed wedding night, during his time as a coal miner, he writes that no onion skin of memory will bring back 'what happened between so much *Fleisch*'. 'Ach ja, das Fleisch,' says Father Fulgentius – one of the monks with whom the still notionally Catholic young man finds post-war board and lodging – and folds his hands defensively into the arms of his habit. In Grass, the flesh is made word.

The object of Grass's final hunger, after food and sex, is art. He calls his chapter about becoming an artist 'The Third Hunger'. Battling his way, alone, with a strong will and professed egoism, up the physical and social rubble mountains of post-war Germany, he becomes first a stonemason and part-time sculptor, then a graphic artist, then a poet, and only at the end, in his late twenties, a writer of prose, inspired by Alfred Döblin's *Berlin Alexanderplatz* and Joyce's *Ulysses*, both discovered and devoured in the library of the well-heeled, cultivated Swiss parents of his first wife, Anna. 'Anna's dowry', he calls it. The memoir ends with his finding, in Paris, what would become one of the most famous first lines of any novel: 'Granted: I am an inmate of a mental hospital.' And the rest is literature.

Like much of Grass's work, *Peeling the Onion* is too wordy. It could have done with the attentions of a red pencil wielded by a more fearless editor. He labours and labours yet again the metaphor of peeling the onion, until we wish that this tiresome vegetable – exhaustively illustrated, in various stages of dismantlement, in Grass's own drawings at the opening of each chapter – had long since been thrown into the rubbish bin. And he uses twice, in fairly trivial contexts, his own most famous syntactic trope, 'Granted: . . .' Wiser, surely, to keep that for something more important: something like, for example, the matter of a great German writer, one of whose main subjects is the entanglement of ordinary Germans in the Nazi past, himself keeping silent for more than sixty years about having been a member of the Waffen-SS. Yet this memoir still stands, and will stand when much else is forgotten, as a fine, mature work, the closing of a circle, a non-fiction companion to the incomparable *Tin Drum*.[2]

I

What of the revelation? On 11 August 2006, the *Frankfurter Allgemeine Zeitung* (*FAZ*) reported on its website that Grass had been a member of the Waffen-SS. Grass had revealed this himself in his then forth-coming memoir, and had confirmed it in an interview with the *FAZ* published in full the following day. This was the literary-political equivalent of a nuclear explosion. I can vividly remember my own sense of almost physical shock. The negative response in Germany was sustained and often savage, as can be seen in a documentation produced by Grass's publisher, *Ein Buch, ein Bekenntnis* ('A Book, a Confession'). A critic said Grass would never have won the Nobel Prize in literature had this been known, and a politician called on him to give it back. Joachim Fest, the well-known historian of Nazism, commented, 'I wouldn't even buy a used car from this man now.' Chancellor Angela Merkel said, 'I would have wished that we had been fully informed about his biography from the outset.' Columnists accused him of making the revelation to get publicity for his new book. Henryk M. Broder, an acerbic commentator, wrote that Grass had clambered his way up from membership in an 'elite troop' – a satirical reference to Grass's own description of how he probably viewed the Waffen-SS as a sixteen-year-old – to being a *Herrenmensch* of the cultural industry.

Grass's reaction to all this has been a curious mixture of surprise, bemusement and taking offence. As I watch the television interviews he has given on the subject, the author, still vigorous and physically imposing despite his nearly eighty years, reminds me of nothing so much as a tired old bear. Cornered, he lashes out. He denounces the 'kangaroo court' of press and television, led by the arts pages of the conservative *FAZ*, and the 'degeneration' of German journalism. This spring, he produced a volume of poems and drawings called *Dummer August* ('Stupid August'), evoking his pain, melancholy and anger during last summer's explosion. In a poem called 'Was Bleibt' ('What Remains') he describes how he spent three years writing his memoir: 'Then, however, a person skilled in the craft of malice cut one sentence from the extensive construction and placed it on a rostrum made of lies.'

'Was Bleibt' is a title made famous by the East German novelist Christa Wolf, herself the object of an earlier attack by the *FAZ* on account of her brief collaboration with the Stasi as a young communist writer. Now Grass dedicates *Dummer August* to Wolf because, as he explained in an interview at the Leipzig book fair, she too has been the object of attempted literary assassination by those horrible conservative hacks in Frankfurt.[3] There is something almost painfully symmetrical in this embattled solidarity of the outstanding German novelists of their generation, the West German tarred with the Nazi brush, the East German with the Stasi.[4] In that interview, Grass also explained how writing these poems kept him going psychologically through that harrowing summer: 'If I had been struck dumb, that would have been worse.' Six decades later, his handsomely produced volume of poems and drawings is thus the old trooper's artistic equivalent of pissing in the *Hauptscharführer*'s coffee pot. It tastes only a little better.

Grass does have half a point about the coverage of this story in the German press. All over the world there is a lamentable pattern of journalists first building up a celebrity to ludicrous heights, then tearing down the unreal statue they have themselves erected. What has happened to Grass is an outsize version of that familiar build 'em up, knock 'em down. There's also a generational edge to some of the German criticism. In effect, impatient younger critics, who themselves were fortunate enough never to be tested by the threats and temptations that Grass faced as a teenager – for they enjoyed what Helmut Kohl once called the 'mercy of a late birth' – are now exclaiming: get off the stage, old man, and let us take your place. This is the age-old literary parricide. The accusation that he was making this painful revelation just as a publicity trick for his new book is simply not worthy of the artistic and moral effort that will be evident to any fair-minded reader of *Peeling the Onion*. The PR charge says more about the mental world of those who make it than about that of the old bear.

Yet I'm afraid that Grass has only half a point. In fact, what is really surprising is that he is so surprised. Recalling the way in which Grass has repeatedly attacked leaders of the Federal Republic such as Helmut Kohl, the bishop of Kohl's home city of Mainz quotes Saint John: 'Let he who is without sin among you cast the first stone.' For more than forty years, ever since he became a famous writer, Günter Grass has been one of the literary world's most inveterate stone-throwers. In thousands of speeches, interviews and articles he has raged against US imperialism and capitalism; against German unification, which he furiously opposed, since a united Germany had 'laid the foundations of Auschwitz'; against Konrad Adenauer, Helmut Kohl and all their journalistic supporters. Like one of the Teutonic knights he admired as a child, he has laid about him to left and right – in recent years, mainly to right – with a bludgeon. He has set himself up as a political and moral authority, and delivered harsh judgements. His language has often been intemperate. Now it is payback time for all those he has criticized, directly or indirectly. In paying him back, some of his critics have fallen into precisely the mode that they previously criticized Grass for adopting: a simplistic, moralistic judgement, elevating the Nazi past to the single yardstick of morality or immorality.[5]

This said, both outrage and amazement seem in order. Outrage not at the fact that he served in the Waffen-SS as a teenager but at the way he has dealt with that fact since. According to the historian Bernd Wegner, a leading authority on the Waffen-SS, the 'Frundsberg' division in which Grass served as a tank gunner 'consisted mainly of members of the *RAD* [*Reichsarbeitsdienst*, 'Reich Labour Service'] who had been conscripted under duress'.[6] Since Grass had previously been conscripted into the Reich Labour Service, it seems likely that his earlier volunteering to fight in the U-boats had nothing to do with his being assigned to the Waffen-SS. There is no suggestion that he was involved in any atrocities. By his own account he hardly fired a shot in anger.

No, his war record is not the cause for outrage. Thousands of young Germans shared the same fate. Many died as a result. The offence is that he should for so many years have made it his stock-in-trade to denounce post-war West Germans' failure to face up to the Nazi past, while himself so spectacularly failing to come clean about the full extent of his own Nazi past. One painfully disappointed reaction comes from his most recent biographer, Michael Jürgs, whose life of Grass appeared in 2002. Grass spent many hours talking to Jürgs, yet allowed him to repeat the standard version that the novelist's war service had been as an auxiliary anti-aircraft gunner (he was also that, briefly, before going into the Waffen-SS), and then in the Wehrmacht. This is not merely 'keeping quiet' about your past. I'd say it counts as lying. What's more, if a conservative German politician had behaved like this, Grass himself would surely have called it lying, adding a few earthy adjectives to boot.

Worse still, knowing full well his own biography, he nonetheless denounced the joint visit by Ronald Reagan and Helmut Kohl to a cemetery in Bitburg in 1985 where, among many war dead, forty-nine Waffen-SS soldiers were buried. Of the forty-nine, thirty-two were under twenty-five years old. The youngest among them may well have been drafted like Günter Grass. He could have been one of them. To denounce the Bitburg visit without acknowledging that he himself had served in the Waffen-SS was an act of breathtaking hypocrisy, doublethink and recklessness.

Even more than outrage, there is sheer amazement. After all, Grass never made any secret of the fact that he had been an enthusiastic young Nazi. The strength of his writing, and his moral authority, came precisely from the fact that he could speak from inside about how ordinary Germans had become complicit with evil. If he had told the full truth, sometime in the 1960s, after the publication of *The Tin Drum*, it would only have strengthened the impact of his work and his voice. In fact it seems that he came close to it. A friend of his, Klaus Wagenbach, who then planned to write his biography, recently went back to the notes he had made from their conversations in 1963 and found there a reference to the SS.[7] But the biography was never written. If only it had been. Grass seems also to have shared the secret about his spell in the SS with at least one other close friend at the time. Why, then, did he take another forty years to acknowledge it in public?

'For decades,' he writes in *Peeling the Onion*:

I refused to acknowledge to myself the word and the double letters. What I accepted with the stupid pride of my youth, I wanted to cover up after the war, out of a growing sense of shame. But the burden remained and no one could lighten it. True, during my training as a tank gunner . . . nothing was to be heard of those war crimes that later came to light, but that claim of ignorance could not obscure the insight that I had been part of a system which had planned, organized and executed the extermination of millions of people. Even if I could be absolved of active complicity, there remained a residue, until today, of what is all too commonly called shared responsibility

[*Mitverantwortung*]. I will certainly have to live with it for the rest of my life.

When interviewers have pressed him on this issue, the answers have been vague and unsatisfactory. 'It oppressed me,' he told Frank Schirrmacher of the *FAZ*, in the original interview that sparked last summer's furore. 'My keeping silent over so many years is among the reasons for writing this book. It had to come out, at last.' Why only now? asked Ulrich Wickert of the German television channel ARD. 'It lay buried in me. I can't tell the reasons exactly.' At the Leipzig book fair this spring, he mused that he had to find the right literary form for this confession, and that, he said, meant waiting until he was of an age to write an autobiography. As if that explained a sixty-year silence.

In the absence of a convincing explanation from Grass himself, let me attempt an inevitably speculative answer. Perhaps he just missed the moment. Had the fact of his brief conscript service in the Waffen-SS come out in Wagenbach's biography in the mid-1960s, it would simply have become part of his story. The suggestion that he would never have been awarded the Nobel Prize if he had confessed to teenage conscript service in the Waffen-SS seems to me far-fetched. But as time went by; as more and more became known about atrocities committed by the Waffen-SS; as, after 1968, the condemnation of the way an older generation had covered up the Nazi past became ever louder; as Grass himself became one of the most strident voices in that chorus; so the price tag on the belated revelation became ever higher. Luther says somewhere that a lie is like a snowball rolling down a hill: the longer it rolls, the larger it gets.

Why come out with it now? As he approaches the end of his life – in his poems, he has a nice line about a new pair of leather shoes acting as if they plan to outlive their wearer – this clearly has oppressed him, psychologically and morally. There has been speculation that he feared researchers would find something in the archives

of the Stasi, who we know gathered potentially compromising material on the Nazi past of prominent West Germans. (It turns out that
the Stasi did not actually have this well-buried detail, but he could
not have known that they did not.) In any case, he must realistically
have reckoned that one day some thorough German academic would
turn up his prisoner-of-war record, with the poisonous three letters
W-SS. (It's reproduced in the documentary volume.) Rather as in
his old age François Mitterrand decided to talk about, and put his
own interpretation on, his Vichy past, so this was Grass's last chance
to say it his way. At the beginning of *Peeling the Onion*, Grass asks
himself why he wants to write this memoir and concludes his list
of reasons: 'because I want to have the last word.' Which, of course,
he won't.[8]

2

How should we judge the Grass affair? Judge it not in the 'kangaroo
court' of immediate press reaction, but calmly, considering all the
available evidence, as in the slow court of history. The first and obvious
point to make is that his achievement as a novelist is unaffected.
Auden said it better than anyone:

> Time that is intolerant
> Of the brave and the innocent,
> And indifferent in a week
> To a beautiful physique,
>
> Worships language and forgives
> Everyone by whom it lives;
> Pardons cowardice, conceit,
> Lays its honours at their feet.

Time that with this strange excuse
Pardoned Kipling and his views,
And will pardon Paul Claudel,
Pardons him for writing well.

('In Memory of W. B. Yeats', 1939)

And time will pardon Günter Grass. For the German language lives through him, as it does, in different ways, through Christa Wolf, and through the poet he befriended in Paris while he was writing *The Tin Drum*, Paul Celan.

His staunchest defenders claim that his standing as a political and moral authority is also unaffected. That seems to me implausible, to put it mildly; but not all his activism is equally affected. Probably his most distinctive political contribution has been to German–Polish reconciliation. A small token of his exemplary attitude is that he refers in his memoir to present-day Gdańsk, formerly Danzig, by its Polish name – something unusual among German writers. Poles were, of course, as shocked as anyone by the initial revelation, and Lech Wałęsa spontaneously said that Grass should be stripped of his honorary citizenship of Gdańsk.

But then Grass wrote a pained, dignified, apologetic letter to the mayor of Gdańsk. For me, the most moving text in the entire documentary record is the mayor's account of how he and his colleagues waited nervously for the novelist's letter (would he say what was needed? would he find the right tone?); received and read it with relief and appreciation; hurried to have it translated into Polish; then asked an actor to read it out loud to a large gathering in the City Hall. There was a moment's silence when the actor finished. Then the audience broke into a storm of applause. The mayor concludes his account, in the German version, 'Danzig versteht seinen Sohn.' Or, as he must have written in the original Polish, 'Gdańsk understands its son.'

So his Polish–German contribution stands. As for his tireless, blunderbuss criticism of the United States, those who like that kind of thing can surely continue to like it; those who don't will like it even less. What is clearly affected, and devalued, is his moralistic grandstanding about the failure of post-war West German conservatives, from Adenauer to Kohl, to face up to the Nazi past.

Yet, even here, let me attempt a rescue which goes beyond the realm of conscious intentions. What will be the effect of Grass's belated revelation? As he approaches the end of his life, as the memories of Nazism fade, as the activities of his SS-Frundsberg division become the object of weekend leisure war games in the United States,[9] Grass suddenly demolishes his own statue – not as a writer of fiction, but as a moral authority on frank and timely facing up to the Nazi past – and leaves its ruins lying as a warning beside the roadside, like Shelley's Ozymandias. Nothing he could say or write on this subject would be half so effective as the personal example that he has now left us. For sixty years even Günter Grass could not come clean about being a member of the Waffen-SS! Look, stranger, and tremble.

When I was starting to think about this mystery, I discussed it with a German friend, just a couple of years younger than the novelist but with a very different wartime biography. 'You know, I have a theory about that,' he said. 'I think Grass never was in the Waffen-SS. He's just convinced himself that he was.' I'm sure my friend didn't mean this literally. Rather, I understood his remark as a kind of poetic insight into the tortured and labyrinthine quality of German memory. 'But don't write it,' he added. 'Otherwise Grass will sue you for claiming he was not in the Waffen-SS.'

2007

The Stasi on Our Minds

One of Germany's most singular achievements is to have associated itself so intimately in the world's imagination with the darkest evils of the two worst political systems of the most murderous century in human history. The words 'Nazi', 'SS' and 'Auschwitz' are already global synonyms for the deepest inhumanity of fascism. Now the word 'Stasi' is becoming a default global synonym for the secret police terrors of communism. The worldwide success of Florian Henckel von Donnersmarck's deservedly Oscar-winning film *The Lives of Others* will strengthen that second link, building as it does on the preprogramming of our imaginations by the first. Nazi, Stasi: Germany's festering half-rhyme.

It was not always thus. When I went to live in Berlin in the late 1970s, I was fascinated by the puzzle of how Nazi evil had engulfed this homeland of high culture. I set out to discover why the people of Weimar Berlin behaved as they did after Adolf Hitler came to power. One question above all obsessed me: what quality was it, what human strain, that made one person a dissident or resistance fighter and another a collaborator in state-organized crime, one a Claus Count Stauffenberg, sacrificing his life in the attempt to assassinate Hitler, another an Albert Speer?

I soon discovered that the men and women living behind the Berlin Wall, in East Germany, were facing similar dilemmas in another German dictatorship, albeit with less physically murderous consequences. I could study that human conundrum not in dusty archives but in the history of the present. So I went to live in East Berlin and ended up writing a book about the Germans under the communist leader Erich Honecker, rather than under Adolf Hitler.[1] As I travelled around the other Germany, I was again and again confronted with the fear of the Stasi. Walking back to the apartment of an actor who had just taken the lead role in a production of Goethe's *Faust*, a friend whispered to me, 'Watch out, Faust is working for the Stasi.' After my very critical account of communist East Germany appeared in West Germany, a British diplomat was summoned to receive an official protest from the East German foreign ministry (one of the nicest book reviews a political writer could ever hope for) and I was banned from re-entering the country.

Yet this view of East Germany as another evil German dictatorship was by no means generally accepted in the West at that time. Even to suggest a Nazi–Stasi comparison was regarded in many parts of the Western left as outmoded, reactionary Cold War hysteria, harmful to the spirit of détente. The *Guardian* journalist Jonathan Steele concluded in 1977 that the German Democratic Republic was 'a presentable model of the kind of authoritarian welfare states which Eastern European nations have now become'. Even self-styled 'realist' conservatives talked about communist East Germany in tones very different from those they adopt today. Back then, the word 'Stasi' barely crossed their lips.

Two developments ended this chronic myopia. In 1989 the people of East Germany themselves finally rose up and denounced the Stasi as the epitome of their previous repression. That they often repressed at the same time – in the crypto-Freudian sense of the word 'repression' – the memory of their own everyday compromises and personal responsibility for the stability of the communist regime was but the other side of the same coin. After 1990, the total takeover of the former East Germany by the Federal Republic meant that, unlike in all other post-communist states, there was no continuity from old to new security services and no hesitation about exposing the evils of the previous secret police state. Quite the reverse.

In the land of Martin Luther and Leopold von Ranke, driven by a distinctly Protestant passion to confront past sins, the forcefully stated wish of a few East German dissidents to expose the crimes of the regime, and the desire of many West Germans (especially those from the class of 68) not to repeat the mistakes made in covering up and forgetting the evils of Nazism after 1949, we saw an unprecedentedly swift, far-reaching and systematic opening of the more than 110 miles of Stasi files. The second time around, forty years on, Germany was bent on getting its *Vergangenheitsbewältigung*, its past-beating, just right. Of course Russia's KGB, the big brother of East Germany's big brother, did nothing of the kind.

After some hesitation, I decided to go back and see if I had a Stasi file. I did. I read it and was deeply stirred by its minute-by-minute record of my past life: 325 pages of poisoned madeleine. Helped by the apparatus of historical enlightenment that Germany had erected, I was able to study in incomparable detail the apparatus of political intimidation that had produced this file. Then, working like a detective, I tracked down the acquaintances who had informed on me and the Stasi officers involved in my case. All but one agreed to talk. They told me their life stories, and explained how they had come to do what they had done. In every case, the story was understandable, all too understandable; human, all too human. I wrote a book about the whole experience, calling it *The File*.[2]

I

It was therefore with particular interest that I sat down to watch *The Lives of Others*, this already celebrated film about the Stasi, made by a West German director who was just sixteen when the Berlin Wall came down. Set in the Orwellian year of 1984, it shows a dedicated Stasi captain, Gerd Wiesler, conducting a full-scale surveillance operation on a playwright in good standing with the regime, Georg Dreyman, and his beautiful, highly strung actress girlfriend, Christa-Maria Sieland. As the case progresses, we see the Stasi captain becoming disillusioned with his task. He realizes that the whole operation has been set up simply to allow the culture minister, who is exploiting his position to extract sexual favours from the lovely Christa, to get his playwright rival out of his way. 'Was it for this we joined up?' Wiesler asks his cynical superior, Colonel Anton Grubitz.

At the same time, he becomes curiously enchanted with what he hears through his headphones, connected to the bugs concealed behind the wallpaper of the playwright's apartment: that rich world of literature, music, friendship and tender sex, so different from his own desiccated, solitary life in a dreary tower-block, punctuated only by brief, mechanical relief between the outsize mutton thighs of a Stasi-commissioned prostitute. In his snooper's hideaway in the attic of the apartment building, Wiesler sits transfixed by Dreyman's rendition of a piano piece called 'The Sonata of the Good Man' – a birthday present to the playwright from a dissident theatre director who, banned by the culture minister from pursuing his vocation, subsequently commits suicide. Violating all the rules that he himself teaches at the Stasi's own university, the secret watcher slips into the apartment and steals a volume of poems by Bertolt Brecht. Then we see him lying on a sofa, entranced by one of Brecht's more elegiac verses.

In the role-reversing culmination of an intricate and gripping plot, the playwright's girlfriend betrays him to the Stasi but the Stasi captain saves him from exposure and arrest – at the cost of his own subsequent career. He is reduced to steaming open letters in a Stasi cellar alongside a junior officer whom we see earlier telling a political joke in the ministry canteen and, in a chilling exchange, being asked for his name and rank by Colonel Grubitz.

After the Wall comes down, the playwright reads his Stasi file, works out from internal evidence how Wiesler – identified in the file as HGW XX/7 – must have protected him, and writes a novel entitled, like the piece of music, *The Sonata of the Good Man*. The film ends with a cinematic haiku. The former Stasi man opens the newly published novel in the Karl Marx Bookshop in east Berlin – we are now in 1993 – and discovers that it is dedicated to 'HGW XX/7, in gratitude'. 'Do you want it gift-wrapped?' asks the shop assistant. 'No,' says Wiesler, 'es ist für mich' – 'it's for me.' Punchline. End of story. Cut to credits.

Watching the film for the first time, I was powerfully affected. Yet I was also moved to object, from my own experience: 'No! It was not really like that. This is all too highly coloured, romantic, even melodramatic; in reality, it was all much greyer, more tawdry and banal.' The playwright, for example, in his smart brown corduroy suit and open-necked shirt, dresses, walks and talks like a West German intellectual from Schwabing, a chic quarter of Munich, not an East German. Several details are also wrong. On everyday duty, Stasi officers would not have worn those smart dress uniforms, with polished knee-length leather boots, leather belts and cavalry-style trousers. By contrast, the cadets in the Stasi university are shown in ordinary, student-type civilian clothes; they would have been in uniform. A Stasi surveillance team would have been most unlikely to install itself in the attic of the same building – a sure give-away to the residents, not all of whom could have been reliably silenced by the kind of chilling warning that Wiesler delivers to the playwright's immediate neighbour across the stairwell: 'One word to anyone and your Masha immediately loses her place to study medicine at university. Understood?'

Some of the language is also too high-flown, old-fashioned and simply Western. A playwright who knew on which side his bread was buttered would never have used the West German word for blacklisting, *Berufsverbot*, in conversation with the culture minister. I never heard anyone in East Germany call a woman *gnädige Frau*, an old-fashioned term somewhere between 'madam' and 'my lady', and a Stasi colonel would not have addressed Christa during an interrogation as *gnädigste*. I would bet my last Deutschmark that in 1984 a correspondent of the West German news magazine *Der Spiegel* would not have talked of *Gesamtdeutschland*.[3] This strikes me as more the vocabulary of the uprooted German aristocracy among whom the director and writer Florian Henckel von Donnersmarck grew up – both of his parents fled from the eastern parts of the *Reich* at the end of the Second World War – than that of the real East Germany in 1984.

But these objections are in an important sense beside the point. The point is that this is a movie. It uses the syntax and conventions of Hollywood to convey to the widest possible audience some part of the truth about life under the Stasi, and the larger truths that experience revealed about human nature. It mixes historical fact (several of the Stasi locations are real and most of the terminology and tradecraft is accurate) with the ingredients of a fast-paced thriller and love story.

When I met von Donnersmarck in Oxford, where he studied politics, philosophy and economics in the mid-1990s, I discussed my reservations with him. While fiercely defending the basic historical accuracy of the film, he immediately agreed that some details were deliberately altered for dramatic effect. Thus, he explained, if he had shown the Stasi cadets in uniform, no ordinary cinemagoer would have identified with them. But because he shows them (inaccurately) in student-type civilian dress and has one of them (implausibly) ask a naive question to the effect of 'isn't bullying people in interrogations wrong?', the viewer can identify with them and is drawn into the story. He argued that in a movie the reality has always to be *verdichtet*, a word which means thickened, concentrated, intensified, but carries a verbal association with *Dichtung*, meaning poetry or, more broadly, fiction. Hence the elevated language ('I beg you, I beseech you' – 'Ich flehe dich an' – says the playwright at one point, asking his girlfriend not to submit again to the minister's piggish lechery). Hence the luxuriant palette of rich greens, browns and subtle greys in which the whole movie is shot, and the frankly operatic staging of Christa's death.

During a subsequent question-and-answer session in an Oxford cinema the director mentioned, in separate answers, two films that he admired: Claude Lanzmann's harrowing Holocaust documentary, *Shoah*, and Anthony Minghella's version of *The Talented Mr Ripley* – a thriller involving murder and stolen identity – which he singled out because 'it doesn't bore me, and for that I'm very grateful.' In *The Lives of Others*, *Shoah* meets *The Talented Mr Ripley*. Von Donnersmarck does care about the historical facts, but he's even more concerned not to bore us. And for that we are grateful. It is just because he is not an East German survivor but a fresh, cosmopolitan child of the Americanized West, a privileged *Wessi* down to the carefully unbuttoned tips of his pink button-down shirt, fluent in American-accented English and the universal language of Hollywood, that he is able to translate the East German experience into an idiom that catches the imagination of the world.

One of the finest film critics writing today, Anthony Lane, concludes his admiring review in the *New Yorker* by adapting Wiesler's punch-line: 'Es ist für mich.' You might think that the film is aimed solely at modern Germans, Lane writes, but it's not: 'Es ist für uns' – 'It's for us.' He may be more right than he knows. *The Lives of Others* is a film very much intended for others. Like so much else made in Germany, it is designed to be exportable. Among its ideal foreign consumers are, precisely, Lane's 'us' – the readers of the *New Yorker*. Or, indeed, those of the *New York Review of Books*.

Does anything essential get lost in this translation? The small inaccuracies and implausibilities are, on balance, justifiable artistic licence, allowing a deeper truth to be conveyed. It does, however, lose something important: the sense of what Hannah Arendt famously called the banality of evil – and nowhere was evil more banal than in the net-curtained, plastic-wood cabins and caravans of the German Democratic Republic. Yet that is extraordinarily difficult to re-create, certainly for a wider audience, precisely because it was so banal, so unremittingly, mind-numbingly boring. (Or could a great screenwriter and director create a non-boring film about boredom? I lay down the challenge here.)

One of the movie's central claims remains troubling. This is the idea, clearly implied in the ending, that the Stasi captain is the 'good man' of the sonata. Now I have heard of Stasi informers who ended up protecting those they were informing on. I know of full-time Stasi operatives who became disillusioned, especially during the 1980s. And in many hours of talking to former Stasi officers, I never met a single one whom I felt to be, simply and plainly, an evil man. Weak, blinkered, opportunistic, self-deceiving, yes; men who did evil things, most certainly; but always I glimpsed in them the remnants of what might have been, the good that could have grown in other circumstances.

Wiesler's own conversion, as shown to us in the film, seems implausibly rapid and not fully convincing – despite a wonderfully enigmatic performance by the East German actor Ulrich Mühe. It would take more than the odd sonata and Brecht poem to thaw the driven puritan we are shown at the beginning. I find it interesting that in a contribution to the accompanying book (which also contains the original screenplay) the film's historical adviser, Manfred Wilke, gives historical corroboration for many aspects of the film, but does not offer a single documented instance of a Stasi officer behaving in this way – and getting away with it. Instead he cites two cases of disaffected officers, a major in 1979 and a captain in 1981, both of whom were condemned to death and executed. Yet I'm prepared to accept that such a conversion and cover-up was just about within the realms of possibility. (If Colonel Grubitz had exposed Wiesler, he would have compromised himself.)

So Wiesler did one good thing, to set against the countless bad ones he had done before. But to leap from this to the notion that he was 'a good man' is an artistic exaggeration – a *Verdichtung* – too far. In negotiating the treacherous moral maze of evaluating how people behave under dictatorships, there are two characteristic mistakes. One is the simplistic, black-and-white, Manichaean division into good guys and bad guys: X was an informer, so he must have been all bad, Y was a dissident, so she must have been all good. Anyone who has ever lived in such circumstances knows how much more complicated things are. The other, equal but opposite, mistake is a moral relativism that ends up blurring the distinction between perpetrator and victim. This kind of moral relativism is frequently to be encountered among liberal-minded Westerners – and, not accidentally, often those who at the time viewed East Germany through rose-tinted spectacles. It is usually accompanied by the argument that the Stasi files cannot be trusted at all: 'Die Akten lügen' – 'The files lie.' Von Donnersmarck himself is very far from this relativism, but his film steers uncomfortably close to it. Its 'good man' is a Stasi captain who falsifies his reports to protect an artist.

This is a fault, but not a fatal one. The net effect of *The Lives of Others* will not, after all, be to unleash a wave of worldwide sympathy for former Stasi officers. It will be to bring home the horrors of that system, in a stylized fashion, to viewers who would have known little or nothing about them before. And this in a memorable, well-made movie. So it deserved the Oscar.

2

According to a report in *Der Spiegel*, when an emotional Florian Henckel von Donnersmarck finally arrived at a late-night German celebration following the award ceremony, he exclaimed, brandishing his Oscar statuette in the air, 'Wir sind Weltmeister!' The phrase implies not masters of the world but world champions (as in soccer) or world masters (as in golf), with subsidiary connotations of artistic mastery, as in *Meistersinger* or *Meisterwerk*. But in what, exactly, are the Germans world masters? In soccer, almost. Their fine perform-ance in the 2006 World Cup produced scenes – unusual for post-war West Germany – of frankly patriotic celebration, and this was prob-ably what von Donnersmarck had in mind. In the export business, certainly, whether it be BMWs to Britain, machine tools to Iran, assembly lines to China or, just occasionally, films. *The Lives of Others* has already netted over $23 million worldwide – a nice little export earner for the German economy.

Some might be tempted to say, especially after watching this film, that Germany is also a world master in the production of cruel dicta-torships. 'Der Tod ist ein Meister aus Deutschland' – 'Death is a master from Germany' – wrote Paul Celan in his incomparable post-Holocaust 'Death Fugue'. In respect of fascism, Hitler's Germany was undoubtedly the world champion – all too literally a world-beater. But can the same be said of Honecker's Germany? Yes, this small country with just 17 million people was a kind of miniature master-piece of psychological intimidation. As Orwell saw, the perfect totalitarian system is the one that does not need to kill or physically torture anyone. I am the last person to minimize the evils of the East German regime; but when set against the millions of deaths in Stalin's Gulag, Mao's enforced famines and Pol Pot's genocide, it is hard to maintain that this was the worst that communism produced.

In that larger scheme of things, East Germany, unlike Nazi Germany, was but a sideshow. The Stasi was modelled on the KGB and not, as many people vaguely imagine, on the Gestapo. As the archives of other Soviet bloc states are opened, we find that their secret police worked in very similar ways. Perhaps the Stasi was that little bit better because it was, well, German; but there are so many larger horrors in the files of the KGB. And we should not forget that the subtle psychological terror of the Stasi state depended, from the first day to the last, on the presence of the Red Army and the willingness of the Soviet Union to use force. When that went, the Stasi state went too.

So why is it that the word 'Stasi' – not 'KGB', 'Red Guards' or 'Khmer Rouge' – is rapidly becoming a global synonym for communist terror? Because the enterprise in which the Germans truly are *Weltmeister* is the cultural reproduction of their country's versions of terror. No nation has been more brilliant, more persistent and more innovative in the investigation, communication and representation – the re-presentation, and re-re-presentation – of its own past evils.

This cultural reproduction has to do with the character of both the perpetrators and the victims. In Hitler's Holocaust, the people of Gutenberg set out to exterminate the people of the book. One of Europe's most talented, profound, creative nations tried to destroy another, with which it had lived in an intense, fecund cultural symbiosis for many years. ('The Germans are a bad love of the Jews,' a Polish peasant woodcarver once observed to a friend of mine.) Afterwards, both nations memorialized the horror with a meticulousness and an artistry never before seen. In Celan's 'Death Fugue', a German poem that whispers with echoes of Hasidic mysticism, that memorialization was itself a new triumph – a living forward out of death – of the German–Jewish symbiosis. Celan himself spoke of how the German language that he loved had survived 'the thousand darknesses of death-bringing speech' ('die tausend Finsternisse todbringender Rede'). Now that language lived again through him, who had himself just eluded the master from Germany.

In the case of communism, the Germans did it to themselves – though not in a sovereign state. The people of Gutenberg oppressed the people of Luther. As soon as it was over, the people of Ranke took up the story. A generation of West German contemporary historians, trained in the study of Nazism, turned their skilled attentions to the GDR, and especially to the dissection of the Stasi. Only the existence and character of West Germany, with its fiercely moral and professional approach to dealing with a difficult past, explains the unique cultural transmission of the Stasi phenomenon. (Imagine that the former Soviet Union had been taken over by a democratic West Russia, equipped and motivated to expose all the evils of the KGB.) And now we have the movie version, produced by a thoroughly Americanized young West German.

Each stage of this process builds on the last. Cognitive scientists tell us that the repetition of words and images strengthens the synapses connecting the neurons in the neural circuits that compute, in our heads, the meaning of those words and images. With time, these mental associations become electrochemically hard-wired. Whether intentionally or not, *The Lives of Others* plugs straight into these preexisting connections in our minds. Take that apparently trivial detail of the Stasi officers' dress uniforms. Why does it matter? Because the sight of Germans in Prussian grey, with long, shining leather boots, shrieks to our synapses: Nazis.

One is not at all surprised to discover that the actor who portrays Wiesler's sinister superior, Colonel Grubitz, made his reputation back in 1984 – the year the film is set – playing, on a West German stage, the role of an SS man. The real everyday Stasi uniforms, dreary numbers made of bargain-basement terylene, completed by cheap mailman's boots, would not have the same effect. In the theatrical way they are shot, the scenes of the playwright Dreyman dancing around the culture minister reminded me strongly of *Mephisto*, István Szabó's brilliant film about the actor-director Gustaf Gründgens and his Faustian pact with Hermann Göring. Another circuit of Nazi–Stasi associations is involuntarily fired.

Then there is the pivotal moment when Dreyman plays the classical 'Sonata of the Good Man' on the piano, while Wiesler listens on his headphones. After he finishes, Dreyman turns to Christa and

337

exclaims, 'Can anyone who has heard this music, I mean really heard it, still be a bad person?' Von Donnersmarck says he was inspired by a passage in which Maxim Gorky records Lenin saying that he can't listen to Beethoven's Appassionata because it makes him want to say sweet, silly things and pat the heads of little people, whereas in fact those little heads must be beaten, beaten mercilessly, to make the revolution. As a first-year film student, von Donnersmarck wondered 'what if one could force a Lenin to hear the Appassionata', and that was the original germ of his movie. (Dreyman actually refers to Lenin's remark.)

So the inspiration for this scene was Russian. But what are the connections that we – especially we of Lane's 'us' – instantly make as we watch? Surely we think of Roman Polanski's *The Pianist*, with the German officer deeply affected by the Polish Jewish pianist's playing of Chopin, and therefore sparing his life – as Wiesler now spares Dreyman. Surely we think, too, of the educated Nazi killers who in the evening listened to the music of Mendelssohn, then went out the next morning to murder more Mendelssohns. Did they not really hear the music? Does high culture humanize? We are back with the deepest twentieth-century German conundrum, conveyed most movingly in music and poetry. Such are the synaptic connections that make *The Lives of Others* resonate so powerfully in our heads.

The Germany in which this film was produced, in the early years of the twenty-first century, is one of the most free and civilized countries on earth. In this Germany, human rights and civil liberties are today more jealously and effectively protected than (it pains me to say) in traditional homelands of liberty such as Britain and the United States. In this good land, the professionalism of its historians, the investigative skills of its journalists, the seriousness of its parliamentarians, the generosity of its funders, the idealism of its priests and moralists, the creative genius of its writers and, yes, the brilliance of its filmmakers have all combined to cement in the world's imagination the most indelible association of Germany with evil. Yet, without these efforts, Germany would never have become such a good land. In all the annals of human culture, has there ever been a more paradoxical achievement?

2007

Orwell in Our Time

Even if you are, as I am, a passionate Orwellian, the question you have to ask of this beautifully produced, stupendously annotated, twenty-volume *Complete Works of George Orwell* is: why Orwell? Why should he, of all writers, have his maudlin teenage love poems edited as if they were lost sonnets by Milton? What is the lasting value of all his hundreds of book reviews and columns? How can you justify three fat volumes of his radio talks, humdrum correspondence as a producer for other people's talks, and even the internal 'Talks Booking Forms' from two years at the Indian Section of the BBC? When Dr Peter Davison says *Complete Works*, he means complete.[1]

Every line treated like Shakespeare. Yet Orwell was no Shakespeare. He was not a universal genius. Nor was he a natural master of the English language. Much of his early writing is painfully bad. A poet friend described the young would-be novelist as 'like a cow with a musket'. He himself later dismissed two of his published novels, *A Clergyman's Daughter* and *Keep the Aspidistra Flying*, both meticulously reprinted here, as 'thoroughly bad books'. When he was dying, he gave instructions that they should 'NOT' (his capitals) be reprinted. Even his final masterpiece, *Nineteen Eighty-Four*, is marred by patches of melodrama and weak writing. Only *Animal Farm* is perfectly composed.

One can immediately think of half a dozen twentieth-century authors who, line for line, page for page, were consistently better writers: Conrad, Joyce, Eliot, Lawrence, Auden, Waugh. So why don't they get this treatment? Why Orwell?

I

One possible answer to this question is: the others should get this treatment too. It's a daunting idea, but worth considering for a moment. There is an extraordinary richness of understanding that comes from having every essay, article, broadcast, review, letter, diary and notebook entry – as well as selected responses from other people – printed in chronological order, day by writing day. The pure literary merit of any individual piece becomes secondary as you navigate the intimate infolding of life and work. You discover multiple connections: between the books Orwell reviewed and those he wrote, between his own love life and those of his characters, between the horrible rats that he catches as a teenager, the rats in a Spanish prison, and the rats that finally break Winston Smith in the melodramatic Room 101 of *Nineteen Eighty-Four* ('Do it to Julia!').

Such editions could even contribute to a new kind of intellectual democracy. Never mind the published biographies. Here is the raw material to make your own. Orwell, the intellectual democrat, would surely have approved. So perhaps every major writer should receive the complete workover, Davison style. All the Conrads and Joyces need is to find their Davisons, ready to invest, for very modest pay, seventeen years of exhausting editorial work. And then for a publishing or philanthropic big-heart to make available the results (this Orwell, too) in affordable form, whether as paperbacks or electronically. At the hardcover price, only university libraries and a few lucky book reviewers will have the intellectual vote.

A more obvious answer to the question 'Why Orwell?' is: the unique fascination and lasting importance of his life and work. Fascination and importance are linked, yet distinct. Fascination first. Davison quotes a well-known comment by Orwell's schoolfriend Cyril Connolly: 'Anything about Orwell is interesting. He was a man, like Lawrence, whose personality shines out in everything he said or wrote.' This is true, and what an eccentric, cussed, contrary, incurably English personality it was.

The bare biographical facts are curious enough: a talented scholar at Eton perversely goes off to become an imperial policeman in Burma, a dishwasher in Paris and a tramp in London; runs a village shop, fights in the Spanish Civil War, abandons left-wing literary London for a farm on a remote Scottish island, and dies of tuberculosis at the moment of literary triumph, aged forty-six. That tall, thin figure, in shabby tweed jacket, ballooning corduroy trousers, and dark shirt, with his odd pencil-line moustache, high, rasping voice, and working man's roll-up cigarettes, is the stuff of anecdote in his lifetime and legend after it. Malcolm Muggeridge notes in his diary five days after Orwell's death: 'Read through the various obituary articles on George by Koestler, Pritchett, Julian Symons, etc., and saw in them how the legend of a human being is created.'

No one wrote better about the English character than Orwell, and he was himself a walking anthology of Englishness. So English in his complicated relationship to class: alert to its subtlest gradations (he famously describes his own family as 'lower-upper-middle class'), hating the snobbery and class distinctions, yet never quite able to escape them. It's a measure of how slowly his beloved England has changed that for fifty years middle-class leftists have wrestled with the same tensions, Orwell's ghost walking always beside them.

Very English, too, in his sense of humour – a large part of his sandpapery charm. Reporting matter-of-factly on Orwell's health after he was shot through the throat by a Francoist sniper's bullet, his commanding officer Georges Kopp wrote: 'Breathing absolutely regular. Sense of humour untouched.' He had that habit of making some outrageous statement – 'All tobacconists are fascists' – and then defying you not to take it seriously. Evelyn Waugh was his political opposite, but they were satirical brothers under the skin. The moralist came with the satirist. Connolly said Orwell couldn't blow his nose without moralizing on conditions in the handkerchief industry.

English, oh so English, in his fumbling relations with women. There are some sad, almost begging letters: 'I hope you will let me make love to you again some time, but if you don't it doesn't matter, I shall always be grateful to you for your kindness to me.' And English, very pre-death-of-Diana English, in emotional understatement that was even more extreme than his comic overstatement. There's no doubt that his marriage to his vivacious, intelligent, resourceful, supportive first wife, Eileen, was deeply important to him. But after her unexpected, early death on the operating table he expressed his grief to Stephen Spender thus: 'She wasn't a bad old stick.'

English, again, in his love of the countryside, animals and gardening. English, above all, in the whole cast of his intelligence, with its deep, stubborn empiricism. He was an inveterate diarist, note-taker and list-maker. These tomes are jam-packed with curious facts and minute observations, from the habits of the hen to the different kinds of German bombs landing on the streets of London. He loved facts. If he had a God, it was Kipling's 'the God of Things as They are'.

Yet there's a complication here, which is also part of the fascination. Orwell put so much of his life into his work. Three of his nine full-length books (now the first nine volumes of the *Complete Works*) are proclaimedly autobiographical. He led the way in the emphatic, frontal use of the word 'I'. That unmistakable Orwell voice is one of defiant unvarnished honesty, of the plain man bluntly telling things as they are. But who exactly is this 'I'? Is it the real man, Eric Blair, or the invented persona, George Orwell? In what sense are the things he tells us actually true?

One of his most powerful early essays describes witnessing a hanging in Burma. But he later told three separate people that this was 'only a story'. So did he ever witness a hanging? He annotates a copy of *Down and Out in Paris and London* for a girlfriend: this really happened, this happened almost like this, but 'this incident is invented.' Anyway, there's a basic untruth in telling the story as if he really was down to his last penny or sou. In England he had family and friends, in Paris a favourite aunt who would certainly have helped out.

Did the avatars of the 'New Journalism' in the United States read him before they wrote? Even if they did not, he is a precursor. The questions the New Journalism raised about the nature of veracity in reporting and the relationship between fictional and non-fictional truths, questions central to the whole business of higher journalism today: all are there in 'Orwell'.

This is already the stuff of a thousand critical studies. Whole departments of English literature seem to have been kept busy disentangling, triangulating, deconstructing and reconstructing fact and fiction in Orwell's work. Still and all, this biographical and critical fascination would not have existed, let alone persisted, multiplying Orwelliana like relics of the true cross, were it not for his huge success and worldwide influence over the last half-century as the author of two books, *Animal Farm* and *Nineteen Eighty-Four*. The fascination cannot, ultimately, be divorced from the importance.

'In terms of the effect he has had on history,' David Remnick has written, 'Solzhenitsyn is the dominant writer of the twentieth century. Who else compares? Orwell? Koestler?' Well, it's an interesting challenge. I would say Orwell. For a start, his influence is so much wider. 'Big Brother', 'newspeak' and 'doublethink' have entered the language. They are used in a thousand, often trivial or wildly inappropriate, contexts. It's an irony Orwell might not have enjoyed that prime evidence for his influence comes from the political-linguistic abuse of terms he invented to warn against such abuse.

Meanwhile, the word 'Orwellian' pops up all over the place, both as an adjective, to describe totalitarian terror, the falsification of history, etc. (compare 'Kafkaesque'), and as a noun, to describe an admirer and conscious follower of his work. Very few writers harvest this double tribute of becoming both adjective and noun. Offhand, I can only think of Marxist, Freudian, Darwinian, Dickensian, Tolstoyan, Joycean and Jamesian. (Partly, to be sure, this is the accident of euphony. 'Solzhenitsynian' is a mouthful, 'Eliotian' sounds like a hair oil.)

No, Orwell is the most influential political writer of the twentieth century. His friend Arthur Koestler certainly does not compare. Who else? Popper? Hayek? Sartre? Camus? Brecht? Aron? Arendt? Berlin? In the 1970s, Solzhenitsyn probably had a greater political impact than any of these. Yet long before Solzhenitsyn, and for much longer – from 1945 to 1990, for the whole span of the Cold War – Orwell was read throughout what we then called 'the West' as the supreme describer of totalitarianism in general, and Soviet totalitarianism in particular.

He even matched Solzhenitsyn on his own ground. Inside what was then called 'the East' anyone who could lay hold of a smuggled underground copy of *Animal Farm* or *Nineteen Eighty-Four* would devour it in a night and recognize it as an extraordinary satirical critique of their own reality. The historian Aleksandr Nekrich wrote that 'George Orwell is perhaps the only Western author to understand the deepest essence of the Soviet world.' The Russian poet Natalya Gorbanyevskaya told me she felt Orwell was an east European.

Except that he wasn't. He was incurably English, and he never went near Russia or eastern Europe. In the 1980s, Polish and Czech friends would show me their samizdat editions of *Animal Farm* and *Nineteen Eighty-Four* and say, 'But how did he do it?' Who told him that in their communal apartment block 'the hallway smelt of boiled cabbage and old rag mats'? How did he understand about everything, from the shortage of razor blades to the deep psychology of double-think? How did he know?

The answer is both complicated and simple. It really starts in the

Spanish Civil War. Because he had joined the heterodox Marxist POUM militia rather than the communist-run International Brigade, he and his wife then got caught up in the violent suppression of the POUM in Barcelona. Friends with whom he had fought at the front were thrown into prison or killed by the Russian-directed communists – supposedly their republican allies. Orwell became a fugitive on the streets. This edition prints a secret report to the Tribunal for Espionage and High Treason in which Eric and Eileen Blair are described as 'rabid Trotskyists' and 'agents of the POUM'. Had they not slipped out of Spain a few days earlier, they could have found themselves, like Georges Kopp, incarcerated, tortured and thrown into a coal bin with giant rats.

This direct experience of communist terror, betrayal and lies is a key to understanding all his subsequent work. Of the Russian agent in Barcelona charged with defaming the POUM as Trotskyist Francoist traitors he writes, in *Homage to Catalonia*, 'It was the first time that I had seen a person whose profession was telling lies – unless one counts journalists.' The tail sting is typical black humour, but also reflects a further, bitter discovery. On returning to England he found that virtually the whole left-wing press was suppressing or falsifying the facts about the Barcelona events. This was the second part of his Spanish experience, and it shocked him even more because it was happening in his own country. Here begins his fascination with what he describes in *Nineteen Eighty-Four* as a basic principle of Oceania's ruling ideology: 'the mutability of the past'. Falsification, airbrushing, rewriting history: in short, the memory hole.

After Spain, he follows with acid passion the development of both totalitarianisms, Nazi and Soviet, but especially the Soviet one. He reads the press closely. One of his many notebooks records the major events leading up to the Second World War, including the Nazi–Soviet pact. The Tehran conference of 1943 gives him the idea of a world divided into three great blocs. He is one of the first to take up the matter of the Katyn massacres of thousands of Polish officers, carried out by the NKVD but attributed by them to the Germans. And he reviews books. Yevgeny Zamyatin's dystopia *We* is an acknowledged influence. An American correspondent's account of life in the Soviet Union contains the central trope of *Nineteen Eighty-Four*: '2 + 2 = 5'. (This was an actual Soviet poster, suggesting the five-year plan could be fulfilled in four.)

Much of the physical feel of the battered, run-down, smelly London in Orwell's imagined 1984 comes from the battered, run-down, smelly London of 1946–8. (What no one could have guessed is that Warsaw and Moscow would still look – and smell! – like that in the real calendar year of 1984.) A few details are also based on his time at the BBC. Davison shows that Room 101 is a personal in-joke. Orwell had attended many boring Indian Section meetings in Room 101, Broadcasting House.

Finally, as with all writers, some things come from very personal sources. To make love in a sun-dappled woodland dell is a recurring fantasy, which he achieved with at least one girlfriend, Eleanor Jaques. In a letter of 1932 he remembers her 'nice white body in the dark green moss'. The white body is back in the woods in *Nineteen Eighty-Four* (Julia's 'body gleamed white in the sun'). Then there's his lifelong thing about rats. And something rather dark: he could describe cruel police oppression and even sadism so well, not just because he had actually been part of an oppressive imperial police but also because there was a streak of cruelty in his own makeup.

All the ingredients are there; but the secret is in the mix. It's in the new mixing that the major weaknesses of his earlier work are magically converted into strengths. His weakness as a novelist is that he is just not sufficiently endowed with the transforming power of the creative imagination. You can say of any of his novels what he later wrote to a correspondent about *Burmese Days*: 'Much of it is simply reporting of what I have seen.' Half his fiction is little more than dressed-up reportage. His weakness as a journalist, a less serious one, but still a weakness, is his penchant for ill-founded, sweeping, violent overstatement: 'No real revolutionary has ever been an internationalist', 'All left-wing parties in the highly industrialized countries are at bottom a sham', 'A humanitarian is always a hypocrite', and so on. As V. S. Pritchett observed, he 'exaggerates like a savage'. This is partly his humour, of course. But the trouble with such a journalistic style is that in the end you don't know whether to take it seriously or not.

Now look what happens in *Animal Farm* and *Nineteen Eighty-Four*. The impact of these books comes precisely from the fact that they are so closely based on real events, details and trends over the three decades after 1917. Just how closely is shown by a letter to his publisher asking that, in the scene when the humans blow up the windmill in *Animal Farm*, the line, 'All the animals including Napoleon flung themselves on their faces', should be changed to 'all the animals except Napoleon', because 'the alteration would be fair to J.S., as he did stay in Moscow during the German advance.' If Russians and east Europeans had this uncanny sense of recognizing their own reality in *Nineteen Eighty-Four*, it's because the starting point was their own reality – with some Nazism and a dash of 1940s London thrown in. But this closely observed reality is then blown up, as on a giant projection screen, by a lover of the savage, darkly humorous overstatement. What mars the journalism makes the masterpiece: first, the small, perfectly formed, Swiftian satirical fable, then the larger, less perfectly formed, but ultimately more powerful dystopia.

Finally, there is the timing. Because of his Spanish experience, Orwell is on the Soviet case while most of his contemporaries are still celebrating our heroic ally of Stalingrad. Famously, *Animal Farm* is rejected by Victor Gollancz, by T. S. Eliot at Faber's (Eliot's thoughtful letter is printed here), and by Jonathan Cape, on advice from an unnamed official at the Ministry of Information. It appears in August 1945, when the British are beginning to realize that they may have to plunge straight into another war, this time a 'cold war' against their former ally. According to the *Oxford English Dictionary*,

Orwell is the first person to use the phrase 'cold war' in English. Recent historians have described a process by which, in 1945 and 1946, Britain tries to bring a reluctant United States into this cold war. The North American publication of *Animal Farm*, in August 1946, is itself a small part of that process. When *Nineteen Eighty-Four* comes out in 1949, just after the Berlin blockade, the new war is fully joined for all to see.

Then Orwell delivers his last masterstroke. He dies. Literary friends hasten to celebrate him, perhaps a mite more generously than they would have done had he continued as a living rival. He is the James Dean of the Cold War, the JFK of English letters. How much less satisfactory had he still been around, as Koestler was, to diminish his own reputation with meanderings into popular science, or, as Solzhenitsyn still is today, busily dismantling his own monument. As Edmund Clerihew Bentley wrote:

> There is a great deal to be said
> For being dead.

To guess which way Orwell might have gone is but a nice parlour game. Whichever way he went, it would have been cussed and contrary. He was committed to a socialism with equality as its central value, but in the last year of his life he was having himself turned into a limited company and putting his adopted son down for Westminster School. More seriously, his last draft work finds him reverting to weak, vaguely Somerset Maughamish fiction, a horrible return of the cow with a musket.

But no, since he dies in 1950 on that marvellous crescendo, his myth and his influence will grow and grow. Left and right will both claim him for their own, and argue over his remains.

2

Orwell was a Cold Warrior of the left, an anti-communist socialist. Forced to choose between Russia and America, he told his former publisher Victor Gollancz in 1947, 'I would always choose America.' But he swiftly moved to puncture an American interpretation of *Nineteen Eighty-Four* as an attack on Britain's Labour government and its brand of socialism. The book's message, he said, was 'Don't let it happen. It depends on you.'

After a brief membership in the Independent Labour Party, he concluded that 'a writer can only remain honest if he keeps free of party labels.' But this did not mean sitting on the fence. Far from it. He exemplified the non-party partisanship of the spectateur engagé. And he followed through. He did not merely go to Spain, as so many leftist writers did; he fought for the republic, and was shot through the throat. Disqualified by illness from fighting against Nazi Germany in the British forces, he became an enthusiastic sergeant in the Home Guard.

He thought the writer's duty in the Cold War was to fight too, not just with his own books but also in voluntary organizations. Here we find him planning one with Arthur Koestler and being vice-chairman of another, the aptly named Freedom Defence Committee. As systematic investigation of possible communist connections of government employees was being introduced in 1948, he signed a Freedom Defence Committee statement saying that such investigation (later known as 'vetting') was acceptable so long as the person being investigated had the right to be represented by a trade union official, MI5 and Special Branch evidence was always corroborated, and the employee could cross-examine his investigator. That was his kind of Cold War politics.

And still you might insist: why Orwell? He was neither a universal genius nor a great novelist. What the whole phenomenon of Eric

Blair tells us about Englishness still matters in the England of Tony Blair, especially as Northern Ireland, Scotland and Wales begin to go their own ways. But that is of interest mainly to us, the English.

He was the most important political writer of the Cold War. But the Cold War is over. Penguin can no longer say, as they did on my 1979 paperback edition of *Nineteen Eighty-Four*, 'First published in 1949, it retains as much relevance today as it had then.' Although today's technology of secret electronic surveillance makes the Thought Police telescreen look primitive, the threat of that kind of centralized, party-state totalitarianism has – unless I am horribly mistaken – receded.

Anyone who wants to understand the twentieth century will still have to read Orwell. His name will go on being invoked, in contexts he never dreamed of. I recently discovered that my eldest son, aged fourteen, has contributed a column to an Apple Mac users' online magazine and there describes some nefarious anti-Apple manoeuvre by Microsoft as 'Orwell-esque'. So for him and his friends Bill Gates is Big Brother.[2] But what is the Orwell his generation should read, an Orwell for the twenty-first century?

In the long summer after I took my first degree at Oxford, I read the whole of Orwell's work, read him self-consciously as example and guide for a would-be writer. The books that affected me most deeply were the *Collected Essays, Journalism, and Letters*, in four Penguin paperback volumes. That handy compendium is now overtaken by Davison's eleven tomes of collected essays, journalism, letters, replies, diaries, notebooks, radio talks and 'Talks Booking Forms'. These should go into paperback or on to CD-ROM. But will any student, even with the longest free summer, read them as I did the old Penguins? What is the essential Orwell for our time?

Animal Farm can be read like *Gulliver's Travels*, at any age. *Nineteen Eighty-Four* is enthralling, and indispensable for understanding modern history. My essential Orwell for our time would add just two more Penguin paperbacks.[3] First, a new selection of his finest and most important essays, articles and letters, with texts and footnotes based on this marvellous edition. Second, *Homage to Catalonia*. Here you would have in concentrated form Orwell's central and enduringly relevant achievement, which is, in his own words, 'to make political writing into an art'.

Homage to Catalonia – which in Orwell's lifetime sold only about fifty copies a year, but now sells more than 10,000 – is a model of how to write about a foreign political crisis, war or revolution. He goes there. He sees for himself. He takes notes, and he takes risks. Then he writes about it in the first person, not in the self-indulgent spirit of 'Look at me, what a brave little Hemingway am I', but because it really is more honest. That 'I' makes explicit the partiality of his view. To rub it in he tells the reader at the end of the book: 'beware of my partisanship, my mistakes of fact, and the distortion inevitably caused by my having seen only one corner of events.'

He uses all his hard-learned writer's craft, chisels away at clean, vivid prose, deploys metaphor, artifice and characteristic overstatement; but all the facts are as accurate as he can make them.[4] It is, as he wrote in praise of Henry Miller, 'a definite attempt to get at real facts'. For all the question marks about the factual basis of some of Orwell's earlier work, his public and private writing after 1937 shows him striving for an old-fashioned, empirical truth, light years removed from the postmodern. This includes, crucially, the unpleasant truths about his own side. These he makes a special point of exposing most bluntly.

True, he invites the reader to 'skip' two chapters of detailed political exposition, full of acronyms. Davison here follows Orwell's later wishes in banishing them to an appendix. I think he should have exercised editorial judgement to ignore those wishes – as he does by reprinting *A Clergyman's Daughter* and *Keep the Aspidistra Flying*. For these chapters are brilliant pieces of clear, vigorous, passionate political writing, and an essential part of a book about what was, as Orwell says, 'above all things a political war'.

You can apply what I call the Homage to Catalonia Test to anything written about any of the defining foreign crises over the last thirty years – Vietnam, Afghanistan, Poland, Nicaragua, South Africa, Rwanda, Bosnia. I must have read twenty books about Bosnia, but I don't think a single one really passes the test.

His great essays straddle politics and literature. They explore Dickens, Kipling and Tolstoy, nationalism, anti-Semitism, Gandhi and boys' weeklies. In 'Politics and the English Language' he shows how the corruption of language is crucial to the making and defending of bad, oppressive politics. But he also shows how we can get back at the abusers of power, because they are using our weapons: words. Freedom depends on writers keeping the word-mirrors clean. In an age of sophisticated media manipulation, this is more vital than ever.

In his best articles and letters, he gives us a gritty, personal example of how to engage as a writer in politics. He takes sides, but remains his own man. He will not put himself at the service of political parties exercising or pursuing power, since that means using half-truths, in a democracy, or whole lies in a dictatorship. He gets things wrong, but then corrects them. Sometimes he joins with others in volunteer brigades or boring committee work, to defend freedom. But if need be, he stands alone, against all the 'smelly little orthodoxies which are now contending for our souls'.

In 'The Prevention of Literature' he suddenly bursts into an old Revivalist hymn:

> Dare to be a Daniel
> Dare to stand alone;
> Dare to have a purpose firm,
> Dare to make it known.

He did. As he himself wrote of Dickens, behind the pages of his work you see the face of a man who is generously angry. This is the great Orwell. We need him still, because Orwell's work is never done.

1998/2009

Orwell's List

So there it was at last, the copy of George Orwell's notorious list of 'crypto-communists' that went into the files of a semi-secret department of the Foreign Office on 4 May 1949. It lay before me in a buff folder on the office table of a senior Foreign Office archivist. Despite all the controversy around it, no unofficial person had been allowed to see the list for more than fifty-four years, since someone typed up this official copy of the original list that Orwell dispatched from his sickbed to a close friend, Celia Kirwan, on 2 May 1949. She had recently begun work in the Foreign Office's Information Research Department (IRD), which was concerned, among other things, with producing anti-communist propaganda. The list contains thirty-eight names of journalists and writers who, as he had written to Celia on 6 April, 'in my opinion are crypto-communists, fellow-travellers or inclined that way and should not be trusted as propagandists'.

Orwell's list, which is divided into three columns headed 'Name', 'Job' and 'Remarks', is eclectic. It includes Charlie Chaplin, J. B. Priestley and the actor Michael Redgrave, all marked with '?' or '??', implying doubt whether they really were crypto-communists or fellow travellers. E. H. Carr, the historian of international relations and Soviet Russia, is dismissed as 'Appeaser only'. The editor of the *New Statesman*,

Kingsley Martin, an old bête noire of Orwell's, gets the gloriously back-handed comment '?? Too dishonest to be outright "crypto" or fellow-traveller, but reliably pro-Russian on all major issues.' Beside the *New York Times* Moscow correspondent Walter Duranty and the former Trotskyist writer Isaac Deutscher ('Sympathizer only'), there are many lesser-known writers and journalists, starting with an industrial correspondent of the *Manchester Guardian*, described as 'Probably sympathizer only. Good reporter. Stupid.'

Over the last decade, 'Orwell's List' has been the subject of many articles with lurid headlines such as 'Big Brother of the Foreign Office', 'Socialist Icon Who Became an Informer' and 'How Orwell's Blacklist Aided Secret Service'. All this speculative denunciation of the author of *Nineteen Eighty-Four* has been based on three incomplete sources: the publication of many (but not all) entries from the strictly private notebook in which Orwell attempted to identify 'cryptos' and 'F.T.' (his abbreviation for fellow travellers), his published correspondence with Celia Kirwan, and the partial release seven years ago of the relevant files from the Information Research Department of the Foreign Office. But in file FO 1110/189 a card was inserted, next to a copy of Orwell's letter to Celia of 6 April 1949, saying a document had been withheld.

There the matter rested, with Her Majesty's Government solicitously guarding one of Orwell's last secrets, until shortly after Celia Kirwan's death last autumn, when her daughter, Ariane Bankes, found a copy of the list among her mother's papers, and subsequently invited me to write about it. After we published the list in the *Guardian*, I asked the British foreign secretary, Jack Straw, to release the original.[1] He agreed, 'since all the information contained in it is now in the public domain', and anyone interested can now read it in its proper place, file FO 1110/189 at the British National Archives.

I

There is the text. What is the context? In February 1949, George Orwell was lying in a sanatorium in the Cotswolds, very ill with the TB that would kill him within a year. That winter, he had worn himself out in a last effort to retype the whole manuscript of *Nineteen Eighty-Four*, his bleak warning of what might happen if Britain succumbed to totalitarianism. He was lonely, despairing of his own wasted health at the age of just forty-five, and deeply pessimistic about the advance of Russian communism, whose cruelty and treacherousness he had personally experienced, nearly at the cost of his own life in Barcelona during the Spanish Civil War. The communists had just taken over Czechoslovakia, in the Prague coup of February 1948, and they were now blockading West Berlin, trying to strangle the city into submission.

He thought there was a war on, a 'cold war', and he feared that the Western nations were losing it. One reason we were losing, he thought, was that public opinion had been blinded to the true nature of Soviet communism. In part, this blinding was the product of understandable gratitude for the Soviet Union's immense role in defeating Nazism. However, it was also the work of a poisonous array of naive and sentimental admirers of the Soviet system, declared Communist Party (CP) members, covert ('crypto-') communists and paid Soviet spies. It was these people, he suspected, who had made it so difficult for him to get his anti-Soviet fable *Animal Farm* published in the last year of the last war.

However, he also knew this was a time in which genuine, idealistic believers in communism were becoming disgusted by what they saw. Some turned into the most acute critics of 'the god that failed', to quote the title of the famous book about communism co-edited by Arthur Koestler and the Labour MP Richard Crossman which appeared in the month of Orwell's death, January 1950, with an introduction by Crossman and essays by, among others, Koestler, Stephen Spender and Ignazio Silone. These writers were especially important to anti-communist leftists like Orwell who were convinced, as he himself wrote, 'that the destruction of the Soviet myth [is] essential if we want to revive the Socialist movement.' At some point in the mid- to late 1940s he had started keeping a private notebook in which he tried to work out who was what: outright member of the CP, agent, 'F.T.', sentimental sympathizer . . .

The notebook, which I have been able to consult without restriction in the Orwell Archive at University College, London, shows that he worried away at the list. It contains entries in pen and pencil, with asterisks in red and blue against some names. There are 135 names in all, of which ten have been crossed out, either because the person had died – like Fiorello La Guardia, the former mayor of New York – or because Orwell had decided they were not crypto-communists or fellow travellers. Thus, for example, the name of the historian A. J. P. Taylor is crossed out, with Orwell's heavily under-lined remark 'Took anti-CP line at Wroclaw Conference', as is that of the American novelist Upton Sinclair, on whom, rejecting his own earlier assessment, Orwell comments: 'No. Denounced Czech coup & Wroclaw conference.' Stephen Spender ('Sentimental sympathizer . . . Tendency towards homosexuality') and Richard Crossman ('Too dishonest to be outright F.T.') are not yet crossed out; but this was before the appearance of *The God That Failed*. The way Orwell agonized over his individual assessments is shown by the entry on J. B. Priestley. This has against it a red asterisk, which is crossed out with black cross-hatching and then encircled in blue with an added question mark.

To this depressed and mortally ill political writer of genius there came, in February 1949, a delightful piece of personal news. Celia Kirwan (née Paget) had returned to London from Paris. Celia was a strikingly beautiful, vivacious and warm-hearted young woman who moved in left-wing literary circles, as did her twin sister Mamaine, then married to Orwell's friend Arthur Koestler. Orwell had met Celia when they spent Christmas together in Wales with Arthur and Mamaine in 1945. He was lonely and in some emotional turmoil after the death of his first wife earlier that year. Celia and he got on very well, and met again several times in London. One evening just five weeks after their first meeting, he sent her a passionate letter, full of tender feeling and rather clumsily proposing either marriage or an affair. It ended, 'good night my dearest love, George.' Celia gently refused him in what she later described as a 'rather ambiguous letter', but they remained close friends. A year later, she went to work for an intellectual review in Paris.

'Dearest Celia,' he now wrote from the Cotswold sanatorium on 13 February, 'how delightful to get your letter and know that you are in England again.' 'I will send you a copy of my new book [that is, *Nineteen Eighty-Four*] when it comes out (about June I think), but I don't think you'll like it; it's an awful book really.' Saying he hoped to see her 'some time, perhaps in the summer' he signed off 'with much love, George'.

Sooner than expected, on 29 March, Celia came to visit him in Gloucestershire; but she also came with a mission. She was working for this new department of the Foreign Office, trying to counter the assault waves of communist propaganda emanating from Stalin's recently founded Cominform. Could he help? As she recorded in her official memorandum of their meeting, Orwell 'expressed his whole-hearted and enthusiastic approval of our aims'. He couldn't write anything for IRD himself, he said, because he was too ill and didn't like to write 'on commission', but he suggested several people who might. On 6 April he followed up with a letter in his neat, rather delicate handwriting, suggesting a few more names and offering his list of those:

who should not be trusted as propagandists. But for that I shall have to send for a notebook which I have at home, and if I do give you such a list it is strictly confidential, as I imagine it is libellous to describe somebody as a fellow-traveller.

Celia circulated the letter to her superior, Adam Watson, who made some comments, then added:

P.S. Mrs. Kirwan should certainly ask Mr. Orwell for the list of crypto-communists. She would 'treat it with every confidence' and send it back after a day or two. I hope the list gives reasons in each case.

Mrs Kirwan did as she was asked, writing from 'Foreign Office, 17 Carlton House Terrace' on 30 April:

Dear George, Thank you so much for your helpful suggestions. My department were very interested to see them . . . They have asked me to say that they would be very grateful if you could let us look at your list of fellow-travelling and crypto journalists: we would treat it with the utmost discretion.

Her letter, at least in the typewritten version contained in file FO 1110/189, has a cooler ending than his: 'Yours ever, Celia'.

Meanwhile, Orwell asked his old friend Richard Rees to send him the notebook from the remote house on the Scottish island of Jura where he had written *Nineteen Eighty-Four*. Thanking him for it on 17 April, he writes:

Cole [that is, the historian G. D. H. Cole] I think should probably not be on the list but I would be less certain of him than of Laski in case of a war . . . The whole business is very tricky, and one can never do more than use one's judgement and treat each case individually.

So we must imagine Orwell lying in his sanatorium bed, gaunt and wretched, going through the notebook, perhaps adding a blue question mark to the red asterisk and black cross-hatching on Priestley, wondering how Cole or Laski, Crossman or Spender, would behave in the event of a real, shooting war with the Soviet Union – and which of the 135 names to pass on to Celia.

On receiving her note, he wrote back at once, enclosing his list of thirty-eight:

> It isn't very sensational and I don't suppose it will tell your friends anything they don't know.

(Note the reference to 'your friends'; Orwell had no illusion that this was just going to her.)

> At the same time it isn't a bad idea to have the people who are probably unreliable listed. If it had been done earlier it would have stopped people like Peter Smollett worming their way into important propaganda jobs where they were probably able to do us a lot of harm. Even as it stands I imagine that this list is very libellous, or slanderous, or whatever the term is, so will you please see that it is returned to me without fail.

The letter was signed 'with love, George'.

On the same day, he wrote again to Richard Rees:

> Suppose for example that Laski had possession of an important military secret. Would he betray it to the Russian military intelligence? I don't imagine so, because he has not actually made up his mind to be a traitor, & the nature of what he was doing would in that case be quite clear. But a real Communist would, of course, hand the secret over without any sense of guilt, & so would a real crypto, such as Pritt [the MP, D. N. Pritt]. The

whole difficulty is to decide where each person stands, & one has to treat each case individually.

At this point, maddeningly, the paper trail goes cold. We know that Celia Kirwan was supposed to come to see Orwell on the next Sunday and that he thanked her on 13 May for sending a bottle of brandy. Did she return the list if she went to visit him again, having had the copy now in file FO 1110/189 typed up in the department? What did they say at that meeting, if it took place? What happened next? Were these names handed on to any other department?

The file itself shows no further action taken with respect to the names listed. In his letter to me, announcing the release of the original, the foreign secretary writes, 'A check of our records confirms that the list is the only document about Orwell's contacts with IRD that has been withheld.' But a good many other IRD files have been withheld, and parts of released documents blanked out, on the grounds that they contain intelligence-related matter and are therefore covered by what Foreign Office archivists call 'the blanket'. Anyway, only part of the truth is ever contained in files.

2

A serious answer to these questions requires a judgement on the nature of this mysterious department, the IRD. I have therefore immersed myself in the published literature about it and read some of the files that have been released to the Public Record Office.[2] I have also talked to several former members of the department at that time. They include Adam Watson, the official who instructed Celia Kirwan to ask Orwell for his list; Robert Conquest, the veteran chronicler of Soviet terror, who subsequently shared an office with Celia Kirwan and himself fell 'madly in love' with her; and the aptly named John Cloake.

The picture that emerges is of an ill-defined outfit, with a very diverse group of people fumbling their way from the recently finished war against fascist totalitarianism, in which most of them had fought, into the new 'cold war' against the communist totalitarianism of Britain's recent wartime ally. IRD was a semi-secret department. Unlike the secret intelligence service, popularly known as MI6, whose very existence was denied by the government, IRD appeared in the lists of Foreign Office departments, but not all its officers were identified there. Much of its funding came from the 'Secret Vote', a governmental appropriation used to fund the secret services and not subject to the usual forms of parliamentary scrutiny. An internal Foreign Office description from 1951 says flatly, 'It should be noted that the name of this department is intended as a disguise for the true nature of its work, which must remain strictly confidential.'[3]

In the beginning, that 'true nature' was mainly to collect and summarize reliable information about Soviet and communist misdoings, to disseminate it to friendly journalists, politicians and trade unionists, and to support, financially and otherwise, anti-communist publications. The department was established by the Labour foreign secretary, Ernest Bevin, and it was particularly interested in authors with good credentials on the left. Bertrand Russell, for example, wrote three short books whose publication was subsidized by the IRD: *Why Communism Must Fail*, *What is Freedom?* and *What is Democracy?* According to IRD veterans, some authors, like Russell, knew perfectly well that the publisher (Background Books) who approached them to write a book was backed by this semi-secret department of the Foreign Office; others, such as the philosopher Bryan Magee, who contributed *The Democratic Revolution*, were outraged when they subsequently learned the source of the publisher's funds. The pattern is familiar from other well-known episodes of the cultural Cold War, such as the CIA funding for *Encounter*.

The better-known of these authors would obviously have been published anyway, but IRD helped to give their work a wider circulation, especially in foreign countries that were already under communism or seen as threatened by it. In Orwell's case, it supported Burmese, Chinese and Arabic editions of his *Animal Farm*, commissioned a rather crude strip-cartoon version of the same book (giving the pig Major a Lenin beard and the pig Napoleon a Stalin moustache, in case simple-minded readers didn't get the point), and organized showings in 'backward' areas of the British Commonwealth of a CIA-financed – and politically distorted – animated film of *Animal Farm*.

The department also established a close working relationship with the overseas services of the BBC. In one file that I have read, IRD officials tried to press Sir Ian Jacob, then head of the BBC's European Service, to adopt its recommendations for the choice of words to describe the Soviet state.[4] (One choice example: 'POLICE STATE. Another useful phrase which underlines this sometimes overlooked but essential aspect of the system.') In this case, the BBC resisted the pressure, and the Foreign Office official overseeing IRD told his subordinates to back off.

However, it seems that some IRD operatives did not stop with these relatively mild means of what Ernest Bevin called 'anticommunist publicity'. Using methods they had learned in the previous war, working for the Political Warfare Executive or for MI6, they apparently tried to combat what they saw as communist infiltration of the trade unions, the BBC or organizations like the National Council for Civil Liberties by identifying members who were or were alleged to be communists, by spreading dark rumours about their activities – and perhaps worse.

So we must imagine Robert Conquest sitting in one room at Carlton House Terrace, scrupulously gathering and sifting information about east European politics. In another office, a former member of the Second World War Political Warfare Executive or of MI6 might be preparing some slightly less scrupulous operation. Next door you could meet the charming professional diplomat Guy Burgess, who worked in IRD for three months – and, being a Soviet agent, told his controllers in Moscow all about it. Down the corridor, though only beginning in 1952, sat a young woman called Fay. The novelist Fay Weldon later recalled that when a visitor came from MI6 she and her colleagues would be told 'Turn your backs!' so this James Bond figure could walk down the corridor unseen. ('Watch the wall, my darling, while the Gentlemen go by.') But they peeked.

As the Cold War intensified, the white propaganda of the early years seems to have been increasingly supplemented with grey and black. By the late 1950s, according to someone who worked for British intelligence agencies at that time, IRD had a reputation as 'the dirty tricks department' of the Foreign Office, indulging in character assassination, false telegrams, putting itching powder on lavatory seats, and other such Cold War pranks . . . little of which will be found in the files, even if the intelligence-related ones are finally released.

All the survivors insist that it is most unlikely that any names supplied by Orwell in 1949 would have been passed on to anyone else, and especially not to MI5, Britain's domestic security service, or MI6, in charge of foreign intelligence. 'In all honesty,' Adam Watson told me, 'I cannot remember any case in which we said [to MI5 or MI6], "Did you realize that X says So-and-so is a crypto-communist?"' However, as Watson himself cautioned me, 'Old men forget.' Clearly no one can ever know exactly what, say, the head of the department, Ralph Murray, might have muttered to a friend from MI6 over a brandy at the Travellers' Club, just around the corner from Carlton House Terrace.

Celia Kirwan always strongly defended Orwell's contribution to the work of IRD. In the 1990s there was fevered speculation about his list. The Marxist historian Christopher Hill said, 'I always knew he was two-faced.' The Labour MP Gerald Kaufman wrote in the *Evening Standard* that 'Orwell was a Big Brother too.' Celia Kirwan insisted:

I think George was quite right to do it ... And, of course, everybody thinks that these people were going to be shot at dawn. The only thing that was going to happen to them was that they wouldn't be asked to write for the Information Research Department.

Some writers today suggest the IRD's anti-communist activities were Britain's equivalent of the McCarthyite witch-hunt. If so, then one is struck by how mild it was by comparison with the American McCarthyism which prompted Arthur Miller to write *The Crucible* and Charlie Chaplin to flee back to Orwell's Britain.

Consider who some of the people on the list were, and what happened to them. Peter Smollett was singled out by Orwell for special mention in his covering letter to Celia. Under 'Remarks' on his list, Orwell noted: ' . . . gives strong impression of being some kind of Russian agent. Very slimy person.' Born in Vienna as Peter Smolka, during the Second World War Smollett was the head of the Soviet section in the British Ministry of Information – one of Orwell's inspirations for the Ministry of Truth. We now know two more things about him. First, according to the Mitrokhin Archive of KGB documents, Smollett–Smolka actually was a Soviet agent, recruited by Kim Philby, with the code name 'ABO'. Second, he was almost certainly the official on whose advice the publisher Jonathan Cape turned down *Animal Farm* as an unhealthily anti-Soviet text. How, then, did the British state prosecute or persecute this Soviet agent? By making him an Officer of the British Empire (OBE). Subsequently, he was the London *Times* correspondent in central Europe. The worst thing that seems to have happened to him is that some of his short stories about post-war Vienna were heavily drawn upon by Graham Greene for *The Third Man*. In the film, he makes an insider-joke phantom appearance as what the viewer must assume is the name of a bar or nightclub called Smolka.

The Labour MP Tom Driberg – 'Usually named as "crypto", but

in my opinion NOT reliably pro-CP' – was, according to the Mitrokhin KGB papers, recruited in 1956 as a doubtless deeply unreliable Soviet agent (code name LEPAGE), after a compromising homosexual encounter with an agent of the KGB's Second Chief Directorate in a lavatory under the Metropole hotel in Moscow. Nonetheless, he ended his life as a celebrated writer and Lord Bradwell of Bradwell-juxta-Mare. E. H. Carr, Isaac Deutscher, the novelist Naomi Mitchison (a 'silly sympathizer') and J. B. Priestley all pursued very successful careers without, so far as we know, any hindrance from the British government. Michael Redgrave went on, ironically enough, to play a leading role in the 1956 film of Orwell's *Nineteen Eighty-Four*.

In other words, nothing bad happened to them even when, as in the case of Smollett, it arguably should have. To be sure, we cannot conclusively say that this was true of all the lesser-known writers and journalists on the list of thirty-eight: that requires further investigation. The only case of anything like a possible 'blacklisting' that I have found so far is that of Alaric Jacob, a minor writer who had attended the same private school as Orwell and followed his subsequent progress with resentment. According to one study of British political vetting, Alaric Jacob joined the BBC monitoring service at Caversham in August 1948, but in February 1951 was 'suddenly refused establishment rights, which meant he would receive no pension'.[5] He complained to his cousin, the same Sir Ian Jacob who had dealings with IRD and later became director general of the BBC. Alaric Jacob's establishment and pension rights were restored shortly after his wife – Iris Morley, who also appears on Orwell's list – died in 1953.

The way in which the BBC collaborated with semi-secret departments like the IRD, and with the intelligence services for secret vetting of its employees, is one of the murkier passages of Britain's Cold War. But a two-year loss of BBC 'establishment rights' is hardly *Darkness at Noon* or a session in Room 101. Anyway, there is no evidence that Orwell's list had anything to do with the temporary blacklisting of Alaric Jacob nearly two years later.

3

'Saints should always be judged guilty until they are proved innocent,' Orwell wrote of Gandhi just a few months before he sent Celia the list. Orwell's rule must now apply to Orwell himself, the Saint George of English political writing. Yet even when all possible files are released and a scrupulous historian has weighed all the available evidence on IRD, the BBC and the rest, his 'innocence' can never finally be proven. Perhaps Orwell would anyway not want to plead innocent but rather growl 'guilty as charged'. It all depends on the charge.

If the charge is that Orwell was a Cold Warrior, the answer is plainly yes. Orwell was a Cold Warrior even before the Cold War began, warning against the danger of Soviet totalitarianism in *Animal Farm* when most people were still celebrating our heroic Soviet ally. He appears in the Oxford English Dictionary as the first writer ever to use the term 'cold war' in English. He had fought with a gun in his hand against fascism in Spain, and was wounded by a bullet through his throat. He fought communism with his typewriter, and hastened his death by the exertion.

If the charge is that he was a secret police informer, the answer is plainly no. IRD was an odd Cold War outfit, but it was nothing like a Thought Police. Unlike that dreadful genius Bertolt Brecht, Orwell never believed that the end justified the means. Again and again, we find him insisting to Richard Rees that you have to treat each case individually. He opposed the banning of the Communist Party in Britain. The Freedom Defence Committee, of which he was vice-chairman, thought political vetting of civil servants a necessary evil, but insisted that the person concerned should be represented by a trade union, that corroborative evidence must be produced, and that the accused should be allowed to cross-examine those giving evidence against him. Hardly the methods of the KGB – or, indeed, of MI5 or the FBI during the Cold War. He told Celia that he approved of the aims of IRD; this does not mean that he would have approved of their subsequent methods.

The list invites us to reflect again on the asymmetry of our attitudes towards Nazism and communism. Orwell liked making lists. In a 'London Letter' to *Partisan Review* in 1942 he wrote, 'I think I could make out at least a preliminary list of the people who would go over' to the Nazi side if the Germans occupied England. Suppose he had. Suppose his list of crypto-Nazis had gone to the Political Warfare Executive. Would anyone be objecting?

The long-overdue publication of the IRD list also highlights the vital distinction, so often blurred, between Orwell's private notebook and the list he sent to Celia at the Foreign Office. Readers may, according to taste, be more shocked or amused by the entries in his notebook. There is about them a touch of the old imperial policeman, a hint of the spy, as well as a generous dose of his characteristic, gruff black humour. (He includes someone from the 'Income Tax Dep't' in his notebook list: bloody communists, those tax inspectors.) But all writers are spies. They peek, like Fay Weldon in Carlton House Terrace. They secretly write things down in notebooks.

One aspect of the notebook that shocks our contemporary sensibility is his ethnic labelling of people, especially the eight variations of 'Jewish?' (Charlie Chaplin), 'Polish Jew', 'English Jew' or 'Jewess'. Orwell's entire life was a struggle to overcome the prejudices of his class and generation; here was one he never fully overcame.

What remains most unsettling about the list he actually sent is the way in which a writer whose name is now a synonym for political independence and journalistic honesty is drawn into collaboration with a bureaucratic department of propaganda, however marginal the collaboration, 'white' the propaganda, and good the cause. In the files of the IRD, you find the kind of bureaucratic language that we now habitually describe as Orwellian or Kafkaesque. Next to the very personal handwritten letter from Orwell ('Dear Celia . . . with love, George') in FO 1110/189 is a typewritten communication from the British embassy in Moscow: 'Dear Department,' it begins, and is signed, surreally, 'yours ever, Chancery'.

Yet perhaps we should not be surprised, for Orwell knew this kind of world from inside, and drew on it for his 'awful book'. While *Nineteen Eighty-Four* was a warning against totalitarianism of both the Nazi (that is, National Socialist) and communist (that is, Soviet Socialist) kind – hence 'Ingsoc' – much of the physical detail was derived from his experience of wartime London, working in the BBC, itself a considerable British bureaucracy in close touch with the Ministry of Information and home to the original Room 101.

The most delicate and speculative part of any interpretation concerns Orwell's relationship with Celia Kirwan. There is, in his letters to Celia, an almost painful eagerness. You sense in them his continued strong feelings for a particularly attractive, warm-hearted and cultured woman. But in all we know about him at this time, you also sense something broader: the more generalized, rather desperate craving of a mortally sick man for affectionate female support. One recalls the emotional turmoil of three years before, when he precipitately proposed not just to Celia but also to two or three other younger women. Lonely, stuck in that Cotswold sanatorium, loathing the thought that he was physically done for at the age of forty-five, did he yearn to combat approaching death with the love of a beautiful woman?

Celia, while remaining a staunch friend, did not encourage any renewal of George's gruff advances. However, soon after their exchange about the list another beautiful young Englishwoman, to whom he had also proposed in that earlier bout of emotional turmoil, returned from Paris, like Celia, and came to see him at the sanatorium. In Sonia Brownell's case, she was on the rebound from a passionate romance with the French philosopher Maurice Merleau-Ponty.

Perhaps sensing some encouragement, Orwell proposed to her again. Egged on by his forceful publisher, Frederic Warburg, Sonia accepted.

In *Nineteen Eighty-Four*, Winston Smith's protest against totalitarian bureaucracy is to have sex with Julia – a character at least partly modelled on Sonia. In real life, was it, at least in part, his desire for Celia's affectionate attention that brought 'Mr. Orwell' into the secret files of the British bureaucracy?

This biographical speculation is not to trivialize his conscious political choice to supply those names to a department of the Foreign Office. Nonetheless, you have to ask yourself this question: had it been a bowler-hatted and pin-striped Mr Cloake who came to visit him on 29 March 1949, would he have offered to send him the list? But it wasn't Mr Cloake. It was his 'dearest Celia'.

Orwell sought desperately to fight his last enemy, death; yet it was his early death that secured his immortality. Tempting as it is to speculate, in the light of the list, about which way he would have gone if he had lived – an iconoclastic left-wing voice on the *New Statesman*? a curmudgeonly old Cold Warrior on *Encounter*? – this is strictly illegitimate. We will never know. One thing, however, is clear: he would have taken definite, strong political stands, and therefore alienated people on the left or the right, and probably both. Only his early death allowed everyone to beatify him in their own way. And he would have written more books – possibly, as his previous novels and last draft story might suggest, less good ones than *Animal Farm* and *Nineteen Eighty-Four*.

How we would all have loved to read his views on the building of the Berlin Wall, on the Vietnam War and on the 1968 student protests. How I would have enjoyed meeting him in central Europe in 1989, aged eighty-six, as the Soviet communist Big Brother finally collapsed. How wonderful it would be to hear his voice today – a voice that we imagine all the more vividly because no recording of it survives – commenting on the propaganda language of the Iraq war, or the continuing miseries of Burma, or the dilemmas of Tony Blair. But the hundred-year-old Orwell growls through the asterisks and crossouts of his notebook, 'Don't be silly. Work it out for yourself.'

2003

Is 'British Intellectual' an Oxymoron?

Is the person sitting next to you an intellectual? Are you? Or would you run a mile from the label? The other night I asked a commentator I consider to be obviously a British intellectual whether he is an intellectual, and he replied, with a flicker of alarm behind his spectacles, 'Oh no!' Why not? 'Because I'm afraid of suffering from Impostor Syndrome'.

In his splendid new book *Absent Minds*, the intellectual historian Stefan Collini charts the long history of this British tradition of denial.[1] Again and again, people who in other European countries would be described as intellectuals deny that they are. What Collini calls 'the absence thesis' claims that we, unlike the French or Poles or Austrians, don't have intellectuals. Intellectuals begin at Calais. 'British intellectual' is an oxymoron, like 'military intelligence'. The river of colloquial English carries a heavy silt of mildly pejorative or satirical epithets: egghead, boffin, highbrow, bluestocking, know-all, telly don, media don, chattering classes, too clever by half. The qualifier 'so-called' travels with the word 'intellectual' like a bodyguard. The inverted commas of irony are never far away.

Collini rightly argues that this places us in a kind of false consciousness. In this as in many other respects we are less exceptional and more European than we think we are. But what does it mean to be an intellectual? Collini distinguishes three different senses. First, there's the subjective, personal sense: someone who reads a lot, is interested in ideas, pursues the life of the mind. That's what people often mean when they say of a friend or relative that he or she is 'a bit of an intellectual'. (Usually this is not unkindly meant, as if talking of a harmless hobby or foible.) Then there's the sociological usage: the intelligentsia as a class, which may be said, for example, to comprise everyone with a university degree. But this sociological usage has never really caught on in Britain, unlike in central and eastern Europe, where it's part of the standard descriptive apparatus.

Last, and most important, is the characterization of a cultural role. Collini attempts to pin this down in a careful definition. An intellectual, in this sense, is someone who first attains a level of creative, analytical or scholarly achievement and then uses available media or channels of expression to engage with the broader concerns of wider publics, for some of which he or she then becomes a recognized authority – or at least a recognized figure and voice. My own attempt at defining the role of the intellectual, in a debate with Czech intellectuals some years ago, was not dissimilar: 'It is the role of the thinker or writer who engages in public discussion of issues of public policy, in politics in the broadest sense, while deliberately not engaging in the pursuit of power.' That last normative caveat seems to me very important, though it is rejected by intellectuals such as Václav Havel who have gone into politics with a large P.

Since the 1980s we have come to describe such persons as 'public intellectuals', a term imported from the US – as was 'highbrow'. But if one means by 'intellectual' someone who plays the role just described, then 'public intellectual' is a pleonasm while 'private intellectual' is an oxymoron. A hermit or recluse may be 'a bit of an intellectual', but engagement with a wider public is the defining feature of an intellectual in this sense. The story is complicated by the fact that you may reach a wider public only after your death. Only eleven people attended Karl Marx's funeral, but he became one of the most influential political intellectuals of all time. There are, so to speak, posthumous publics.

When British intellectuals decry or dismiss the term intellectual, they are sometimes merely expressing British empiricism's dislike of various continental forms of more abstract theorizing. This is part of what Orwell was getting at when, in a private letter, he described Jean-Paul Sartre as 'a bag of wind'. As the poet James Fenton puts it in his 'Manila Manifesto', 'We say to France: AUT TACE AUT LOQUERE MELIORA SILENTIO – either shut up or say something worth saying.' 'Where's the beef?' is the Anglo-Saxon question to Derrida, Althusser or Heidegger. But this is merely the clash of different intellectual traditions. Also, typically, the further you go to the right in Britain, the greater the suspicion of intellectuals. British communists talked quite happily of 'Communist Party intellectuals' (which helps explain Orwell's hostility to the tag), while the conservative historian and journalist Paul Johnson, an intellectual if ever there was one, has written a whole book saying how awful intellectuals are.

The plain fact is that Britain has one of the richest intellectual cultures in Europe today. There are probably more genuine, substantial, creative debates about ideas, policies and books – and reaching a wider public – in Britain than there are in France, the homeland of *les intellectuels*. The South Bank of the Thames is less elegant but more intellectually alive than the left bank of the Seine.

Nowhere else outside the US has such an array of think tanks. Every month seems to bring a new literary festival, with large audiences queuing up to hear eggheads and boffins galore. We have the best universities in Europe, and some British academics still manage to escape the ghastly, Soviet-style clutches of the government-imposed Research Assessment Exercise, and other bureaucratic nightmares, for sufficient time to share their knowledge with a wider public. We have the BBC, especially BBC radio, to help them do that, in programmes such as Melvyn Bragg's *In Our Time* and Andrew Marr's *Start the Week*. In laying out his vision for the future of the BBC, its director general, Mark Thompson, has reaffirmed his commitment to the third leg of the Reithian tripod: to educate, as well as to inform and entertain.

We have commercial book publishers who manage to bring serious work to a wider readership. (The state of our bookshops is a worry, but fortunately there's always Amazon.) We have first-rate intellectual journals: *Prospect*, the *TLS*, *Guardian Review*, the *London Review of Books*, openDemocracy.net, to name just a few. Through the English language, and the intensity of cultural exchange across the Atlantic, we are also plugged into the big debates not just in the United States but throughout the English-speaking world. The Internet and the blogosphere provide extraordinary opportunities for any thinking person to try their hand at being a (public) intellectual. If they have interesting things to say, a public will find them – and not just a British public but a worldwide one.

In sum: British intellectuals have never had it so good. So does it matter that they go on denying that they exist? Perhaps not. Perhaps it's even a useful safeguard against that exaggerated sense of one's own importance sometimes encountered among intellectuals on the continent; against, so to speak, becoming Bernard Henri-Lévy. Let the French keep the word; we'll be content with the thing.

2006

'Ich bin ein Berliner'

When you are young, you cannot imagine that the old were ever young. As you get older, that becomes easier. Isaiah Berlin was in his sixties when I first met him in Oxford. Britain's most celebrated public intellectual, an iconic figure with his heavy-rimmed spectacles, dark three-piece suit and unforgettable, much-imitated, bubbling, allusive, rapid-fire conversation, had characteristically agreed to spend an evening with a small undergraduate society. To a nineteen-year-old student, he seemed close to Methuselah – although, as I would discover over a quarter-century of closer acquaintance, this was a Methuselah with a vast appetite and talent for gossip.

Henry Hardy's meticulously edited first volume of his letters, covering the years 1928–46, shows what Isaiah Berlin was like when he was young.[1] His life unfolds in a sequence of expanding circles. The first circle is his close and supportive Russian-Jewish family, which had moved from Riga to England in 1921. There is a moving early letter from the nineteen-year-old Shaya, as he was then known, to his spirited, musical, romantically aspiring mother, Marie, consoling her ('I know that your position is not sweet') for the frustrations of living with the pedestrian caution of his merchant father, Mendel Berlin. It ends with this admonition: 'Remember: Life is Good; and

always will be Good however ugly it looks . . .' Somehow that remained
Isaiah's personal belief through all the horrors of the twentieth century,
and this fundamentally optimistic, life-affirming attitude is one of
the qualities that made him such a stimulating person.

The entire volume is punctuated by such affectionate, loyal, reassuring letters to 'Ma and Pa', who are constantly worrying about his
health, appearance and so forth. Sometimes, reading them feels like
eavesdropping. At the age of twenty-four, already a lecturer at New
College, Oxford, he writes:

> My dear mother: in answer to your questions in order: 1) I am
> taking my medicine. 2) I feel much better. The stomach is less
> troublesome. I am taking care about diet. 3) I have not taken
> the new handkerchiefs with me so far as I know. I'll look again,
> but I think not. 4) I have had 2 baths! 5) Nails etc. fairly, not
> very, clean. Doing my best.

No doubt Methuselah, too, had a fussing Jewish mother. Hardy
also inserts at various points extracts from Mendel Berlin's rather
touching private biographical sketch of his son, writing of Isaiah as
'you'.

The second circle is Oxford, to which he came as an undergraduate
in 1928 and where he died in 1997. Oxford was at the heart of Isaiah's
life – 'London is heaven,' he writes from Washington in 1944, 'but
Oxford seventh heaven' – and these letters speak to us of a time
when Oxford still confidently considered itself to be central to British
culture, and beyond. He approvingly quotes a comment by the German
scholar Ernst Robert Curtius that 'the barometers of culture in
England were in Oxford & Cambridge & not in London.' (No longer
true, if it ever was.) And from his wartime stay in the United States
he reports back, 'After Oxford, Harvard is a desert.'

Isaiah Berlin's Oxford, like Isaiah's world altogether, was all about
particular people. Crowds of them tear through these pages in a melee

of vivid, thumbnail sketches, gossip, congratulation, condolence, written as he spoke: generous, witty, occasionally waspish, and overflowing with *joie de vivre*. We are told that he plunged into the social life of his undergraduate college, small, 'cosy' Corpus Christi, joining every student society, and 'his rooms were a place of resort' for other students seeking company and conversation. His genius for friendship was there from the beginning.

At the outset, the company is not so striking, with fellow classicists going on to join the Colonial Service for life, or so they fondly imagined: 'Jerry's career seems to be completely settled. I am happier about it than I can say, in spite of a slightly bitter letter about Africa from Cruikshank which I unexpectedly received.' But soon he is moving into grander company, titled, rich, the *haute volée*, or, as Isaiah himself puts it, 'mildly vile body society' – presumably an allusion to Evelyn Waugh's *Vile Bodies*. Now the first-ever Jewish scholar to be elected a Fellow of All Souls College, Oxford, he goes to stay with Victor Rothschild and his wife in Cambridge, in the company of Aldous Huxley ('dull', 'too unspontaneous'), and is flown back from Cambridge to Oxford in a private plane.

Here is Isaiah's third circle: high society. English high society, initially, but soon stretching well beyond. One remark attributed to him in later life was that 'there are 567 people in the world and I know all of them.' Yet he was far too ironical an observer ever to have been a snob, and 'snobbish' appears in these pages as a severely critical epithet. Rather, he was characterized by an insatiable appetite and ability, apparent already when in his early twenties, to get to know an extraordinary range of people, spanning especially politics, diplomacy, literature (Stephen Spender is an early, important and lifelong friend, Elizabeth Bowen a regular correspondent), journalism, music and, of course, academia. By the end of his life, he really did seem to know – or to have known – 'everyone'. This came with a quality, of which he was wholly aware, of being something of a conversational chameleon – agreeing with each interlocutor, flattering them by that generous agreement, before going on to add something original of his own. Describing a tense *ménage à trois* between two philosophers and one woman he says, self-ironically, 'I play my usual precarious delicate and tactful part of friend of all the world.' In his later years, I sometimes felt, he had raised this to a utilitarian principle: chameleonism justified as bringing the greatest happiness to the greatest number.

In these letters from the 1930s, he is a witty social observer, tossing off some striking lines: '[Richard] Crossman is trying to sell his soul again & finding no buyers even among those who think he had one'; tutoring undergraduates is 'like striking matches on soap'; 'David Cecil still runs in and out, with a voice like a crate of hens carried across a field.' But the torrent of gossip in his letters about long-dead dons and 'mildly vile body society', recounted in a consciously heightened and slightly bright-young-thing style, can occasionally pall. The full title of All Souls College is 'The College of All Souls of the Faithful Departed', but at times this feels like All Souls of the Frivolous Departed. 'There may be a lot of theatrical nonsense here,' as he self-deprecatingly remarks at the end of one letter to Elizabeth Bowen, confessing that 'I can never trust myself to re-read letters.'

It's perhaps not surprising that we don't hear so much about his serious intellectual pursuits, although there are glimpses of the intense excitement of his regular Thursday philosophy sessions with A. J. (Freddie) Ayer, J. L. Austin and Stuart Hampshire, and some fine literary exchanges with Stephen Spender. In a letter to Spender from All Souls, written in 1935, he comments on the German poet Stefan George and his book of 1900, *Der Teppich des Lebens* ('The Tapestry of Life'):

Your remarks on George I think are absolutely true. I think he was a divine poet sometimes the Teppich des Lebens is magnificent, so are odd things in the other books: as for the passages you quote, I think he was a persecuted megalomaniac, nor can any of the pleas of his closest followers save him from the fact that he was a man of repulsive views or actual modes of living, that he ruined many of his friends, exploited them, used them, etc. as sometimes Wagner did, did not simply burn them up as George Sand or Dostoyevsky did, or tortured them as Lawrence sometimes must have done (is this nonsense?) but definitely used them coldly & that not in virtue of his nature but in virtue of what he believed himself to be, or at any rate in virtue of the part he was determined to act.

More surprising is how relatively little the threatening politics of Europe in the 1930s intrude. From one of the earliest of his regular annual trips to the Salzburg music festival with Stephen Spender, in 1931, he records his 'first glimpse of a real Nazi – a great corpulent creature in the official brown uniform, with a red & black Swastika on his sleeve, & wearing a small black demi-astrakhan hat with silver symbols embroidered thereon.' There's a trip to Ruthenia in 1933: '5 principal languages, 7 subsidiary ones, 4 frontiers, picturesque and mad Jews, petty Ukrainian squabblers.' There are echoes of the arguments about appeasing Hitler over the dinner table at All Souls. Adam von Trott, a German aristocrat at Oxford, later to be executed for his part in the resistance to Hitler, moves in and out of Berlin's circle. But, for the most part, the disintegrating European world is heard like echoes from a busy street the other side of a high college wall.

This may partly just reflect what Isaiah thought fitting matter for letter-writing, as well as the accident of which letters have survived and found their way to his Boswell, Henry Hardy, who begins this volume by appealing to anyone who possesses others to come forward. Indeed, to read this book properly you need to have Michael Ignatieff's excellent memoir/biography of Isaiah in the other hand.[2] Yet you also glimpse how, in other circumstances, Isaiah might have remained no more than just a great Oxford character, a local legend but not a figure of any wider significance, like his early exemplar Maurice Bowra, on whose conversational voice and style, Ignatieff suggests, Berlin's famous voice and style were originally modelled. What saved him from this fate, what made him a thinker not just of national but of international importance, were the three wider circles of his life: his Jewish engagement, in relation to Zionism, Palestine and later Israel; America, where he went in 1940; and Russia.

For me, this book explodes into electrifying life with Isaiah's first trip to Palestine, in 1934. It goes without saying that Isaiah was deeply conscious of his own Jewishness, but one sees in these pages how, while being fully accepted as a brilliant young member of English society, he was still clearly identified as 'a Jew'. After meeting him at a dinner in New College, Virginia Woolf wrote to her nephew Quentin Bell, 'There was the great Isaiah Berlin, a Portuguese Jew by the look of him; Oxford's leading light; a communist, I think, a fire eater.'

Now, in Palestine, the two identities, English and Jewish, are in tension, if not outright conflict. He lodges at the Pension Romm on King George Avenue, Jerusalem, with Russian-Jewish friends of his parents, Yitzchok and Ida Samunov, while his travelling companion, John Foster, a gentile Fellow of All Souls, puts up at the grander King David Hotel. 'There has been trouble there,' Isaiah explains in a letter to his parents, '– all the Jewish employées were suddenly dismissed – labour trouble – so it is unpopular for Jews to stay there at the moment.' A childhood Jewish friend is working illegally on 'a Palestine paper'. But 'tonight Foster & I dine with a lot of young [British] officials & Yitzchok wants me to "pump" them. This I will not do.'

One moment he is sitting with an Oxford contemporary and friend in the colonial administration, the next with a Jewish family friend who feels horribly oppressed by it. 'And yet,' he writes to his parents, 'the atmosphere, though hectic, is beautiful: Jews. Everywhere Jews. On the holidays you feel rest: a lot of Hebrew singing not too loud & vulgar in the Jewish suburbs of Jerusalem, people going about in

Talésim openly etc.' However, 'Jewish opinion is v. bitter against the English. Not so much abt. policy in general as abt. small rudenesses, brutalities, insults.' And, he adds, 'the English are C3' – meaning of low quality. Palestine, he writes to Marion and Felix Frankfurter, is 'staffed by public school men – of an inferior brand'. 'As for the Jews they are most odd and fascinating, & I felt equally uneasy with them & away from them.'

Small wonder he spoke of himself in Britain as a 'Metic' – the ancient Greek word for an alien living in a Greek city, having some but not all the rights of citizenship. And it was this sense of foreignness, critical distance, never quite being fully at home, that fed his intellectual growth. Often the difference between an academic and an intellectual lies precisely in this stubborn grain of alienation. All intellectuals are mental Metics. In Berlin's case, it seems fair to assume that his central philosophical argument about value pluralism grew out of such experiences and tensions.

Berlin's more than five years in America, which occupy nearly half this volume, came about in a most improbable way – because he was trying to get to Russia. By the summer of 1940, most of his British friends were either in military or government service. Isaiah was disqualified from the former by his weak left arm, damaged at birth, and, Hardy suggests, from the latter by his foreign origins. Frustrated, he drafted a letter to Lord Halifax, the then foreign secretary, offering his services as a kind of informal cultural-political listening-post and investigator for Britain in Russia ('no Russian on merely hearing me speak would assume that I was any sort of foreigner'). The letter appears not to have been sent in this form, but perhaps a similar one was.

At around the same time, he received a visit from Guy Burgess, then known as a louche, drunken British diplomat, but in fact also a Soviet agent. Burgess suggested that Berlin should become British press attaché in Moscow, and that he, Burgess, should accompany him, first to America, to obtain the necessary Soviet documents, and then to Moscow. Presumably, Burgess felt Isaiah would be useful cover for his own trip to visit his secret Soviet masters. Lord Halifax soon thereafter signed a courier's passport requesting 'free passage for Mr Isaiah Berlin, proceeding to Moscow, via USA and Japan'.

In slightly Chekhovian fashion, Isaiah then sits around in Washington, sighing 'to Moscow!' while, unbeknown to him, none other than the traveller-diplomat Fitzroy Maclean irritably but in fact wisely puts the kibosh on Burgess's unconventional scheme, after John Foster has urged the government to block it. (The story is meticulously reconstructed by Henry Hardy.) Fortunately, his talents are then seized upon by the British Information Service and embassy. His task is both to report upon and to attempt to influence the Jewish community and organized labour in the United States. To influence them, that is, to be more sympathetic to the British cause in the war against Hitler, which, at this point, the United States has not yet entered. 'The Jews here are a tough nut,' he writes cheerfully to his parents from New York, 'but I hope to crack them for the benefit of H.M.G. [His Majesty's Government].' Yet he is equally adept at getting to know the upper crust of New Deal Washington, such as the Alsop brothers and Philip and Katherine Graham. His genius for friendship is put to good use.

Isaiah's reporting from New York and Washington was so rich and vivid that it even came to the attention of Winston Churchill, prompting a famous episode when Irving Berlin was invited to lunch by Clementine Churchill and then quizzed about American politics by the British prime minister, labouring under the misapprehension that he was talking to the I. Berlin who had penned those brilliant dispatches.

Hardy includes here one sample of Isaiah's reportorial talent, a list of 'Things Which Americans Hold Against the British', including everything from imperialism and the class system to 'British lack of forthrightness in speech'. Englishmen in America substitute caution and reserve for tact, do not allow themselves to agree or disagree vehemently with the American speaker's point of view, but are expected to remark that it is 'very interesting'. The British diplomat who forwards this list to the Foreign Office in London describes its author as 'A v. clever Jew who works in the British Propaganda dept here. [The paper] has the schadenfreude of the Jew finding that another race [Hardy adds here 'sic'] is disliked also – but it is very shrewd and about 60 per cent of it is accurate.'

In private, meanwhile, Isaiah is confessing how much he misses England. (Like many British writers of his generation, Isaiah uses Britain and England interchangeably, but England carries the more positive charge of affection.) 'How much nicer England is,' he writes to his parents from New York in August 1940. And six months later, 'wish I were in England.' It is New York, particularly, he finds hard to take. He later recalled, with some hyperbole:

> I used to stand on the 44th floor of the Rockefeller Building, and look down into the street with a certain desire to commit suicide. All these little ants running around, one more, one less, it couldn't make any difference. I felt somehow I was just a cypher, a number, no individual personality at all. In Washington I felt quite different.

He is at pains to conceal this deeper discontent from his ever-loving, ever-caring, ever-worrying parents. 'Flourishing,' he repeatedly cables them (thus giving the title to the British edition of these letters, sadly missing from the American one). Or even 'PLEASE SUGGEST SYNONYMS FOR FLOURISHING = BERLIN.' On one occasion, however, he is forced to concede, 'I must admit that perhaps it was not very wise or true to cable you, as I did yesterday, that I was "flourishing", which was an exaggeration.' He writes this from New York Hospital, where he is recovering from pneumonia. Yet even then he concludes: 'I am, au fond, flourishing.'

'Mother would like America v. much,' he writes, 'open, vigorous,

2 x 2 = 4 sort of people, who want yes or no for an answer. No nuances.' But Isaiah himself is much less sure. 'There is no social mystery,' he confides in Mary Fisher, a close Oxford friend, 'no special social mazes which in principle cannot be represented by a definite plan, as e.g. Oxford, Cambridge, Bloomsbury, even Edinburgh I expect. This is very grave. There is a total lack of salt, pepper, mustard etc.' 'Everything is clear, explicit, floodlit even,' he writes to Marion Frankfurter, giving America a more positive spin to his American correspondent:

I am myself a little disturbed by this terrific clarity & emphasis: where nothing is taken for granted, everything is stated in so many unambiguous terms, no secret seasoning is tasteable, everything is what it is and proclaims itself sometimes at great length, to be so. But it is superior to the nuances and evasions of England or France. Aesthetically inferior but morally superior.

A very English ambivalence about America is perfectly expressed.

Isaiah clearly did a superb job in Washington and New York. He made many friends for life. In 1945, *Time* magazine published an article on his impact, despite a telegram from Isaiah to the proprietor, Henry Luce – and of course he knew Luce, as he seemed to know everybody – trying to stop publication of the article. In a characteristic flurry of hyphenated adjectives, *Time* reported:

Dark-skinned, raven-haired Berlin's main job was to compile weekly reports on the US scene, which he accumulated in part in an interminable round of dinners and cocktail parties. Hostesses and guests were charmed by his Oxford-accented observations on the world and its great; Reporter Berlin was charmed with what he learned.

The second use of the word 'charmed' is questionable, at least without some secret seasoning. *Time*'s story needs to be read beside a frank, affecting judgement by Mendel Berlin, in his family memoir, summarizing Isaiah's American years in his slightly erratic Russian English:

> You have enlarged and expanded your personality, came into contact with a greater and larger world than academic Oxford ... and gained a great deal of self-confidence. You have obtained a knowledge of politics and diplomacy and cannot so easily be led up the garden, as many academicians were and are.

Made with a father's careful, loving eye, that judgement seems to me about right. But Isaiah himself was restless, not least, it seems, because the Holocaust (which, remarkably, hardly appears at all in these pages; and I mean the terrible thing itself, not the word, which only came into wider usage later) was creating an increasingly acute tension between his Jewish and English/British self, as prefigured in Palestine ten years before. 'The Jewish issue is certainly about to boil up seriously here,' he writes to his parents from the British embassy in Washington in January 1944, 'and I try as much as possible to have nothing to do with it, without success, as everything ultimately comes to rest on my desk and I have to perform miracles of diplomatic contortion.' And he continues:

> Everyone is most kind and charming and polite; this country is undoubtedly the largest assemblage of fundamentally benevolent human beings ever gathered together, but the thought of staying here remains a nightmare. On the very first day after even the European war is over, I shall probably make a frantic attempt to return to Oxford.

Yet before he got back to that nest of high college walls and secret seasoning, he was to plunge into the deepest and darkest circle of his experience: Russia. For, unlike Chekhov's three sisters, Isaiah did finally get to Moscow – for four months from September 1945 to January 1946. We know from his other writings, especially the moving 'Meetings with Russian Writers in 1945 and 1946', that this sixth circle of Berlin's world largened, deepened and informed everything he subsequently said and wrote, even more than Palestine and America. This was his first and only direct experience of totalitarian rule, which was deforming the lives of his close relatives, including his uncle Lev, or Leo, Berlin, a professor of dietetics, whom he sought out and visited. Leo Berlin was arrested in 1952 and accused of belonging to a British spy ring that included Isaiah. He was interrogated and tortured until he 'confessed'. Released after Stalin's death, he died of a heart attack when he saw his torturer on the street.

Through no fault of the editor, the Russian part of this book is disappointing. Only a handful of letters survive and they add very little. Hardy has to fall back on other sources, and reprints Isaiah's official report of one of his trips to Leningrad, where he had lived as a child. But, as Hardy notes, Berlin 'deliberately underplays, indeed slightly falsifies' his encounters and talk through the night with the poet Anna Akhmatova, which had such a great impact on both of them. To understand it, you have to go back to Isaiah's own writings, Ignatieff's biography, and, of course, Akhmatova's 'Poem without a Hero', with this extraordinary poetic tribute to Isaiah, written as a dedication on the tenth anniversary of her second meeting with him in her bare apartment in the Fontanny Dom:

> He will not be a beloved husband to me
> But what we accomplish, he and I,
> Will disturb the Twentieth Century.

This was a long, long way from the tittle-tattle of Corpus Christi College in 1928.

After a few last months in Washington, Isaiah, now aged

thirty-seven, would return to New College, Oxford, 'in the dim recesses of which,' he wrote to Averell Harriman, 'I shall think with some nostalgia but no regret of the world to which I do not think I shall ever be recalled.' Yet nor would he ever entirely leave it. Shaya had become Isaiah, recognizably the Isaiah that I would meet in another college thirty years later: an Oxford figure enlarged and made unique by the three wider circles of Palestine–Israel, America and Russia.

Over the next two decades, from about 1946 to 1966, he would produce that great outpouring of work – not pure philosophy or monographs, but lectures and essays in the history of ideas, biography and political theory – which would lay the solid foundation of his intellectual reputation. He would argue and defend a complex, nuanced, pluralist version of liberalism (a 'liberalism of fear' in Judith Shklar's perfect phrase) which would not so much 'disturb the Twentieth Century' as attempt to find a civilized answer to the century's terrible disturbances. His subtle, tolerant and life-affirming answer was such that some of us are still moved to say, 'Ich bin ein Berliner.'

2004

The Literature of Fact

For much of my life, I have worked on frontiers. Night, fog, armed guards, tension. Walk just a few paces down the snow-covered Friedrichstrasse in Berlin, through a musty East German checkpoint, and you move from a world called West to a world called East. Nothing changes, and everything changes. Or a sandbagged border post between Milošević's Serbia and liberated Kosovo: fresh-faced Canadian soldiers pass you tenderly from one darkness to another. But also – and sometimes almost as tense – the frontiers between politics and culture, between continental Europe and the Anglosphere, between academia and journalism, left and right, history and reportage.

I like crossing frontiers. So much is revealed at them. In this essay, I want to explore the one between the literature of fact and the literature of fiction. I deliberately use the less familiar 'literature of fact', rather than that lumpen term from an English-language publisher's catalogue, 'non-fiction'. It exists in Polish, *literatura faktu*, and in some Scandinavian languages: *facklitteratur* in Swedish, *faglitteratur* in Norwegian. 'Literature of fact': the phrase is beautiful, and contains the key word – fact. But first, what of its other half, that large word 'literature'?*

---

*This essay began life as a contribution to a symposium on 'Witness Literature' organized by the Swedish Academy to mark the 100th anniversary of the first award of the Nobel Prize in Literature in 1901. Hence the opening reflections on the nature of literature and witness.

It seems to me self-evident that these adjacent territories of fact and fiction can both belong to literature, as France and Germany both belong to Europe. 'Literature' is often taken to mean invented worlds. The twentieth century sustained the nineteenth's romantic privileging of the creative imagination. But who could possibly argue that the works of Thucydides, Macaulay and Nietzsche, that George Orwell's *Homage to Catalonia* and V. S. Naipaul's *Among the Believers*, are not literature? Wherever the boundary of literature lies, it is not here.

The frontier between the literature of fact and the literature of fiction is open, unmarked. Some very fine writers stray across it quite casually, as one does when traveling in the Masai Mara – no border posts, same shrubland, same dust, same lions, but suddenly you are in Tanzania, not Kenya. These frontier crossings come in many forms. In the reportage of that master traveller Ryzsard Kapuściński, we find haunting claims that would certainly not survive the attentions of a fact-checker at the *New Yorker*. (I open his *Shah of Shahs* at random and read: 'The Iranian Shiites have been living underground, in the catacombs, for eight hundred years.') With Kapuściński, we keep crossing from the Kenya of fact to the Tanzania of fiction, and back again, but the transition is nowhere explicitly signalled.

Paul Theroux's travel book *The Great Railway Bazaar*, which is full of amusing incidents and wonderfully entertaining dialogue, concludes with an elaborate plea for its own strict, reportorial accuracy. He describes in detail the four thick notebooks in which he wrote things down as they happened, 'remembering to put it all in the past tense'. On this railway trip through Asia, he writes, he had learned 'that the difference between travel writing and fiction is the difference between recording what the eye sees and discovering what the imagination knows. Fiction is pure joy – how sad that I could not reinvent the trip as fiction.' At which I found myself thinking, 'Well, you did, you did.' Perhaps I am wrong, but even the production of four weather-stained notebooks containing words identical to those on the printed page would not dissuade me, for the invention can come at the moment of recording.

The historian Simon Schama begins his stimulating and avowedly experimental *Dead Certainties (Unwarranted Speculations)* with a compelling eyewitness account of the Battle of Quebec by a soldier who fought in it. At the end of the book, Schama reveals that this account was fiction, 'constructed from a number of contemporary documents'. So you were in Tanzania after all. Schama suggests that history as storytelling, as literature, must reclaim the ground it has lost to history as science, or pseudoscience. I entirely agree; but from this particular literary device it is not a long step to the postmodernist conclusion that any historian's 'story' is as good as any other's.

Sometimes the frontier transgression comes not in the text itself, but in the context established by the writer. According to the biography of Jerzy Kosinski by James Park Sloan, Elie Wiesel was initially lukewarm to Kosinski's novel *The Painted Bird*, which tells of a Jewish child in hiding alone during the war in a Polish village, thrown into a slurry pit by anti-Semitic Polish peasants, and struck dumb by the experience. Then Wiesel gathered from Kosinski himself that the book was closely based on Kosinski's own childhood experience, and so he hailed it as a 'chronicle' and 'a poignant first-person account'. The novel was celebrated as a 'testament', a work of witness. Later, it turned out that Kosinski was never in hiding alone, thrown into a slurry pit or struck dumb. The work was discredited on the very grounds that had established it. Kosinski's self-justification was interesting for our purpose. 'I aim at truth, not facts,' said the novelist, 'and I'm old enough to know the difference.'

Now I want to mount a defence of this frontier, so open, ill marked, often transgressed; a difficult defence, against the spirit of the times ('Who cares? It's all entertainment anyway'), yet one that seems to me of the first importance precisely when it comes to the moral and artistic quality of witness.

Of course Kosinski had a point. Just as literature extends both sides of this frontier, so does truth. Truth is the other continent to which the states of fact and fiction equally belong. 'Ah,' you may say, 'but these are two different kinds of truth.' Yet that is exactly what needs to be examined, for in saying that both belong to literature we are suggesting – and I think rightly – that in many ways it is actually the same kind of truth.

Nor shall we naively suppose that 'witness' can be found only on one side of the line. 'You who harmed an ordinary man . . .' writes Czesław Miłosz, in one of his most famous poems:

> Do not feel safe. The poet remembers.
> You may kill him – another will be born.
> Deeds and words shall be recorded.

The poet remembers: *Poeta pamięta!* Poems and novels are an essential part of the literature of witness. But I do suggest that any meaningful notion of witness depends on having a clear delineation of this frontier, and knowing which side you are supposed to be on at any one time. Ian McEwan's novel *Atonement* imagines a novelist who tries at the end of her life to atone for a terrible thing she did as a child by telling the truth about it. But since she does so in a novel, no one can know what is invented and what is real. She cannot atone, because she is God in this invented world.

Words like 'witness', 'testimony', 'evidence' and, of course, 'fact' have their sober offices in a court of law. And witnesses in literature, as in law, often testify to a particular kind of fact: the fact as something someone has done, often to someone else. In sixteenth- and seventeenth-century English the most common meaning of the word 'fact' was 'an evil deed or crime'. 'He is . . . hanged,' wrote a sixteenth-century authority, 'neere the place where the fact was committed.' (The usage survives in the English phrase 'accessory after the fact'. In German, *Tatsache* means fact and *Tatort*, scene of the crime.) When we say 'witness literature' we think first of witnesses to those 'facts' that are committed by human beings on other human beings, whether in war, apartheid, holocaust or gulag.

In defending this line, we must start by conceding much to those who would blithely stroll across it. For a start, all historians, journalists and lawyers know that witnesses are wildly unreliable. They forget, lie, exaggerate, get confused. That's why, so biblical scholars tell us, the Bible reflects the Jewish law of multiple witness. And Jesus chose twelve witnesses to his acts. But (as that example suggests) even multiple corroboration achieves only a very rough approximation to the original reality. I spent some time at the end of the 1990s talking to Serb and Albanian witnesses to atrocities in Kosovo. Turning from Serb to Albanian, and back again, I often wanted to say to them what Chaim Weizmann's father, a famous village peacemaker, reportedly used to exclaim after hearing one side of an argument: 'From what you tell me, I can see that you are entirely in the wrong. Now I shall hear the other side; perhaps you are in the right after all.'

Moreover, the evidential basis on which history is written is often extraordinarily thin. Sometimes, we have only one witness. During the Velvet Revolution in Prague, in 1989, crucial decisions were taken by a group around Václav Havel, meeting in a curious glass-walled room in the subterannean Magic Lantern theatre. Most of the time, I was the only outsider present, and certainly the only one with a notebook open, trying to record what was being said. I remember thinking: if I don't write this down, nobody will. It will be lost for ever, as most of the past is, like bathwater down the drain. But what a fragile foundation on which to write history.

Of course, others who were there will add their recollections. But what use are recollections? The problem with memory is at the heart of the problem with witness. When I set out some years ago to explore my Stasi file, I thought, 'This is the perfect way to test the credibility of secret police files. After all, if I know anything at all, I know what I myself did and said.' But as I read the file, talked to the people who had informed on me and the secret police officers who had spied on me, I found that I didn't really know even that. Or rather, what I thought I knew kept changing with every new revelation. We don't simply forget; we re-remember. Memory is a rewritable CD that is constantly being rewritten. And rewritten in a particular way: one that both makes sense of the story to us and makes it more comfortable for us. Isn't it curious how, if two people separately describe to you an argument between them, both seem to have won?

Philosophers have long been on to this in their different ways. Thomas Hobbes wrote that 'Imagination and Memory are but one thing.' One of Nietzsche's deepest apothegms reads: '"I did that," says my memory. "I can't have done that," says my pride, and remains adamant. Finally, memory gives way.' Schopenhauer ascribed it to vanity rather than pride. More recently, the neuroscientist Michael Gazzaniga has suggested, after studying patients whose left and right brain hemispheres are disconnected, that human beings have what he labels 'the interpreter' located specifically in the left brain, whose job it is to string together our experiences into narratives that seem to make sense. In short, we all have a novelist in our heads. A novelist called Memory ceaselessly redrafting the short story we call 'My Life'.

Yet that is only half the ground we defenders of the line must concede, the better to advance. Suppose for a moment that there was no involuntary exercise of the creative imagination through memory. Suppose we had a perfect, impartial, scientific record of what really happened. (With the new technology of video cameras we can get closer to it than ever before, though with only two of the four senses deployed by a human witness. Cameras cannot smell or touch.) Even then, we would still have almost nothing – and much too much. To study five years of the French Revolution in just one corner of Paris you would have to sit for five years in front of a screen.

To create the literature of fact, we have in many ways to work like novelists. We select. We cast light on this object, shadow on that. We imagine. We imagine what it is like to be that old Albanian woman weeping over the body of her murdered son, or what it was like to be a fourteenth-century French serf. No good history or reportage was ever written without a large imaginative sympathy with the people you are writing about. Our characters are real people; but we shape them like characters, using our own interpretation of their personalities. Then we talk of 'Michelet's Napoleon', 'Taine's Napoleon' and 'Carlyle's Napoleon', for each Napoleon is in some important sense the author's creation.

The property of deliberate imagining is certainly not confined to the Tanzania of fiction. Imagination is the sun that illuminates both countries. But this leads us into temptation. A voice in your ear whispers, 'You know that Kenyan in the slouch hat really did say that awfully funny thing you think he almost said. Just write it down. No one will ever know. And look, just across the frontier there is that gorgeous flower – the one missing novelistic detail that will bring the whole story alive. Pop across and pick it. No one will notice.' I know this voice. I have heard it. But if we claim to write the literature of fact, it must be resisted.

Why? For moral reasons, above all. Words written about the real world have consequences in the real world. If, in my book *The File*, I had identified as a Stasi informer someone who was not, in fact, a Stasi informer – and I nearly did – that man could have found his life ruined. Friends would have shunned him, he would probably have lost his job – and worse. (At least one person exposed as a Stasi informer committed suicide.) On a larger scale, the Balkan wars of the last decade have been fuelled by bad history, written by all sides. As the historian Eric Hobsbawm observes, 'The sentences typed on apparently innocuous keyboards may be sentences of death.' There is also a moral obligation to the victims, whether living or dead. How would we feel – how would the survivors feel – if we learned that events described in Primo Levi's *If This is a Man* had been deliberately invented or ornamented?

These moral reasons are sufficient; but there are artistic ones too. Writers often cross this frontier because they think their work will be enhanced as a result. Reportage or history will become Literature. Paragraph for paragraph, that may be true. But as a whole, the work is diminished.

We also need to ask 'How?' (often an even more difficult question than 'Why?'). How does one determine when this frontier has been crossed, given everything I have said about the unreliability of witnesses, the involuntary creativity of memory, and the necessity of deliberate imagining? A simplistic, nineteenth-century positivist answer about scientific truth won't do. For the truth achieved by the literature of fact is in many ways the same as that achieved by the literature of fiction. If we are convinced that human beings might have acted, thought or felt in this way, it is in large measure as a result of the writer's art and imagination.

I would suggest that, as well as satisfying all the truth-tests that apply to fiction, the literature of fact must pass two further, special truth-tests: those of 'facticity' and of veracity. First, facticity. Are those things in the text that claim to be facts actually facts, or are they merely, to use Norman Mailer's vivid coinage, factoid? Dates, places, events, quotations. Did the informer identified in my Stasi file with the incongruous code name 'Smith' actually sign a formal undertaking to work for the secret police as an 'unofficial collaborator' or did he not? Everything else – causes, motives, consequences – is, strictly speaking, speculation; this is fact. (As a matter of fact, I know 'Smith' did sign, because I have studied the original document.) Many alleged facts can be externally verified. The discipline of history and the craft of reporting have developed rules, procedures, specialist skills for testing evidence. Some even merit the label 'scientific'. (An analysis of the ink used in 'Smith's' pledge, for example.) To pass this basic test of facticity does not make a text true, but to fail does make it untrue.

Yet much of the time, especially with 'witness literature', the witness is alone at the scene he or she describes. Alone with his or her eyes, conscience and imagination. If we find witnesses accurate on things we know, we are more likely to believe them on things we don't; but sometimes, there is little that we can know or check. What test works here? The best I can come up with is the quite unscientific litmus of veracity. Do we feel, as we read the text, that the writer is making what George Orwell, in praising Henry Miller, called 'a definite attempt to get at real facts'?

For me, the model of such veracity is Orwell's own *Homage to Catalonia*. Actually, Orwell got some of his externally verifiable facts wrong – not least because most of his notes were stolen during a secret police search of his hotel room in Barcelona. But we never for a moment doubt that he is trying to tell it exactly as it was. And when we reach his plea of veracity at the end of the book, it is the very opposite of Paul Theroux's. Orwell writes, in that wonderfully plain, conversational style that he worked so hard to achieve, 'In case I have not said this somewhere earlier in the book I will say it now: beware of my partisanship, my mistakes of fact, and the distortion inevitably caused by my having seen only one corner of events.' In effect, he says, 'Don't believe me!' – and so we believe him.

Veracity is revealed in tone, style, voice. It takes us back to the artistic reasons for defending this line. You can often tell just from internal, stylistic evidence when a writer has strayed. Take a now notorious example: the book published in 1995 as *Bruchstücke* (*Fragments*) by Binjamin Wilkomirski, which purported to be the memories of a man who survived the Nazi death camps as a Polish-Jewish child. It is now established beyond reasonable doubt that the author was a Swiss musician of troubled past and disturbed mind, originally called Bruno Grosjean, who had never been near a Nazi death camp – but had imagined himself into that past, that other self. Reading *Fragments* now, one is amazed that it could ever have been hailed as it was. The wooden irony ('Majdanek is no playground'), the hackneyed images (silences broken by the sound of cracking skulls), the crude, hectoring melodrama (his father squashed against the wall by a transporter, dead women with rats crawling on their stomachs). Material which, once you know it is fraudulent, is obscene. But even before one knew that, all the aesthetic alarms should have sounded. For every page has the authentic ring of falsehood.

Compare this with the great books of true witness. Of course there are large variations in tone and style between these works. Many nonetheless have a certain voice in common: one of pained, sober, yet often ironical or even sarcastic veracity, which speaks from the very first line. Take, for example, and contrast with Wilkomirski, the first line of Primo Levi's *If This is a Man*:

> It was my good fortune to be deported to Auschwitz only in 1944, that is, after the German Government had decided, owing to the growing scarcity of labour, to lengthen the average life-span of the prisoners destined for elimination; it conceded noticeable improvements in the camp routine and temporarily suspended killings at the whim of individuals.

How could we not believe this?

The facts need not always be ugly. 'I will bring you,' writes the English poet Craig Raine, 'the beauty of facts.' It is, no doubt, a rather Anglo-Saxon sentiment. Yet facts, like artifacts, can be beautiful. On a white shelf at my home in Oxford, I have two objects. One is a rounded natural stone, some three inches high, of a delicate grey colour tinged with a very pale pink, moulded into contours by the cold sea washing across a pebble beach on the north-easternmost tip of mainland Britain, at the Duncansby Stacks, where I picked it up during a contented afternoon spent with my family. The other is a jagged piece of the Berlin Wall made of a gritty composite barely deserving the name of stone, with a patch of garish graffiti on one side. They sit there, the rough and the smooth, the unnatural and the natural, facing each other, rather brightly lit on the white shelf – a stone poem for the literature of fact.

It may seem a grave limitation for any writer to leave the facts as facts, but self-limitation is a key to art. On this frontier we should stand.

2001

7.
Envoi

Elephant, Feet of Clay

What is the elephant in all our rooms? It is the global triumph of capitalism. Democracy is fiercely disputed. Freedom is under threat even in old-established democracies such as Britain. Western supremacy is on the skids. But everyone does capitalism. Americans and Europeans do it. Indians do it. Russian oligarchs and Saudi princes do it. Even Chinese communists do it. And now the members of Israel's oldest kibbutz, that last best hope of egalitarian socialism, have voted to introduce variable salaries based on individual performance. Karl Marx would be turning in his grave. Or perhaps not, since some of his writings eerily foreshadowed our era of globalized capitalism. His prescription failed but his description was prescient.

Here is the great fact about the early twenty-first century, so big and taken for granted that we rarely stop to think how extraordinary it is. It was not ever thus. 'Can capitalism survive?' asked the British socialist thinker G. D. H. Cole, in a book published in 1938 under the title *Socialism in Evolution*. His answer was no. Socialism would succeed it. Most readers of the *Manchester Guardian* in 1938 would probably have agreed.

What are the big ideological alternatives being proposed today? Hugo Chávez's 'twenty-first-century socialism' still looks like a local

403

or at most a regional phenomenon, best practised in oil-rich states. Islamism, sometimes billed as democratic capitalism's great competitor in a new ideological struggle, does not offer an alternative economic system (aside from the peculiarities of Islamic finance) and anyway does not appeal beyond the Muslim *umma*. Most anti-globalists, *alter-mondialistes* and, indeed, green activists are much better at pointing out the failings of global capitalism than they are at suggesting systemic alternatives. 'Capitalism should be replaced by something nicer,' read a placard at a May Day demonstration in London a few years back.

Of course there's a problem of definition here. Is what Russian or Chinese state-owned companies do really capitalism? Isn't private ownership the essence of capitalism? One of America's leading academic experts on capitalism, Edmund Phelps of Columbia University, has an even more restrictive definition. For him, what we have in much of continental Europe, with multiple stakeholders, is not capitalism but corporatism. Capitalism, he says, is 'an economic system in which private capital is relatively free to innovate and invest without permission from the state, green lights from communities and regions, from workers, and other so-called social partners'. In which case most of the world is not capitalist. I find this much too restrictive. Surely what we have across Europe are multiple varieties of capitalism, from more liberal market economies like Britain and Ireland to more coordinated stakeholder economies like Germany and Austria.

In Russia and China, there's a spectrum from state to private owner-ship. Other considerations than maximizing profit play a large part in the decision-making of state-controlled companies, but they, too, operate as players in national and international markets and increasingly they also speak the language of global capitalism. At the 2007 World Economic Forum in Davos, I heard Gazprom's Alexander Medvedev defend the company's record by saying that it is one of the world's top five in market capitalization and constantly looking for value for its shareholders – who happen to include the Russian state. At the very least, this suggests a hegemony of the discourse of global capitalism. China's 'Leninist capitalism' is a very big border-line case, but the crab-like movement of its companies towards what we would recognize as more rather than less capitalist behaviour is far clearer than any movement of its state towards democracy.

Does this lack of any clear ideological alternative mean that capitalism is secure for years to come? Far from it. With the unprecedented triumph of globalized capitalism over the last two decades come new threats to its own future. They are not precisely the famous 'contradictions' that Marx identified, but they may be even bigger. For a start, the history of capitalism over the last hundred years hardly supports the view that it is an automatically self-correcting system. As George Soros (who should know) points out, global markets are now more than ever constantly out of equilibrium – and teetering on the edge of a larger disequilibrium. Again and again, it has needed the visible hands of political, fiscal and legal correction to complement the invisible hand of the market. The bigger it gets, the harder it can fall.

An oil tanker is more stable than a sailing dinghy, but if the tanker's internal bulkheads are breached and the oil starts swilling from side to side in a storm, you have the makings of a major disaster. Increasingly, the world's capital is like oil in the hold of one giant tanker, with ever fewer internal bulkheads to stop it swilling around.

Then there is inequality. One feature of globalized capitalism seems to be that it rewards its high performers disproportionately, not just in the City of London but also in Shanghai, Moscow and Mumbai. What will be the political effects of having a small group of super-rich people in countries where the majority are still super-poor? In more developed economies, such as Britain and America, a reasonably well-off middle class with a slowly improving personal standard of living may be less bothered by a small group of the super-rich – whose antics also provide them with a regular diet of tabloid-style entertainment. But if a lot of middle-class people begin to feel they are personally losing out to the same process of globalization that is making those few fund managers stinking rich, while at the same time outsourcing their own middle-class jobs to India, then you may have a backlash. Watch Lou Dobbs on CNN for a taste of the populist and protectionist rhetoric to come.

Above all, though, there is the inescapable dilemma that this planet cannot sustain six and a half billion people living like today's middle-class consumers in its rich North. In just a few decades, we would use up the fossil fuels that took some 400 million years to accrete – and change the earth's climate as a result. Sustainability may be a grey and boring word, but it is the biggest single challenge to global capitalism today. However ingenious modern capitalists are at finding alternative technologies – and they will be very ingenious – some-where down the line this is going to mean richer consumers settling for less rather than more.

Marx thought capitalism would have a problem finding consumers for the goods that improving techniques of production enabled it to churn out. Instead, it has become expert in a new branch of manu-facturing: the manufacture of desires. The genius of contemporary capitalism is not simply that it gives consumers what they want but that it makes them want what it has to give. It's that core logic of ever-expanding desires that is unsustainable on a global scale. But are we prepared to abandon it? We may be happy to insulate our lofts, recycle our newspapers and cycle to work, but are we ready to settle for less so others can have more? Am I? Are you?

2007

Decivilization

Before our attention wanders on to the next headline story, let's learn the big lesson of Hurricane Katrina. This is not about the incompetence of the Bush administration, the scandalous neglect of poor black people in America, or our unpreparedness for major natural disasters – though all of those apply. Katrina's big lesson is that the crust of civilization on which we tread is always wafer thin. One tremor, and you've fallen through, scratching and gouging for your life like a wild dog.

You think the looting, rape and armed terror that emerged within hours in New Orleans would never happen in nice, civilized Europe? Think again. It happened here, all over our continent only sixty years ago. Read the memoirs of Holocaust and Gulag survivors, Norman Lewis's account of Naples in 1944, or the recently republished anonymous diary of a German woman in Berlin in 1945. It happened again in Bosnia just ten years ago. And that wasn't even the *force majeure* of a natural disaster. Europe's were man-made hurricanes.

The basic point is the same: remove the elementary staples of organized, civilized life – food, shelter, drinkable water, minimal personal security – and we go back within hours to a Hobbesian state of nature, a war of all against all. Some people, some of the time, behave with heroic solidarity; most people, most of the time, engage in a ruthless fight for individual and genetic survival. A few become temporary angels, most revert to being apes.

The word civilization, in one of its earliest senses, referred to the process of human animals being civilized – by which we mean, I suppose, achieving a mutual recognition of human dignity, or at least accepting in principle the desirability of such a recognition. (As the slave-owning Thomas Jefferson did, even if he failed to practise what he preached.) Reading Jack London the other day, I came across an unusual word: decivilization. The opposite process, that is, the one by which people cease to be civilized and become barbaric. Katrina tells us about the ever-present possibility of decivilization.

There are intimations of this even in normal, everyday life. Road rage is a good example. Or think what it's like waiting for a late-night flight which is delayed or cancelled. At first, those carefully guarded cocoons of personal space we carry around with us in airport waiting areas break down into flickerings of solidarity. The glance of mutual sympathy over the newspaper or laptop screen. A few words of shared frustration or irony. Often this grows into a stronger mani-festation of group solidarity, perhaps directed against the hapless check-in staff of BA, Air France or American Airlines. (To find a common enemy is the only sure way to human solidarity.)

But then a rumour creeps out that there are a few seats left on another flight at Gate 37. Instant collapse of solidarity. Angels become apes. The sick, infirm, elderly, women and children are left behind in the stampede. Dark-suited men, with degrees from Harvard or Oxford and impeccable table manners, turn into gorillas charging through the jungle. When, having elbowed aside the competition, they get their boarding card, they retreat into a corner, avoiding other people's gaze. The gorilla who got the banana. (Believe me, I have been that ape.) All this just to avoid a night at the Holiday Inn in Des Moines.

Obviously the decivilization in New Orleans was a thousand times worse. I can't avoid the feeling that there will be more of this, much more of it, as we go deeper into the twenty-first century. There are just too many big problems looming which could push humanity back. The most obvious threat is more natural disasters as a result of climate change. If this cataclysm is interpreted by American politicians such as John McCain as – to use the hackneyed phrase that they will themselves undoubtedly use – a 'wake-up call' to alert Americans to the consequences of the United States continuing to pump out carbon dioxide as if there were no tomorrow, then the Katrina hurricane cloud will have a silver lining. But it may already be too late. If recent indications are correct that not just the icecaps but the permafrost in Siberia is thawing, which thawing would itself then generate further emissions of natural greenhouse gases, then we may be launched on an unstoppable downward spiral. If that were so, if large parts of the world were tormented by unpredictable storms, flooding and temperature changes, then what happened in New Orleans would seem like a tea party.

In a sense, these too would be man-made hurricanes. But there are also the more direct threats of humans towards other humans. Thus far, terrorist attacks have provoked outrage, fear, some restrictions of civil liberties, and the abuses of Guantánamo and Abu Ghraib, but they have not resulted in mass hysteria or scapegoating. Least of all in London, the world capital of phlegmatism. But suppose we ain't seen nothing yet. Suppose there's a dirty bomb or even a small nuclear weapon exploded by a terrorist group in a major city. What then?

Almost having the force of a flood is the pressure of mass migration from the poor and overpopulated South of the planet to the rich North. (Not accidentally, anti-immigration populists routinely use the flood metaphor.) If natural or political disaster were to put still more millions on the move, our immigration controls might one day prove to be like the levees of New Orleans. But even with current levels of immigration, the resulting encounters – especially those between Muslims and indigenous Europeans – are proving to be explosive. How civilized will we remain? In the way some Europeans and some

Muslim migrants are talking about each other, I see the advancing shadow of a new European barbarism.

And then there is the challenge of accommodating the emerging great powers, particularly India and China, into the international system. Especially in the case of China, where late-communist leaders use diversionary nationalism to stay in power, there is a danger of war. Nothing decivilizes more quickly and surely than war.

So never mind Samuel Huntington's 'clash of civilizations'. That, as the old Russian saying goes, was long ago and not true anyway. What's under threat here is simply civilization, the thin crust we lay across the seething magma of nature, including human nature. New Orleans opened a small hole through which we glimpsed what always lies below. The Big Easy shows us the Big Difficult, which is to preserve that crust.

In political preaching mode, we may take Katrina as an appeal to get serious about addressing these challenges, which means the great blocs and the great powers of the world – Europe, America, China, India, Russia, Japan, Latin America, the UN – reaching for a new level of international cooperation. But, on a sober analysis, we may venture a more pessimistic conclusion: that somewhere around the year 2000 the world reached a high point in the diffusion of civilization, to which future generations may look back with nostalgia and envy.

2005

The Mice in the Organ

On Christmas Eve, 1818, the curate of Oberndorf in Austria, Josef Mohr, dropped in to see the second organist, Franz Gruber, who was a schoolteacher in the next village. He had written this little carol, he said. Could Franz do him a tune, for choir and guitar accompaniment?

By when?

Oh, by this evening, please. The choir should sing it at midnight mass.

So Gruber sat down and tossed off a quick number. 'Si-er-lent Night, Ho-er-ly Night.'

Now here's the point: we would not be hearing the tune of 'Silent Night' in hundreds of thousands of churches, chapels and homes across the world tomorrow evening; the text would not exist in 300 languages, from Catalan to Tagalog; there would not be, at Bronner's Christmas Wonderland in Frankenmuth, Michigan, a 56-foot tall replica of the chapel in Oberndorf which commemorates the original Church of St Nicholas; you would not be able to buy an electrified 'Silent Night'-playing model of that chapel as a 'corporate gift' for $29.99; none of this would have happened were it not for the mice in the organ of St Nicholas's.

Because there were mice in the organ – the story goes that it was mice, but perhaps it was rats, or just dust – the instrument had to be repaired. This brought Karl Mauracher, a master organ-builder from the Ziller valley, to the church in Oberndorf. He heard the carol and brought a copy back to the Ziller valley. There he played or sang it to a family of singing sisters, the Strassers, who seem to have been something vaguely like the Julie Andrews gang in *The Sound of Music*. The Strasser sisters incorporated 'Silent Night' into their repertoire as they travelled around German-speaking central Europe, selling gloves and trilling songs.

Another group of singing sisters, the Rainers, supposedly performed the new folk hit before the emperors of Austria and Russia, as well as taking it to America in 1839. (It seems that you could not cross the road in central Europe without being waylaid by a band of Austrian singing sisters.)

Thus 'Silent Night' began its journey to becoming the world's most famous carol. To be sure, it's a pretty good tune. The words are not bad either, at least those of the first verse, although I slightly prefer this Taiwanese Ho-Lo-Oe version:

> Peng-an mi! Seng-tan mi!
> Ching an-cheng! Chin kng-beng!
> Kng chio lau-bu chio Eng-hai,
> Chin un-sun koh chin kho-ai,
> Siong-te su an-bin,
> Siong-te su an-bin.

But it's the tune that works the magic. Much of its charm comes from its simplicity. Was this because Franz Gruber only had a few hours to dash it off and then rehearse the choir in the new number, as well as cutting the firewood, milking the goat and plucking the Christmas goose? Or because the organ had broken down, so the music had to be simple for the guitar? Or just because he knew the limited musical abilities of his village choir? Whatever the cause, the simplicity makes the universality.

Yet there are probably hundreds of other equally beautiful tunes out there, and certainly as many amateur Christmas hymns of equal quality. What made this the all-time world hit, probably still even more widely known than the Beatles' 'Yellow Submarine'? Answer: the mice in the organ. In other words: chance, luck, fortune. Or rather, as is usual in these cases, a whole string of lucky coincidences – assuming, in the generous spirit of this season, that your definition of luck stretches to embrace ending up as a corporate gift at Bronner's Christmas Wonderland.

Napoleon knew this when he famously asked of one of the senior officers commended to his attention: 'Is he lucky?' Machiavelli makes the point in *The Prince*: 'I believe that it is probably true that fortune is the arbiter of half the things we do, leaving the other half or so to be controlled by ourselves.'

Yet most of the time we act as if the proportion of our destiny that we can control is very much larger. We feel that if people are successful or rich, they must be especially able; if companies prosper, they must be well-managed. And we constantly succumb to what Henri Bergson calls 'the illusions of retrospective determinism'. Because something happened, it somehow had to happen. There must have been good reasons for it. It's as if we can't live with the idea that so much is the result of chance. If so, why put in so much effort?

The religion that 'Silent Night' celebrates also has this insight: 'The race is not to the swift, nor the battle to the strong, neither yet bread to the wise, nor yet riches to men of understanding, nor yet favour to men of skill; but time and chance happeneth to them all.' However, Christianity suggests another larger pattern, in which effort in this life is rewarded in the next. A memorial in the chapel at Oberndorf shows Josef Mohr listening from a window in heaven to children singing his carol down on Earth.

But how about living with the plain, knowable truth: that at the end of the day, half of it is luck. Is that really so unbearable? Is it more consoling to think that tragedy strikes for a reason or without reason? On account of an errant gene, a devil, a socio-economic cause, or simply owing to chance? If you know that half of anyone's good fortune can be ascribed, precisely, to fortune, does that make it better or worse to contemplate?

Of course, the good fortune does not come without the other half. You have to do the business as well. So, serene in the knowledge that half of what follows will be down to luck, just go ahead and write that song. Pop round and ask a friend to dash off a tune in time for the evening performance. Then sit back and wait for the mice in the organ. Either way, you'll always have the song.

2004

Notes

The Strange Toppling of Slobodan Milošević

1. For an account of those demonstrations see 'The Serbian Tragedy' in my *History of the Present: Essays, Sketches, and Dispatches from Europe in the 1990s* (New York: Vintage Books, 2001).
2. This story has a bloody aftermath. In 2006, this same General 'Legion' (so called because of his earlier service in the French Foreign Legion) was condemned to forty years in prison for having organized the assassination of Zoran Djindjić in 2003. See the chapter by Ivan Vejvoda in Adam Roberts and Timothy Garton Ash (eds.), *Civil Resistance and Power Politics: The Experience of Non-Violent Action from Gandhi to the Present* (Oxford: Oxford University Press, 2009).
3. To say 'the last' was premature. Although Milošević was the last leader to have remained in power continuously from the communist to the post-communist period, the Orange Revolution in Ukraine and the Rose Revolution in Georgia arguably belong in this series.

Orange Revolution in Ukraine

1. Smaller parts of today's Ukraine fell to inter-war Romania and Czechoslovakia.
2. The pro-independence movement Rukh set the terms of debate during 1991 but failed to win elections.
3. Keith A. Darden, 'Blackmail as a Tool of State Domination: Ukraine under Kuchma', *East European Constitutional Review*, Vol. 10, Nos. 2/3 (2001), pp. 67–71.
4. See Ivan L. Rudnytsky, *Essays in Modern Ukrainian History* (Edmonton:

Canadian Institute for Ukrainian Studies, 1987), pp. 447–61.

5. See Oxana Shevel, 'Nationality in Ukraine: Some Rules of Engagement', *East European Politics and Societies*, Vol. 16, No. 2 (2002), pp. 386–413.

6. Text in 'Temnyk po khvorobi Iushchenka', *Ukrains'ka pravda*, 1 October 2004. A *temnyk* was a secret instruction issued by Kuchma's aides to television stations, guiding the presentation of certain topics.

7. This was a reference to a well-known line by the poet Ivan Franko, 'It's time to live for Ukraine!' But 'It's time' was also a slogan in Belgrade in 2000 and Prague in 1989.

8. See 'The Serbian Tragedy' in Timothy Garton Ash, *History of the Present: Essays, Sketches, and Dispatches from Europe in the 1990s* (New York: Vintage Books, 2001).

9. C. J. Chivers, 'How Top Spies in Ukraine Changed the Nation's Path', *New York Times*, 17 January 2005.

10. This modifies slightly Iaroslav Hrytsak, 'Re: birth of Ukraine', *Krytyka* (Kiev), 1–2 (2005).

11. Online edition of *Pravda*, 3 December 2004.

12. For a fuller treatment of this theme, see Timothy Snyder, *The Reconstruction of Nations: Poland, Ukraine, Lithuania, Belarus, 1569–1999* (New Haven: Yale University Press, 2003).

13. Reported in *Rzeczpospolita*, 27 January 2005, p. 6.

14. See Timothy Garton Ash, 'The $65 Million Question', in the *Guardian*, 16 December 2004, and Michael McFaul, 'What Democracy Assistance is . . . and is Not', in *Hoover Digest*, No. 1 (2005).

15. *Financial Times*, 20 December 2004. On earlier liberation projects, see Timothy Snyder, *Sketches from a Secret War: A Polish Artist's Mission to Liberate Soviet Ukraine* (Yale University Press, 2006).

16. Quoted by Richard Pipes in *National Review*, 27 December 2004.

17. RBC News, 10–11 January 2005, 6,130 respondents.

1989!

1. The title page says 'Stephen Kotkin, with a contribution by Jan T. Gross', and the preface says the book originated in a Princeton seminar co-taught by the authors, but the book nowhere specifies the exact nature of Gross's 'contribution'. Since Gross is an outstanding historian of modern Poland, I am assuming that this contribution came particularly in the chapter on Poland, which suffers least from the weakness I identify in this essay.

2. The most important set of articles is his 'The Collapse of East European

Communism and the Repercussions within the Soviet Union', published in three parts in the *Journal of Cold War History,* Vol. 5, No. 4 (Fall 2003); Vol. 6, No. 4 (Fall 2004); Vol. 7, No. 1 (Winter 2007). But see also his research reports published by the Cold War International History Project, and his chapter in Adam Roberts and Timothy Garton Ash (eds.), *Civil Resistance and Power Politics: The Experience of Non-Violent Action from Gandhi to the Present* (Oxford: Oxford University Press, 2009).

3. Gorbachev Foundation Collection, Hoover Institution Archives, Adamishin, Box 1, p. 26. I owe this reference to an unpublished paper by my Stanford colleague Norman Naimark on 'The Superpowers and 1989 in Eastern Europe', and my analysis of the role of the superpowers has been enriched by conversations with him.

4. Personal information from Robert Conquest.

Velvet Revolution in Past and Future

1. Despite extensive inquiries with leading Czech and Western historians of the velvet revolution, I have not (yet) been able to pin down the first use.

2. Mao Zedong, *Report of an Investigation into the Peasant Movement in Hunan,* quoted in George Lawson, *Negotiated Revolutions: The Czech Republic, South Africa and Chile* (Burlington, VT: Ashgate, 2005), p. 51.

3. I am well aware that the guillotine was not introduced until a later stage in the French Revolution.

4. See my account in *The Magic Lantern: The Revolution of '89 Witnessed in Warsaw, Budapest, Berlin, and Prague* (New York: Random House, 1990), p. 113.

5. Quoted in an excellent article by John K. Glenn, 'Competing Challengers and Contested Outcomes to State Breakdown: The Velvet Revolution in Czechoslovakia', *Social Forces,* Vol. 78, No. 1 (September 1999), pp. 187–211. Note also that the Slovak counterpart of the Civic Forum was actually called the Public Against Violence.

6. On this see Adam Roberts and Timothy Garton Ash (eds.), *Civil Resistance and Power Politics: The Experience of Non-Violent Action from Gandhi to the Present* (Oxford: Oxford University Press, 2009). For this essay, I have drawn on the findings of that multiauthor volume, and the Oxford University research project behind it: cis.politics.ox.ac.uk/research/Projects/civ_res.asp.

7. Quoted in Lawson, *Negotiated Revolutions,* p. 72.

8. See 'Orange Revolution in Ukraine', pp. 31–45 in this book.

9. See Roger Cohen, 'Iran: The Tragedy and the Future', *New York Review,* August 13, 2009.

10. Quoted in Lawson, *Negotiated Revolutions,* p. 90. On this, see also my *The Magic Lantern,* p. 154, and Krishan Kumar, *1989: Revolutionary Ideas and Ideals* (Minneapolis: University of Minnesota Press, 2001).

11. Hannah Arendt, *On Revolution* (New York: Viking, 1963), p. 36.

12. When my earlier *New York Review* essay '1989!' was reprinted in a supplement to the *Guardian* (24 October 2009), it was illustrated with a dramatic photograph of a young man with a machine gun running through the streets of Bucharest, Romania, in December 1989. Ah yes, the reader inwardly exclaims, *that's* revolution. But what happened in Romania was profoundly unrepresentative of 1989: it was the exception, not the rule.

13. See Adrian Karatnycky and Peter Ackerman, *How Freedom Is Won: From Civic Resistance to Durable Democracy* (New York: Freedom House, 2005).

14. I am most grateful to my colleague at the Hoover Institution, Professor Abbas Milani, for his translation and elucidation of this interesting document.

15. This emerges very clearly both from the studies in Roberts and Garton Ash, *Civil Resistance and Power Politics,* and from those in Valerie Bunce, Michael McFaul, and Kathryn Stoner-Weiss (eds.), *Democracy and Authoritarianism in the Postcommunist World* (Cambridge: Cambridge University Press, 2009).

Are There Moral Foundations of European Power?

1. 732 is the date generally given, but two French scholars argue that it actually occurred in 733; see J. H. Roy and J. Deviosse, *La Bataille de Poitiers–Octobre 733* (Paris: Gallimard, 1966).

The Twins' New Poland

1. Norman Davies, *Heart of Europe: A Short History of Poland* (Oxford: Oxford University Press, 1984), p. 462. The Preface is dated 1983.

2. Britain has been especially welcoming to workers coming from the so-called 'new accession countries' of central and eastern Europe. Of the more than 290,000 people who have formally applied to work in Britain since their countries joined the EU on 1 May 2004, some 170,000 come from Poland. See the report in the *Guardian,* 23 November 2005. If all 290,000 are actually working in the UK, that would be equivalent to 1 per cent of the country's total workforce.

3. This was told to me by friends in Warsaw, talking of their own teenage children. It is confirmed in a fascinating guide to the new slang used by young Poles: Bartek Chaciński, *Wypasiony: Słownik Najmłodszej Polszczyzny* (Kraków: Znak, 2005), p.36, using the Polish phonetic spelling 'esesman'.

4. Conversation in London, 10 November 2005. Subsequent quotations from Wałęsa are also from that conversation.

5. See David Ost, *The Defeat of Solidarity: Anger and Politics in Postcommunist Europe* (Ithaca: Cornell University Press, 2005), pp. 187, 229.

6. Of course, the word 'liberal' now means very different things in different European and North American contexts. But most of these politicians have generally endorsed some combination of economic liberalism (with a strong belief in free markets, sometimes known as 'neoliberal'), political liberalism (more or less 'left liberal') and cultural liberalism (about beliefs and life styles); so 'liberal' seems an appropriate shorthand term.

7. The real employment figures, including the black economy and those working abroad, are probably somewhat higher.

8. World Bank, *Growth, Poverty and Inequality: Eastern Europe and the Former Soviet Union* (2005), drawing on World Bank, *Growth, Employment and Living Standards in Pre-Accession Poland* (2004).

9. Surveys conducted by CBOS, available on www.cbos.pl, and see *Gazeta Wyborcza*, 16 December 2005.

10. Conversation in Warsaw, 5 November 2005.

'O Chink, where is thy Wall?'

1. See Adam Roberts and Timothy Garton Ash (eds.), *Civil Resistance and Power Politics: The Experience of Non-Violent Action from Gandhi to the Present* (Oxford: Oxford University Press, 2009).

Islam in Europe

1. See note 1 to 'Are There Moral Foundations of European Power?' page 418 for the dating to 733 rather than the more traditional date of 732.

2. Originally the title of an obscure journal, the term 'Eurabia' seems to have been popularized by a writer called Bat Ye'or. The jacket copy of her *Eurabia: The Euro-Arab Axis* (Madison, NJ: Fairleigh Dickinson University Press, 2005) summarizes its thesis: 'This book is about the transformation of Europe into "Eurabia", a cultural and political appendage of the Arab/Muslim world. Eurabia is fundamentally anti-Christian, anti-Western, anti-American, and anti-Semitic.' Much of Ms Ye'or's argument, which has a strong element of conspiracy theory, is built around the alleged secret guiding influence of an organization called the Euro-Arab Dialogue (EAD).

Here is an example of her fair and balanced tone: 'Is the European Union's covert war against Israel, through its Palestinian Arab allies, the secret

Schadenfreude fulfilment of an interrupted Holocaust?' She describes the United Nations as 'an international anti-Semitic tribunal, seeking to impose on Israel the Islamic condition of dhimmitude'. Bruce Bawer, in *While Europe Slept: How Radical Islam is Destroying the West from Within* (New York: Doubleday, 2006), uncritically repeats Ye'or's thesis, going on to suggest that 'Europe may simply persist in its passive ways, tamely resigning itself to a gradual transition to absolute sharia law and utter dhimmitude.' Despite these dubious antecedents, the word 'Eurabia' recently gained the ultimate seal of transatlantic respectability – to be used on an *Economist* cover. See the *Economist*, 24–30 June 2006.

3. Jonathan Laurence and Justin Vaisse, *Integrating Islam: Political and Religious Challenges in Contemporary France* (Washington, DC: Brookings Institution, 2006).

4. Estimates of their number vary wildly, from as low as 3 million to as high as 30 million. In 2003, when advancing Russia's case for being a member of the Organization of the Islamic Conference, Vladimir Putin named a suspiciously round number of 20 million. See the authoritative discussion by Edward W. Walker in *Eurasian Geography and Economics*, Vol. 46, No. 4 (2005), pp. 247–71. I am most grateful to John Dunlop for this reference.

5. See the very useful article by Timothy M. Savage, 'Europe and Islam: Crescent Waxing, Cultures Clashing', *Washington Quarterly*, Vol. 27, No. 3 (Summer 2004), pp. 25–50.

6. Until the closing minutes of the World Cup final, I hoped that Zidane's brilliant and disciplined performance as captain of the French team would provide an inspiring example for millions of French Muslims. Then his vicious but exquisitely executed headbutt of the white, presumably Catholic, Italian defender Marco Materazzi suggested a different kind of inspiration for European Muslims. Popular culture subsequently gave the story an unexpected twist, as a catchy and amusing song, ironically celebrating Zidane's headbutt (*coup de boule*), became an instant hit in France. It can be heard at www.koreus.com/media/zidane-coup-boule-mix.html.

7. Note that I refer specifically to adult women. There is an argument that teenage girls might actually feel liberated by the ban on wearing the hijab in schools from what they themselves feel to be oppressive parental, communal or religious authority. But what, then, of the rights of teenage girls who would freely choose to wear a headscarf?

8. For this and more detail on the alienation of the younger generation of British Muslims, see my column in the *Guardian*, 10 August 2006.

9. This brief summary of Ramadan's position draws on presentations I have heard him make as a visiting fellow at St Antony's College, Oxford. The intense controversies around him have resulted in his being made to feel unwelcome in much of French-speaking Europe and in his being refused a US visa to take up a permanent chair at Notre Dame University. A systematic presentation of his argument from Islamic law and jurisprudence is *To be a European Muslim: A Study of Islamic Sources in the European Context* (Leicester: The Islamic Foundation; the date of first publication is given as 1999/1420 H).

Mr President

1. Quotations are from my own notes, occasionally augmented by the notes and recollections of Lionel Barber and Michael McFaul, with whom I have worked to reconstruct the meeting. Although Barber and I both made our notes soon afterwards, the quotations should be read with all the obvious caveats. In future, we hope to use the Freedom of Information Act to obtain the official minute of the meeting, but it seems likely that the fruitier passages will not appear in an official record.

2. I was not, of course, suggesting that US Marines should start planning a 'Black Hawk Down' into Macedonia. My point was that a timely NATO and EU diplomatic and peacekeeping effort there had a reasonable prospect of success, while a failure to get involved, to prevent what at that time threatened to be a downward spiral into Slav–Albanian civil war, would have direct knock-on effects for the rest of Europe.

3. For more on that equally bizarre encounter, see 'The Chequers Affair' in my *History of the Present: Essays, Sketches and Despatches from Europe in the 1990s* (New York: Vintage Books, 2001).

4. This was the same President of Macedonia, Boris Trajkovski, who told me a few months later that 'so far as I know, world leaders are all praising Macedonia'. See 'Is there a Good Terrorist?'.

Anti-Europeanism in America

1. Mark Steyn, *Jewish World Review*, 1 May 2002.
2. Jonah Goldberg, *National Review Online*, 16 July 2002.
3. Quoted by Martin Walker, UPI, 13 November 2002.
4. *Guardian*, 13 November 2002.
5. Jonah Goldberg believes he coined this term and relates it etymologically to a wiener sausage – as a metaphor for the European spine. However, an earlier

coinage seems to be P. J. O'Rourke's *Rolling Stone* essay 'Terror of the Euroweenies'.

6. *Policy Review*, No. 113 (June/July 2002). A book-length version was subsequently published as *Paradise and Power* (London: Atlantic Books, 2003).

7. Attributed to him by the London *Times*, 9 July 2002, quoting what someone told the *Times* journalist that Shirley Williams said that Tony Blair said that President Bush said to him. Blair's spokesman, Alastair Campbell, denied that Bush said anything of the sort.

8. Jean-François Revel, *L'Obsession anti-américaine* (Paris: Plon, 2002).

9. 12 June 2001. For an Englishman this does raise an urgent question: what on earth is 'British bologna'?

10. Jonah Goldberg was the only person I met who was prepared to accept that he was 'anti-European', so long, he explained, as one means by 'European' a certain kind of know-it-all, bureaucratic, liberal internationalist in Paris or Brussels.

11. IPSOS US-Express, 3–5 December 2002. I am most grateful to Michael Petrou for arranging this.

12. *Weekly Standard*, 26 August 2002.

13. See my 'Bosnia in Our Future', in Timothy Garton Ash, *History of the Present: Essays, Sketches, and Dispatches from Europe in the 1990s* (New York: Vintage Books, 2001). In this case the British government was very much among the Europeans.

14. The *Economist* ran a cover drawing in 1984 entitled 'How to Recognise a European through American Eyes'. Distinguishing characteristics of the European were 'An Angry Eye on Reagan. A Blind Eye on Russia. Limp-Wristed. Weak-Kneed. No Guts. Cold Feet. Snooty. Too Big for His Boots. But in Need of US Support'.

15. 'The Collapse of "The West"', *Foreign Affairs*, Vol. 72, No. 4 (September/October 1993).

16. See Kalypso Nicolaïdis and Robert Howse, '"This is my EUtopia ...": Narrative as Power', *Journal of Common Market Studies*, Vol. 40, No. 4 (November 2002).

17. See, for example, Will Hutton, *The World We're In* (London: Little, Brown, 2002), and my debate with him in *Prospect*, May 2002.

18. See his 'The End of the West' in the *Atlantic Monthly*, November 2002, and his *The End of the American Era: US Foreign Policy and the Geopolitics of the Twenty-First Century* (New York: Knopf, 2002).

19. Email to the author from Ambassador Thomas W. Simons, 16 May 2002, quoted with his kind permission. Michael Ledeen puts it less kindly:

'Conversation is much better in America,' he writes, and 'Europeans have gone brain dead.' This in the journal of the American Enterprise Institute, *The American Enterprise*, December 2002. The issue, entitled 'Continental Drift: Europe and the US Part Company', is a veritable anthology of American right-wing views of Europe, including Mark Steyn's remarkable comment, 'I find it easier to be optimistic about the futures of Iraq and Pakistan than, say, Holland or Denmark.'

20. See my 'The Capital Makes Up Its Mind', *New York Times*, 12 December 2002. This impression is confirmed by an August 2002 opinion poll by the Pew Research Centre for the People and the Press.

21. *Special Providence: American Foreign Policy and How It Changed the World* (London: Routledge, 2002).

22. This is borne out by the IPSOS US-Express, 3–5 December 2002, poll. Asked 'out of the following six countries, which one, in your opinion, exhibits the strongest reaction of solidarity with the United States in its efforts against Iraq?' 59 per cent said Britain. This was followed by Israel, 11 per cent; Canada, 7 per cent; France, 4 per cent; Germany, 3 per cent; and Russia, 3 per cent.

23. Stanley Hoffmann, 'The High and the Mighty', *American Prospect*, 13 January 2003.

24. See, for example, Ronald D. Asmus and Kenneth M. Pollack, 'The New Transatlantic Project', *Policy Review*, No. 115 (October/November 2002).

Beauty and the Beast in Burma

1. It's an irony so obvious it barely needs pointing out that one of the last Orwellian regimes in the world prevails in the country where Orwell was himself an imperial policeman. Curiously, Orwell's *Burmese Days* was on sale in my Rangoon hotel – presumably as a sound anti-colonialist text for visiting businessmen or tourists.

2. Several charities try to alleviate the effects of this disastrous policy by giving those Burmese students who can get out of the country the chance to pursue higher education abroad. Notable among them are Prospect Burma, a British-based charity originally established with the money from Aung San Suu Kyi's Nobel Peace Prize, and the New York-based Burma Project, one of the many valuable initiatives supported by George Soros.

3. The best introductions to this highly intricate subject are Martin Smith, *Burma: Insurgency and the Politics of Ethnicity* (London: Zed Books, 2nd, updated, edn, 1999; distributed in the US by St Martin's) and Bertil Lintner, *Burma in Revolt: Opium and Insurgency since 1948* (Boulder, Colo.: Westview, 1994). I

am grateful to a number of leading Burma specialists for their generous help in the preparation of this article.

The Brown Grass of Memory

1. Translations are generally my own and, for the purposes of this essay, stay as close as possible to the German original: *Beim Häuten der Zwiebel* (Göttingen: Steidl, 2006). On a rapid perusal, Michael Henry Heim's translation *Peeling the Onion* (New York: Harcourt, 2007) seems to me a characteristically skilful attempt to render the unrenderable.

2. Grass has a powerful imagination, but in his best fiction he draws from life. Take, for example, the fantastical performing dwarfs that appear in *The Tin Drum*. You might think they must have been invented. But in *Peeling the Onion*, Grass recalls how, on his way to join the Waffen-SS, he saw a group of dwarfs performing in the bomb shelter of a Berlin railway station. Volker Schlöndorff, director of the wonderful film version of *The Tin Drum*, says he concluded, while working on the film, that 'nothing in these novels is invented.'

3. See http://www.zdf.de/ZDFmediathek/inhalt/29/0,4070,5255773-5,00.html.

4. For more on Nazi–Stasi echoes see the next chapter in this volume, 'The Stasi on Our Minds'.

5. I owe this observation to my Stanford colleague Amir Eshel, whose forth-coming book on the place of historical memory in German and Israeli literature promises to deliver more fascinating insights in this area.

6. Bernd Wegner, *The Waffen-SS: Organization, Ideology and Function* (Oxford: Basil Blackwell, 1990), p. 370, note 60.

7. Klaus Wagenbach, 'Grass sprach schon 1963 über SS-Mitgliedschaft', *Welt-online*, 25 April 2007.

8. It seems worth adding that at a remarkable event with Günter Grass and Norman Mailer, interviewed separately and together by Andrew O'Hagan at the New York Public Library, to coincide with the American publication of *Peeling the Onion*, Mailer – who said that he found the book 'one of the very finest, if not the finest piece of war writing that I have ever read' – gave a strikingly acute and sympathetic 'guess as a novelist' about Grass's behaviour:

> I think probably he felt he couldn't get into it before this. Because, one, he wasn't ready to write about it [that is, hadn't found the appro-priate literary form], and, two, there was so much to lose. There was so much to lose as the years went by. There was more and more to

lose in terms of what he believed in . . . And so now he's paying the dues. But I must say, that I'm happy to be here tonight with him, and I honour the man.

Mailer, who indicated that this might be one of his last public appearances, also told the audience that the Grass story had prompted him to start 'searching my own life, asking what have I held on to for a long, long time and never written about, and indeed . . . may never write about? And it seems to me that stabbing my wife, Adele, is probably what I will never write about.'

An audio recording of the event can be found at www.nypl.org/research/chss/pep/pepdesc.cfm?id=2678.

9. 'We are not a politically oriented group,' says this organization on its website, 'and only seek to enjoy the fast paced and exciting atmosphere of WWII reenacting': www.frundsberg.org.

The Stasi on Our Minds

1. *'Und willst Du nicht mein Bruder sein...' Die DDR heute* (Reinbek: Rowohlt, 1981). Parts appeared in English in *The Uses of Adversity: Essays on the Fate of Central Europe* (New York: Random House, 1989).
2. Reissued in 2009 by Atlantic Books, with a new Afterword.
3. A post-war term for Germany as a whole, sometimes intended to include not just East Germany but also the former German eastern territories, such as Silesia, given to Poland after 1945.

Orwell in Our Time

1. Peter Davison (ed.), *The Complete Works of George Orwell*, 20 vols. (London: Secker & Warburg, 1998).
2. Curiously enough, the magazine is called *1984*. However, I am told that this refers not to Orwell but to the year in which the Mac was launched.
3. Penguin more or less followed this suggestion; see *Orwell and Politics* (London: Penguin, 2001) and *Orwell and Spain* (London: Penguin, 2001).
4. If his facts are nonetheless sometimes wrong, this is at least partly because all his papers – including, probably, his Spanish war diary – were taken during a secret police search of his hotel room in Barcelona. Davison makes the intriguing suggestion that these may now be in an NKVD dossier on Orwell that, according to one source, still exists in the Soviet archives.

Orwell's List

1. *Guardian Review*, 21 June 2003, reprints the whole list.
2. A detailed but tendentious account is Paul Lashmar and James Oliver, *Britain's Secret Propaganda War, 1948–1977* (Stroud: Sutton, 1998). A shorter but much more nuanced treatment is in Hugh Wilford, *The CIA, the British Left and the Cold War: Calling the Tune?* (London: Frank Cass, 2003). See also W. Scott Lucas and C. J. Morris, 'A Very British Crusade: The Information Research Department and the Beginning of the Cold War', in *British Intelligence, Strategy and the Cold War*, ed. Richard J. Aldrich (London: Routledge, 1992); Phillip Deery, 'Confronting the Cominform: George Orwell and the Cold War Offensive of the Information Research Department, 1948–50', in *Labour History*, No. 73 (November 1977); *IRD: Origins and Establishment of the Foreign Office Information Research Department, 1946–48* (London: FCO Historians' History Notes, No. 9, August 1995); and the brief, accusatory treatment in Frances Stonor Saunders, *Who Paid the Piper? The CIA and the Cultural Cold War* (London: Granta, 1999).
3. Minute of 21 April 1951, in FO 1110/383.
4. See FO 1110/191.
5. Mark Hollingsworth and Richard Norton-Taylor, *Blacklist: The Inside Story of Political Vetting* (London: Hogarth Press, 1988).

Is 'British Intellectual' an Oxymoron?

1. Stefan Collini, *Absent Minds: Intellectuals in Britain* (Oxford: Oxford University Press, 2006).

'Ich bin ein Berliner'

1. Isaiah Berlin, *Flourishing: Letters 1928–1946*, ed. Henry Hardy (London: Chatto & Windus, 2004).
2. Michael Ignatieff, *Isaiah Berlin: A Life* (New York: Metropolitan Books, 1998).

Acknowledgements

Honour and thanks to Robert Silvers and Rea Hederman at the *New York Review of Books*; Alan Rusbridger, Georgina Henry and the whole Comment team at the *Guardian*; David Goodhart at *Prospect*; Margaret MacMillan and many friends and colleagues at St Antony's College, Oxford, and in the wider University, with a special word of thanks to the invincibly good-humoured and humorous Denise Line; John Raisian and another remarkable group of scholars at the Hoover Institution and at Stanford University more broadly; Ian McEwan, scalpel upon scalpel; Ralf Dahrendorf, to whom, on his eightieth birthday, this book is dedicated; Tony Judt, partner in thought; Adam Roberts, exemplary perfectionist; Tim Snyder, this time especially for our collaboration on Ukraine; Georges Borchardt, William Frucht, John Palmer and the remarkable team at Yale University Press; above all, as always, to the moot – and to my parents, who made this all possible.

Beyond these specific thanks, let me add a generic thank you to the almost innumerable scholars, students, journalists, activists, specialists of every kind, in so many different countries and disciplines, who helped me on particular topics. Some are mentioned by name in the essays and notes, but I wish to acknowledge them all very warmly.

Index